Legal Executions in North Carolina and South Carolina

Also by Daniel Allen Hearn
and from McFarland

Legal Executions in Delaware, the District of Columbia, Maryland, Virginia and West Virginia: A Comprehensive Registry, 1866–1962 (2015)

Legal Executions in Georgia: A Comprehensive Registry, 1866–1964 (2015)

Legal Executions in Illinois, Indiana, Iowa, Kentucky and Missouri: A Comprehensive Registry, 1866–1965 (2015)

Legal Executions in New Jersey: A Comprehensive Registry, 1691–1963 (2005)

Legal Executions in New England: A Comprehensive Reference, 1623–1960 (1999; paperback 2008)

Legal Executions in New York State: A Comprehensive Reference, 1639–1963 (1997; paperback 2008)

Legal Executions in North Carolina and South Carolina

A Comprehensive Registry, 1866–1962

Daniel Allen Hearn

McFarland & Company, Inc., Publishers
Jefferson, North Carolina

LIBRARY OF CONGRESS CATALOGUING-IN-PUBLICATION DATA

Hearn, Daniel Allen, 1958–
Legal executions in North Carolina and South Carolina : a comprehensive registry, 1866–1962 / Daniel Allen Hearn.
p. cm.
Includes bibliographical references and index.

ISBN 978-0-7864-9539-9 (softcover : acid free paper) ♾
ISBN 978-1-4766-1715-2 (ebook)

1. Executions and executioners—North Carolina—History—Chronology. 2. Executions and executioners—South Carolina—History—Chronology. I. Title.

HV8699.U5H394 2015
364.6609756'0904—dc23 2015002186

BRITISH LIBRARY CATALOGUING DATA ARE AVAILABLE

Cover image Craig Colvin/Dreamstime.com

Printed in the United States of America

McFarland & Company, Inc., Publishers
Box 611, Jefferson, North Carolina 28640
www.mcfarlandpub.com

Table of Contents

Preface

This book joins several books from McFarland that chronicle the use of capital punishment in the United States on a case-by-case basis. Previous volumes have included New York (Hearn, 1997), the New England states (Hearn, 1999), New Jersey (Hearn, 2005), California (O'Hare, Berry and Silva, 2006), other Western and Midwestern states (R. Michael Wilson, 2010, 2011 and 2012), and Tennessee (Lewis Laska, 2011). Only those cases that resulted in an actual execution are covered. The present volume (North Carolina and South Carolina) is meant to provide a reliable historical reference that will in turn provide grist for further study by scholars, lawyers, researchers, policy makers and others regardless of their opinions on the always contentious issue of capital punishment. Several long-held misconceptions about death penalty usage will, however, be brought to light as these pages unfold.

The executions covered in this book begin in 1866, the first full year after the Civil War. Complications with record-keeping, destruction of records, and incomplete data prevented me from going back further in this work. There is simply too much information lost to history to claim that what I might uncover is at all complete. I do hope to go further back in history in another book at some point in the future. The current volume ends in 1962, the year of the last execution in South Carolina before the death penalty was abolished in 1972. North Carolina's last execution before abolishment was in 1961.

There have previously been three serious attempts to compile a complete census of legal executions in the United States of America. None succeeded because of a combination of factors, chief among which was the excessive difficulty one encounters when ferreting out the far-flung pieces of such a puzzle. There was no centralized record keeping until very recent times. Each of the more than 50 states and territories of this nation had its own ways of doing things and its own methods of record keeping. These ranged from concise and well organized to haphazard. Some states (like Pennsylvania) had restrictive privacy laws which barred them from divulging even innocuous information like a person's age on a death certificate that is more than 100 years old. The Southern states have proven to be especially problematic for this kind of research. There have been too many courthouse fires, too much wartime vandalism (1861–1865), and too many natural disasters like hurricanes, floods and tornadoes that resulted in the loss of irreplaceable records. In other cases, officials found it easier to send old court records to the county landfills than to preserve them. Many such stories have been told to me by courthouse personnel who now resent their predecessors for having had no sense of the historical value of documents.

Another impediment, which I also encountered particularly in the South, was pervasive reticence about such matters. Murders, sexual assaults and executions were not regarded as suitable topics for polite conversation. Everybody knew about them but few would speak on the subject—especially to strangers. When I set about this project 30 years ago, many Southern archivists, records managers and local officials were leery of me when they heard my Yankee accent and learned that I was from New England. They became more cordial when I explained that I was not a crusader or cultural imperialist. Many agreed with my belief that the longstanding policy of silence about criminal matters had been a mistake because it had given rise to a pernicious myth that they were trying to hide something. In my opinion, a more forthcoming attitude would have gone a long way to dispel much of the calumny and misinformation that has been bandied about. Only within the last decade has this ice begun to thaw.

The actual record of capital punishment shows, in my opinion, that the southern states have little or nothing of which to be ashamed. It is true that they executed more criminals than their northern and western neighbors, but all that proves is that they were more serious about law enforcement—hardly a derogatory trait.

As stated above, there have been three organized efforts to compile a historical census of American executions by the rule of law. The first of these was a noteworthy endeavor on the part of George P. Upton (1834–1919), a longtime reporter, contributor and editorialist for the *Chicago Tribune*. Beginning in the year 1877 and ending 40 years later in 1917, Upton gathered and published annual lists of legal executions *purported to be* authoritative. No one thought to question their accuracy and for many decades they were accepted as gospel by capital punishment scholars. The reality—sad to say—is much different. Upton's compilations are of poor quality, being incomplete to a large degree and riddled with errors. Dozens of the names on his lists do not hold up to independent confirmation. I have found some to be apocryphal. Some were actually lynchings or even attempted lynchings. There are incorrect dates and incorrect locations. Most troubling of all is the presence on Upton's lists of numerous condemned criminals who were not executed at all. They were reprieved for various reasons but Upton nonetheless chalked them up as having been executed. It is now apparent that Upton's annual inventories were haphazardly thrown together by poorly paid cub reporters who made little or no effort to verify their accuracy. Upton unwisely put his imprimatur on them. The result has been decades of flawed studies and misinformation based on this obsolete and untrustworthy source. The late capital punishment scholar Raymond T. Bye (1892–1976) made extensive use of Upton's material and consequently his findings must now be called into serious question. The following comparison chart of legal executions (using the Carolinas as a sampling) confirms this.

Legal Executions, Upton and Hearn

	North Carolina		South Carolina	
Years	*Upton*	*Hearn*	*Upton*	*Hearn*
1890–95	20	27	47	56
1896–00	21	27	15	26
1901–05	21	31	8	15
1906–10	10	21	25	46
1911–17	22	32	31	42
Total:	**94**	**138**	**126**	**185**

The Upton figures are reproduced from *Capital Punishment in the United States* by Raymond T. Bye (University of Pennsylvania, 1919). My numbers are compiled from my own research as set forth in this book. Professor Bye somehow failed to report 103 legally imposed Carolina executions within a 27-year period.

The second attempt to compile a national database of American executions was that of Temple University professor Negley K. Teeters (1896–1971) and his youthful research assistant Charles J. Zibulka during the 1960s. Teeters began naturally enough with his home state of Pennsylvania and made research inroads into neighboring New York before infirmity of years overtook him. Alas, his published works show evidence not only of haste but of flawed methodology. Teeters relied imprudently on secondhand printed sources instead of original archival material. He used error-prone late–19th-century county histories without seeming to realize that they were heavily edited for content by stuffy Victorian censors. Even worse, he neglected to study Pennsylvania's abundant 18th- and early 19th-century newspapers in order to assimilate the precious information they contain. As a result of this, Teeters missed many reported executions. He also suffered the embarrassment of having to acknowledge having done so. Zibulka was being groomed to succeed Teeters in this historical fact-finding endeavor, but the young man (University of Washington '66) was reportedly killed in a car accident and no one could be found to take his place.

The third attempt of this kind was begun in 1970 by Major Watt Espy, Jr. (1933–2009), an independent researcher residing in Headland, Alabama. His initial approach to the task was a letter writing campaign to several hundred circuit and superior court clerks nationwide along with town and county historians, querying them for information about old death penalty cases in their respective jurisdictions. The responses he received were a mixed bag, as could be expected. Some were vague. Some were worthless, for the most part, whereas others were meticulous. A lot of the respondents were people of mature years, nearly all of them now deceased. They had long memories and in many instances a willingness to share information with a fellow Southerner. Espy tried to pin down independent confirmation of what these well-meaning folks told him, but the task was a formidable one. Important bits of data like exact dates and unpublished forensic details had become fuzzy in the minds of many Espy correspondents over the course of their lifetimes. Espy lacked funds to take research trips that might have advanced his project. He also found himself depending more and more on secondhand source materials, as Professor Teeters had done. In so doing, Espy unwittingly integrated other people's mistakes into his own work. Additionally, many of those who provided information to Espy turned out to be persons who were more interested in playing up the politics of capital punishment than in researching it objectively. Espy complained about this to me in numerous conversations, accusing the academic left of withholding or suppressing historical information that did not comport with their preconceptions.

The heyday of Espy's self-styled "Capital Punishment Research Project" began in 1977 when he entered into an agreement with the University of Alabama Law Center to set up shop there. The situation was enhanced seven years later when the National Science Foundation recognized the importance of Espy's mission by awarding the University of Alabama a grant "to support development of a comprehensive computer database on the history of capital punishment in the United States." The result was what has come to be known as *Executions in the United States, 1608–1987: The Espy File*, originally made available through the Inter-University Consortium for Political and Social Research at the University of Michigan. For Espy himself it was a short-lived hurrah. He had returned to his home in Headland, Alabama, by the summer of 1987, much the worse for the experience. It was there where I first met him. "The Project was a disaster!" he told me. "Too many cooks had spoiled the soup!" Several unauthorized versions of *The Espy File* have cropped up on the Internet over the years.

To illustrate the inadequacy of *The Espy File*, the following comparison chart speaks volumes, again using the Carolinas as an example:

Legal Executions, Espy and Hearn

	North Carolina		South Carolina	
Year	*Espy*	*Hearn*	*Espy*	*Hearn*
1866	2	7	0	3
1867	0	7	2	2
1868	6	13	0	0
1869	1	5	1	2
1870	1	5	2	5
1871	1	11	0	8
1872	1	7	3	6
1873	0	5	0	2
1874	0	4	3	5
1875	1	5	7	11
1876	1	3	1	6
1877	3	5	10	13
1878	8	9	6	10
1879	13	12	3	3
1880	7	9	4	5
1881	4	4	10	10
1882	7	7	10	10
1883	5	5	6	6
1884	2	2	8	9
1885	6	10	3	4
1886	6	6	4	4
1887	3	3	3	5
1888	0	3	5	8
1889	3	7	2	6
1890	5	6	5	7
1891	1	4	6	9
1892	3	5	10	13
1893	1	2	9	11
1894	6	6	6	8
1895	3	4	6	8
1896	1	3	1	3
1897	5	6	1	3
1898	1	5	1	9
1899	5	5	5	7
1900	6	8	3	4
1901	3	3	3	4
1902	7	7	1	2
1903	3	3	2	3
1904	8	10	0	2
1905	6	8	3	4
1906	4	4	7	13
1907	6	8	3	3
1908	3	5	5	12

Year	*Espy*	*Hearn*	*Espy*	*Hearn*
1909	1	2	3	9
1910	2	2	3	9
1911	8	9	5	5
Total:	**169**	**269**	**181**	**291**

The disparities in these figures are quite large: Espy fails to report 210 legal executions within only two jurisdictions during a 45-year period, 100 in North Carolina and 110 in South Carolina. A similar rate of omission occurs in the Espy listings for nearly every state of the former Confederacy, including Espy's home state of Alabama, as well as the three border states of Kentucky, Maryland and Missouri. Consequently, any death penalty research (whether published or unpublished) that relied on *The Espy File* must now be regarded as suspect.

All of this leads up to the following question: How accurate and complete is the Hearn inventory? No claims of perfection are made. The law of averages and the widely scattered sources from which the body of this book was assembled make it inevitable that I shall have missed at least something. I do, however, feel justified in calling the present volume a substantial improvement over what has previously been available. Additions and corrections are welcome so long as they are supported by sound documentation.

My methodology in gathering this information can be easily explained. I investigated every known source until it was exhausted. My first rule was to eschew secondhand accounts for which I could not also find independent confirmation. I sought out original archival materials wherever and whenever possible. These consisted of official government records on both state and local levels such as courthouse files, jail rosters, death certificates, census records, coroners' inquests, appellate data (both published and unpublished), gubernatorial correspondence, clemency applications and individual prison inmate files. I rummaged through courthouse vaults, antique file cabinets, attics, cellars, musty old boxes that were heaped atop each other, and so forth. I spent countless hours and close to 30 years picking my way through volumes upon volumes of old newspapers, most on microfilm but some still in original hard copy. I also learned a valuable lesson by so doing: that there is no substitute for the old methods of painstaking research. I scoured those 18th-, 19th- and 20th-century newspapers one page at a time—month by month, year by year and title by title—until I had mined them for every tidbit. I have no regrets for having done it the hard way because in so doing I captured an enormous amount of information that might otherwise have been missed. I learned that the worst mistake that one can make (besides taking secondhand sources at their word) is to depend entirely on digital imagery and computerized search engines when studying historical newspapers. The newer technology does help on occasion, but scanned imaging often misses more than it captures. Old newsprint is frequently faded, light-toned, slightly blurred or otherwise defective in some way which fools electronic eyes.

I had also made it a point to do everything at my own expense. I spent many thousands of dollars, all of it my own money, on travel, photocopying, records requests, research fees, library guest passes, parking, gratuities, donations to historical societies, etc. I didn't want to be obligated to anyone. Nor did I want to have to tailor my findings to suit the political agenda of some biased organization. Sometimes I had to bear the ridicule of others who likened me to Don Quixote. Throughout, I kept in mind the words of my ninth-grade history teacher who told me 40 years ago that the road to truth is a long and curvy one. So I chugged on undauntedly. I became such a familiar face at some libraries that a couple of them even bent their rules by allowing me to take rolls of newspaper microfilm home with me after I had purchased an old hand-cranked microfilm reader. I continued this work through the 1980s and 1990s. Then, ever so gradually and ever so grudgingly, the forgotten files began to give up their secrets. Many of them were brittle with age. Many were held together with old metallic fasteners that had fused solid from rust. Some were putrid with coal dust. Some of them contained the actual bullets that had killed people and the semiliterate pleas for mercy crudely scrawled on cheap note paper by condemned men. There were fragile bundles of documents wrapped in once colorful ribbons that had since become faded and dry rotted and which crumbled in my hands. I was probably the first person to handle many of them since they had been filed away. Most telling of all were the macabre death warrants—calligraphic works of art—heavily festooned with black trimmings, black borders, black ink and black sealing wax—signed on their reverse sides by long-dead sheriffs stating that at exactly such and such hour on such and such date they had caused the person named in the warrant to be hanged by the neck until dead.

In the text that follows, I have opted not to use "politically correct" phraseology, but rather to reflect the language of the times. This is not because I am a vulgarian by nature but rather because I do not feel entitled to throw perfume on the harsh reality of the past. I acknowledge that some readers may not agree with this decision.

I have chosen to identify sexual assault victims only if their names were previously made public by a newspaper or a published appellate report, or if the person in question came forward voluntarily. Names are also provided if the case is so old that it has been legally declassified. Names are withheld if they do not meet these criteria or if I agreed not to divulge them as a condition of being granted access to the files. Confidentiality is also maintained in cases where there is a possibility that the victim might still be alive.

Additional tabulation of the data in this book reveals that 1,152 legal executions took place on Carolina soil during the century after the Civil War: 621 in the North State and 531 in the Palmetto State. Their distribution by specific felony is as follows:

North Carolina	**South Carolina**
455 for Murder	442 for Murder
126 for Rape	80 for Rape or Attempted Rape
34 for Aggravated Burglary	9 for Arson
4 for Highway Robbery	
2 for Arson	

The demographic breakdown of North Carolina's executed murderers is 341 blacks, 108 whites, and six Native Americans. Of the black persons who were legally put to death, 189 were condemned for killing white people, 150 for killing their fellow blacks, one for killing multiple victims who were both black and white, and one for killing multiple victims who were both white and American Indian. The white men who were executed for murder had in 100 instances killed people of their own race. Seven died for murdering blacks. One was executed for killing multiple victims who were both black and white. All six of the executed Native American killers had been convicted of murdering white people.

The demographic breakdown of North Carolina's executed sex offenders is 113 black males, 11 white males and two Native American males. Among the black men, there were 11 legal executions for black-on-black rape, one for the rape of a Native American woman, and 101 for the rape of white females. All of the executed white rapists had attacked females of their own race.

South Carolina executed 461 blacks, 68 whites and two Native Americans. Of the blacks who were legally put to death, 229 had been condemned for murdering white people, 140 for black-on-black homicide, two for killing a Chinese man and six for killing multiple victims both black and white. The white men who were executed for murder had in 60 instances killed persons of their own race. Three met their ends for murdering blacks. Sex offenders numbered as follows: 75 black males legally put to death for attacking white females and five white males for doing the same. There were no executions for rape of non-white victims.

This book will not address the questions of possible racial bias (in prosecution, conviction and sentencing) that have been contentiously debated for several decades. Its purpose is not to present an argument. Instead, I hope that by providing the most complete accounting to date of the executions that did occur in North Carolina and South Carolina and the crimes of which the condemned persons were convicted, the book will better inform anyone studying the complex issues surrounding capital punishment in the United States, regardless of their opinions or preconceptions.

Part One
Persons Executed in North Carolina
(Listed Chronologically)

1866

James Nixon, Donaldson Ruffin and Richard Williams (blacks, ages not recorded). *Aggravated Burglary.* Their crime was committed on an uncertain date in either 1865 or 1866 in Jones County. Executed for a nocturnal break-in at the house of 45-year-old Jacob F. Scott Esq. (white), almost undoubtedly under circumstances of a violent nature. This seems probable given the appalling state of lawlessness which prevailed in the Neuse River counties at this time and the fact that three men paid for it with their lives. They were hanged at Trenton on June 1, 1866. Sources: *Raleigh Daily Sentinel*, 6/7/66 (2:2); *Wilmington (NC) Daily Journal*, 5/9/66 (4:1), 5/17/66 (4:1) & 6/7/66 (4:1). See also: NC Governor's Papers Box 196 (May 7–15, 1866) containing mercy petition of John Williams (a 4th condemned prisoner in this case). The original trial papers are lost. See also: 1860 & 1870 U.S. Census (Jones Co., NC), which notes Mr. Scott, the only person of that surname which fits the party mentioned in the Williams mercy petition.

Charles Parks (black, age not recorded). *Murder.* The crime was committed on an unspecified date in either 1865 or 1866 in Mecklenburg County. Uxoricide. Executed for the murder of his wife (black, name unknown), she having been beaten and choked to death. Motive: unknown. The original trial papers have not survived. He was hanged at Charlotte on June 29, 1866. Source: *Western Democrat* (Charlotte, NC), 5/15/66 (3:1) & 7/3/66 (3:2).

Henry Queary (black, age not recorded). *Rape.* The crime was committed on 7/30/1866 in Cabarrus County. Indecent assault on the person of 28-year-old Josephine Queary (white, the wife of his former owner), she having been attacked in her own home. He was hanged at Concord on September 7, 1866. Source: *Wilmington (NC) Daily Journal*, 8/9/66 (4:1) & 9/11/66 (4:1). See also: NC Governor's Papers Box 198 (Aug 1–4, 1866), in which there is a formal request for authorization of a special court to try this offender. See also: 1860 U.S. Census (Cabarrus Co., NC) which notes the female party.

Augustus Williams and Lewis Williams (blacks, ages not recorded). *Highway Robbery.* The crime was committed on 6/25/1866 in New Hanover County. Specifically executed for forcibly stopping a wagon driven by a young freedman named John Loftin (black) while it was en route from Wilmington to Camp Whiting and stealing from it the following items: a newly butchered pork loin, a slab of bacon, three jars of molasses, half a bushel of corn meal, an 8-lb. sack of flour and a knife. The culprits also fired a musket at the wagon driver (Loftin) when he attempted to bolt from the scene. The shot tore away part of the coat that he was wearing. These bandits were also the prime suspects in a similar crime upon the person of a white man (Benjamin Mills) that same week. Mills lost his groceries and $3.25 in silver. Both of the robbers were hanged at Wilmington on December 21, 1866. Sources: *Wilmington (NC) Daily Journal*, 9/7/66 (3:1), 9/26/66 (3:1) & 10/20/66 (3:1); *Charleston (SC) Mercury*, 12/24/66 (4:2).

1867

William Johnson (black, age not recorded). *Murder.* The crime was committed on 1/4/1867 in Chatham County. Executed for the murder of 77-year-old John A. Johnson (white, his former owner), who was knocked from his horse and his skull broken in two places. Motive: highway robbery. The killer was hanged at Pittsboro on April 26, 1867. Sources: *Wilmington (NC) Daily Journal*, 1/22/67 (3:3); *Norfolk Virginian*, 1/25/67 (1:4); *Chatham (NC) Record*, 11/4/1886 (3:1) in retro. See also: Chatham County Superior Court minutes (Spring Term 1867), pg. 9; NC State Archives.

Green Hodges (black, age not recorded). *Rape.* The crime was committed on 1/7/1866 in Mecklenburg County. Indecent assault on the person of 41-year-old Jane Spears (white), she having been chased down and tackled by her assailant. He was hanged at Charlotte on June 14, 1867. Sources: *Western Democrat* (Charlotte, NC), 6/18/67 (3:2); Supreme Court Case File no. 8949 (NC State Archives). See also: 1870 U.S. Census (Mecklenburg Co., NC), which notes the female party.

John Brinkley (white, age 30). *Murder.* The crime was committed on 4/20/1867 in Lenoir County. Executed for the murder of Jonathan A. Costin (white, age not recorded), an oyster vender, who was shot in the head by means of an unspecified type of firearm, stripped naked and his body dragged into a creek by means of a rope tied around one of his ankles. Motive: highway robbery. The killer was hanged at Kinston on July 12, 1867. Sources: *Journal of Commerce* (New Bern, NC), 4/23/67 (1:4); *Wilmington (NC) Daily Journal*, 7/17/67 (3:2). See also: 1850 & 1860 U.S. Census (Craven Co., NC), which notes Brinkley.

Lewis Albritton (black, age not recorded). *Highway Robbery.* The crime was committed on 7/18/1867 in Craven County. Specifically executed for stopping 39-year-old Cicero Green and his wife (whites) on the highway one mile west of New Bern and stealing $30 from them. Also confirmed to have murdered Craven County Deputy Sheriff Bryan Williams (white, age 28) four days later when that officer attempted to arrest him on the Neuse Road. A handgun was used on that occasion. Albritton was also the prime suspect in the robbery and burning of the Wood & West Mercantile Company in

Kinston, NC. He was hanged at New Bern on August 16, 1867. Sources: *New Bern (NC) Republican*, 7/23/67 (3:1), 7/25/67 (3:2) & 7/27/67 (3:1); *Journal of Commerce* (New Bern), 8/17/67 (1:2). See also: 1860 U.S. Census (Craven Co., NC), which notes Green and Williams.

Franklin Smith (white, age not recorded). *Rape.* The crime was committed on or about 12/2/1866 in New Hanover County. Indecent assault on the person of 8-year-old Susan Smith (white), his foster daughter. He was hanged at Wilmington on August 30, 1867. Source: *Wilmington (NC) Daily Journal*, 12/8/66 (3:1), 4/12/67 (3:1) & 8/31/67 (4:3). Appeal: 61 NC 302–303.

Banvester Haywood (black, age not recorded). *Murder.* The crime was committed on 5/3/1866 in Craven County. Shotgun slaying of Tellishia Keyes (black female, age not recorded), she having been blasted in the face at point-blank range. Motive: obnoxious drunk. Haywood was hanged at New Bern on September 20, 1867. Sources: *Wilmington (NC) Daily Journal*, 5/9/66 (4:1); *Journal of Commerce* (New Bern), 5/31/67 (1:2) & 9/21/67 (1:2). Appeal: 61 NC 376–379.

Anderson Marslettur (black, age not recorded). *Murder.* The crime was committed on 8/28/1867 in Halifax County. Uxoricide. Executed for the hatchet murder of his wife (black, name not specified), she having been completely decapitated. The original trial papers have not survived. Motive: uncertain. The trial jury was comprised of 3 blacks and 9 whites. Marslettur was hanged at Halifax on November 29, 1867. Sources: *Wilmington (NC) Daily Journal*, 9/7/67 (3:3); *Raleigh Weekly Register*, 11/2/67 (3:5); *Raleigh Daily Sentinel*, 12/3/67 (2:4).

1868

Squire Woods (black, age not recorded) **and Willis Weatherly** (black, age about 20). *Murder.* The crime was committed on 11/13/1865 in Rockingham County. Musket slaying of Dick Wright (black, age not recorded), the victim having succumbed to his wound on 3/31/1866. Motive: gambling dispute. Both killers were hanged at Wentworth on January 3, 1868. Sources: *Richmond (VA) Whig*, 1/10/68 (3:4); NC Governor's Papers Box 205 (Nov 1–6, 1867) and State Supreme Court Case No. 8910 (unpublished); NC State Archives.

Washington Hicks (black, age not recorded). *Highway Robbery.* The crime was committed on 7/18/1867 in Craven County. Specifically executed for "feloniously and violently" making an assault on the person of 39-year-old Cicero Green (white) "to the bodily fear and danger of his life" and stealing from him a silver watch. (This was the same incidence of robbery for which Lewis Albritton was hanged in 1867.) Hicks was a notorious outlaw and bandit who led a gang of renegade freedmen that had terrorized the Neuse River counties since the time of Emancipation. He and his cronies interpreted the word "Freedom" as a license to run wild. Hicks was hanged at New Bern on February 14, 1868. Sources: *New Bern Republican*, 7/18/67 (3:1); *Wilmington (NC) Daily Journal*, 2/18/68 (3:2). See also: Craven County Superior Court Criminal Action Papers (1867), NC State Archives.

Needham Evans and Richard Jackson (blacks, ages not recorded). *Murder.* The crime was committed on 12/24/1867 in Pitt County. Gunshot slaying of 56-year-old Willis Briley (white). Motive: home invasion. Both offenders were hanged at Greenville on February 14, 1868. Source: *Petersburg (VA) Daily Index*, 1/3/68 (2:3), 2/10/68 (2:3) & 2/25/68 (2:3). See also: 1860 U.S. Census (Pitt Co., NC), which notes the murdered man.

William Wright Parker (white, age 17). *Murder.* The crime was committed on 3/29/1863 in New Hanover County. Executed for the wartime murder of William Childress (white, age not recorded), a boon companion with whom he had been out whoring that night. The victim was slashed to death with a knife and his body dumped in a creek. Motive: robbery and gross perfidy. Parker was hanged at Wilmington on February 28, 1868. Source: *Wilmington (NC) Daily Journal*, 10/18/66 (3:1), 10/12/67 (3:1) & 2/29/68 (3:1). Appeal: 61 NC 462–467.

Jim Knight (black, age about 43) **and John Taylor** (black, age about 32). *Murder.* The crime was committed on 8/9/1866 in Edgecombe County. Executed for the murder of 21-year-old John H. Cutchen (white), a store clerk who was battered to death with a hammer. Motive: robbery. The killers were hanged at Tarboro on April 3, 1868. Sources: *New York Herald*, 4/4/68 (4:1); *Tarboro (NC) Southerner*, 4/9/68 (3:2); *Wilmington (NC) Daily Journal*, 8/14/66 (2:3). See also: 1860 U.S. Census (Edgecombe Co., NC), which notes Cutchen.

Thomas Dula (white, age 36). *Murder.* The crime was committed on 5/28/1866 in Wilkes County. Fatal stabbing and illegal burial of 23-year-old Laura Foster (white). Motive: because she had infected him with venereal disease. Venue changed from Wilkes County to Iredell County. Dula was hanged at Statesville on May 1, 1868. Sources: *Raleigh Weekly Standard*, 10/31/66 (4:6); *New York Herald*, 5/2/68 (7:5). See also: 1860 U.S. Census (Caldwell Co., NC), which notes both parties; *Famous Detective Cases*, 7/35; *Front Page Detective*, 3/54.

Reuben Wright (white, age 63). *Murder.* The crime was committed on 6/26/1867 in Stokes County. Ax murder of about 42-year-old Silas Hairston (black), the victim's headless body having been dumped in a river. Motive: adultery and wife stealing. This white man who hankered for a black woman was hanged at Danbury on May 19, 1868. Sources: *Wilmington (NC) Daily Journal*, 7/9/67 (3:4) & 5/31/68 (3:4); *New York Herald*, 5/23/68 (8:3) & 5/27/68 (4:1). See also: 1860 U.S. Census (Stokes Co., NC), which notes the killer; and 1860 U.S. Census (Stokes Co., NC, slave schedule), which notes the victim under the ownership of Ruth Hairston.

George Washington (black, age 17). *Arson.* The crime was committed on an unknown date in Lenoir County. Although the legal execution of this juvenile offender is confirmed by three different North Carolina newspapers, none of them specified anything other than his age and the nature of his transgression. The fire that he was convicted of setting must have been no ordinary conflagration. Lenoir County Superior Court records were themselves destroyed by fire in 1880. Washington was hanged for his crime at Kinston on May 22, 1868. Sources: *Raleigh Daily Sentinel*, 6/1/68 (2:3); *Wilmington Morning Journal*,

6/2/68 (3:4); *Tarboro (NC) Southerner*, 6/4/68 (4:4).

Rufus F. Ludwick, alias "Ludwig." (white, age 21). *Murder.* The crime was committed on 6/4/1867 in Rowan County. Uxoricide. Executed for the murder of 19-year-old Milly Campbell Ludwick (white, his bride of 11 days) who was shot through the head with a rifle, her throat cut and her weighted body dumped in a creek. Motive: elusive; it was never explained with any degree of certainty. This tragic young husband was hanged at Salisbury on June 27, 1868. Source: *New York Herald*, 7/1/68 (5:4). See also: 1850 U.S. Census (Pope Co., AR), which notes the killer as a minor and the correct variation of his surname.

Tom Ryan (black, age not recorded). *Murder.* The crime was committed on 8/29/1868 in Martin County. Fatal stabbing of 33-year-old James R. Leggett (white), the victim having been knifed multiple times. Motive: personal grudge with racial overtones. Ryan had approached Leggett in a country store and accused that man of "having mistreated" him. Then he pulled out a knife and went on the attack. He ran out of the place yelling that he would get his gun and "kill every damned white man in Jamesville." Ryan was hanged at Williamston on November 6, 1868. Sources: *Wilmington (NC) Daily Journal*, 10/18/68 (3:3); *Tarboro (NC) Southerner*, 11/12/68 (3:1). See also: 1860 U.S. Census (Martin Co., NC), which notes the murdered man.

1869

Augustus Holmes (black, age not recorded). *Murder.* The crime was committed on 6/9/1867 in Edgecombe County. Enfield rifle slaying of Matthew King (black, age not recorded). Motive: because the killer thought that the victim had said bad things about him. Holmes was hanged at Tarboro on January 1, 1869. Sources: *Tarboro (NC) Southerner*, 6/13/67 (3:1) & 1/7/69 (3:1); *New York Herald*, 1/5/69 (4:1).

Augustus Baker (black, age 26) **and James Thomas** (black, age not recorded). *Murder.* The crime was committed on 5/24/1868 in Halifax County. Murder of Wade Ditcher (black, age not recorded), who was clubbed to death and dumped in a river. Motive: gambling dispute. The killers were hanged at Halifax on June 4, 1869. Sources: *Wilmington (NC) Daily Journal*, 6/4/68 (3:4); *New York Herald*, 6/5/69 (5:1); *Tarboro (NC) Southerner*, 6/10/69 (2:4). See also: 1860 U.S. Census (Halifax Co., NC), which notes Baker as a free Negro.

John Smith (black, age not recorded). *Murder.* The crime was committed on 6/14/1868 in Orange County. Strangulation murder of Smith Green (black, age not recorded) by means of a leather strap. Motive: apparent conspiracy. Venue changed from Orange County to Chatham County. Smith was hanged at Pittsboro on August 6, 1869. Source: Chatham County Superior Court Minutes (Spring Term 1869), pg. 106. Also State Supreme Court case file no. 9359 (State vs. Nero Davis, a co-defendant in this case whose death sentence was later commuted), NC State Archives; *Chatham (NC) Record*, 11/4/1886 (3:1) in retro.

Benjamin Douglass (black, age not recorded). *Murder.* The crime was committed on December 30, 1868 in Moore County. Shotgun slaying of Dennis Thomas (black, age not recorded). Motive: uncertain. The killer was hanged at Carthage on October 1, 1869. Source: State Supreme Court case file no. 9188; NC State Archives.

1870

Lewis Hines (black, age not recorded). *Rape.* The crime was committed on 4/29/1869 in Edgecombe County. Indecent assault on the person of 18-year-old Sarah Johnson (white), she having denounced him in open court as "a nasty stinking rascal" who had attacked her in a field while dressed in his Sunday clothes. He was hanged at Tarboro on January 14, 1870. Sources: *Tarboro (NC) Southerner*, 1/20/70 (3:2); *New York Herald*, 1/17/70 (6:4). See also: 1870 U.S. Census (Edgecombe Co., NC), which notes the female party.

Bob Gunn and Tom Young (blacks, ages not recorded). *Murder.* The crime was committed on 12/25/1869 in Orange County. Executed for the murder of 29-year-old Reuben Blalock (white), a barkeep who was blackjacked by means of a cog wheel tied to a rope, his throat cut, a pillow case stuffed into his mouth and a cord tightly knotted around his neck. Motive: robbery. Both culprits were hanged at Hillsboro on April 1, 1870. Sources: *Hillsborough (NC) Recorder*, 4/6/70 (3:1); *Wilmington (NC) Daily Journal*, 12/30/69 (3:3) & 1/5/70 (3:3); *New York Herald*, 1/11/70 (5:5) & 4/2/70 (8:1).

Andrew Tarpley (black, age 14). *Rape.* The crime was committed on April 6, 1870 in Alamance County. Indecent assault on the person of 11-year-old Bettie Loy (white), the details of which were so heinous that his age was disallowed as a mitigating factor. Tarpley was hanged at Graham on August 26, 1870. Sources: *New York Herald*, 9/4/70 (5:6); NC Governor's Papers Box 224 (Aug 21–31, 1870); NC State Archives. See also: 1870 U.S. Census (Alamance Co., NC), which notes the culprit and the revelation that his mother had borne him when she was eleven years old.

William Stimson (black, age not recorded). *Rape.* The crime was committed on 6/28/1870 in Wake County. Sentenced to death by an all-black jury for indecently assaulting 66-year-old Nancy Bunn (white) during the course of a home invasion. He ransacked the woman's house, set it ablaze and dragged the feeble occupant outdoors by means of a lariat into some woods, where he raped her. Stimson was hanged at Raleigh on November 4, 1870. Sources: *Daily Sentinel (Raleigh NC)*, 11/5/70 (3:1); *Wilmington (NC) Daily Journal*, 7/2/70 (3:5); *New York Herald*, 11/5/70 (5:1). See also: 1860 U.S. Census (Wake Co., NC), which notes the female party.

1871

Dumer Harget (black, age 31). *Murder.* The crime was committed on 5/1/1870 in Carteret County. Musket slaying of Absalom Fisher (black, age not recorded), whose body was then weighted with irons and dumped in a river. Motive: adultery with the victim's wife. Harget was hanged at Beaufort on February 3, 1871. Sources: *Wilmington (NC) Daily Journal*, 7/15/70 (3:2); *New York Herald*, 2/4/71 (7:1). See also: Carteret County Superior Court Criminal Action Papers (1870); NC State Archives.

Henderson Oxendine (black, age 47). *Murder.* The crime was committed on 10/4/1870 in Robeson County. Executed for the ambush killing of 36-year-old Stephen Davis (white), a posse man whose party was fired upon with rifles and shotguns. Motive: resisting arrest. This was just one incident in a decade long (1864–1874) imbroglio called the "Lowry War," which convulsed Robeson and Bladen Counties. An outlaw gang headed by a mixed-blood (Tuscarora-Lumbee) Native American named Henry Berry Lowry had holed up in the more inaccessible regions of that area and swelled their numbers with a motley collection of renegades, malcontents and riffraff, according to published accounts. They were known alternately as the "Lowry Gang" and the "Swamp Angels." They terrorized the entire district with every species of crime. It took ten years for authorities and bounty hunters to finally root them out. The cost was enormous in terms of lives and property damage. It was also a major factor in why this part of North Carolina lagged behind in its social and economic development. Henderson Oxendine was hanged at Lumberton on March 17, 1871. He was the only member of the "Lowry Gang" to meet his end by legal means. The bones of innumerable others remain in the swamps to this day. Sources: *Richmond (VA) Whig*, 10/11/70 (4:6); *New York Herald*, 3/21/71 (4:5); *Wilmington (NC) Daily Journal*, 3/11/71 (3:2) & 3/19/71 (3:3). See also: 1870 U.S. Census (Robeson Co., NC), which notes Oxendine, and (Bladen Co., NC), which notes Davis.

Madison Youngblood (black, age not recorded). *Murder.* The crime was committed on 2/13/1870 in Johnston County. Shotgun slaying of Miles Draughton (white, age not recorded), a professional gambler who was murdered in his bed. Motive: robbery. The killer was hanged at Smithfield on May 5, 1871. Sources: *Daily Journal (Wilmington NC)*, 2/20/70 (3:4); *New York Herald*, 5/6/71 (9:1).

Ned McLendon (black, age not recorded). *Rape.* The crime was committed on 6/21/1870 in Richmond County. Indecent assault on the person of 25-year-old Sallie L. Usher (white), she having been pounced on when she went to a spring to draw water on an oppressively hot day. The trial jury was comprised of 8 blacks and 4 whites. McLendon was hanged at Rockingham on June 2, 1871. Sources: *Wilmington (NC) Daily Journal*, 6/4/71 (3:3); *New York Herald*, 6/6/71 (8:1). See also: 1870 U.S. Census (Richmond Co., NC), which notes the female party.

Henderson Young (black, age not recorded). *Murder.* The crime was committed on 12/27/1870 in Mecklenburg County. Shotgun slaying of 45-year-old Edward Smith (white) accompanied by the near-fatal beating of that man's wife and the ransacking and burning of his home. Motive: robbery. The killer was hanged at Charlotte on July 14, 1871. Sources: *Wilmington (NC) Daily Journal*, 12/31/70 (3:4); *Charlotte (NC) Democrat*, 7/18/71 (3:1); *New York Herald*, 7/15/71 (7:2). See also: 1870 U.S. Census (Mecklenburg Co., NC), which notes Mr. Smith.

Ned Myers (black, age 54) **and Lewis Coppedge** (black, age 17). *Murder.* The crime was committed on 5/20/1871 in Anson County. Murder of 37-year-old James W. Redfearn (white), who was battered to death with pieces of wooden fence rail. Motive: mugging. Both killers were hanged at Wadesboro on July 21, 1871. Source: *New York Herald*, 7/26/71 (6:5). See also: 1860 U.S. Census (Anson Co., NC), which notes Mr. Redfearn; and 1870 U.S. Census (Anson Co., NC), which notes the culprits.

Alfred Mackey (black, age not recorded). *Murder.* The crime was committed on 7/5/1871 in Columbus County. Ax murder of 44-year-old John Stancill (white, a former lieutenant in the 20th NC Regiment, CSA), who was butchered as he dozed on the portico of his store one lazy afternoon. Motive: robbery. Mackey was hanged at Whiteville on October 27, 1871. Sources: *Wilmington (NC) Daily Journal*, 7/7/71 (3:1); *New York Herald*, 10/28/71 (5:3). See also: 1870 U.S. Census (Columbus Co., NC), which notes the murdered man.

William B. Parker (white, age 50). *Murder.* The crime was committed on 12/4/1870 in Guilford County. Murder of 60-year-old Thomas Price (black) by allowing a pack of ferocious dogs to tear him apart. The victim was then finished off by having his brains beaten out with a fence rail. Motive: because the killer suspected Price of burning his barn. Parker was hanged at Greensboro on October 27, 1871. Sources: *New York Herald*, 10/28/71 (5:2); *Norfolk Virginian*, 10/31/71 (1:7). See also: 1870 U.S. Census (Guilford Co., NC), which notes both parties.

Mack Swann (black, age not recorded). *Rape.* The crime was committed on 8/4/1871 in Johnston County. Indecent assault on the person of 69-year-old Keziah "Kizzie" Peeden (white), she having been snatched in broad daylight as she was walking homeward, dragged into woods and brutally manhandled to such an extent that two of her ribs were broken. The trial jury was comprised of six blacks and six whites. Swann was hanged at Smithfield on November 3, 1871. Sources: *New York Herald*, 11/9/71 (5:4); *Norfolk Virginian*, 11/11/71 (3:1). See also: 1870 U.S. Census (Johnston Co., NC), which notes the woman in this case. Also: Johnston County Superior Court Minutes (Fall Term 1871), pg. 340.

Pompey Lyon (black, age 31). *Murder.* The crime was committed on 10/21/1871 in Orange County. Fatal stabbing of Baker Tilley (black, age not recorded). Motive: fracas at a husking bee. The killer was hanged at Hillsboro on December 15, 1871. Source: *New York Herald*, 12/16/71 (5:1). See also: 1870 U.S. Census (Orange Co., NC), which notes the culprit.

1872

Govan Adair (white, age 25) **and Columbus Adair** (white, age 27). *Murder.* The crime was committed on 4/26/1871 in Rutherford County. Two brothers executed for the massacre of 51-year-old Silas Weston and family (blacks) who were all shot with handguns, slashed with knives and their cabin burnt. The other homicide victims were: David Weston (age 5), Theodosia Weston (age 6), and William Herbert Steadman, alias Lee (age 10), the latter apparently having been the illegitimate result of a relationship that Weston's wife had at the age of 14 or 15. She survived the slaughter along with the youngest member of the family, Mary Weston (age 15 mo.), although both were believed by the killers to have been slain as well, the baby's throat being cut in its cradle. Motive: terrorism. The primary victim (Silas Weston) had dared to testify against Klansmen (the Adairs) for stealing liquor. Venue changed from Rutherford County to Henderson County. The Adairs were hanged at Hendersonville on July 12, 1872. Source: *New York Herald*, 7/19/72 (8:1). See also: 1870 U.S. Census (Rutherford Co., NC), which notes all parties but erroneously classified two of the child victims as white, an impossibility since their parents were "mulatto." The kids in question were probably so light-toned that the census taker erred.

Newton V. Chandler (white, age 26). *Rape*. The crime was committed on 4/1/1871 in Gaston County. Indecent assault on the person of a 28-year-old white female identified only as "Miss Bradshaw" during the course of an armed home invasion in which her father was robbed of his money. Venue changed from Gaston County to Mecklenburg County. Chandler was hanged at Charlotte on August 9, 1872. Sources: *Charlotte (NC) Democrat*, 8/13/72 (3:2); *Wilmington (NC) Daily Journal*, 8/13/72 (3:3); *New York Herald*, 8/10/72 (10:1). See also: 1860 U.S. Census (Cleveland Co., NC), which notes the culprit.

Nathaniel Caldwell (black, age 30). *Murder*. The crime was committed on April 1, 1872, in Mecklenburg County. Baby killer. Executed for the murder of less than 1-year-old Dovey Davidson (black), his female bastard child that he had begotten by a 16-year-old "mulatto girl" named Ann Eliza Davidson. The tiny victim was buried alive. Motive: unwanted paternity. Caldwell was hanged at Charlotte on August 23, 1872. Sources: *Pomeroy's Democrat* (New York), 6/1/72 (3:5); *Charlotte (NC) Democrat*, 8/27/72 (3:2). Appeal: 67 NC 119–122. See also: 1870 U.S. Census (Mecklenburg Co., NC), which notes the killer as "Nathan Caldwell," a married man. Also: State Supreme Court case file no. 10260 (NC State Archives).

York Lattimore (black, age 42) **and Jerry Thompson** (black, age 24). *Murder*. The crime was committed on an unspecified date in the spring of 1872 in Rutherford County. Both executed for the murder (by undisclosed means) of 20-year-old Samuel Martin (black). Motive: rivalry for a white whore. The trial papers were presumably lost in a 1907 courthouse fire. The killers were hanged at Rutherfordton on November 8, 1872. Sources: *Daily Phoenix* (Columbia, SC), 11/27/72 (2:3); *Raleigh Daily News*, 11/13/72 (3:1). See also: 1870 U.S. Census (Rutherford Co., NC), which notes all parties.

Thomas Johnson (black, age 21). *Rape*. The crime was committed on 9/16/1871 in Davidson County. Indecent assault on the person of 62-year-old Susan Thompson (white), a pedestrian whom he had encountered while tramping along some RR tracks. The woman was beaten and choked into submission. The miscreant was hanged at Lexington on December 13, 1872. Sources: *Wilmington (NC) Daily Journal*, 11/16/72 (2:2) & 12/17/72 (2:3); *New York Herald*, 12/14/72 (5:5).

1873

Orren Mercer (black, age 35). *Murder*. The crime was committed on 4/15/1872 in Edgecombe County. Baby killer. Executed for the murder of his bastard child (a 5-month-old black male infant of no known name), by pouring concentrated lye, or "caustic potash," as the substance was then known, down its throat. Motive: because he had been ordered to pay child support. Mercer was hanged at Tarboro on January 16, 1873. Sources: *Tarboro Southerner*, 1/16/73 (3:1); *New York Herald*, 1/19/73 (5:1); *Wilmington (NC) Daily Journal*, 4/25/72 (3:3).

George Lea (black, age 28). *Rape.* The crime was committed on 3/20/1873 in Caswell County. Indecent assault on the person of 74-year-old Ann Kearsey (white), a maiden woman. She was described rather callously as "tottering with infirmity, stooped, decrepit, emaciated and shriveled. Her few and straggling hairs were whitened by her great age, her eyes red, bleared and sunken in their sockets, her gums toothless and her very skeleton nearly protruding through the yellowish and parchment like skin that covers it." The culprit terrorized "this poor old creature" with a razor to more effectively accomplish his purpose. A published description of the rapist himself was equally overdone: "His features were remarkable for nothing save a total absence of any intellectual expression and the presence instead of every animal characteristic peculiar to a savage, the eyes being large, dull and heavy, the jaw large, the lips thick, nose wide and forehead reclining. In appearance he did not belie his nature, instincts and deeds as a brute. The fiend's eyes glared with a brutal lust and his breath was hot and sickening with the foul stench of the vilest pine top whiskey." George Lea was hanged at Yanceyville on May 6, 1873. Sources: *New York Herald*, 5/7/73 (7:5); *Wilmington (NC) Daily Journal*, 5/8/73 (4:4).

Bayless Henderson (white, age 26). *Murder.* The crime was committed on 9/15/1872 in Jackson County. Handgun slaying of 72-year-old Nimrod Simpson Jarrett (white), the victim having been basely shot from behind. Motive: highway robbery. Regarded by many as a Southern traitor in addition to a murderer, Henderson was hanged at Sylva on June 6, 1873. Sources: *Charlotte (NC) Democrat*, 10/1/72 (3:4); *Raleigh Daily News*, 6/8/73 (3:1) & 6/15/73 (3:1). Appeal: 68 NC 348–351. See also the Civil War enlistment record of Bayless Henderson (3rd Mounted Infantry, East Tennessee, USA) which notes his age.

Aaron Stroud (black, age 16). *Rape.* The crime was committed on 12/21/1872 in Orange County. Indecent assault on the person of "not quite 4-year-old" Martha E. Stroud (white), a daughter of his former owner. She was "severely lacerated" in a female way. Her attacker was hanged at Hillsboro on June 30, 1873. Source: *New York Herald*, 7/1/73 (5:4). See also: 1870 U.S. Census (Orange Co., NC), which notes both parties.

Hardy Jones (black, age 63). *Murder.* The crime was committed on 2/1/1872 in Craven County. Shotgun slaying of Robert Miller (black, age not recorded), a posse man. Motive: resisting arrest. Jones was hanged at New Bern on August 8, 1873. Sources: *New York Herald*, 8/9/73 (5:5); *Wilmington (NC) Daily Journal*, 8/10/73 (1:4). See also: 1870 U.S. Census (Craven Co., NC), which notes the killer.

1874

Joseph Baker (white, age 28). *Murder.* The crime was committed on 2/17/1873 in Mecklenburg County. This man was a CSA veteran condemned by an all-white jury for the fatal stabbing of a black man named Newton Wilfong (age not recorded) in a saloon brawl. Baker was hanged at Charlotte on January 16, 1874. Sources: *Wilmington (NC) Daily Journal*, 1/20/74 (1:4); *Charlotte (NC) Democrat*, 1/20/74 (3:3); *New York Herald*, 1/17/74 (8:5). Appeal: 69 NC 126–128.

John Allen Ketchey (white, age 30). *Rape.* The crime was committed on 6/15/1872 in Rowan County. Indecent assault on the person of 17-year-old Millie Bersherer (white), she having been accosted on a public road (the culprit having smeared himself with blackface for that purpose) and dragged into woods against her will. Ketchey was hanged at Salisbury on June 26, 1874. Sources: *New York Herald*, 6/27/74 (9:6); *Wilmington (NC) Daily Journal*, 6/27/74 (4:4) which gives "Beecher" as the victim's surname.

John Allen Blake (black, age 23). *Rape.* The crime was committed on 6/22/1874 in Wake County. Indecent assault on the person of 18-year-old Lucy Haley (white), she having been traumatized to such an extent that "she lost her mind" and was left "a raving maniac." Her attacker was hanged at Raleigh on July 24, 1874. Sources: *Daily News (Raleigh NC)*, 7/25/74 (1:4); *Evening Star (Washington, D.C.)*, 7/27/74 (1:4).

George Berry (black, age 28). *Murder.* The crime was committed on 9/10/1873 in Columbus County. Fatal stabbing of 22-year-old Cain Cooper (black). Motive: drunken brawl. Berry was hanged at Whiteville on October 30, 1874. Source: *Wilmington (NC) Daily Journal*, 10/31/74 (4:3). See also: 1870 U.S. Census (Duplin Co., NC), which notes the victim.

1875

Aaron Bonner (black, age not recorded). *Rape.* The crime was committed on 8/10/1874 in Beaufort County. Indecent assault on the person of 25-year-old Margaret Kipps (white). The trial jury was comprised of 7 blacks and 5 whites. Bonner was hanged at Washington on March 5, 1875. Sources: *Wilmington (NC) Daily Journal*, 11/13/74 (4:4) & 3/12/75 (4:5); *Tarboro (NC) Southerner*, 3/12/75 (3:3); Beaufort County Superior Court Minutes (Fall Term 1874), pg. 247–248. See also: 1850 U.S. Census (Beaufort Co., NC), which notes the victim was a minor.

George Cunningham (white, age 19). *Murder.* The crime was committed on 6/6/1874 in Buncombe County. Ax murder of Daniel Sternberg (white, age not recorded), a traveler from Kansas who he met in a roadside campground. Motive: gambling dispute. Venue changed from Buncombe County to Madison County. The killer was hanged at Marshall on May 28, 1875. Source: *Raleigh Daily News*, 10/18/74 (3:1) & 6/8/75 (3:1). Appeal: 72 NC 432–440. See also: a well-done feature article on this case which appeared in the *News-Times* (Hendersonville, NC) on 9/21/1986, pg. B-1.

Cornelius Williamson (black, age 39). *Murder.* The crime was committed on 6/17/1874 in Northampton County. Handgun slaying of Samuel Presson (white, age not recorded), a railroad bridge tender. Motive: attempted robbery. Williamson was hanged at Jackson on August 27, 1875. Sources: *Wilmington*

(NC) Daily Journal, 6/20/74 (1:3) & 8/29/75 (4:4); *Petersburg (VA) Index & Appeal*, 8/28/75 (3:4). Articles about this case in the *Chicago Times*, 6/5/75 (4:1) & 6/19/75 (3:4), are erroneous, having been telegraphed prematurely by an evidently over-eager reporter.

Lawyer Bryan (black, age 17). *Murder.* The crime was committed on 5/4/1874 in Onslow County. Shotgun slaying of 41-year-old Michael T. Langley (white), the victim having been blasted from behind. Motive: indiscernible. Venue changed from Onslow County to Carteret County. Bryan was hanged at Beaufort on September 3, 1875. Sources: Carteret County Criminal Action Papers (1875), NC State Archives; *Raleigh Weekly News*, 3/31/75 (3:2); *Wilmington (NC) Daily Journal*, 3/7/75 (4:5); *Courier-Journal* (Louisville, KY), 11/23/75 (2:1). See also: 1870 U.S. Census (Onslow Co., NC), which notes Michael "Langly." The bill of costs for this case included $3.55 for lumber to build the gallows, $20 for a carpenter to construct it along with a coffin, 50 cents for a rope, $10 for the hangman, $5 for the gravedigger and $10 for an attending physician since none could be found who would do the job without pay.

William H. Hall (white, age not recorded). *Murder.* The crime was committed on 9/12/1874 in Buncombe County. Shotgun slaying of Andrew J. Gillespie (white, age not recorded), his stepfather-in-law. Motive: family feud. Hall was hanged at Asheville on October 1, 1875. Source: *People's Press* (Salem NC), 7/15/75 (2:1) & 11/25/75 (2:4). Appeal: 73 NC 122–126. See also: Buncombe County Superior Court Criminal Action Papers (1868–1875), *State vs. William & Clara Hall*; NC State Archives.

1876

Burwell Newsome (black, age 18). *Rape.* The crime was committed on 12/23/1875 in Bertie County. Indecent assault on the person of 28-year-old Ellen Outland (white), a poor woman who worked in the fields. Her attacker was hanged at Windsor on May 23, 1876. Source: *New York Herald*, 5/24/76 (7:4). See also: 1870 U.S. Census (Bertie Co., NC), which notes the female party.

Isaac Berry (black, age about 45). *Murder.* The crime was committed on or about 10/10/1872 in Caldwell County. Uxoricide. Executed for the murder of Sophie Berry (black, age not recorded), she having been battered with a blunt instrument and her body dumped over an embankment, where it was then covered with pine branches. Motive: bigamy on his part. Berry was hanged at Lenoir on June 1, 1876. Source: Nancy Alexander, *Here I Will Dwell: The Story of Caldwell County* (self-published, 1956), pgs. 152–154. The original records on which Ms. Alexander based her account have since gone missing, but there is independent verification to be found in the NC Governors Papers (Box 232) Oct. 12–31, 1872, NC State Archives. The proof is in the form of a letter about Berry's status as a fugitive. It also mentions that he had another wife and two outside children in Buncombe County and was believed to be hiding out with them.

William Messimer (white, age 22). *Murder.* The crime was committed on 5/15/1875 in Rowan County. Hanged on his 24th birthday for the murder of 74-year-old Sarah Heilig (white, his mother-in-law), she having been felled with a rock, then beaten to death and her body thrown down a well. Motive: avarice. Venue changed from Rowan County to Iredell County. The killer was executed at Statesville on December 22, 1876. Sources: *Wilmington (NC) Daily Journal*, 5/26/75 (4:5); *New York Herald*, 12/23/76 (5:2). See also: 1860 U.S. Census (Rowan Co., NC), which notes the slain woman.

1877

Simon Ragland (black, age not recorded). *Rape.* The crime was committed on 12/12/1875 in Edgecombe County. Indecent assault on the person of 21-year-old Cornelia Bidgood (white), she having been accosted on a footpath, beaten, gagged and raped. Venue changed from Edgecombe County to Martin County. The culprit was hanged at Williamston on January 22, 1877. Sources: *Tarboro (NC) Southerner*, 12/17/75 (3:3) & (3:5); *New York Herald*, 1/23/77 (5:6). See also: 1870 U.S. Census (Edgecombe Co., NC), which notes the female party.

Hillman Morgan (black, age not recorded). *Murder.* The crime was committed on 6/3/1870 in Franklin County. Executed for the murder of John Crudup (black, age not recorded), who was shot in the belly with a handgun and finished off by having his head smashed with a rock. Motive: thief caught in the act. Morgan was hanged at Louisburg on November 2, 1877. Sources: *People's Press* (Salem, NC), 7/8/70 (3:2); *Raleigh Observer*, 11/6/77 (3:6).

Nathan Perry Overton (white, age 33) **and Noah Taylor** (black, age 31). *Murder.* The crime was committed on 10/31/1874 in Edgecombe County. Ax murder of about 25-year-old William Grimes (white), a store clerk. Motive: robbery. Venue changed from Edgecombe County to Beaufort County. The killers were hanged at Washington on November 2, 1877. Sources: *Enquirer-Southerner* (Tarboro, NC), 11/6/74 (3:3); *Raleigh Observer*, 11/6/77 (2:5); *New York Herald*, 11/3/77 (3:6).

Hilliard Morgan (black, age 35). *Aggravated Burglary.* The crime was committed on 2/8/1877 in Wayne County. Executed for a nocturnal break-in at the house of 65-year-old Thomas Yelverton (white), during which a substantial amount of money was stolen. The culprit was caught on 7/6/1877 with some of the loot still in his possession. He was hanged at Goldsboro on December 21, 1877. Source: *New York Herald*, 12/22/77 (3:2). See also: 1870 U.S. Census (Carteret Co., NC), which notes Morgan, and (Wayne Co., NC), which notes the homeowner in this case.

1878

Arden Nelson (black, age 22). *Murder.* The crime was committed on 4/20/1877 in Bertie County. Murder of 37-year-old Jehu Webb (white, a store clerk), who was struck down from behind with a persimmon club. Motive: robbery. The loot consisted of $3.50 in money and a new suit of clothes off the store rack. Venue changed from Bertie County to Washington County. Nelson was hanged at Plymouth on January 18, 1878. Source: *New York Herald*, 1/22/78 (10:2). See also: 1870 U.S. Census (Bertie Co., NC), which notes Webb, and (Beaufort Co., NC), which notes Nelson.

John Shallington, alias "John Chalton," alias "Lewis Phillips." (black, age 28). *Murder.* The crime was committed on or about 8/15/1877 in Greene County. Shotgun slaying of 16-year-old Serena Thompson (black), his stepdaughter. Motive: because she had dared to become affianced to another young man when the killer treated her like his personal concubine. Shallington was hanged at Snow Hill on April 12, 1878. Sources: *Goldsboro (NC) Messenger*, 4/11/78 (3:3) & 4/15/78 (3:3); *New York Herald*, 4/13/78 (5:6); *Jackson (MI) Weekly Citizen*, 4/16/78 (4:4).

Henry Roberts (black, age not recorded). *Murder.* The crime was committed on 2/16/1878 in Cleveland County. Executed for the murder of Gus Ware (black, age not recorded), who was battered with a hickory club and his body put on railroad tracks, where it was mangled by a passing train. Motive: rivalry for a white whore. Roberts was hanged at Shelby on May 24, 1878. Sources: *New York Herald*, 5/25/78 (3:4); *Jackson (MI) Weekly Citizen*, 5/28/78 (8:2).

Harris Atkinson (black, age 38), **Noah Cherry** (black, age 64) **and Robert Thompson** (black, age 42). *Murder.* The crime was committed on 2/12/1878 in Wayne County. Ax murders of James Patrick Worley and Apsilla Jane Snipes Worley (a married white couple, ages not recorded), the woman having also been gang raped. Motive: self-explanatory. The three culprits were hanged at Goldsboro on June 14, 1878. Source: *Goldsboro (NC) Messenger*, 2/18/78 (3:2); *New York Herald*, 2/14/78 (10:3) & 6/15/78 (10:1); *Tarboro Southerner*, 6/27/78 (3:5). See also: Johnston County Marriage Register (1874), which notes the Worleys on January 27 of that year.

James Laxton (black, age about 43). *Rape.* The crime was committed on 4/14/1876 in Caldwell County. Indecent assault on the person of 17-year-old Nancy L. Barlow (white), she having reportedly been attacked and beaten up in her own home. Venue changed from Caldwell County to Iredell County. The rapist was hanged at Statesville on October 25, 1878. Sources: *New York Herald*, 10/26/78 (8:5); *National Police Gazette*, 11/9/78 (10:3). Appeal: 78 NC 484–489. Note that the aforesaid newspapers published conflicting accounts of Miss Barlow's character.

William Rainey (black, age not recorded). *Murder.* The crime was committed on 3/28/1878 in Warren County. Executed for the murder of 21-year-old James Taylor (black), who was beaten to death with an ax handle. Motive: robbery and gross perfidy. The two young men were tramping their way across country to their homes in Granville County. Rainey knew that Taylor had $3.75 in his pockets. The former coveted that paltry sum (consisting of 3-cent and 5-cent coins) and basely murdered his companion to gain possession thereof. Rainey also killed Taylor's dog when it tried to defend its master. Corpse and carcass were found side by side. Rainey was hanged at Warrenton on November 8, 1878. Source: *New York Herald*, 11/9/78 (3:6). See also: 1870 U.S. Census (Granville Co., NC), which notes Taylor.

William Jefferson (black, age 31). *Rape.* The crime was committed on 5/3/1878 in Warren County. Serial rapist specifically executed for an indecent assault on the person of 36-year-old Amanda Myrick (black), she having been ravished in the presence of her elderly grandmother after she had assiduously provided the culprit with a meal. Jefferson had also raped a 16-year-old black girl named Melissa Darndell in Granville County earlier that same day. He admitted to eight other rapes in addition to the one for which he was executed. He had reportedly spent the years 1866–1871 in the Virginia State Penitentiary for a sexual assault committed near Boydton. Upon his release from prison, he went to Weldon, North Carolina, to reclaim a wife there, only to wind up murdering another black man who had taken up with the woman during his absence. The body was dumped in a river and the homicide went undetected until Jefferson himself divulged it while awaiting execution. He was hanged at Warrenton on December 6, 1878. Sources: *New York Herald*, 12/7/78 (5:2); *National Police Gazette*, 12/21/78 (11:1). See also: 1870 U.S. Census (Warren Co., NC), which notes Amanda Myrick.

1879

John Edwards (white, age 65). *Murder.* The crime was committed on 10/9/1877 in Johnston County. Shotgun slaying of 46-year-old Kader J. Ballard (white). Motive: landlord-tenant dispute. Edwards was hanged at Smithfield on February 14, 1879. Sources: *New York Herald*, 2/15/79 (5:6); *National Police Gazette*, 3/1/79 (7:2). See also: 1870 & 1880 U.S. Census (Johnston Co., NC), which note the Ballard family.

Richard Leach (black, age 29). *Serial Burglar.* The crime was committed on 6/1/1878 in Bladen County. Specifically executed for nocturnally entering the home and store of 43-year-old John D. Currie (white) and rifling those places of money, food, mercantile goods and jewelry. He first got into the detached house and deftly lifted valuables from its bedrooms as the homeowner and his wife slept. Then he went into their pantry and actually had the nerve to sit down and make a meal for himself with victuals that he found there. Next, using a key that he had found in the bedroom, the culprit entered the Currie General Store and plundered it as well. Venue changed from Bladen County to Cumberland County. Leach was hanged at Fayetteville on May 9, 1879. Sources: State Supreme Court case file no. 12340 (NC State Archives); *Raleigh Observer*, 5/11/79 (2:5); *New York Herald*, 5/10/79 (3:4). See also: 1870 U.S. Census (Bladen Co., NC), which notes "J.D. Currie."

Henry F. Andrews (white, age 29), **Louis Carlton** (black, age 33) **and Henry Alfonso Davis** (white, age 32). *Aggravated Burglary.* The crime was committed on 6/15/1878 in Orange County. Serial burglars and bandits. Specifically executed for breaking into the house of 40-year-old Margaret Lydia Johnston Herndon (white) and severely wounding the homeowner with an ax. The attack occurred on the 20th anniversary of the victim's marriage to her deceased husband, an estimable citizen of Chapel Hill. It was the culmination of a crime spree that had terrorized that town for several months at the hands of these culprits. They were all hanged at Hillsboro on May 16, 1879. Source: *New York Herald*, 5/17/79 (5:1). See also: 1850 U.S. Census (Orange Co., NC), which notes the victim by her maiden name. Also: Orange County Marriages (1779–1868), Vol. H, pg. 136.

Jessie Davis (black, age 41). *Rape.* The crime was committed on 12/25/1877 in

Franklin County. Indecent assault on the person of 29-year-old Margaret Champion (white), she having been attacked in her home by an armed intruder who menaced her with a butcher knife. Venue changed from Franklin County to Johnston County. Davis was hanged at Smithfield on June 13, 1879. Sources: *New York Herald*, 6/14/79 (5:5); *National Police Gazette*, 6/28/79 (7:1). See also: 1870 & 1880 U.S. Census (Franklin Co., NC), which respectively note the culprit and the lady.

Edward Foy (black, age 19). *Rape.* The crime was committed on 4/30/1878 in Carteret County. Indecent assault on the person of 27-year-old Adelia Hanners (white), she having been attacked while at home and a loaded pistol held to her head while the culprit forced himself on her. Foy was hanged at Beaufort on June 20, 1879. Source: *New York Herald*, 6/21/79 (5:6).

Robert Jones (black, age about 45). *Murder.* The crime was committed on 12/26/1877 in Edgecombe County. Executed for the murder of Rudolph Eaton, a dissipated white man and local vagrant (age not recorded), who had his head smashed in with a pine knot. Motive: drunken row. The two had been huddled in a shed sharing a bottle of liquor. An argument flared and both wound up dead: one at the scene and the other on the gallows. Jones was hanged at Tarboro on June 25, 1879. Sources: *Tarboro Southerner*, 6/26/79 (3:4); *New York Herald*, 6/26/79 (10:1).

John Davis (black, age 29). *Murder.* The crime was committed on 12/19/1878 in Brunswick County. Shotgun slaying of Henry McDuffie (black, age not recorded). Motive: rivalry for a female. Davis was hanged at Southport on July 11, 1879. Source: *New York Herald*, 7/12/79 (4:2). See also: 1870 U.S. Census (Brunswick Co., NC), which notes Davis.

Robert McCorkle (black, age about 60). *Murder.* The crime was committed on 11/7/1878 in Catawba County. Shotgun slaying of 50-year-old John Wesley Wyckoff (white). Motive: adultery with the victim's wife. She got a life sentence. Venue changed from Catawba County to Alexander County. The killer was hanged at Taylorsville on August 15, 1879. Source: *New York Herald*, 8/16/79 (5:3). See also the murdered man's enlistment record (49th NC Infantry), dated 3/19/62.

Thomas Pinckney Bowman (white, age not recorded). *Murder.* The crime was committed on or about 5/1/1877 in Guilford County. Uxoricide. Executed for the fatal and deliberate poisoning (strychnine) of Thurza Ann Cannon Bowman (white, age not recorded), a physically infirm woman. Motive: so he could be free to carry on with a black concubine. Venue changed from Guilford County to Randolph County. Bowman was hanged at Asheboro on August 29, 1879. Source: *New York Herald*, 8/30/79 (4:1). Appeal: 80 NC 394–400.

Robert Boswell (black, age not recorded). *Murder.* The crime was committed on 8/21/1877 in Orange County. Ax murder of Nancy Blackwell (black, age not recorded), his purported "wife," who was deliberately chased down in a pea patch. Her mangled corpse was then dragged into the cabin they shared and the whole place set on fire. The resultant blaze incinerated their two bastard children, who were presumably asleep at the time. Boswell is further confirmed to have had a hand in the fatal and purposeful poisoning of another black man named Ned Lyon (age not recorded) the previous month so that he could abscond with that man's wife. Motive: adultery. Boswell was hanged at Hillsboro on October 31, 1879. Source: *New York Herald*, 11/1/79 (2:6).

1880

Allen Mathis (black, age about 28). *Murder.* The crime was committed on 9/22/1878 in Pender County. Ax murder of 48-year-old Reuben Herring (black) and illegal burial of his body in a well that he filled in with dirt. Motive: adultery. Venue changed from Pender County to New Hanover County. The killer was hanged at Wilmington on January 9, 1880. Sources: *Morning Star* (Wilmington, NC), 1/10/80 (1:5); *New York Herald*, 1/10/80 (5:1). See also: 1870 U.S. Census (New Hanover Co., NC), which notes the murdered man.

Joe Gillespie (black, age 23). *Murder.* The crime was committed on 12/17/1878 in Iredell County. Accomplice in the murder of 38-year-old William G. Fowler (white), a storekeeper who was clubbed to death as he walked home from work. The victim's skull was broken in seven different places. Defensive wounds were also found on his hands as evidence of homicidal intent. Motive: mugging for the sake of a few coins amounting to less than five dollars. Venue changed from Iredell County to Alexander County. The principal culprit, Julius Davidson, was lynched by outraged citizens. Gillespie was legally hanged at Taylorsville on January 30, 1880. Sources: *The Landmark* (Statesville, NC) 1/30/80 (2:3) & 2/6/80 (3:2); *New York Herald*, 1/31/80 (4:4). See also: 1870 U.S. Census (Iredell Co., NC), which notes Gillespie and (Wilmington, NC) which notes Mr. Fowler.

Henry Horne (black, age not recorded). *Serial Burglar.* The crime was committed on 2/25/1880 in Mecklenburg County. Specifically executed for a nocturnal break-in at the house of 53-year-old Daniel H. Byerly (white), during which personal items were stolen from the homeowner's bedroom. Horne was apprehended that same night when he perpetrated an identical crime at the house of 51-year-old Robert M. Oates (white), the homeowner having seized him in the act. It was the culmination of a long series of nighttime burglaries that had beset the city of Charlotte, the culprit stealing even the very clothes that his victims had laid out for the next day's use. Horne was hanged at Charlotte on May 7, 1880. Sources: *New York Herald*, 5/8/80 (4:6); *Charlotte (NC) Observer*, 5/8/80 (3:2). See also: 1880 U.S. Census (Mecklenburg Co., NC), which notes Messrs. Byerly and Oates.

Robert Outerbridge (black, age not recorded). *Murder.* The crime was committed on 9/17/1879 in Bertie County. Shotgun slaying of 28-year-old Peter Freeman (black). Motive: adultery. The killer was hanged at Windsor on June 11, 1880. Source: *Tarboro Southerner*, 6/17/80 (3:6). Appeal: 82 NC 535–539. See also: 1870 U.S. Census (Bertie Co., NC), which notes Freeman.

Alex Howard (black, age 40). *Murder.* The crime was committed on 7/24/1878 in Sampson County. Mutilation murder of about 60-year-old Batel Autry (white). Motive: robbery and home invasion. Venue changed from Sampson County to Wayne County. The killer was hanged at Goldsboro on July 9, 1880. Source: *New York Herald*, 7/10/80 (6:1). See also: 1870 U.S. Census (Sampson Co., NC), which notes Howard.

Stephen Richardson (black, age 35). *Murder.* The crime was committed on 7/19/1880 in New Hanover County. Murder of 61-year-old Lucy Phinney (black, his mother-in-law), who was battered to death with a spade. Motive: family tension. The trial jury was comprised of 7 blacks and 5 whites. The killer was hanged at Wilmington on September 3, 1880. Source: *New York Herald*, 9/4/80 (4:5). See also: 1880 U.S. Census (Wilmington, NC), which notes both parties.

Peter Leach (black, age 27). *Murder.* The crime was committed on 1/6/1879 in Robeson County. Shotgun slaying of Sam Townsend (black, age not recorded). Motive: adultery and wife swapping. Described as "a bad nigger" by the correspondent of a Northern newspaper, Leach was the brother of Richard Leach, alias Lee, who had been executed at Fayetteville the previous year. Peter Leach was himself hanged at Lumberton on September 24, 1880. Source: *New York Herald*, 9/25/80 (4:3). See also: 1880 U.S. Census (Robeson Co., NC), which notes this killer.

Charles Pearson, alias "Henry Williams" (black, age 23). *Murder.* The crime was committed on 8/17/1880 in Catawba County. Murder of 24-year-old Harrison Kinder (black), the victim having been fatally slashed with a razor. Motive: possibly deranged. The murdered man was standing on a railroad station platform waiting for a train with his girlfriend when the killer attacked him for no apparent reason. Pearson was hanged at Newton on October 22, 1880. Source: *New York Herald*, 10/23/80 (8:4). See also: 1880 U.S. Census (Rowan Co., NC), which notes Kinder.

Daniel Keith (white, age 33). *Murder.* The crime was committed on 1/28/1880 in Cleveland County. Child killer. Executed for the murder of 9-year-old Alice Ellis (black), she having had a pillow case put over her head and her brains pounded out with a rock. Motive: sexual assault. Venue changed from Cleveland County to Rutherford County. The killer was hanged at Rutherfordton on December 17, 1880. Sources: *Raleigh News & Observer*, 12/19/80 (2:5); *New York Herald*, 12/18/80 (4:4), which erroneously said that the killer was a Negro. Also: 1880 U.S. Census (Cleveland Co., NC), which notes Keith and confirms that he was white.

1881

Marshall Baxter (black, age 24). *Murder.* The crime was committed on or about 12/20/1880 in Mecklenburg County. Executed for the murder of 28-year-old Robert Hennigan (black), who was clubbed on the head and thrown into a creek, his body having been found on 1/28/1881. Motive: speculative; no one was ever able to figure this out, and Baxter himself shed no light on the matter. The killer was hanged at Charlotte on April 29, 1881. Source: *New York Herald*, 4/30/81 (3:4). See also: 1880 U.S. Census (Mecklenburg Co., NC), which notes both parties.

Allen Johnson (black, age 25). *Murder.* The crime was committed on 1/30/1880 in Mecklenburg County. Executed for an act of gross betrayal in the beating death of a 60+-year-old black man known only as "Old Blind Crump," a sightless object of public compassion who had placed his trust in Johnson to act as his guide. Motive: robbery. Johnson and two equally heartless accomplices battered the victim with sticks and threw his body in a swamp. They stripped Old Crump of his pants, his boots and three 5-cent coins which they divided up among them. Both of the other guilty parties died in prison so that Johnson went to the gallows alone. He was hanged at Charlotte on October 28, 1881. A pauper's grave awaited him almost next to that of the man that he had so basely slain. Sources: *Charlotte (NC) Observer*, 2/1/80 (3:2) & 10/29/81 (3:2); *New York Herald*, 10/29/81 (5:7).

Henry Lovett (black, age 22). *Murder.* The crime was committed on 7/19/1880 in Columbus County. Fatal stabbing of 60-year-old Argilus P. Williams (black). Motive: obnoxious drunk. Lovett was hanged at Whiteville on November 4, 1881. Source: *New York Herald*, 11/5/81 (8:3). See also: 1880 U.S. Census (Columbus Co., NC), which notes both parties and the victim's correct name in particular.

Augustus Smith (black, age 21). *Rape.* The crime was committed on 9/29/1881 in Johnston County. Indecent assault on the person of 7-year-old Lillian Johnson (white), she having also been thereby infected with a "loathsome disease." Smith was hanged for this atrocity at Smithfield on November 18, 1881. Sources: *Raleigh News & Observer*, 11/22/81 (2:5); *New York Herald*, 11/19/81 (8:1).

1882

Matilda Carter (black female, age 22), **Joseph Hay** (black, age 25) **and Eldridge Scales** (black, age 26). *Murder.* Their crime was committed on December 17, 1880, in Rockingham County. Murder of 40-year-old Nash Carter (black, the husband of Matilda), who was pounced on in his sleep by four assailants (his wife and three of her male lovers), dragged across his bedroom floor by means of a lariat, and had his head held taut by that instrument while his throat was cut. Matilda Carter held a bucket to catch the blood as it spurted from her husband's neck during this attack. Then she stomped up and down on his body to make sure that no breath remained in it. Motive: sexual profligacy. All three male attackers had committed adultery with the female catalyst. She bore a reputation among her fellow blacks as extremely promiscuous. She had already borne six children by the age of 22, most of them by different fathers. She was hanged along with two of her cohorts at Wentworth on January 13, 1882. Sources: *Raleigh News & Observer*, 1/14/82 (1:3); *New York Herald*, 1/14/82 (8:1). See also: 1880 U.S. Census (Rockingham Co., NC), which notes the Carters and Joseph Hay.

John Alexander Morris (black, age 28). *Murder.* The crime was committed on 8/10/1880 in Lincoln County. Murder of Joseph Roark (black, age not recorded), who was shot twice with a handgun and then clubbed so badly that most of his bones were smashed. Motive: to remove a hostile witness in a pending court case. Venue changed from Lincoln County to Cleveland County. Morris was hanged at Shelby on January 27, 1882.

Source: *New York Herald*, 1/28/82 (8:1). See also: 1880 U.S. Census (Lincoln Co., NC), which notes the killer.

Stephen Effler (white, age 21). *Murder.* The crime was committed on 1/6/1881 in McDowell County. Uxoricide. Fatal beating of 22-year-old Margaret Grindstaff Effler (white), her neck being broken and her ribs crushed inward (as proof that she had been stomped on), among other traumatic injuries. Motive: sheer brutality. The killer was hanged at Marion on May 19, 1882. Sources: *Raleigh News & Observer*, 5/20/82 (2:4); *New York Herald*, 5/20/82 (5:3). See also: 1880 U.S. Census (Yancey Co., NC), which notes both parties.

Philip Faison (black, age 33). *Murder.* The crime was committed on 5/25/1882 in Sampson County. Shotgun slaying of 62-year-old Henry Sillers (black) who was murdered in his own doorway. Motive: a personal feud that had raged ever since Faison (who was a married man) had begotten a bastard child by the victim's daughter. Faison was hanged at Clinton on July 11, 1882. Source: *Raleigh News & Observer*, 7/12/82 (1:5); *New York Herald*, 7/12/82 (5:4). See also: 1870 & 1880 U.S. Census (Sampson Co., NC), which respectively note "Sellers" [*sic*] and Faison.

Iverson Slade (black, age about 23). *Murder.* The crime was committed on 6/7/1882 in Caswell County. Handgun slaying of 20-year-old Dora White (black, his sister-in-law) who was shot three times in her own house. Motive: because she had dared to give refuge to the killer's estranged wife. Slade was hanged at Yanceyville on December 29, 1882. Sources: *Raleigh News & Observer*, 12/30/82 (1:4); *New York Herald*, 12/30/82 (6:3). See also: 1880 U.S. Census (Caswell Co., NC), which notes Dora White.

1883

Jerome Holt (black, age 23). *Rape.* The crime was committed on 2/16/1883 in Alamance County. Indecent assault on the person of a 47-year-old white female identified only as "the wife of William Terrell," together with the near-fatal beatings of that woman's 67-year-old husband and unnamed son. Holt was hanged at Graham on March 23, 1883. Sources: *Raleigh News & Observer*, 3/24/83 (1:5); *New York Herald*, 3/24/83 (6:2). See also: 1880 U.S. Census (Alamance Co., NC), which notes "Gerome" Holt.

Robert Henderson (black, age 20). *Murder.* The crime was committed on 10/29/1882 in Granville County. Uxoricide. Fatal beating of pregnant 18-year-old Frances Henderson, she having been mistreated to such an extent that almost every bone in her body was broken. Motive: the killer was a bully. The trial jury was comprised of 3 whites and 9 blacks. Henderson was hanged at Oxford on June 1, 1883. Source: *Oxford (NC) Torchlight*, 11/7/82 (3:2) & 6/5/83 (3:5). See also: Granville County Superior Court Criminal Action Papers (1882–1883), NC State Archives (*State vs. Henderson*).

Henry Jones (black, age 22). *Murder.* The crime was committed on 2/14/1882 in Wake County. Cop killer. Shotgun slaying of 22-year-old Alvis H. Blake (white), a sheriff's deputy. Motive: resisting arrest. Jones was hanged at Raleigh on August 27, 1883. Sources: *Raleigh*

News & Observer, 8/28/83 (4:2); *New York Herald*, 8/28/83 (3:4). See also: 1880 U.S. Census (Wake Co., NC), which notes the slain deputy.

Bert Ellis (black, age 23). *Murder.* The crime was committed on 10/19/1883 in Cleveland County. Murder and attempted murder of 63-year-old William Logan and 53-year-old Lizzie Logan (whites, a married couple). The woman was manually strangled and a pile of cotton heaped atop her, which was then set on fire. The man was similarly mistreated but survived. He managed to crawl from the pyre despite the killer's belief that he was dead. Motive: robbery and home invasion. Ellis was hanged at Shelby on December 14, 1883. Sources: *Raleigh News & Observer*, 12/15/83 (1:5); *New York Herald*, 12/15/83 (3:5). See also: 1880 U.S. Census (Cleveland Co., NC), which notes the Logans.

Guilford Soon (black, age about 40). *Rape.* The crime was committed on 5/8/1883 in Lenoir County. Indecent assault on the person of 48-year-old Eliza Jones (white), she having been terrorized in her little cottage and very nearly murdered. The culprit, after having held the woman captive for several hours, had decided to kill her and pulled a knife on her for that purpose. She squirmed loose from his grip and fled outdoors where neighbors, who were law abiding black folks, rescued her. The miscreant also stole the woman's money in addition to other articles of value. Soon's father, Ben Soon, had reportedly murdered his master (he then being a slave) in Pitt County in 1863 and was shot dead by Union occupation forces. The younger Soon—the rapist—was hanged at Kinston on December 20, 1883. Sources: *Raleigh News & Observer*, 12/21/83 (1:5); *New York Herald*, 12/21/83 (4:6). See also: 1880 U.S. Census (Lenoir Co., NC), which notes Mrs. Jones.

1884

Benjamin Gilliam (black, age 28). *Murder.* The crime was committed on 4/4/1883 in Pamlico County. Executed for the murder of 34-year-old Henry Carter (black) who was clubbed to death with a tree branch specially hewn for that purpose. Motive: adultery on the part of the killer and the victim's wife. Gilliam was hanged at Bayboro on February 29, 1884. Sources: *Raleigh News & Observer*, 3/1/84 (1:4); *New York Herald*, 3/1/84 (6:1). See also: 1880 U.S. Census (Pamlico Co., NC), which notes both parties.

Enoch Brown (black, age about 40). *Murder.* The crime was committed on 8/17/1883 in Halifax County. Uxoricide. Ax murder of Lucy Brown (black, age not recorded) and illegal burial of her remains that were found exactly one month later. Motive: unspecified. The killer was hanged at Halifax on May 2, 1884. Sources: *Raleigh News & Observer*, 3/1/84 (1:4) & 5/3/84 (1:6); *Roanoke News* (Weldon, NC), 5/8/84 (3:6).

1885

Irving Lang (black, age not recorded). *Murder.* The crime was committed on 8/21/1884 in Pitt County. Ax murder of 41-year-old Moses Barrett (black). Motive: barnyard brawl. The killer was hanged at Greenville on February 23, 1885. Sources: *The Landmark* (Statesville,

NC), 2/27/85 (3:3); *New York Herald*, 2/25/85 (10:2). See also: Pitt County Criminal Action Papers (1880–1884); NC State Archives (*State vs. Lang*). Also: 1880 U.S. Census (Pitt Co., NC), which notes Barrett.

Eaton Mills (black, age 46). *Murder.* The crime was committed on 12/22/1882 in Halifax County. Handgun slaying of 34-year-old John Henry Ponton (black), who was shot down on a public road. Motive: indecent proposal(?). The culprit had long been notorious in the county, the bane of blacks and whites alike. He was hanged at Halifax on July 17, 1885. Sources: *Raleigh News & Observer*, 7/18/85 (1:4); *Roanoke News* (Weldon, NC), 7/23/85 (3:3). See also: 1880 U.S. Census (Halifax Co., NC), which notes both parties.

Tom Gee (black, age 60+). *Murder.* The crime was committed on 9/29/1884 in Cumberland County. Ax murder of about 50-year-old Mary Hughes (white), a known prostitute. Motive: robbery. The hovel in which she dwelled was ransacked. Another account says that Gee had lived with the victim and that she had nagged him for having a roving eye. Gee was hanged at Fayetteville on August 7, 1885. Sources: *Fayetteville (NC) Observer*, 10/2/84 (3:3); *Raleigh News & Observer*, 8/8/85 (1:5); *New York Herald*, 8/8/85 (10:1). Appeal: 92 NC 707–714.

Joseph O. Howard (white, age not recorded). *Murder.* The crime was committed on 10/29/1884 in Cumberland County. Murder of 44-year-old Cullen L. Blackman (white), who was found dead in his barn with his throat cut. Motive: drunken row. The killer was hanged at Fayetteville on August 7, 1885. Source: *Raleigh News & Observer*, 8/8/85 (1:5). Appeal: 92 NC 722–728. See also: 1880 U.S. Census (Cumberland Co., NC), which notes the murdered man.

Tom McNeill (black, age 23). *Murder.* The crime was committed on 8/10/1884 in Cumberland County. Fratricide. Handgun slaying of 33-year-old Simon McNeill (black). Motive: drunken brawl. The killer was hanged at Fayetteville on August 7, 1885. Sources: *Raleigh News & Observer*, 8/8/85 (1:5); *New York Herald*, 8/8/85 (10:1). See also: 1880 U.S. Census (Cumberland Co., NC), which notes both parties.

Isaiah Richardson, Edward Sauders and John Swanner (blacks, ages not recorded). *Aggravated Burglary.* Their crime was committed on 9/13/1885 in Gates County. Executed for a nocturnal break-in at the country store of Willey & Eggleston mercantile partners, the culprits being armed with a handgun, a carbine and a briar hook. Stolen goods included clothing, cash in excess of $150 and six revolvers taken from a gun case. The live-in store clerk (who was asleep in an overhead room at the time) was smart enough to lie low during this incursion. Homicidal intent was proven by the fact that one of the burglars stood in wait for the clerk meaning to gaff him with the briar hook if he ventured down the stairs. The three night prowlers were hanged at Gatesville on December 7, 1885. Sources: *Raleigh News & Observer*, 12/8/85 (1:7); *New York Herald*, 12/8/85 (3:6).

Anderson Davis and Nelson Stewart (blacks, ages not recorded). *Aggravated Burglary.* The crime was committed on 9/21/1885 in Mecklenburg County. Both executed for a nocturnal break-in at the house of 48-year-old Samuel G. Strickland (white), the stolen goods having been found in their cabin the following day. The homeowner had apparently been terrorized. The culprits were hanged at Charlotte on December 9, 1885. Sources: *Raleigh News & Observer*, 12/10/85 (1:7); *Daily Charlotte Observer*, 12/10/85 (7:2). See also: 1880 U.S. Census and 1897 Charlotte NC City Directory, which both note Mr. Strickland.

1886

Louis Kilgore (black, age 40). *Murder.* The crime was committed on 9/25/1885 in Henderson County. Handgun slaying of Mattie Henderson (white), a known prostitute. Motive: carousal turned deadly. Kilgore was hanged at Hendersonville on May 21, 1886. Sources: *New York Herald*, 5/9/86 (13:5); *Raleigh News & Observer*, 5/22/86 (1:6). See also: 1880 U.S. Census (Henderson Co., NC), which notes the killer.

George McNair (black, age 15). *Rape.* The crime was committed on 5/22/1884 in Onslow County. Indecent assault on the person of 9-year-old Kizzie A. Edens (white), it being noted that the assailant was "the size of an ordinary man," which in turn suggests that the victim suffered traumatic injuries to her privy parts. McNair was hanged at Jacksonville on June 1, 1886. Source: *Raleigh News & Observer*, 6/2/86 (1:4). See also: NC State Supreme Court case file no. 14567 (NC State Archives); 1880 U.S. Census (Onslow Co., NC), which notes the culprit.

Frank Gaston (black, age not recorded). *Rape.* The crime was committed on 3/21/1886 in Rowan County. Indecent assault on the person of 40-year-old Jerome Shepard (white), a female inmate of the county almshouse, who was jumped while gathering firewood near that institution. Her attacker was hanged at Salisbury on July 2, 1886. Sources: *North Carolina Herald* (Salisbury) 3/25/86 (3:3) & 7/8/86 (3:3); *Carolina Watchman* (Salisbury), 5/6/86 (3:2). See also: 1850 U.S. Census (Rowan Co., NC), which notes the victim as a minor.

Andrew Jackson Lambert (1/8th Cherokee, age 40). *Murder.* The crime was committed on 12/17/1884 in Swain County. Executed for the handgun slaying of Richard Wilson (white, age not recorded). Motive: obnoxious drunk or so it was alleged. Lambert was hanged at Bryson City on July 9, 1886. Sources: *Raleigh News & Observer*, 7/11/86 (2:3); *New York Herald*, 7/10/86 (6:6). Appeal: 93 NC 580–586. See also: 1880 U.S. Census (Swain Co., NC), which notes Lambert, alias "Jack Lambert." Considerable controversy exists about this case and the purported "innocence" of the executed man based on a reported deathbed confession 30 years after the fact. Stories like this were common in 19th and early 20th century newspapers, and were a favorite ploy of anti-death penalty crusaders. They were also a tactic sometimes used by grumpy old men to stir up trouble after they were gone. It is unwise to put faith in such stories because hoaxes abound. The Swain County Historical Society and descendants of the executed man have amassed a file on this case that is heartfelt but unconvincing.

George Moore, alias "Robert Hall" (black, age not recorded). *Rape.* The crime was committed on 5/10/1886 in Mecklenburg County. Indecent assault on the person of Sarah Moore (his own daughter, black, age not recorded) who he had been mistreating in that manner for a long time. Moore was hanged at Charlotte on July 29, 1886. Source: *Raleigh News & Observer*, 7/30/86 (1:6). See also: Mecklenburg County Criminal Superior Court Minutes (June term, 1886), pg. 159.

Alliday Wrenn (black, age 27). *Aggravated Burglary.* The crime was committed on 9/11/1886 in Chatham County. Executed for a violent break-in at the house of 78-year-old Ann Welch (white), during which the homeowner and her maiden daughter (Ann Marie Welch, white, age 54) were brutalized and sexually assaulted. The culprit used an ax to hew down both the outer and inner doors of the aforesaid premises and get at the terrified occupants. He left both women severely beaten and traumatized. Wrenn was hanged at Pittsboro on November 11, 1886. Source: *Chatham (NC) Record*, 9/16/86 (3:1), 11/4/86 (3:1) & 11/11/86 (3:2). See also: 1880 U.S. Census (Chatham Co., NC), which notes the female parties.

1887

Henry Artis (black, age 35). *Murder.* The crime was committed on 11/5/1886 in Wayne County. Ax murder of 20-year-old Ida Louisa Dickerson (black), his stepdaughter. Motive: jealousy lest she seek the companionship of other males. The trial jury was comprised of six whites and six blacks. Artis was hanged at Goldsboro on March 11, 1887. Source: *Goldsboro (NC) Messenger*, 3/14/87 (5:4). See also: 1880 U.S. Census (Wayne Co., NC), which notes both parties.

Albert Taborn (black, age 26). *Aggravated Burglary.* The crime was committed on 3/14/1887 in Granville County. Executed for a break-in at the house of 34-year-old Patrick Booth (white, a physician), during which the homeowner's wife, Belle E. Booth (white, age 27), was sexually assaulted. The culprit had made it a point to strike when Dr. Booth was out of town. His brother, John Taborn, feared that Albert might be lynched, so he made matters worse by setting a huge warehouse fire the next evening to provide cover for a jailbreak that proved unsuccessful. The blaze spread out of control, and by the time that it was over, more than half the business district of Oxford, North Carolina, lay in ashes. Albert Taborn's trial jury was comprised of 10 blacks and 2 whites. News accounts reported that Albert's father had been executed for a capital crime years earlier in this county. It might have actually been his grandfather, as records confirm the execution of a "Washington Taborn" there on April 9, 1834. Albert Taborn was hanged at the Granville County Jail on June 18, 1887. Sources: *The Free Press* (Halifax, NC), 4/25/34 (1:3); *New York Herald*, 3/16/87 (7:3); *Salisbury (NC) Herald*, 5/16/87 (2:3); *Kansas City Times*, 6/19/87 (1:5); *Raleigh News & Observer*, 6/19/87 (1:4). See also: 1880 U.S. Census (Granville Co., NC), which notes all parties.

Archibald Martin (black, age not recorded). *Murder.* The crime was committed on 4/2/1887 in Richmond County. Shotgun slaying of another black man named William Henry McNeil, age not recorded. Motive: because the victim had allegedly insulted the killer's wife. The trial jury was composed "almost entirely of negroes." Martin was hanged at

Rockingham on July 12, 1887. Sources: *Raleigh News & Observer*, 7/13/87 (1:5); *Rockingham (NC) Rocket*, 7/14/87 (3:3).

1888

Stephen Freeman (black, age not recorded). *Rape.* The crime was committed on 11/9/1887 in New Hanover County. Indecent assault on the person of 23-year-old Ada Bogan Sellers (white), a young woman who even the state's attorney conceded to be of vile character because she had given birth to a "mulatto child" at the age of 16 and been run out of her native Anson County for that reason. This, however, did not give anybody a right to rape her. Freeman was hanged for his crime at Wilmington on July 11, 1888. Source: *Morning Star* (Wilmington, NC), 11/30/87 (1:5) & 7/12/88 (1:4). Appeal: 100 NC 429–438.

James Byers (white, age about 40). *Murder.* The crime was committed on 8/25/1886 in Wilkes County. Handgun slaying of Henry Edwards (white, age not recorded), who was shot down on a public road during an armed confrontation about a stolen horse. Motive: resisting a citizen's arrest. Byers was hanged at Wilkesboro on July 13, 1888. Source: *The Landmark* (Statesville, NC), 11/11/86 (3:6) & 7/19/88 (3:2). Appeal: 100 NC 512–518.

William Houston (black, age not recorded). *Murder.* The crime was committed on 5/21/1888 in Forsyth County. Handgun slaying of Kate Cosby (black, age not recorded), a known prostitute. Motive: atavistic male jealousy. The killer was hanged at Winston-Salem on July 19, 1888. Sources: *Raleigh News & Observer*, 7/20/88 (1:2); *People's Press* (Salem, NC), 7/26/88 (4:2).

1889

John Yancey (black, age 43). *Murder.* The crime was committed on 4/7/1888 in Caswell County. Executed for the murder of 26-year-old Bob Oliver (black), who was waylaid and beaten to death with a heavy stick. Motive: rivalry for a female. The killer was hanged at Yanceyville on January 25, 1889. Source: *Raleigh News & Observer*, 1/26/89 (1:3). See also: Caswell County Superior Court Criminal Action Papers (*State vs. Yancey*), NC State Archives. Also: 1880 U.S. Census (Caswell Co., NC), which notes both parties.

Amma Ellis (black, age 31). *Murder.* The crime was committed on 9/4/1888 in Sampson County. Patricide. Fatal stabbing of 53-year-old John Allen Ellis (black), who was knifed multiple times with a blade specially sharpened for that purpose. Motive: family row. Amma Ellis was hanged at Clinton on January 29, 1889. Source: *New York Herald*, 1/30/89 (7:4). Appeal: 101 NC 765–769. See also: 1870 U.S. Census (Sampson Co., NC), which notes both parties.

Howard Anderson (white, age 27). *Murder.* The crime was committed on 7/28/1888 in Wayne County. Executed for the willful murder of 37-year-old William H. Porter (white), a barbecue vendor who was bludgeoned with a rock when he refused to let the killer purchase his wares on credit. Anderson was hanged at Goldsboro on February 27, 1889. Source: *Raleigh News & Observer*, 2/28/89 (4:2). See also: 1880 U.S. Census (Wayne Co., NC), which notes both parties.

Eli Ward (black, age 26). *Aggravated Burglary.* The crime was committed on 1/12/1889 in Northampton County. Executed for a break-in at the house of 58-year-old William Henry Farmer (white), during which an effort was made to murder the homeowner by slashing him with a razor. Ward was hanged at Jackson on May 3, 1889. Sources: *Roanoke (NC) News*, 5/9/89 (3:2); *Raleigh News & Observer*, 5/4/89 (1:3). See also: 1880 U.S. Census (Rich Square, NC), which notes "Ely Ward" and "Henry Farmer."

Lee Carson, alias "Charlie Armstrong" (black, age 33). *Aggravated Burglary.* The crime was committed on or about 10/15/1888 in Cleveland County. Executed for a nocturnal break-in at the house of 50+-year-old Angeline Dean (white), who came home to find "all her furniture, provisions and clothing stolen." Suspected accomplice in the murder of James Philbeck (white, age 65), who was shot in the face with a handgun when he answered a knock on his door in the same county on the evening of 11/21/1888, his wife being shot as well (albeit not fatally) and his residence robbed. Carson's brother, John Carson, alias "Van Canady," subsequently confessed to the homicide. He was lynched by outraged citizens on 12/2/1888. A search of the killer's home turned up a substantial cache of stolen goods including items taken from Angeline Dean. This no doubt weighed heavily on the minds of jurors when they returned a death penalty verdict in the Lee Carson burglary case. Lee Carson was hanged at Shelby on May 13, 1889. Source: *The New Era* (Shelby, NC), 11/30/88 (3:2), 12/7/88 (3:2), 4/19/89 (3:2) & 5/17/89 (1:2).

William Weddington (black, age not recorded). *Murder.* The crime was committed on 5/6/1888 in Union County. Cop killer. Executed for the murder of 25-year-old John Pearce (white), who was bludgeoned with a floorboard that had been pried up for that purpose. Motive: resisting arrest. Venue changed from Union County to Mecklenburg County. The killer was hanged at Charlotte on July 11, 1889. Source: *Charlotte (NC) Chronicle*, 5/8/88 (4:4) & 7/12/89 (4:1). Appeal: 103 NC 364–374.

Matthew Banks (black, age 16). *Rape.* The crime was committed on 7/7/1889 in Pasquotank County. Indecent assault on the person of 15-year-old Florence Swain (white), she having been snatched off a public road and brutalized although she was "a small and delicate girl." The rapist was hanged at Elizabeth City on November 29, 1889. Source: *North Carolinian* (Elizabeth City, NC), 7/10/89 (3:3), 9/25/89 (3:2) & 12/4/89 (3:2). See also: 1880 U.S. Census (Pasquotank Co., NC), which notes both parties.

1890

John Claude Parrish (white, age 39). *Rape.* The crime was committed on numerous occasions throughout the years 1887 and 1888. Indecent assault on the person of 13-year-old Esther Parrish (white, his own daughter), including at least one time when he compelled her to bend over a fence rail to more effectively accomplish his purpose. This doting parent was hanged for his crimes at Raleigh on January 10, 1890. Sources: *Raleigh News & Observer*, 1/11/90 (4:2); *Macon (GA) Telegraph*, 1/11/90 (1:2). Appeal: 104 NC 679–694. See also: 1880 U.S. Census (Raleigh, NC), which notes Parrish as a jailbird.

Elijah Moore (black, age 26). *Murder.* The crime was committed on 10/17/1888 in Guilford County. Fatal stabbing of 23-year-old Laura Hyatt (black). Motive: lovers' quarrel. Moore was hanged at Greensboro on February 7, 1890. Source: *Charlotte (NC) News*, 2/8/90 (4:1). Appeal: 104 NC 743–751. See also: 1880 U.S. Census (Guilford Co., NC), which notes both parties.

Manley Pankey (black, age about 19). *Murder.* The crime was committed on 8/3/1889 in Montgomery County. Shotgun slaying of about 19-year-old Chambers Leak (black). Motive: the killer became wrathful when the victim reproved him for making inappropriate dinner conversation. Pankey was hanged at Troy on February 7, 1890. Sources: *Montgomery Vidette* (Troy, NC), 8/8/89 (3:1) & 2/13/90 (3:2); *Charlotte (NC) News*, 2/8/90 (4:1).

John B. Wilson (white, age 39). *Murder.* The crime was committed on 9/22/1888 in Yancey County. Handgun slaying of 44-year-old Thomas Edge (white). Motive: obnoxious drunk. Wilson was hanged at Burnsville on February 7, 1890. Source: *Charlotte (NC) News*, 2/8/90 (4:1). Appeal: 104 NC 868–873. See also: 1880 U.S. Census (Yancey Co., NC), which notes Edge, and 1870 U.S. Census (Yancey Co., NC), which notes Wilson.

William S. Shackelford, alias "James S. Davis" (white, age 42). *Murder.* The crime was committed on 11/15/1889 in Chatham County. Executed for the murder of 32-year-old John D. Horton (white), who was battered to death with a bootjack and buried in his tobacco barn. Motive: despoliation; the killer hoped to thereby acquire the victim's farm. Shackelford was also reported to have been a practitioner of willful incest who had murdered two infants begotten on his eldest daughter. He allegedly had to get out of his native South Carolina for that reason. He was hanged at Pittsboro on March 28, 1890. Sources: *The Landmark* (Statesville, NC), 11/28/89 (2:4); *Raleigh News & Observer*, 3/29/90 (1:5). See also: 1880 U.S. Census (Chatham Co., NC), which notes Horton; *Front Page Detective*, 11/54.

Stephen Jacobs (Croatan, age about 45). *Murder.* The crime was committed on 1/11/1889 in Robeson County. Shotgun slaying of 52-year-old Candice Earp (white), who was fired upon as she stood in her own doorway. Motive: unknown. The killer was hanged at Lumberton on October 10, 1890. Sources: *Morning Star* (Wilmington, NC), 10/11/90 (4:5); *Wilmington (NC) Messenger*, 10/11/90 (1:3). See also: State Supreme Court case file no. 16413 (NC State Archives).

1891

Henry W. Brabham (black, age 21). *Murder.* The crime was committed on 4/11/1891 in Mecklenburg County. Executed for the murder of 45-year-old John B. Mocca (an Italian storekeeper), who was struck down from behind in his place of business with a railroad coupling pin that had been made into a slung shot. Motive: robbery. The killer was hanged at Charlotte on July 2, 1891. Sources: *Charlotte (NC) Chronicle*, 4/13/91 (4:1); *Raleigh News & Observer*, 7/3/91 (1:3). See also the slain man's burial record in Elmwood Cemetery (Charlotte, NC), which notes his age.

Ben Bostick (black, age 20). *Murder.* The crime was committed on 8/7/1891 in Moore County. Shotgun slaying of 27-year-old Jerome C. Currie (white). Motive: the killer resented having been told that he was lying down on the job. Bostick was hanged at Carthage on September 29, 1891. Source: *Carthage (NC) Blade*, 8/11/91 (1:3) & 9/29/91 (1:3). See also: 1880 U.S. Census (Moore Co., NC), which notes the murdered man.

James Johnson (black, age not recorded). *Murder.* The crime was committed on 8/2/1891 in Bladen County. Child killer. Executed for the murder of 10-year-old Florence Sutton (black), who was strangled and buried face down in a shallow grave. Motive: sexual assault. Johnson was hanged at Elizabethtown on December 11, 1891. Sources: *Wilmington (NC) Messenger*, 8/4/91 (1:5); *Morning Star* (Wilmington), 8/4/91 (1:4), 8/5/91 (1:4) & 12/12/91 (1:4).

Badger Lawson (black, age 22). *Murder.* The crime was committed on 9/29/1891 in Person County. Executed for the murders of 58-year-old William Dixon and 38-year-old Fannie Dixon (whites, a married couple), who were battered to death with rocks and their bodies consumed by fire when the killer torched their house. Motive: disagreement over a bill. Lawson was hanged at Roxboro on December 26, 1891. Source: *Person County Courier*, 10/8/91 (3:4), 10/29/91 (3:4) & 1/7/92 (3:3). See also: 1880 U.S. Census (Person Co., NC), which notes the Dixons.

1892

Caroline Shipp (black female, age 20). *Murder.* The crime was committed on 3/31/1891 in Gaston County. Baby killer. Executed for using rat poison to get rid of her 11-month-old bastard child, a male infant (black, name not recorded) whose paternity she assigned to a rover named Ed Brown. The condemned mother asseverated her innocence to the last, blaming her most recent lover for the deed, but she could not satisfactorily explain why she herself had bought the poison. Nor could she counter the fact that the accused man, Mack Farrar, had provided an alibi for his whereabouts at the time of the crime. The guilty girl was hanged at Dallas, North Carolina, on January 22, 1892. Source: *Gastonia (NC) Gazette*, 1/28/92 (1:1).

John Cox (black, age 21). *Murder.* The crime was committed on 9/6/1888 in Jones County. Handgun slaying of William Sutton (black, age not recorded). Motive: rivalry for a female. Cox was hanged at Trenton on May 13, 1892. Sources: *State Chronicle* (Raleigh, NC), 5/14/92 (1:4); *Kinston (NC) Free Press*, 5/19/92 (3:4).

Charles Blackman (black, age about 25). *Murder.* The crime was committed on 4/17/1892 in Guilford County. Uxoricide. Handgun slaying of pregnant 23-year-old Mary Morehead Blackman (black), who was in the act of nursing an infant at the time. Motive: fickle husband; the killer had become obsessed with another woman and wanted out of his marriage. He was hanged at Greensboro on July 14, 1892. Source: *Greensboro (NC) Patriot*, 4/20/92 (3:3) & 7/20/92 (3:3). See also: 1880 U.S. Census (Guilford Co., NC), which notes the victim by her maiden name.

Charles W. Reynolds (white, age 25) **and Judge Merriman Headen** (black, age not recorded). *Murder.* The crime was committed on 8/16/1892 in Guilford County. Handgun slaying of 87-year-old Salathiel Swaim (white), who was shot in the head at point-blank range as he dozed in a chair on the front porch of his home. Motive: robbery; the victim was known to have money in his pockets. The killers were hanged at Greensboro on October 20, 1892. Source: *Greensboro (NC) Patriot*, 8/17/92 (3:2), 9/7/92 (3:3) & 10/26/92 (3:2). See also: 1880 U.S. Census (Guilford Co., NC), which notes Reynolds and Swaim.

1893

John Hambright (black, age not recorded). *Murder.* The crime was committed on 1/6/1891 in Cleveland County. Shotgun slaying of Jenks Macobson (black, age not recorded). Motive: rivalry for a female. Hambright was hanged at Shelby on February 17, 1893. Source: *Raleigh News & Observer*, 2/18/93 (1:7). Appeal: 111 NC 707–715.

Sam Neely (black, age 15). *Aggravated Burglary.* The crime was committed on 6/1/1893 in Gaston County. Executed for a nocturnal break-in at the house of 41-year-old William Allen (white), the homeowner having been shot in his bed with murderous intent. His youth irrespective, the culprit was described as an ex-convict with a belligerent mentality. He was a hired hand on the Allen farm when capital felony was added to his record. Neely "used all the skill of a professional burglar in entering Mr. Allen's house" shortly before midnight on the above date. He made his way to his employer's bedroom unseen and there found a loaded pistol atop a fireplace mantle. This weapon he placed muzzle to the head of Mr. Allen as that man and his wife lay asleep in their bed. One shot was fired. The bullet did not pierce Mr. Allen's skull, but did inflict a nasty flesh wound ranging downward from the pate to the forehead. The man's survival was regarded as a miracle. The motive of the would-be murderer was attributed to having been reprimanded for insolence. Sam Neely was hanged at Dallas, North Carolina, on December 1, 1893. Sources: *The Landmark* (Statesville, NC), 6/15/93 (1:7); *Daily Charlotte Observer*, 12/2/93 (4:4). See also: 1880 U.S. Census (Gaston Co., NC), which notes Wm. Allen of South Point Twp.

1894

Dan Gilchrist (black, age 19). *Murder.* The crime was committed on 2/9/1893 in Richmond County. Ax murder of 46-year-old Frank McKay (black), his father-in-law. Motive: personal enmity to a high degree, reason uncertain. The crime was exacerbated by the fact that the killer induced the victim's sons (ages 15 and 16) to observe the violent death of their father. Gilchrist was hanged at Rockingham on January 5, 1894. Source: *Daily Charlotte Observer*, 1/6/94 (1:7). See also: 1880 U.S. Census (Richmond Co., NC), which notes the killer, and (Robeson Co., NC), which notes the murdered man.

Peter DeGraff (white, age 24). *Murder.* The crime was committed on 7/20/1892 in Forsyth County. Handgun slaying of about 20-year-old Ellen Smith (white), the mother of his bastard child. Motive: lovers' quarrel. DeGraff had (by his own admission) "ruined the lives and characters" of several "young girls during his life." This almost certainly figured in the trial court's decision to hang him. DeGraff was executed at Winston-Salem on February 8, 1894. Source: *Daily Charlotte Observer*, 7/22/92 (1:3) & 2/9/94 (2:3). See also: 1880 U.S. Census (Forsyth Co., NC), which notes the killer.

Calvin Coley (white, age 20) **and Thomas Coley** (white, age 25). *Murder.* Their crime was committed on 6/30/1892 in Franklin County. Ax murder of Samuel Tucker (a Jewish peddler, age not recorded). Motive: robbery. The victim came from Richmond, Virginia. His bones were taken there for burial in a denominational cemetery 18 months after his death. The killers (brothers) were described as ill-bred roughnecks who had no religious instruction or formal education. Both were hanged at Louisburg on July 13, 1894. Sources: *Daily Charlotte Observer*, 2/2/94 (4:3); *Raleigh News & Observer*, 7/14/94 (1:3). Appeal: 114 NC 879–885.

Orange Page (black, age 45). *Murder.* The crime was committed on 1/16/1894 in Wake County. Executed for the murder of 100-year-old Rosa Haywood, a.k.a. "Old Aunt Rosa" (black), who was found dead in her bed with a broken neck. Motive: robbery. A lowlife by any description, Page had run out on his wife and children, leaving them to fend for themselves in an Edgecombe County sharecropper shack. He came to Raleigh and there situated himself in the bed of a black woman named Martha Smith. She was the geriatric caretaker of Old Aunt Rosa Haywood, an enfeebled but much beloved fixture in the black community. "Auntie" had a pouch that she kept close to her person. It contained coins to the value of $12 which were meant to pay her anticipated funeral expenses. Page and his lover felt that they could put that money to a better purpose. So they murdered the helpless centenarian and absconded with her coins. The crime enraged Raleigh blacks to a degree not seen in living memory. Two Negro detectives hunted down the guilty parties. Page was found in Edgecombe County. He had gone crawling back to the wife whom he had previously abandoned. The detectives pulled him out from under a feather mattress upon which he had commanded his wife and young children to sit in an effort to elude the searchers. Orange Page was hanged at Raleigh on August 3, 1894. Sources: *Raleigh News & Observer*, 8/4/94 (1:2); *Daily Charlotte Observer*, 5/17/94 (1:5) & 8/4/94 (1:5).

Bob Madkins, alias "Matkins" (black, age 19). *Rape.* The crime was committed on 5/20/1894 in Alamance County. Indecent assault on the person of 19-year-old Mary Phillips (white), she having been attacked on a public road and further outraged at gunpoint, a pistol being held to her head. The attacker was hanged at Graham on August 10, 1894. Source: *Daily Charlotte Observer*, 5/22/94 (2:3), 5/29/94 (2:2) & 8/11/94 (1:6). See also: 1880 U.S. Census (Alamance Co., NC), which notes "Matkins" as a minor.

1895

George Mills (white, age 29). *Murder.* The crime was committed on 6/20/1894 in Wake County. Executed for the murder of pregnant 17-year-old Ianna E. Wimberly (white, his niece) who was battered to death with a heavy stick after being lured to an empty house under the pretense of seeing someone who could alleviate her condition. Motive: scandalous paternity. Mills insisted that the victim's father and two brothers were all in the habit of using her for sex. Mills himself was an unemployable scapegrace described as borderline mentally retarded, nearly blind, unkempt and nasty in his personal deportment. He was a brother of Miss Wimberly's mother, Sarah Mills Wimberly by name. The true paternity of the unwanted child (or product of incest, as it was alleged) was ascribed to George Mills when he admitted wielding the murder weapon. He was hanged at Raleigh on May 3, 1895. Sources: *Daily Charlotte Observer*, 6/23/94 (1:7), 1/18/95 (1:5) & 5/4/95 (1:5); *Raleigh News & Observer*, 5/3/95 (2:1) & 5/4/95 (2:1). See also: 1880 U.S. Census (Wake Co., NC), which notes the murdered girl and her family. Also: 1870 U.S. Census (Pitt Co., NC), which notes Mills and his sister—the future Mrs. Wimberly—as minors.

Anderson Brown (black, age 33). *Murder.* The crime was committed on 3/2/1895 in Rowan County. Handgun slaying of 23-year-old Callie Roberts (black), she having been murdered in her bed. Motive: brutish male jealousy. The killer was hanged at Salisbury on July 25, 1895. Source: *Raleigh News & Observer*, 7/26/95 (1:1). See also: 1880 U.S. Census (Rowan Co., NC), which notes Brown, and (Davidson Co., NC), which notes "Cally" Roberts.

Whit Farrand, alias "Ferron, Ferrand and Ferrin" (black, age 34). *Murder.* The crime was committed on 2/20/1895 in Rowan County. Cop killer. Shotgun slaying of 54-year-old Henry C. Owen (white). Motive: resisting arrest. The killer was hanged at Salisbury on July 25, 1895, the same place and date as Anderson Brown (above). Source: *Charlotte Daily Observer*, 2/21/95 (1:7) & 7/26/95 (1:7). See also: 1880 U.S. Census (Wake Co., NC), which notes "Ferrin" as a convicted horse thief.

George Washington (black, age 18). *Murder.* The crime was committed on 10/23/1895 in Edgecombe County. Shotgun slaying of 30-year-old Charles Neville (white). Motive: mugging. The victim had just received his pay. He was a railroad man who tended the water tank at Tarboro Depot. His money, watch and folding knife were found in the killer's pockets. The latter was hanged at Tarboro on December 4, 1895. Sources: *Raleigh News & Observer*, 12/5/95 (1:6); *Daily Charlotte Observer*, 10/25/95 (3:4) & 12/6/95 (2:3). See also: 1880 U.S. Census (Halifax Co., NC), which notes Neville as a teenager, which is inconsistent with his being 18 in 1895.

1896

Thomas Covington (white, age 26). *Murder.* The crime was committed on 9/26/1894 in Catawba County. Handgun slaying of about 55-year-old James Brown (white), the victim having been shot three times with his own weapon. Motive: burglary. Brown owned a cotton mill that employed many local residents, Covington among them. The mill had an outlet store on the same site. There was a pilferage problem there and Brown took means to catch the thief. He hid out in the store by night armed and ready. Covington fell into this trap. A struggle took place inside the darkened store. The intruder wrested a loaded pistol from Mr. Brown and shot him dead. Covington later admitted his guilt as well as the fact that he had been stealing from his employer up until that time. He was hanged at Newton on February 13, 1896. Source: *Daily Charlotte Observer*, 9/28/94 (1:7), 10/18/94 (1:5) & 2/14/96 (2:2). See also: 1880 U.S. Census (Catawba Co., NC), which notes the killer as a youngster.

Edward Fairley, alias "Frank McRae" (black, age 19). *Rape.* The crime was committed on 4/22/1896 in Robeson County. Indecent assault on the person of 17-year-old Susan J. McNair (black), who was severely beaten, choked and lacerated by the culprit's teeth. He was hanged at Lumberton on June 19, 1896. Sources: *Charlotte Daily Observer*, 6/20/96 (1:4); *Wilmington (NC) Morning Star*, 6/20/96 (1:5).

Henry Dowden (black, age not recorded). *Murder.* The crime was committed on 2/22/1896 in Halifax County. Handgun slaying of 37-year-old Matthew M. Dodd (white), a locomotive engineer who was shot dead in his cab. Motive: obnoxious drunk. Dowden was hanged at Halifax on July 2, 1896. Sources: *Raleigh News & Observer*, 2/23/96 (5:1) & 7/3/96 (3:2); *Roanoke (NC) News*, 2/27/96 (3:1) & 7/9/96 (3:1).

1897

Monroe Johnson (black, age 40). *Aggravated Burglary.* The crime was committed on 1/8/1896 in Mecklenburg County. Executed for a nocturnal break-in at the house of 69-year-old Cowan Alexander Shields (white), during which that man's unmarried daughter (Maggie Shields, white, age 28) was terrorized in her bedroom. The culprit also fired five shots from a handgun during this intrusion. One bullet struck the homeowner himself, inflicting a serious but non-fatal wound. The culprit was hanged at Charlotte on February 8, 1897. Source: *Charlotte Daily Observer*, 1/12/96 (6:4), 4/16/96 (4:2), 2/7/97 (6:1) & 2/9/97 (4:1). See also: 1880 U.S. Census (Mecklenburg Co., NC), which notes all parties.

George Brodie (black, age about 20). *Rape.* The crime was committed on 7/30/1897 in Vance County. Indecent assault on the person of about 18-year-old Nannie Catlett (white), she having been accosted at knifepoint as she went to draw water from a spring. The trial jury was comprised of 9 whites and 3 blacks. It was further reported that the non-white residents of that area were disgusted by what Brodie had done. He was hanged at Henderson on September 1, 1897. Sources: *Charlotte Daily Observer*, 7/31/97 (8:1), 8/1/97 (8:1) & 9/2/97 (1:5); *The Gazette* (Raleigh, NC), 8/28/97 (1:2).

Doc Black, alias "Doc Kelly" (black, age 23). *Rape.* The crime was committed on 6/21/1897 in Greene County. Indecent assault on the person of 52-year-old Janie Stepp (white), a maiden woman. The culprit was hanged at Snow Hill on September 1, 1897. Sources: *Kinston (NC) Free Press*, 9/4/97 (1:5); *Charlotte Daily Observer*, 9/5/97 (4:3); *Raleigh News & Observer*, 9/4/97 (6:3). See also: 1880 U.S. Census (Greene Co., NC), which notes the victim.

Wiley Wright, alias "Sam Wright" (black, age not recorded). *Murder.* The crime was committed on 10/2/1897 in Wayne County. Executed for the murder of about 35-year-old Alonzo Carr (white, a storekeeper), who was struck down from behind with a heavy stick in his place of business and his throat cut with a knife that had been specially sharpened for that purpose. Motive: robbery and gross perfidy. The killer was hanged at Goldsboro on November 10, 1897. Source: *Goldsboro Headlight*, 10/7/97 (3:3) & 11/11/97 (3:1).

Edgar Purvis (black, age not recorded). *Murder.* The crime was committed on 8/14/1897 in Harnett County. Handgun slaying of 27-year-old James N. Blackwell (white), a railroad flagman. Motive: resentment for having been put off a train, the killer being a hobo who was stealing a ride. Purvis was hanged at Lillington on November 17, 1897. Sources: *The Post* (Charleston, SC), 8/16/97 (1:3), 8/17/97 (8:1) & 8/19/97 (5:5); *Raleigh News & Observer*, 9/11/97 (2:1) & 11/18/97 (4:4).

Robert Sonly Ryan (white, age 41). *Murder.* The crime was committed on 12/4/1897 in Guilford County. Uxoricide. Handgun slaying of 37-year-old Eliza Jennings Ryan (white), who was shot three times. Motive: robbery. The killer was unanimously described as an alcoholic wife beater who attributed his failed life to everybody's fault except his own. He was a fugitive from justice on the aforesaid date, there being outstanding warrants against him for spousal abuse and nonsupport. The harried Mrs. Ryan had been reduced to taking in boarders just to be able to feed and clothe the couple's seven children because Mr. Ryan contributed nothing toward that end. Eliza Ryan collected her rents on the day of her death. She was en route to pay her grocery bill when she was confronted by her husband on a sidewalk. He demanded the rent money. Then he pulled out a pistol and shot the woman when she balked at this. The law made short work of Robert Sonly Ryan. He was dangling at the end of a rope three weeks later, hanged at Greensboro on December 23, 1897. Sources: *Charlotte Daily Observer*, 12/5/97 (8:4) & 12/24/97 (4:3); *Raleigh News & Observer*, 12/24/97 (1:2). See also: 1896 Greensboro City Directory and 1880 U.S. Census (Guilford Co., NC), which note this ill-fated couple.

1898

John Evans (black, age about 21). *Rape.* The crime was committed on 10/23/1897 in Richmond County. Indecent assault on the person of 24-year-old Lillie Cole (white), she having been attacked as she walked to work in company with her two younger sisters. The rapist was hanged at Rockingham on April 1, 1898. Sources: *Charlotte Daily Observer*, 10/24/97 (8:3) & 10/30/97 (1:4); *Raleigh News & Observer*, 4/2/98 (3:2). See also: 1900 U.S. Census (Richmond Co., NC), which notes the victim and her family.

Hatton Perry (black, age 17). *Rape.* The crime was committed on 2/8/1897 in Beaufort County. Indecent assault on the person of 16-year-old Annie Smith (white). The condemned youth had the full benefit of every post-conviction maneuver that his defense team could concoct. He was hanged at Washington, North Carolina, on May 12, 1898. Source: *Washington (NC) Progress*, 2/24/97 (3:6) & 5/18/98 (3:3). Appeals: 121 NC 533–537 and 122 NC 1018–1023. See also: 1880 U.S. Census (Beaufort Co., NC), which notes the culprit as a baby.

Mit Sadler (black, age about 20). *Murder.* The crime was committed on 1/8/1898 in Cleveland County. Handgun slaying of Will Wells (white, age not recorded) who was shot once and then shot again as he lay writhing on the ground. Motive: armed confrontation. Both parties had drawn pistols on each other. Wells somehow had his own weapon snatched from him and was shot dead when he demanded its return. The killer was hanged at Shelby on May 27, 1898. Source: *Charlotte Daily Observer*, 5/28/98 (2:1).

John Jack Mays (white, age 39). *Murder.* The crime was committed on 6/18/1898 in Surry County. Murder of 66-year-old Martha Thompson Higgins (white, a Confederate widow), who was cremated in the ruins of her burning house after having been subjected to other undisclosed acts of violence. Motive: robbery. The killer was hanged at Dobson on November 11, 1898. Sources: *The Landmark* (Statesville, NC), 6/28/98 (1:7) & 11/15/98 (4:4); *Charlotte Daily Observer*, 10/9/98 (8:1). See also: Record of Burials for Thompson Family Cemetery (Dobson, NC), as well as the killer's gravestone as shown on CemeteryCensus.com.

John Brooks (black, age 20). *Rape.* The crime was committed on 4/18/1898 in Brunswick County. Indecent assault on the person of a matronly white female identified only as "Mrs. M.A. Chaires" (age not specified), she having been severely beaten as well as raped by an intruder in her home. The culprit was hanged at Southport on November 26, 1898. Sources: *Charlotte Daily Observer*, 4/30/98 (3:3) & 11/27/98 (1:3); *Wilmington (NC) Messenger*, 11/27/98 (5:1).

1899

James Booker, alias "Chavis" (black, age 22). *Murder.* The crime was committed on 8/29/1896 in Wake County. Musket slaying of 37-year-old Mahala White (black). Motive: jilted lover. The killer was hanged at Raleigh on January 18, 1899. Sources: *Charlotte Daily Observer*, 8/30/96 (1:8) & 4/1/98 (3:1); *Raleigh News & Observer*, 1/19/99 (6:4). See also: 1880 U.S. Census (Wake Co., NC), which notes both parties.

Joe Jackson, alias "Old Joe Jackson" (black, age 50+). *Rape.* The crime was committed on 9/18/1898 in Mecklenburg County. Indecent assault on the person of 16-year-old Minnie Brown (white, a mentally retarded girl), she having been attacked in broad daylight as she walked across a field with her little brother, age 10. "Old Joe" was hanged at Charlotte on May 18, 1899. Source: *Charlotte Daily Observer*, 9/20/98 (8:3), 10/29/98 (6:1) & 5/19/99 (6:1).

Julius Alexander (black, age 49). *Rape.* The crime was committed on 2/24/1899 in Mecklenburg County. Indecent assault on the person of 58-year-old Julia Mullis (white), she having been attacked in broad daylight as she walked across a rail yard. The rapist was hanged at Charlotte on August 24, 1899. Source: *Charlotte Daily Observer*, 2/25/99 (6:1), 2/26/99 (6:1) & 8/25/99 (5:1). See also: 1880 and 1900 U.S. Census (Mecklenburg Co., NC), which respectively note the culprit and the victim.

Avery Kale (white, age 19). *Murder.* The crime was committed on 8/13/1898 in Catawba County. Shotgun slaying of 28-year-old George E. Travis (white). Motive: smoldering resentment; Travis had been given a job from which Kale had been fired. The killer was hanged at Newton on October 19, 1899. Source: *Charlotte Daily Observer*, 10/20/99 (2:1). See also: 1880 U.S. Census (Catawba Co., NC), which notes both parties as minors.

Elijah Joyner (black, age 27). *Murder.* The crime was committed on 4/25/1899 in Pitt County. Murder of 20-year-old Robert Sheppard (white), a clerk in the employ of his maternal uncle Theodore Turnage, whose remains were found in the burned wreckage of his uncle's country store. There was enough left of the decedent to show that his throat had been cut. Motive: robbery. The killer was hanged at Greenville on November 10, 1899. Sources: *The Landmark* (Statesville, NC), 4/28/99 (2:1), 5/19/99 (1:6) & 9/26/99 (2:5); *Charlotte Daily Observer*, 11/11/99 (1:4). See also: 1880 U.S. Census (Farmville, NC), which notes both parties as minors.

1900

William Truesdale (black, age 24). *Murder.* The crime was committed on 8/23/1899 in Mecklenburg County. Murder of about 20-year-old Janie Brown (black) who was found in a wooded area with her head smashed in. Motive: paternity suit. The victim was described as "a wronged colored girl" from Greensboro. Truesdale had reportedly abandoned a wife and child in Camden, South Carolina, in favor of being a drifter. He sometimes earned honest pay as a hotel waiter, but never in the same location for any appreciable length of time. It was during one such stint at Greensboro, North Carolina, that he met and seduced Janie Brown. She soon found herself in the family way. Truesdale was noncommittal, so she had him arrested on a charge of bastardy. He was allowed to go free when he promised to marry Janie Brown. He honored that pledge by jumping on the first train out of town. Janie Brown traced him to Charlotte, North Carolina. She went there to enforce her claim with the help of local authorities. Truesdale put on a show of welcome and then basely murdered her. It is not clear if she had already become a mother by then. The killer was hanged at Charlotte on February 8, 1900. Source: *Charlotte Daily Observer*, 8/25/99 (6:1) & 2/9/00 (6:1). See also: 1880 U.S. Census (Kershaw Co., SC), which notes young Truesdale.

Reuben Ross (black, age not recorded). *Rape.* The crime was committed on 9/30/1899 in Robeson County. Indecent assault on the person of 20-year-old Bettie Ingram (white), she having been twice attacked in her own home. A special investigation into the victim's character was held before the governor allowed the execution to proceed. Aspersions cast on the young woman were found to be baseless. Ross was hanged at Lumberton on February 9, 1900. Source: *Charlotte Daily Observer*, 1/20/00 (3:1) & 2/10/00 (3:1).

Robert Fortune (black, age 21) **and John Henry Taylor** (black, age 23). *Murder.* The crime was committed on 12/21/1899 in Nash County. Both executed for the handgun slaying of 57-year-old Robert Hester (white), who was shot three times. Motive: highway robbery. They are confirmed to have also murdered another man named Lawrence Jackson under similar circumstances near Weldon, North Carolina, three days earlier. The killers were hanged at Nashville,

North Carolina, on March 15, 1900. Source: *The Graphic* (Nashville, NC), 2/8/00 (3:3) & 3/22/00 (1:1). See also: 1880 U.S. Census (Granville Co., NC), which notes Mr. Hester.

Thomas Jones (black, age 29). *Murder.* The crime was committed on 3/21/1900 in Wake County. Mass killer. Child killer. Baby killer. Executed for the ax murders of 33-year-old Ella Jones and 14-year-old Ida Jones (blacks, a mother and daughter who were not kin to their destroyer) and the burning of their home, in which inferno four more of the woman's offspring perished, the youngest a babe at her breast. The other dead were: Jesse Jones (age 6), Nancy Jones (age 3), Cleveland Jones (age 2) and the baby, whose name and gender are not specified in news accounts. Motive: paternity suit. The killer had sired the youngest victim out of wedlock and been taken to task for it. He was hanged at Raleigh on August 31, 1900. Source: *Raleigh News & Observer*, 3/23/00 (1:1), 8/31/00 (6:1) & 9/1/00 (6:1).

William Edwards (black, age 27). *Murder.* The crime was committed on 9/2/1899 in Rowan County. Cop killer. Handgun slaying of 25-year-old William J. Kerns (white). Motive: obnoxious drunk. Edwards was hanged at Salisbury on September 3, 1900. Source: *Charlotte Daily Observer*, 9/3/99 (5:1), 9/5/99 (3:3) & 9/4/00 (1:4).

Chauncey Davis (black, age 27). *Arson.* The crime was committed on 5/8/1899 in Edgecombe County. Executed for willfully setting fire to an inhabited dwelling place with the resultant loss of human life. He had fired the house of 30-year-old Lavinia Battle (black), in the subsequent course of which a young man named Henry Bunn (black, age 21) perished while engaged in rescue efforts. The incendiary was hanged at Tarboro on September 28, 1900. Sources: *Tarboro Southerner*, 10/4/00 (4:2); *Charlotte Daily Observer*, 9/29/00 (1:7). See also: 1880 U.S. Census (Edgecombe Co., NC), which notes Battle and Bunn as minors.

Archie Kinsauls (white, age 31). *Murder.* The crime was committed on 10/27/1898 in Sampson County. Fatal stabbing of 23-year-old John C. Herring (white). Motive: fracas at a political rally. The killer was hanged at Clinton on September 28, 1900. Sources: *The Landmark* (Statesville, NC), 11/4/98 (2:2); *Raleigh News & Observer*, 9/29/00 (1:6). See also: 1880 U.S. Census (Sampson Co., NC), which notes Herring as a minor, and 1900 U.S. Census (Wilmington, NC), which notes Kinsauls as a prisoner.

1901

John Ruffin (black, age 17). *Rape.* The crime was committed on 8/23/1900 in Alamance County. Indecent assault on the person of 9-year-old Gertrude Skeen (black), she having been torn in such a way that an emergency operation was needed to save her life. The rapist was hanged at Graham on February 1, 1901. Sources: *Charlotte Daily Observer*, 8/24/00 (8:3); *Raleigh News & Observer*, 1/5/01 (5:2) & 2/2/01 (1:4). See also: 1900 U.S. Census (Alamance Co., NC), which notes both parties.

William Monroe (black, age 20). *Rape.* The crime was committed on 8/13/1901 in Mecklenburg County. Indecent assault on the person of pregnant 16-year-old

Lida Philmon Martin (white, a newlywed), who was attacked in the parlor of her home, beaten, choked and felled with a wooden chair to better effect the culprit's purpose. The rapist was hanged at Charlotte on September 13, 1901. Source: *Charlotte Daily Observer*, 8/14/01 (5:1) & 9/14/01 (6:1). See also: 1910 U.S. Census (Mecklenburg Co., NC), which notes the victim as still living where the attack happened.

Louis Council (black, age 28). *Rape.* The crime was committed on 5/29/1900 in Cumberland County. Indecent assault on the person of 17-year-old Lonie M. West (white), she having been jumped in a pig pen and forcibly dragged into nearby bushes irrespective of mud and swine feces. The rapist was hanged at Fayetteville on November 2, 1901. Source: *Charlotte Daily Observer*, 11/3/01 (1:5). See also: 1880 U.S. Census (Cumberland Co., NC), which notes Council, and 1900 U.S. Census there which notes the victim.

1902

Frank Johnson, alias "Dudley Johnson," alias "Frank Wilson" (white, age about 25) **and Ben Foster** (black, age 23). *Aggravated Burglary.* The crime was committed on 2/8/1901 in Buncombe County. Both executed for a nocturnal break-in at the United States Post Office located at Emma (a village four miles west of Asheville), during which the keeper thereof (Samuel Alexander, white, age 24) was shot in the rear end. The culprits were suspected serial burglars who had been active throughout the greater Asheville area. They had forced Alexander to open the Post Office safe, threatening him with death if he refused. A gun battle erupted when the harried postal employee got a chance to reach for a pistol that was kept there for security purposes. Johnson and Foster were also wounded by gunfire. Two other accomplices who were not triggermen were also sentenced to death but reprieved on humanitarian grounds. Johnson and Foster were hanged at Asheville on February 26, 1902. Sources: *Asheville (NC) Daily Gazette*, 2/26/02 (1:4) & 2/27/02 (1:2); *Raleigh News & Observer*, 2/27/02 (1:1). See also: 1900 U.S. Census (Buncombe Co., NC), which notes Foster as a chain ganger.

John Henry Rose (white, age 24). *Murder.* The crime was committed on 7/27/1901 in Wilson County. Shotgun slaying of 38-year-old Thomas Farmer (white), the victim having been blasted from ambush. Motive: because Rose thought that Farmer had reported him to authorities for making moonshine. The killer was hanged at Wilson on February 26, 1902. Source: *Charlotte Daily Observer*, 9/7/01 (2:1) & 2/27/02 (1:2). See also: 1900 U.S. Census (Wilson Co., NC), which notes both parties.

Frank Shaw (black, age 36). *Murder.* The crime was committed on 11/27/1901 in Robeson County. Shotgun slaying of 34-year-old Mary Eliza Ferguson (black, his stepsister) and the deliberate smashing of her head with the butt of that weapon to make sure that she was dead. Motive: rejected suitor. Shaw was hanged at Lumberton on April 14, 1902. Sources: *The Robesonian* (Lumberton, NC), 12/3/01 (2:2) & 4/15/02 (3:2); *Charlotte Daily Observer*, 4/10/02 (4:4). See also: 1880 U.S. Census (Robeson Co., NC), which notes the victim as daughter of Wash Ferguson, and 1900 U.S. Census (Robeson Co., NC), which notes Shaw.

Archie Conley (black, age 23). *Murder.* The crime was committed on 11/22/1901 in Rowan County. Fatal stabbing of Gus Davis (black, age not recorded), who was knifed multiple times and his head nearly severed. Motive: belligerent attitude. The victim was attacked when he refused the killer's demand that he give him a cigarette. Conley was hanged at Salisbury on July 8, 1902. Source: *Charlotte Daily Observer*, 11/23/01 (6:3) & 7/9/02 (1:3). Appeal: 130 NC 683–687.

Dick Fleming (black, age 35). *Rape.* The crime was committed on 2/18/1902 in Rowan County. Indecent assault on the person of 36-year-old Belle Livengood (white), who was attacked by two or possibly three nocturnal home invaders who broke down her door, smashed up her furniture and forced themselves on her. Fleming was hanged at Salisbury on July 8, 1902. Source: *Charlotte Daily Observer*, 7/9/02 (1:3). See also: 1900 U.S. Census (Rowan Co., NC), which notes both parties.

Calvin Elliott (black, age about 20). *Rape.* The crime was committed on 9/27/1902 in Lincoln County. Indecent assault on the person of 37-year-old Julia K. Brown (white), she having been attacked in a tiny cottage that she inhabited along with her semi invalid husband and three small children. None were able to offer much resistance on account of physical infirmity. The victim's husband, Caleb Brown, was described as an "imbecile" due to a previous head injury. The rapist "knocked him down" in order to get at his wife. Elliott was hanged at Lincolnton on November 25, 1902. Source: *Charlotte Daily Observer*, 11/26/02 (1:1). See also: 1900 U.S. Census (Lincoln Co., NC), which notes the family Brown.

1903

John Broadnax (black, age 16). *Murder.* The crime was committed on 3/19/1903 in Rockingham County. Handgun slaying of 57-year-old Arthur Sidney Blair (white) and serious wounding of that man's female housekeeper (Sallie Walker, white, age 33), they having been shot twice and three times respectively. Motive: home invasion. The killer was hanged at Wentworth on May 22, 1903. Sources: *The Robesonian* (Lumberton, NC), 3/24/03 (2:4); *Charlotte Daily Observer*, 4/15/03 (7:1); *Raleigh News & Observer*, 5/23/03 (1:3). See also: 1900 U.S. Census (Rockingham Co., NC), which notes the victims in this case.

Wilfred Roseboro (black, age 24). *Murder.* The crime was committed on 7/30/1903 in Iredell County. Murder of 46-year-old Dovie C. Beaver (white), she having been choked, raped, her head split open and her body thrown down a well. Motive: sexual assault and theft of a handgun. The killer was hanged at Statesville on September 10, 1903. Source: *Charlotte Daily Observer*, 8/2/03 (1:1) & 9/11/03 (8:1). See also: 1900 U.S. Census (Iredell Co., NC), which notes both parties.

Cyrus Dixon (white, age 22). *Murder.* The crime was committed on 11/21/1901 in Jones County. Shotgun slaying of 35-year-old Godfrey A. Webber (white) through deliberate malice of lying in wait for him with homicidal intent. Motive: adultery with the victim's wife. Dixon was hanged at Trenton on December 1, 1903. Source: *Charlotte Daily Observer*, 12/2/03 (2:1). See also: 1900 U.S. Census (Jones Co., NC), which notes Dixon, and (Craven Co., NC), which notes Webber; *Front Page Detective*, 6/58.

1904

Jabel Register (white, age 29). *Murder.* The crime was committed on 3/29/1903 in Columbus County. Shotgun slayings of 58-year-old Jesse Soles (a white man) and 40-year-old James Staley (a black man), two illicit distillers, and the burning of their bodies. Motive: robbery. The killer was hanged at Whiteville on February 25, 1904. Sources: *Charlotte Daily Observer*, 5/2/03 (1:2); *Raleigh News & Observer*, 2/26/04 (1:7). Appeal: 46 SE 21–24. See also: 1900 U.S. Census (Columbus Co., NC), which notes Register and Soles, and (Bladen Co., NC), which notes Staley.

Will Boggan (black, age not recorded). *Murder.* The crime was committed on 2/28/1903 in Anson County. Handgun slaying of 38-year-old John A. Sullivan (white). Motive: quarrel about an overcoat. The killer was hanged at Wadesboro on February 25, 1904. Source: *Raleigh News & Observer*, 2/26/04 (6:4). Appeal: 133 NC 761–769. See also: 1900 U.S. Census (Anson Co., NC), which notes both parties but does not specify Boggan's age.

Alfred Daniels (black, age 33). *Murder.* The crime was committed on 9/12/1903 in Jones County. Shotgun slaying of 77-year-old Furnifold G. Simmons (white). Motive: poaching on the victim's land. The added fact that Simmons was the father of a United States senator was certainly not a palliative factor in determining the killer's fate. He was hanged at Trenton on May 19, 1904. Sources: *Charlotte Daily Observer*, 9/15/03 (1:2) & 11/3/03 (1:3); *Raleigh News & Observer*, 5/20/04 (1:1). See also: 1900 U.S. Census (Jones Co., NC), which notes both parties.

Frank Davis (white, age 30). *Murder.* The crime was committed on 9/30/1903 in Lenoir County. Shotgun slaying of 36-year-old Charles F. Pate (white). Motive: vindictiveness. The victim had "superseded" Davis in a job. The killer was hanged at Kinston on May 19, 1904. Source: *Daily Free Press* (Kinston, NC), 10/1/03 (1:4), 10/13/03 (1:4) & 5/19/04 (1:3). See also: 1900 U.S. Census (Lenoir Co., NC), which notes both parties.

Adam Hunt (black, age 26). *Murder.* The crime was committed on 11/7/1903 in Person County. Fatal beating of 25-year-old Fleetwood Wilkins (white), a frail storekeeper. Motive: robbery. The killer was hanged at Roxboro on June 15, 1904. Sources: *Charlotte Daily Observer*, 11/13/03 (1:4); *The Landmark* (Statesville, NC), 6/17/04 (2:4). See also: 1900 U.S. Census (Manchester, VA), which notes the killer, and (Halifax Co., VA), which notes the victim.

Jesse Allen (black, age 20). *Rape.* The crime was committed on 5/26/1904 in Granville County. Indecent assault on the person of 9-year-old Jennie Oakley (white), the details being unfit for publication. The rapist was hanged at Oxford on September 9, 1904. Sources: *Winston-Salem Journal*, 7/15/04 (2:1); *The Landmark* (Statesville, NC), 8/9/04 (1:6); *Raleigh News & Observer*, 9/10/04 (1:3).

Ben Clark (black, age about 25). *Murder.* The crime was committed on 8/27/1904 in Cleveland County. Cop killer. Handgun slaying of 36-year-old Barnett Edgar Hamrick (white), the police chief of Shelby. Motive: obnoxious drunk. The killer was hanged at Shelby on October 28, 1904. Sources: *Charlotte Daily Observer*, 8/29/04 (1:7); *Raleigh News &*

Observer, 10/29/04 (1:2). See also: 1880 U.S. Census (Cleveland Co., NC), which notes the victim as a minor.

Dave Brown (black, age 34) **and Neil Sellers** (black, age 34). *Murder.* The crime was committed on 9/3/1904 in Bladen County. Mutilation murder of 21-year-old Blanche Packer (white), she having been dragged from her home, beaten with a fence rail and slashed all over with a knife. Motive: sexual assault. The killers were hanged at Elizabethtown on November 16, 1904. Sources: *Charlotte Daily Observer*, 9/4/04 (1:3) & 9/6/04 (8:1); *Raleigh News & Observer*, 11/17/04 (1:3).

Reuben Johnson (black, age 21). *Murder.* The crime was committed on 5/17/1904 in Washington County. Uxoricide. Handgun slaying of 22-year-old Maggie Webb Johnson (black), she having been shot five times. Motive: suspected infidelity. The killer was hanged at Plymouth on December 17, 1904. Source: *Roanoke Beacon* (Plymouth, NC), 5/20/04 (4:1) & 12/23/04 (5:3). See also: Washington County Marriage Register entry dated 6/12/01, and 1900 U.S. Census (Washington Co., NC), which notes the victim by her maiden name.

1905

Walter Partridge (black, age 16). *Rape.* The crime was committed on 2/1/1905 in Cumberland County. Indecent assault on the person of 25-year-old Lillie Ida Rogers Hales (white, a recent widow), who was pounced on as she walked along with her 4-year-old son, beaten up and cut with scissors. The rapist was hanged at Fayetteville on April 6, 1905. Sources: *Charlotte Daily Observer*, 4/5/05 (3:3) & 4/7/05 (3:1); *The Robesonian* (Lumberton, NC), 2/7/05 (6:2). See also: 1900 U.S. Census (Cumberland Co., NC), which notes the culprit as having been born in June 1888.

Daniel Teachey (white, age 33). *Murder.* The crime was committed on 3/4/1903 in Duplin County. Handgun slaying of 25-year-old William Robert Rivenbark (white). Motive: rivalry for a black whore. The killer was hanged at Kenansville on July 20, 1905. Source: *Charlotte Daily Observer*, 7/21/05 (1:7). Appeal: 138 NC 422–430. See also: 1880 & 1900 U.S. Census (Duplin Co., NC), which note both parties.

Joseph W. Hammons (white, age 49). *Murder.* The crime was committed on 4/29/1905 in Forsyth County. Uxoricide. Handgun slaying of 28-year-old Henrietta Conway Hammons (white), she having been gunned down on a public sidewalk while in the act of picking up her small child. Motive: duped bridegroom. Hammons had married the victim believing her to be a widow. He later discovered that she was a liar who had not been previously married and that her child was a bastard. So he got hold of a gun and made good on a pledge that he had made to the effect that no woman would scam him in such a way and live to talk about it. Hammons was hanged at Winston-Salem on September 2, 1905. Source: *Charlotte Observer*, 9/3/05 (1:1). See also: 1900 U.S. Census (Patrick Co., VA), which notes the victim by her maiden name.

Ashton Moore (black, age 19). *Rape.* The crime was committed on 4/24/1905 in Sampson County. Indecent assault on the person of 11-year-old Kanella Brewington (black), she having been attacked while working the fields. The rapist was hanged at Clinton on September 2, 1905. Source: *Charlotte Observer*, 9/3/05 (1:1) & (1:2). See also: 1900 U.S. Census (Sampson Co., NC), which notes both parties.

Will Adams (black, age 30). *Murder.* The crime was committed on 1/22/1904 in Wake County. Child killer, etc. Executed for the ax murders of 30-year-old Mollie Bridgers and 5-year-old Lillie Bridgers along with the grievous wounding of 8-year-old William Bridgers (blacks, a mother and her offspring), who were slaughtered in a cotton patch close to their home. Motive: uncertain; the killer gave no reason. He was hanged at Raleigh on September 14, 1905. Source: *Raleigh News & Observer*, 9/15/05 (5:1). See also: 1900 U.S. Census (Wake Co., NC), which notes the victims, and (Wilmington, NC), which notes the culprit.

Peter Smith (white, age 63). *Rape.* The crime was committed on 11/8/1904 in Madison County. Executed for an indecent assault on the person of 15-year-old Eva Suttles (white), who was lured from her home with a contrived story and then raped at knifepoint. Prime suspect in the October 1901 murder of pregnant 16-year-old Hannah Plemmons (white), whose head was found by a reaper mowing a field not far from the site of the Suttles ordeal. The rapist was hanged at Marshall on October 2, 1905. Source: *Charlotte Daily Observer*, 10/3/05 (1:1). See also: 1900 U.S. Census (Madison Co., NC), which notes Smith and the Plemmons girl. See also: Tom Rusher, *Until He is Dead: Capital Punishment in Western North Carolina History* (Boone, NC: Parkway Publishers, 2003), pgs. 130–173. Although erudite and well-intentioned, Rusher blundered badly in his book by citing incorrect statistics on pgs. 132 and 161.

Preston Daniels (black, age 23). *Murder.* The crime was committed on 6/19/1905 in Martin County. Handgun slaying of 28-year-old William Eborn (black). Motive: male bravado. The murder was perpetrated aboard an excursion train, Daniels and his girlfriend being seated together in the Jim Crow car. Daniels got up to get a drink only to find Eborn sitting in his spot when he returned. He assumed right away that Eborn was trying to put the moves on his girl and ordered him to leave. Eborn was said to have muttered something as he rose from the seat, whereupon Daniels pulled out a gun and shot him dead. Daniels was hanged at Williamston on December 16, 1905. Source: *Raleigh News & Observer*, 12/17/05 (12:1). Appeal: 139 NC 549–554. Martin County Superior Court Minutes Book (June 1905) pgs. 343–344. See also: 1900 U.S. Census (Nash Co., NC), which notes the killer and (Beaufort Co., NC), which notes Eborn.

Will Carter (black, age 17). *Rape.* The crime was committed on 10/22/1905 in Duplin County. Indecent assault on the person of 6-year-old Virginia James (white), the daughter of Mr. and Mrs. Howard James. The child's parents had left her in the care of a trusted family servant while they went to church. It was then that the culprit made his move. He was hanged at Kenansville on December 20, 1905. Sources: *The Landmark* (Statesville, NC), 10/27/05 (1:6); *Raleigh News & Observer*, 12/21/05 (1:7).

1906

Bob Mitchell (black, age 56). *Murder.* The crime was committed on 6/12/1905 in Bertie County. Uxoricide. Executed for the murder of 32-year-old Susan R. Mitchell (black), who was bludgeoned with a wagon board and then cremated in a burning outhouse. Motive: presumed marital problems. The killer was hanged at Windsor on March 1, 1906. Source: *Raleigh News & Observer*, 3/2/06 (3:1). See also: 1900 U.S. Census (Bertie Co., NC), which notes both parties.

Henry Scott (black, age about 25). *Murder.* The crime was committed on 10/10/1905 on the high seas. Executed under federal authority for the handgun slayings of five persons aboard the merchant schooner *Harry A. Berwind*, which was then en route from Mobile, Alabama, to Philadelphia, Pennsylvania, with an 8-man crew. The homicide victims consisted of the skipper, Edward B. Rummill (white, age 45) of Hancock Co., Maine; 1st mate John T. Hall; ship's engineer C.L. Smith (full name not recorded); ship's cook John Falbe (whites, ages not recorded); and a Negro crewman named John S. Coakley, age not recorded. All of the victims were thrown overboard after being shot about 30 nautical miles southeast of Cape Fear. Motive: disgruntled employee, or crewman in this case. There was also a strong element of racial animosity as well. The culprit had originally made it a point to murder only the white people aboard the vessel. The lone black victim was slain for a different reason: because he had signaled to another ship that there was trouble aboard the *Berwind.* The killer was hanged at Wilmington on July 6, 1906. Sources: *Wilmington (NC) Messenger*, 7/7/06 (1:1); *Raleigh News & Observer*, 7/7/06 (1:3). See also: 1900 U.S. Census (Hancock Co., ME), which notes the murdered skipper.

Henry Bailey (black, age not recorded). *Murder.* The crime was committed on 6/21/1906 in Craven County. Shotgun slaying of 34-year-old John Macon Lancaster (white). Motive: landlord-tenant dispute. Bailey was hanged at New Bern on August 31, 1906. Source: *New Bern Weekly Journal*, 6/22/06 (4:6) & 9/4/06 (1:5). See also: 1880 U.S. Census (Craven Co., NC), which notes the victim as a minor.

Ben Williams (black, age not recorded). *Murder.* The crime was committed on 2/19/1906 in Wake County. Handgun slaying of 20-year-old Alex Clark (black). Motive: rivalry for a female. Williams was hanged at Raleigh on December 20, 1906. Sources: *Raleigh News & Observer*, 2/20/06 (5:1) & 12/21/06 (5:1); *Times-Dispatch* (Richmond, VA), 4/7/06 (8:6). See also: 1900 U.S. Census (Petersburg, VA), which notes Clark.

1907

Henry Walker (black, age 30). *Aggravated Burglary.* The crime was committed on 11/6/1906 in Alamance County. Executed for a violent break-in at the house of 64-year-old Lynn Banks Holt (white, a wealthy cotton magnate), the homeowner having been shot in the head with a handgun and painfully wounded. Motive: disgruntled former employee. Walker had previously been a coachman in Mr. Holt's employ. He had been fired from that job for using profanity in the presence of Mrs. Holt. Seething with resentment in the aftermath of his dismissal, Walker effected an entry to the Holt residence at a late hour and shot Mr. Holt with intent to commit murder. One bullet struck Holt in the head but did not penetrate his skull. A disfiguring wound resulted. Holt died of natural causes on 10/25/1920. Henry Walker was hanged at Graham on January 8, 1907. Sources: *Greensboro (NC) Daily Record*, 11/7/06 (1:5) & 1/8/07 (1:2); *Charlotte Daily Observer*, 11/10/06 (1:7) & 1/9/07 (1:5). See also: 1900 U.S. Census (Alamance Co., NC), which notes both parties. Also: 1920 Alamance County death cert. no. 254.

Sylvester Barrett (black, age 29). *Murder.* The crime was committed on 1/20/1906 in Pitt County. Cop killer. Handgun slaying of Walter J. Lovett (white, age not recorded), the constable of Farmville Township. Motive: resisting arrest. Barrett was hanged at Greenville on January 15, 1907. Sources: *Daily Reflector* (Greenville, NC), 1/22/06 (1:1); *Charlotte Daily Observer*, 1/16/07 (4:4). See also: 1900 U.S. Census (Pitt Co., NC), which notes Barrett.

Frank Bohannon (black, age not recorded). *Murder.* The crime was committed on 7/31/1906 in Guilford County. Shotgun slaying of 35-year-old R.E. Betchman (white, full name not given), who was deliberately blasted in the crotch with a double-barreled weapon. Motive: disgruntled employee. The victim was foreman on a railroad track crew. He had fired Bohannon the previous day for being drunk and disorderly. Bohannon was hanged at Greensboro on February 8, 1907. Sources: *Greensboro Daily News*, 8/1/06 (1:1); *Raleigh News & Observer*, 2/9/07 (2:1).

John H. Hodges (white, age 50). *Murder.* The crime was committed on February 25, 1906, in Durham County. Uxoricide. Handgun slaying of 36-year-old Mattie High Hodges (white), she having been pulled from her sickbed and shot dead in the presence of their six children. Motive: impending divorce. The killer was hanged at Durham on February 8, 1907. Sources: *Charlotte Daily Observer*, 2/26/06 (1:1); *Raleigh News & Observer*, 2/9/07 (1:1). See also: 1900 U.S. Census (Durham Co., NC), which notes both parties.

Freeman Jones (black, age about 35). *Aggravated Burglary.* The crime was committed on 6/17/1906 in Durham County. Executed for a violent break-in at the house of about 58-year-old "Mrs. John W. Barker" (white), a so-called "half witted woman" who lived with her 83-year-old mother. She was terrorized and dragged outdoors with intent to commit rape at 3 o'clock in the morning. The culprit was hanged at Durham on February 8, 1907. Sources: *Greensboro Daily Record*, 6/18/06 (4:3) & 6/19/06 (1:2); *Raleigh News & Observer*, 2/9/07 (1:1). Also: Durham County Superior Court Minutes Book (August 1906), pg. 351.

Tom Walker (black, age about 30). *Murder.* The crime was committed on 3/2/1907 in Cumberland County. Cop killer. Handgun slayings of about 46-year-old Jefferson A. Chason and 30-year-old Owen Lockamy (whites), respectively the police chief of Fayetteville and one of his lesser-ranking officers. Motive: speakeasy raid turned deadly. The killer sold alcoholic beverages contrary to law. "You've hunted me down like dogs!" shouted Walker at the officers. "And now I will kill you like dogs!" He was hanged at Fayetteville on April 15, 1907. Sources: *Charlotte Daily Observer*, 3/3/07 (1:1) & 3/4/07 (1:1); *Raleigh News & Observer*, 4/16/07 (1:4). See also: 1900 U.S. Census (Cumberland Co., NC), which notes Lockamy.

Will Banks (black, age not recorded). *Murder.* The crime was committed on 5/1/1906 in Ashe County. Handgun slaying of 45-year-old Frank McMillan (black, his uncle). Motive: hard feelings instigated by a third party. The victim had a teenage son who skipped out on a $1.50 loan and then told lies about the lender (Banks) in order to dodge repayment. Banks became exasperated and went to physically confront the defaulter. Frank McMillan told Banks that no one could put hands on his son save he. A brawl erupted during which Banks pulled out a gun and shot Frank McMillan. The shooter was hanged at Jefferson on August 20, 1907. The scene was said to have resembled a saturnalia and gave rise to a movement to transfer executions to the State Prison in Raleigh. Source: *Charlotte Daily Observer*, 8/23/07 (9:1). Appeal: 143 NC 652–658. State Sup. Court file no. 22796 (NC State Archives). See also: 1900 U.S. Census (Ashe Co., NC), which notes McMillan.

James Rucker (black, age not recorded). *Rape.* The crime was committed on 1/14/1907 in Buncombe County. Indecent assault on the person of 6-year-old Susie Rucker-Upshire (black, his stepdaughter) whose fundament he slit with a knife to better effect his purpose. This child rapist and child mutilator was hanged at Asheville on August 20, 1907. Sources: *Charlotte Daily Observer*, 1/15/07 (7:5) & 2/14/07 (8:4); *Raleigh News & Observer*, 8/21/07 (1:3). See also: Buncombe County Superior Court Criminal Action Papers (*State vs. Rucker*, 1907); NC State Archives.

1908

Sam Murchison, alias "Sam Melvin" (black, age 38). *Murder.* The crime was committed on 2/23/1908 in Cumberland County. Cop killer. Handgun slaying of 54-year-old James H. Benton (white), the police chief of Fayetteville. Motive: resisting arrest. The killer was hanged at the county jail on April 16, 1908. Sources: *Charlotte Daily Observer*, 3/27/08 (1:2); *Raleigh News & Observer*, 4/17/08 (1:7). See also: 1900 U.S. Census (Cumberland Co., NC), which notes both parties.

David Bryant (black, age 15). *Rape.* The crime was committed on 1/31/1908 in Jones County. Indecent assault on the person of 13-year-old Nannie Basden (white), she having been accosted on a public road, choked into semiconsciousness, and dragged nearly 100 yards to a spot where she was raped. The culprit was hanged at Trenton on May 7, 1908. Sources: *New Bern Daily Journal*, 2/2/08 (1:5) & 5/8/08 (1:6); Jones County Superior Court Minutes Book (Spring Term 1908), pgs. 243–245. See also: 1900 U.S. Census (Jones Co., NC), which notes Bryant as having been born in Nov. 1892.

Lewis Fletcher (black, age 23). *Murder.* The crime was committed on 8/9/1908 in Mecklenburg County. Handgun slaying of George Boyd (black, age not recorded, who was attacked while on his way to church, the killer making it a point to shoot him in the mouth. Motive: because the victim had said something uncomplimentary about the killer's womenfolk. Fletcher was hanged at Charlotte on November 20, 1908. Source: *Charlotte Daily Observer*, 8/10/08 (6:2), 8/22/08 (6:1), 8/28/08 (6:2), 11/20/08 (8:5) & 11/21/08 (6:1).

Henry E. Harvey (black, age 22). *Murder.* The crime was committed on 7/19/1908 in Richmond County. Handgun slaying of 26-year-old Hugh Price (black), the victim having been shot multiple times. Motive: gambling dispute. Harvey was hanged at Rockingham on December 17, 1908. Source: *Charlotte Daily Observer*, 7/21/08 (1:3), 9/15/08 (1:7) & 12/18/08 (1:6). See also: 1900 U.S. Census (Roanoke, VA), which notes both parties, who were laborers from that city.

Will Graham (black, age 39). *Rape.* The crime was committed on 10/13/1908 in Cabarrus County. Indecent assault on the person of 16-year-old Pearl Tucker (white), she having been attacked in a field. Graham was reported to have also attempted to force himself "upon the person of a little girl of his own people" several weeks earlier but escaped prosecution by bribing her parents. He was hanged at Concord on December 18, 1908. Sources: *Charlotte Daily Observer*, 11/7/08 (1:3); *Raleigh News & Observer*, 12/18/08 (5:5) & 12/19/08 (1:6). See also: 1900 U.S. Census (Cabarrus Co., NC), which notes both parties.

1909

Jackson Palmer, alias "Will Ward" (black, age not recorded). *Rape.* The crime was committed on 1/19/1909 in Sampson County. Indecent assault on the person of Mollie McLeod (white, age not recorded), she having been attacked in her own home by a besotted intruder, choked, menaced with a knife and dragged back into the house for more when she attempted to flee. The rapist was hanged at Clinton on March 3, 1909. Sources: *The Robesonian* (Lumberton, NC), 1/25/09 (4:6); *Raleigh News & Observer*, 1/20/09 (5:1) & 3/4/09 (1:5).

Robert Robeson, alias "Roberson" (black, age not recorded). *Murder.* The crime was committed on 8/12/1908 in Martin County. Handgun slaying of 31-year-old Charles H. Whichard (white), who was shot three times. Motive: dispute over wages. The killer was hanged at Williamston on June 12, 1909. Sources: *Richmond (VA) Times-Dispatch*, 8/13/08 (1:6); *Raleigh News & Observer*, 5/6/09 (2:7) & 6/13/09 (16:7). Appeal: 150 NC 837–845. See also: 1880 U.S. Census (Martin Co., NC), which notes Whichard as a small child.

1910

Henry Spivey (black, age not recorded). *Murder.* The crime was committed on 12/10/1908 in Bladen County. Shotgun slaying of Frank Shaw (black, age not recorded), his father-in-law, who was struck in the face with a load of buckshot. Motive: family problems. Spivey's wife had left him (on account of his brutality) and taken refuge with her father. The latter caught Spivey in the act of splashing kerosene on the exterior of his house, it being his intention to destroy the place. Spivey was also armed with a shotgun at the time. Shaw succumbed after seven days in agony. The killer was hanged at Elizabethtown on March 11, 1910. Sources: *Charlotte Daily Observer*, 3/17/09 (7:2);

Morning Star (Wilmington, NC), 3/12/10 (1:6); *Winston-Salem Journal*, 5/31/09 (3:5) & 3/12/10 (8:3). Appeal: 151 NC 676–686.

Walter Morrison (black, age 34). *Rape.* The crime was committed on 5/27/1909 in Robeson County. Indecent assault on the person of 29-year-old Polly A. Rodgers (a Croatan), she having been purposely lured to a prearranged spot with a contrived story that her husband had been injured in an accident. The rapist had been released from the county chain gang exactly 17 days earlier. He had a lengthy criminal record. On March 18, 1910 he became the first condemned criminal to be executed at the North Carolina State Prison. Source: *The Robesonian* (Lumberton, NC), 5/31/09 (3:5) & 3/21/10 (1:1). See also: 1910 U.S. Census (Robeson Co., NC), which notes Archie and Polly Rodgers.

1911

Philip Mills (black, age 23). *Murder.* The crime was committed on 9/8/1910 in Transylvania County. Uxoricide. Filicide. Baby killer. Executed for the murder of 20-year-old Martha Gaston Mills (black), who was battered beyond recognition with the butt of a shotgun. She had reportedly attempted to flee with their infant son (unnamed) in her arms. The baby was knocked to the ground and died as well. Motive: marital estrangement. Mills was executed on February 10, 1911. Source: *Charlotte Daily Observer*, 9/11/10 (1:2) & 2/11/11 (1:6). See also: 1910 U.S. Census (Transylvania Co., NC), which shows the killer living with his parents. Also: Transylvania County Marriage Register entry dated 12/12/1908.

Nathan Montague (black, age 27). *Murder.* The crime was committed on 12/19/1910 in Granville County. Executed for the atrocious murders of 62-year-old James Leyton Saunders, 19-year-old Mattie Saunders, and 3-year-old Irene Overton (whites, a father, daughter and granddaughter), who were all slashed to death with a large jackknife and cremated inside their burning house. Motive: sexual assault of the 19-year-old female victim. The killer had spent the earlier part of that day killing hogs on the Saunders farm. The murder weapon was the same one he used in the porcine abattoir. The culprit was executed on February 15, 1911. Source: *Greensboro (NC) Daily News*, 12/21/10 (1:3) & 2/16/11 (6:3). See also: 1900 & 1910 U.S. Census (Granville Co., NC), which note all parties.

James B. Allison (white, age 43). *Murder.* The crime was committed on 7/5/1910 in Buncombe County. Murder of 37-year-old Floyd McGhee (white), who was shot five times (including four bullets in the back) with a handgun and then finished off by having his skull smashed with a hammer. Motive: rivalry for a female. Allison had reportedly committed four other homicides during the preceding 12 years but euchred his way out of trouble each time with pleas of self-defense. He was executed on February 24, 1911. Source: *Greensboro (NC) Daily News*, 7/6/10 (2:4) & 8/7/10 (1:2). Also: 1911 Wake Co. death cert. no. 100; 1910 U.S. Census (Asheville, NC), which notes both parties.

Lewis West (black, age 24). *Murder.* The crime was committed on 2/3/1911 in Wilson County. Cop killer. Handgun slaying of 41-year-old George W. Mumford (white), who was shot multiple times. Motive: resisting arrest. Lewis West was executed on May 5, 1911. Source: *Charlotte Daily Observer*, 2/4/11 (1:1). See also: 1911 Wilson Co. death cert. no. 13 and Wake Co. death cert. no. 206.

Norman Lewis (black, age 21). *Murder.* The crime was committed on 9/18/1910 in Nash County. Cop killer. Shotgun slaying of 46-year-old James M. Stalling, the police chief at Spring Hope. Motive: resisting arrest. The killer was executed on May 12, 1911. Source: *Charlotte Daily Observer*, 9/20/10 (1:4), 9/21/10 (1:2) & 5/13/11 (3:5). See also: 1910 U.S. Census (Nash Co., NC), which notes Stalling, and 1911 Wake Co. death cert. no. 221.

George Nowall Marshall (black, age 28). *Rape.* The crime was committed on 9/16/1911 in Warren County. Indecent assault on the person of 21-year-old Lizzie Abbott Chaplin (white), she having been forced at gunpoint. The culprit also shot and seriously wounded the young woman's father. He was executed on October 27, 1911. Source: *Charlotte Daily Observer*, 9/18/11 (1:6), 9/19/11 (1:2), 9/20/11 (11:3) & 10/28/11 (4:6). See also: 1910 U.S. Census (Warren Co., NC), which notes both parties, and 1911 Wake Co. death cert. no. 498.

Ross French (Cherokee, age 20). *Murder.* The crime was committed on 10/4/1911 in Swain County. Child killer. Executed for the murder of 15-year-old Ethel Shuler (white), who was found lying in the middle of a road with her throat cut. Motive: attempted sexual assault. French was reportedly a tribesman from the Birdtown Reservation. His people tried to disassociate themselves from him by saying that he was a mongrel. He was executed on November 24, 1911. Source: *Charlotte Daily Observer*, 10/9/11 (1:1), 10/14/11 (1:4), 10/28/11 (4:5), 11/25/11 (1:2) & 11/26/11 (2:1). See also: 1910 U.S. Census (Swain Co., NC), which notes both parties.

Zachary Taylor Love (black, age 28). *Murder.* The crime was committed on 8/12/1911 in Haywood County. Rifle slaying of 29-year-old Fred Morehead (black), the shot having carried away half of his head. Motive: rivalry for a female. The killer was executed on December 1, 1911. Sources: *Charlotte Daily Observer*, 8/17/11 (8:5) & 10/5/11 (8:2); *Greensboro (NC) Daily Record*, 12/1/11 (1:6). See also: 1910 U.S. Census (Haywood Co., NC), which notes both parties.

Louis Sandlin (white, age 42). *Murder.* The crime was committed on 6/27/1911 in New Hanover County. Uxoricide. Handgun slaying of 53-year-old Dova Sandlin (white), she having been shot three times. Motive: marital estrangement. The killer was executed on December 29, 1911. Source: *Charlotte Daily Observer*, 12/30/11 (7:1). See also: 1911 New Hanover Co. death cert. no. 392 and Wake Co. death cert. no. 624.

1912

Brad Bagley, alias "Grant Bagley" (black, age 32). *Murder.* The crime was committed on 8/15/1911 in Martin County. Cop killer. Shotgun slaying of 43-year-old William R. White (white, the police chief of Williamston), who was blasted twice in the back as he walked by the Martin County courthouse. Motive: vengeance; the killer hated the police chief for having broken up his illegal liquor business. Bagley was executed on May 17, 1912. Source:

Charlotte Daily Observer, 8/17/11 (9:5). See also: 1910 U.S. Census (Martin Co., NC), which notes the murdered man. Also: 1912 Wake Co. death cert. no. 232, which notes the killer as "Brad Bradley."

Arthur B. Wilkins (black, age 26). *Murder.* The crime was committed on 10/19/1911 in Nash County. Uxoricide. Shotgun slaying of 21-year-old Ida Wilkins (black) and illegal burial of her body in a pig pen. Motive: marital estrangement. The killer was executed on June 21, 1912. Sources: *Greensboro (NC) Daily News*, 10/21/11 (1:6); *Greensboro (NC) Daily Record*, 5/23/12 (1:6). Also: 1912 Wake Co. death cert. no. 308; 1910 U.S. Census (Nash Co., NC), which notes this ill-fated couple.

1913

There were no legal executions in North Carolina this year.

1914

Redden W. Cobb (white, age 23). *Murder.* The crime was committed on 5/3/1913 in Halifax County. Handgun slaying of 48-year-old Thomas Shaw (white), a storekeeper. Motive: armed robbery. Cobb was executed on March 6, 1914. Source: *Greensboro (NC) Daily News*, 3/7/14 (6:2). See also: 1913 Halifax Co. death cert. no. 565, and 1914 Wake Co. death cert. no. 7044.

Sidney Thurman Finger (black, age 21). *Murder.* The crime was committed on 2/24/1914 in Rowan County. Murder of 25-year-old Preston Lyerly (white, a storekeeper), who was shot with a handgun, mutilated with an ax, and his place of business burned down around him. Motive: armed robbery. The killer was executed on June 19, 1914. Source: *Charlotte Daily Observer*, 2/25/14 (1:3), 2/26/14 (1:5) & 5/7/14 (2:3). See also: 1914 Rowan Co. death cert. no. 187, and Wake Co. death cert. no. 319; 1900 U.S. Census (Lincoln Co., NC), which notes that the killer had been born in Oct. 1892.

Grady Lane (black, age 19). *Murder.* The crime was committed on 10/28/1912 in Moore County. Handgun slaying of George McCain (black, age not recorded). Motive: robbery. Lane was executed on August 21, 1914. Source: *Greensboro (NC) Daily News*, 8/22/14 (7:2). Appeal: 166 NC 333–340.

Jim Cameron (black, age 24). *Murder.* The crime was committed on 8/11/1913 in Moore County. Handgun slaying of 33-year-old John Archibald Blue (white), the manager of a railroad work camp commissary. Motive: squabble over store credit. The prevalent story was that Cameron had been denied a loan but he attempted to justify himself by saying that Mr. Blue had slammed a door in his face. Cameron was executed on August 28, 1914. Sources: *Charlotte Daily Observer*, 8/13/13 (3:4), 8/28/13 (2:5) & 12/12/13 (1:6); *Greensboro (NC) Daily News*, 8/29/14 (3:4). See also: 1900 U.S. Census (Moore Co., NC), which notes Mr. Blue. Also: NC Deaths Collection (1908–1967), NC State Archives, entry dated 8/28/14, which notes Cameron. Appeal: 166 NC 379–388.

Harvey Gannaway (black, age 35). *Murder.* The crime was committed on

6/17/1914 in Forsyth County. Uxoricide. Executed for the murder of 28-year-old Sallie Ann Preston Gannaway (black), she having been shot dead with a handgun and her head cracked open with an iron rod. Motive: because the killer didn't like the clothes she wore to a revival meeting. Gannaway was put to death on October 16, 1914. Source: *Winston-Salem Journal*, 6/18/14 (1:5). See also: 1914 Forsyth Co. death cert. no. 312, and Wake Co. death cert. no. 270.

Howard Craig (black, age 22). *Rape.* The crime was committed on 10/6/1914 in Stanly County. Indecent assault on the person of 13-year-old Vera Odessa Coggin (white), the details of which are too revolting for repetition here. The rapist was executed on December 4, 1914. Source: *Greensboro (NC) Daily News*, 10/29/14 (8:6) & 12/5/14 (1:7). See also: 1914 Wake Co. death cert. no. 56.

1915

Willie Bell (black, age 23). *Murder.* The crime was committed on 3/8/1915 in Durham County. Murder of 61-year-old Burkett N. Mann (white), who was fatally beaten on the head with a billiard cue. Motive: mugging. Bell was executed on July 8, 1915. Source: *Greensboro (NC) Daily News*, 3/10/15 (2:2), 3/29/15 (6:5) & 7/9/15 (7:7). See also: 1915 Durham Co. death cert. no 94, and Wake Co. death cert. no. 327.

Charles E. Trull (white, age 21). *Murder.* The crime was committed on 5/16/1914 in Mecklenburg County. Murder of 50-year-old Sidney Swain (white), who was fatally bludgeoned with a four-foot-long galvanized iron pipe. Motive: mugging. The killer was executed on September 3, 1915. Source: *Charlotte Daily Observer*, 5/18/14 (1:7) & 9/3/15 (7:5). See also: 1914 Mecklenburg Co. death cert. no. 264, and 1915 Wake Co. death cert. no. 409.

1916

Jeff Dorsett (black, age 26) **and Edward Walker** (black, age 25). *Murder.* The crime was committed on 1/20/1915 in Guilford County. Handgun slaying of 34-year-old John M. Swaim (white). Motive: highway robbery. This double execution became otherwise noteworthy for the fact that the state prison warden (who had personally performed it) dropped dead at his desk a few minutes later on January 28, 1916. Source: *Greensboro (NC) Daily News*, 1/21/15 (1:2) & 1/29/16 (1:1). See also: 1915 Guilford Co. death cert. no. 298, and 1916 Wake Co. death cert. nos. 499 & 500.

James Cooper (black, age 25). *Murder.* The crime was committed on 3/28/1915 in Rowan County. Shotgun slaying of 19-year-old Lucinda Price (black). Motive: adultery turned lethal. The killer was executed on February 11, 1916. Source: *Charlotte Daily Observer*, 11/22/15 (1:4). See also: 1915 Rowan Co. death cert. no. 49, and 1916 Wake Co. death cert. no. 419.

Ernest Lowry (black, age 23) **and George Poston** (black, age 22). *Murder.* The crime was committed on 3/7/1915 in Gaston County. Murder of 45-year-old Grant Davis (black), who was clubbed to death for the sake of some money that he was known to have in his pockets, he being a dispenser of illegal whiskey. Motive: robbery. The killers were executed on February 25, 1916. Source: *Greensboro (NC) Daily Record*, 2/26/16 (1:7). See also: 1915 Gaston Co. death cert. no. 494, and 1916 Wake Co. death cert. nos. 446 & 447.

Lawrence Swinson (black, age about 23). *Aggravated Burglary.* The crime was committed on 4/8/1916 in New Hanover County. Serial Burglar. Specifically executed for breaking and entering the house of 33-year-old Henry C. Mason (white) at No. 105 Queen Street, Wilmington, and attempting to fire a pistol at the homeowner with murderous intent. The weapon did not function properly because its firing pin was warped, a mischance to which the intended victim owed his survival. The culprit was executed on July 7, 1916. Source: *Morning Star* (Wilmington, NC), 5/11/16 (5:2). See also: 1916 Wake Co. death cert. no. 348; 1920 U.S. Census (New Hanover Co., NC), which notes Mr. Mason.

Willie Black (black, age 14). *Rape.* The crime was committed on 3/31/1916 in Greene County. Indecent assault on the person of 6-year-old Mattie Tyson (white), who suffered traumatic injuries as a result. This case was of a highly aggravated nature. The culprit had come upon the victim at play with another young child in a tobacco barn. Screams brought their mother running to the scene. She was then attacked as well, being beaten senseless with a club. The rapist then resumed his inhumanity to the violated child before fleeing into nearby woods. Angry men pursued him, but Black fought back with a cache of weapons consisting of a loaded pistol and two shotguns. He severely wounded two of his pursuers before escaping from the scene. The local sheriff later caught up with him and saw to it that he was whisked away to the state prison in Raleigh for safekeeping. A lynch mob soon learned that Black's father (Joseph Black, age 54) had furnished him with weapons. So it turned its wrath on him instead of his son. Joseph Black was dragged from the Greene County jail and literally shot to pieces. Willie Black—who had caused all the trouble—was tried and executed pursuant to law. Accounts differ as to the exact age of Willie Black. His death certificate says that he was aged 18 when he died. Newspaper accounts say "about 16," whereas the 1910 Census says that he was born in 1902. He was legally put to death on July 21, 1916. Sources: *Charlotte Daily Observer*, 4/2/16 (23:5); *Greensboro (NC) Daily News*, 4/6/16 (9:1). See also: 1916 Wake Co. death cert. no. 382; 1910 U.S. Census (Greene Co., NC), which notes Joseph and Willie Black.

Arthur Smith (black, age 26). *Murder.* The crime was committed on 3/26/1916 in Cumberland County. Uxoricide. Ax murder of 30-year-old Fannie Atkins Smith (black), whose mutilated body was found in a roadside ditch. Motive: because she had threatened to leave him. Smith was a brother of Octavius Smith (another murderer of that vicinity), who had butchered his wife and three children the previous year and escaped to parts unknown. Arthur Smith was executed on August 1, 1916. Source: *Charlotte Daily Observer*, 3/27/16 (2:6) & 3/31/16 (10:5). See also: 1916 Cumberland Co. death cert. no. 11, and Wake Co. death cert. no. 401.

John Savage (black, age 51). *Murder.* The crime was committed on 3/22/1916 in Washington County. Fatal beating of 78-year-old George H. Bowen (white), the victim having been attacked in his bedroom by burglars. Motive: housebreaking. A pair of wrought iron fireplace tongs were among the objects used in this deadly assault and battery. Bowen died of his injuries on 4/20/1916. His adult daughter was also beaten up by the culprits when she ran to her father's aid. John Savage was put to death on August 4, 1916. Source: *Charlotte Daily Observer*, 3/25/16 (12:2) & 8/5/16 (1:5). See also: 1916 Wake Co. death cert. no. 402; NC Deaths Collection (1908–1967), NC State Archives, which notes the murdered man.

1917

Bunk Maske (black, age 23). *Murder.* The crime was committed on 3/17/1917 in Union County. Cop killer. Handgun slaying of 39-year-old Edgar R. Williams (white). Motive: resisting arrest. Maske was executed on May 25, 1917. Source: *Greensboro (NC) Daily News*, 3/18/17 (10:2). See also: 1917 Wake Co. death cert. no. 243; 1910 U.S. Census (Union Co., NC), which notes Williams.

Charles Williams (black, age 60). *Murder.* The crime was committed on 6/30/1917 in Iredell County. Cop killer. Shotgun slaying of 36-year-old John H. Miller (white). Motive: resisting arrest. Williams was executed on September 25, 1917. Source: *The Landmark* (Statesville, NC), 9/28/17 (1:1). See also: 1917 Iredell Co. death cert. no. 2, and Wake Co. death cert. no. 448.

Lee Perkins (black, age 23). *Aggravated Burglary.* The crime was committed on 8/22/1917 in Craven County. Executed for breaking into the house of 41-year-old Willis A. Wilson (white) with intent to ravish that man's daughters, four of whom shared the same bedroom. Perkins and an accomplice were caught in the very act of terrorizing those girls. Perkins was put to death on October 10, 1917. Sources: *Greensboro (NC) Daily News*, 8/24/17 (5:3) & 10/11/17 (2:3); *Winston-Salem Journal*, 9/9/17 (2:4) & 9/13/17 (2:5). See also: 1917 Wake Co. death cert. no. 224; 1910 U.S. Census (Craven Co., NC) which notes the homeowner.

Jeremiah Terry (white, age 65). *Murder.* The crime was committed on 7/15/1916 in Guilford County. Handgun slaying of 54-year-old John R. Stewart (white). Motive: acrimonious lawsuit. Terry was executed on November 9, 1917. Source: *Greensboro (NC) Daily Record*, 7/17/16 (1:1), 7/17/16 (2:3) & 11/9/17 (1:5). See also: 1916 Guilford Co. death cert. no. 403; 1870 U.S. Census (Guilford Co., NC), which notes the killer as a young fellow.

1918

Earle Neville (black, age 22). *Rape.* The crime was committed on 9/20/1917 in Wake County. Indecent assault on the person of 31-year-old Sybil Hawkins Celey (white), she having been accosted in her home by an armed intruder (Neville), forced to cook a meal for him at gunpoint, robbed of her money and then sexually assaulted. The rapist and home invader was executed on March 15, 1918. Source: *Greensboro (NC) Daily News*, 9/21/17 (1:7) & 10/8/17 (7:3). See also: 1918 Wake Co. death cert. no. 491, as well as the victim's gravestone in Oakwood Cemetery, Raleigh.

Willie Williams (black, age 19). *Rape.* The crime was committed on 12/26/1917 in Buncombe County. Indecent assault on the person of 43-year-old Bessie McDowell (white), a widowed mother of three. He was caught on 2/28/1918 and executed on April 26, 1918. Source: Buncombe County Superior Court Minutes (March Term 1918) pg. 426. See also: 1918 Wake Co. death cert. no. 2399; 1910 U.S. Census (Buncombe Co., NC), which notes the female party; *Winston-Salem Journal*, 3/9/18 (1:4).

Frank Moore (black, age 20). *Murder.* The crime was committed on 7/28/1917 in Duplin County. Handgun slaying of 31-year-old Walter Heath (white), a restaurateur. Motive: violation of the Jim Crow law. Already known as a punk and a troublemaker, Moore sauntered into the victim's place of business in open defiance of its legally sanctioned "Whites Only" status. He behaved in a deliberately obnoxious manner, whereupon the proprietor (Heath) forcibly ejected him. Moore came back a short time later armed with a revolver and shot the restaurant owner dead in his doorway. Moore was executed for this crime on May 24, 1918. Source: *Greensboro (NC) Daily News*, 7/30/17 (1:6) & 12/7/17 (12:3). See also: 1918 Wake Co. death cert. no. 5240; 1910 U.S. Census (Duplin Co., NC), which notes Mr. Heath.

Herbert Perry (black, age 33). *Rape.* The crime was committed on 8/16/1917 in Granville County. Indecent assault on the person of 14-year-old Katie May (white) on the porch of her cabin, a pistol being held to her head throughout. The rapist was executed on May 25, 1918. Sources: *Public Ledger*, (Oxford, NC), 11/21/17 (1:1); *Greensboro (NC) Daily News*, 5/26/18 (1:7). See also: 1918 Wake Co. death cert. no. 119.

Lonnie Council (black, age 37). *Murder.* The crime was committed on 2/8/1918 in Durham County. Murder of 41-year-old Robert Jones (black), who was beaten on the head with a heavy broomstick. Motive: adultery with the victim's wife. The killer was executed on June 7, 1918. Source: *Greensboro (NC) Daily News*, 2/12/18 (10:3). See also: 1918 Durham Co. death cert. no. 20, and Wake Co. death cert. no. 8576.

Baxter Cain (black, age 31). *Murder.* The crime was committed on 8/25/1917 in Rowan County. Murder of 30-year-old Abel Harris (black), who was bludgeoned with a heavy iron trolley switch key and stabbed 17 times in the head and neck. Motive: robbery. A one-legged man, Cain was employed as a watchman in the Salisbury trolley barns. He was due to be fitted with a new artificial leg but lacked the $50 required for its purchase. Becoming desperate, he guilefully persuaded Harris to substitute for him on the job while he supposedly kept an appointment to pick up his new limb. Cain then concealed himself in the trolley barns and murdered Harris as described. He stole a moneybag containing the previous day's trolley receipts, hoping that everybody would think that Harris had been slain by a bandit. Cain used the ill-gotten money to pay for his prosthetic leg. He also assured himself that he had established a foolproof alibi for his whereabouts at the time of the murder. But he proved too clever for his own good. It so happened that one of the dollar bills that was among the robbery loot had doodle marks on it that a trolley motorman remembered as being among his fares. Cain was executed for his crime on September 13, 1918. Source: *Charlotte Observer*, 8/28/17 (10:3). See also: 1917 Rowan Co. death cert. no. 167, and 1918 Wake Co. death cert. no. 16559.

Napoleon Spencer (black, age 15). *Murder.* The crime was committed on 3/5/1918 in Forsyth County. Handgun slayings of 27-year-old Harvey Hester and 24-year-old Alvie Siewers Hester (whites, a married couple). Motive: home invasion. Venue changed from Forsyth County to Surry County. The killer was executed on December 20, 1918. Sources: *Charlotte Observer*, 3/8/18 (2:1); *Greensboro (NC) Daily News*, 3/10/18 (12:1). See also: 1918 Forsyth Co. death cert. nos. 155 & 235, plus Wake Co. death cert. no. 32870, which notes 6/17/1902 as the killer's date of birth.

1919

James Henry Warren (black, age 19). *Murder.* The crime was committed on 12/19/1918 in Greene County. Shotgun slaying of 43-year-old Joseph Denver Hughes (white), a storekeeper. Motive: not certain. It was an odd aspect of this case that the killer had first purchased ammo from the victim before returning a few minutes later with a gun loaded with that same ammo and killing him with it. Warren was executed on April 26, 1919. Source: *Greensboro (NC) Daily News*, 12/21/18 (4:7) & 4/27/19 (4:4). See also: 1918 Greene Co. death cert. no. 31492, and 1919 Wake Co. death cert. no. 9038.

Tom Gwynn (black, age 22). *Rape.* The crime was committed on 4/29/1919 in Catawba County. Indecent assault on the person of 16-year-old Ruth Hildebrand (white), she having been attacked as she walked home from school. The culprit was described as having "presented a monstrous appearance for a human being. His hair was shaggy and his clothes very dirty and ragged and upon the whole hardly had the appearance of a human being." This rapist was executed on June 27, 1919. Source: *Charlotte Observer*, 5/28/19 (3:4). See also: 1919 Wake Co. death cert. no. 14431; 1910 U.S. Census (Catawba Co., NC), which notes the female party.

Aaron Allabrook, alias "Dupree" (black, age 28). *Murder.* The crime was committed on 12/18/1913 in Hoke County. Shotgun slaying of 24-year-old McCormick Brown (white). Motive: disgruntled employee. The killer was executed on November 14, 1919. Sources: *The Robesonian* (Lumberton, NC), 12/19/13 (1:1); *Raleigh News & Observer*, 11/15/19 (8:2). See also: 1913 Hoke Co. death cert. no. 4524, and 1919 Wake Co. death cert. no. 489.

1920

Churchill Louis Godley (white, age 33). *Rape.* The crime was committed on 5/20/1919 in Johnston County. Indecent assault on the person of 9-year-old Mamie Beasley (white), she having been lured into a taxi and brought to a remote location with nefarious intent. The rapist was put to death on January 16, 1920. Sources: Johnston County Superior Court Criminal Action Papers (*State vs. Godley*, 1919); NC State Archives; *Greensboro (NC) Daily News*, 1/17/20 (1:7). Also: 1920 Wake Co. death cert. no. 28.

Joseph A. Cain (white, age 37) **and Sanford Gardner Cain** (white, age 41). *Murder.* Their crime was committed on 7/23/1918 in Surry County. Handgun slaying of 57-year-old Riley Easter (white). Motive: moonshiners' feud. The killers were executed on March 5, 1920. Source: *Greensboro (NC) Daily News*, 7/24/18 (2:1) & 3/5/20 (1:3). See also: 1918 Surry Co. death cert. no. 119, and 1920 Wake Co. death cert. nos. 159 & 160.

Ralph Connor (black, age 20). *Murder.* The crime was committed on 8/3/1919 in Iredell County. Cop killer. Handgun slaying of 34-year-old Robert Lloyd Cloaninger (white), who was shot multiple times, initially in the back. Motive: riot at a camp meeting. The killer was executed on September 20, 1920. Source: *The Landmark* (Statesville, NC), 8/5/19 (1:1) & 9/20/20 (1:7). See also: 1919 Iredell Co. death cert. no. 103, and 1920 Wake Co. death cert. no. 452.

Andrew Jackson (black, age 30). *Rape.* The crime was committed on 9/14/1920 in Lincoln County. Indecent assault on the person of 38-year-old Bettie E. Keever (white) under circumstances that were later described as revolting in the extreme. Initial accounts said that it was an "attempted" felony and that the culprit "failed in his purpose," but this was a lie commonly put forth in such cases to protect the victim's good name and deter would-be lynchers. The rapist himself was described as "a negro of gorilla proportions and intelligence." He was executed on November 5, 1920. Sources: Lincoln County Superior Court Minutes (October Term, 1920), pgs. 462–466; *Lincoln County (NC) News*, 9/16/20 (2:1) & 10/7/20 (1:2). See also: 1920 Wake Co. death cert. no. 545; 1920 U.S. Census (Lincoln Co., NC), which notes the female party.

Jim McDonald, alias "Arthur McDowell," alias "Arthur Cunningham" (black, age 26). *Rape.* The crime was committed on 6/30/1920 in Davidson County. Indecent assault on the person of 48-year-old Minnie McCarn (white), she having been "severely choked and bruised" in addition to the primary felony. The rapist was executed on December 3, 1920. Sources: Davidson County Superior Court Criminal Action Papers (*State vs. Jim McDonald*, 1920); NC State Archives; *Greensboro (NC) Daily News*, 7/1/20 (1:5) & 12/4/20 (4:7). See also: 1920 Wake Co. death cert. no. 593.

Tom Johnson (black, age 19). *Rape.* The crime was committed on 5/13/1920 in Guilford County. Indecent assault on the person of 19-year-old Mattie Andrews Sartin (white), she having been attacked in her own bed and nearly strangled as she lay napping with her 2-month-old infant child. The rapist was executed on December 3, 1920. Source: *Greensboro (NC) Daily News*, 5/14/20 (3:3) & 12/4/20 (4:7). See also: 1920 Wake Co. death cert. no. 592; 1910 U.S. Census (Guilford Co., NC), which notes the victim by her maiden name.

1921

William Hopkins (black, age 21). *Murder.* The crime was committed on 1/15/1921 in Sampson County. Handgun slaying of 30-year-old Louis E. Ramey (white), a storekeeper. Motive: armed robbery. Hopkins was executed on March 21, 1921. Source: *Greensboro (NC)*

Daily News, 3/22/21 (4:5). See also: 1921 Sampson Co. death cert. no. 46, and Wake Co. death cert. no. 104.

Luke Frazier (black, age 33). *Murder.* The crime was committed on 3/6/1921 in Craven County. Shotgun slaying of 36-year-old John Mann (black), a boatman. Motive: because he resented the victim's refusal to provide him with passenger transport. Frazier was executed on May 27, 1921. Source: *Raleigh News & Observer*, 5/28/21 (3:1). See also: 1921 Craven Co. death cert. no. 396, and Wake Co. death cert. no. 208.

Frank Henderson (white, age 33). *Murder.* The crime was committed on 8/24/1920 in Madison County. Uxoricide. Manual strangulation of 29-year-old Ella Henderson (white). Motive: presumed infidelity, or so he said. The killer was executed on October 10, 1921. Source: *Charlotte Observer*, 8/30/20 (1:6) & 10/11/21 (1:1). See also: 1921 Wake Co. death cert. no. 447; 1920 U.S. Census (Madison Co., NC), which notes this ill-fated couple.

James Thomas Harris (white, age 53). *Murder.* The crime was committed on 9/3/1920 in Buncombe County. Shotgun slaying of 60-year-old Fredric Wilhelm Monnish (white). Motive: "The Unwritten Law," or so it was alleged. Harris was executed on October 20, 1921. Sources: *Winston-Salem Journal*, 9/4/20 (1:4); *Greensboro (NC) Daily Record*, 10/20/21 (1:7). See also: 1880 U.S. Census (Sullivan Co., TN), which notes Harris as a minor; 1920 U.S. Census (Tuscaloosa, AL), which notes Mr. Monnish; 1920 Buncombe Co. death cert. no. 191, and 1921 Wake Co. death cert. no. 463.

Henry Caldwell (black, age 32). *Murder.* The crime was committed on 11/14/1920 in Wayne County. Handgun slaying of 39-year-old Herman Jones (white), a storekeeper. Motive: armed robbery, or so it was said. Caldwell had flashed a phony police badge in the victim's face and accused him of dispensing illegal liquor. Jones balked at this, whereupon Caldwell shot him. Caldwell was executed on October 31, 1921. Sources: *The Robesonian* (Lumberton, NC), 11/18/20 (8:1); *Greensboro (NC) Daily News*, 11/1/21 (3:4). Appeal: 181 NC 519. See also: 1921 Wake Co. death cert. no. 483; 1920 U.S. Census (Wayne Co., NC), which notes Mr. Jones.

William Westmoreland (white, age 37). *Murder.* The crime was committed on 10/20/1920 in Iredell County. Handgun slaying of 34-year-old James H. Nantz (white, a jitney driver) and illegal disposal of his body by dumping it down an abandoned well. Motive: robbery. The killer was executed on November 21, 1921. Source: *The Landmark* (Statesville, NC), 2/3/21 (1:1) & 2/7/21 (1:1). See also: 1920 Iredell Co. death cert. no. 429, and 1921 Wake Co. death cert. no. 627.

Claude Morehead (black, age 22). *Murder.* The crime was committed on 9/12/1920 in Guilford County. Uxoricide. Executed for the murder of 30-year-old Alma Mathis Morehead (black), she having had a chair smashed over her head. Motive: marital discord. The killer was executed on November 30, 1921. Source: *Greensboro (NC) Daily News*, 9/13/20 (5:3) & 9/14/20 (13:1). See also: 1920 Guilford Co. death cert. no. 320, and 1921 Wake Co. death cert. no. 646.

1922

Angus Murphy (black, age 36) **and Jasper Thomas** (black, age 20). *Rape.* The crime was committed on 8/4/1922 in Moore County. Indecent assault on the person of 22-year-old Gertrude Ketchen (white), she and her 38-year-old husband having been attacked as they slept in a tourist camp. The male victim was disabled by a gunshot. The young woman ran from their tent screaming with a baby in her arms. The culprits chased her down. Mrs. Ketchen was then pistol whipped, raped and robbed of her intrinsic valuables. Both of the miscreants were executed on September 15, 1922. Source: *Charlotte Observer*, 8/15/22 (1:3) & 8/16/22 (1:5). See also: 1922 Wake Co. death cert. nos. 462 & 463; 1920 U.S. Census (Dade Co., FL), which notes Mr. and Mrs. Ketchen.

McIver Burnett (black, age 17). *Rape.* The crime was committed on 7/29/1922 in Wake County. Indecent assault on the person of about 19-year-old Melissa McGhee (white, a recent bride), who was attacked in her own home. The culprit was a "trusty" on the Wake County chain gang serving a 30-day sentence for vagrancy. He had been given the plum position of water boy on account of his youth and the fact that he was up until then a nonviolent offender. He called at the victim's home for the purpose of drawing water from her well, but finding her alone and unprotected made use of the occasion to force himself on her. Burnett was executed on October 12, 1922. Sources: *Charlotte (NC) News*, 7/31/22 (5:5); *Charlotte Observer*, 9/14/22 (1:5) & 10/13/22 (1:7); *Raleigh News & Observer*, 10/13/22 (1:4). See also: 1922 Wake Co. death cert. no. 546.

1923

Robert Williams (black, age 25). *Murder.* The crime was committed on 1/25/1923 in Columbus County. Cop killer. Handgun slaying of 42-year-old Bradley Cribb (white), the police chief of Fair Bluff. Motive: armed robbery gone awry. The killer was a professional bandit who had been terrorizing the countryside between Lumberton and Cape Fear. He had escaped from custody on five prior occasions. He was executed on March 1, 1923. Source: *The Robesonian* (Lumberton, NC), 1/29/23 (1:2). See also: 1923 New Hanover Co. death cert. no. 170, and Wake Co. death cert. no. 161.

William M. Hardison (black, age 15). *Murder.* The crime was committed on 8/5/1922 in Onslow County. Shotgun slaying of 38-year-old Cyrus M. Jones (white), the victim having been deliberately lured into an ambush. Motive: pique. Jones had given Hardison a ride in his automobile to a so-called "Negro Dance" four months earlier. It was agreed then that Jones would pick up Hardison later that night for a return ride home. Jones kept the rendezvous, but Hardison declined to leave with him because he had by then decided that he would rather dance the night away. So Jones drove away and Hardison was left to find his own way home. Hardison resented this (or so the story goes) because he felt that Jones was still bound by his word to provide him with a ride home regardless of the time. Hardison brooded over this imaginary slight for four months. Then he shot and savagely beat the man whom he felt had done him wrong. It was a senseless and unnecessary crime for which Hardison paid with his life on

April 27, 1923. Sources: *Charlotte Observer*, 8/7/22 (1:7) & 8/8/22 (2:4); *Greensboro (NC) Daily Record*, 8/9/22 (1:8) & 10/27/22 (3:4). See also: 1922 Onslow Co. death cert. no. 42, and 1923 Wake Co. death cert. no. 173.

Wiley Perry (black, age 29). *Murder.* The crime was committed on 10/30/1921 in Granville County. Cop killer. Shotgun slaying of 26-year-old Roy H. Aiken (white), a special deputy who was assisting the local chief of police at Creedmoor. Motive: resisting arrest. Perry was executed on May 9, 1923. Source: *Greensboro (NC) Daily News*, 10/31/21 (1:6) & 11/5/21 (7:3). See also: 1921 Granville Co. death cert. no. 39–5491, and 1923 Wake Co. death cert. no. 297.

Dan Milton Nobles (white, age 36). *Murder.* The crime was committed on 9/23/1922 in Columbus County. Sniper killing of 32-year-old Henry Bishop Nobles (white), his cousin. Motive: speculative. The killer denied his guilt to the last but did mutter something about so-called "lewd behavior." He was executed on June 26, 1923. Sources: *Charlotte (NC) News*, 9/28/22 (5:3); *Winston-Salem Journal*, 6/27/23 (1:1). See also: Columbus Co. World War I draft registration card no. 160, which notes the victim's full name and date of birth; 1922 Florence Co., SC, death cert. no. 13720 (H.B. Nobles having died in the hospital there), and 1923 Wake Co. death cert. no. 406.

Edward Dill (black, age 42). *Rape.* The crime was committed on 3/30/1922 in Beaufort County. Indecent assault on the person of Mattie E. Williams (white, age not recorded), she having been accosted on a public road and forcibly outraged there. The rapist was executed on June 28, 1923. Sources: *Greensboro (NC) Daily Record*, 6/12/22 (8:3); *Greensboro (NC) Daily News*, 9/28/22 (3:3). Appeal: 184 NC 645–653. See also: 1923 Wake Co. death cert. no. 413.

James Miller (black, age 38). *Murder.* The crime was committed on 9/29/1922 in Lenoir County. Handgun slaying of 42-year-old John Sutton (white), a farmer who had nabbed him for pilfering his crops. Motive: resisting a citizen's arrest. The killer was executed on October 5, 1923. Sources: *Greensboro (NC) Daily Record*, 9/30/22 (1:4), 10/2/22 (1:5) & 10/5/23 (1:5); *The Landmark* (Statesville, NC), 1/15/23 (4:7). See also: 1923 Wake Co. death cert. no. 578, and 1920 U.S. Census (Kinston, NC), which notes Mr. Sutton.

John G. Goss (black, age 44). *Rape.* The crime was committed on 9/26/1923 in Mitchell County. Indecent assault on the person of 62-year-old Margaret Alice Parker Thomas (white), she having been accosted on a public road and menaced at knifepoint. Goss was a "trusty" on the Mitchell County chain gang. He had originally been sent up from New Hanover County under a 15-year sentence for an attempted rape committed there in 1913. He ran away from the chain gang ten years into his term and then committed the crime that sealed his doom. He was executed on December 7, 1923. Sources: *Greensboro (NC) Daily Record*, 9/30/23 (1:7); *Winston-Salem Journal*, 10/23/23 (1:7). See also: 1923 Wake Co. death cert. no. 699; 1910 U.S. Census (Mitchell Co., NC), which notes Mrs. Thomas.

Lee Washington (black, age 20). *Rape.* The crime was committed on 11/9/1923 in Nash County. Indecent assault on the person of a married white female (age not recorded) identified only as "Mrs. A.J. Herring." She was raped at gunpoint by an armed intruder (Washington) who had forced his way into her home, terrorizing both her and her 3-year-old daughter. This rapist and home invader was executed on December 28, 1923. Source: *The Graphic* (Nashville, NC), 11/15/23 (1:7). See also: 1923 Wake Co. death cert. no. 745.

1924

Vance Morgan (black, age 22). *Murder.* The crime was committed on 11/28/1923 in Union County. Murder of 54-year-old A. Butler Funderburk (white, a storekeeper, full name not recorded), who was beaten on the head with a heavy metal wrench. Motive: robbery. The killer was executed on November 28, 1924. Source: *Greensboro (NC) Daily Record*, 11/28/24 (10:1). See also: 1923 Union Co. death cert. no. 43, and 1924 Wake Co. death cert. no. 619; 1870 U.S. Census (Lancaster Co., SC), and the victim's gravestone at Spring Hill Baptist Church (Tradesville, SC), which pointedly neglected to specify his entire name either as a baby or as a middle-aged corpse.

1925

Kenneth Hale (black, age 24) **and John Leak** (black, age 18). *Murder.* The crime was committed on 8/7/1924 in Davidson County. Murder of 30-year-old Charles Garwood (white, a cab driver), who was beaten to death with an iron bar. Motive: robbery and carjacking. The killers were executed on January 5, 1925. Source: *Greensboro (NC) Daily Record*, 8/9/24 (1:1) & 1/5/25 (1:7). See also: 1924 Davidson Co. death cert. no. 22, and 1925 Wake Co. death cert. nos. 133 & 134.

David Jones (black, age 21). *Murder.* The crime was committed on 8/30/1924 in Chowan County. Handgun slaying of 53-year-old Samuel Humphrey Small (white). Motive: highway robbery. The victim was returning home with his farm wagon after having sold a load of watermelons. The killer was executed on February 18, 1925. Source: *The Independent* (Elizabeth City, NC), 9/5/24 (1:1). See also: 1924 Chowan Co. death cert. no. 29, and 1925 Wake Co. death cert. no. 197.

Charles William Stewart (white, age 55) **and William Elmer Stewart** (white, age 23). *Murder.* The crime was committed on 7/29/1924 in Brunswick County. Cop killers. Executed for the ambush slayings of U.S. Deputy Marshal Samuel Lilly (white, age 46) and City of Wilmington Special Prohibition Officer Leon George (white, age 51), who were riddled with rifle and shotgun fire in the performance of their duty. Motive: resisting arrest. The killers were executed on April 17, 1925. Source: *Greensboro (NC) Daily Record*, 7/30/24 (1:7) & 4/17/25 (1:4). See also: 1924 Brunswick Co. death cert. nos. 74 & 75; 1925 Wake Co. death cert. nos. 321 & 322.

Leonard Walton (black, age 27). *Murder.* The crime was committed on 7/15/1923 in Hoke County. Shotgun slaying of 25-year-old Jeneral Dewey Castleberry (white). Motive: retaliation for a "road rage" incident. Walton was executed on April 21, 1925. Source: *Greensboro (NC) Daily Record*, 4/21/25 (1:7). Appeal: 124 SE 842–844. See also: 1923

Cumberland Co. death cert. no. 163, and 1925 Wake Co. death cert. no. 331.

William Henry Singleton (black, age 17). *Murder.* The crime was committed on 3/7/1925 in Craven County. Shotgun slaying of 45-year-old Henry N. Banks (white). Motive: payroll robbery. The killer was executed on May 8, 1925. Sources: *Sun-Journal* (New Bern, NC), 3/9/25 (1:7); *Greensboro (NC) Daily Record*, 3/9/25 (10:2) & 5/8/25 (1:5). See also: 1925 Craven Co. death cert. no. 57, and Wake Co. death cert. no. 253.

James Collins (black, age 19). *Murder.* The crime was committed on 7/19/1924 in Anson County. Handgun slaying of 37-year-old Adam Chalmers Sedberry (white). Motive: because the victim had asked him to repay a loan. Collins was executed on June 5, 1925. Source: *Winston-Salem Journal*, 7/20/24 (1:5), 7/22/24 (1:7) & 7/28/24 (1:4). See also: 1924 Anson Co. death cert. no. 48, and 1925 Wake Co. death cert. no. 309.

Willie Williams (black, age 24). *Murder.* The crime was committed on June 22, 1924, in Scotland County. Shotgun slaying of 44-year-old Frank Green (black). Motive: obnoxious drunk, or so it appeared. Williams was executed on June 12, 1925. Source: *The Robesonian* (Lumberton, NC), 6/15/25 (2:7). Appeal: 127 SE 675–677. See also: 1924 Scotland Co. death cert. no. 14, and 1925 Wake Co. death cert. no. 326; 1910 U.S. Census (Richmond Co., NC), which notes Green.

George Henry Love (black, age 30). *Murder.* The crime was committed on 1/13/1923 in Haywood County. Handgun slaying of 40-year-old William Brock (white), the victim having been "waylaid at night." Motive: personal grudge. The killer was executed on June 19, 1925. Source: *Greensboro (NC) Daily Record*, 2/10/23 (1:5) & 6/19/25 (12:3). Appeal: 189 NC 766–774. See also: 1923 Haywood Co. death cert. no. 11, and 1925 Wake Co. death cert. no. 334.

John McMillan, alias "Thomas Hamilton" (black, age 18). *Rape.* The crime was committed on 8/3/1925 in Moore County. Indecent assault on the person of 24-year-old Willie Idell Sides (white), she having been jumped while drawing water from a spring and dangerously struck on the head. She died of pellagra on 4/23/1930. The rapist was executed on October 2, 1925. Source: *Moore County News* (Carthage, NC), 8/6/25 (3:2), 8/13/25 (1:4) & 8/20/25 (1:3). See also: 1925 Wake Co. death cert. no. 531, and 1930 Rowan Co. death cert. no. 320.

Thomas Robinson (black, age 26). *Rape.* The crime was committed on 8/12/1925 in New Hanover County. Indecent assault on the person of a 19-year-old white female (name withheld) who was employed as a nurse at James Walker Memorial Hospital, she having been attacked during a thunderstorm while running to get out of the rain. The rapist was executed on October 2, 1925. Source: *Greensboro (NC) Daily Record*, 8/13/25 (1:6), 9/2/25 (1:7) & 10/2/25 (1:2). See also: 1925 Wake Co. death cert. no. 532.

1926

William Webster Dawkins, alias "John Wesley Dawkins" (black, age 20). *Murder.* The crime was committed on 8/2/1924 in Forsyth County. Shotgun slaying (by lying in wait) of 52-year-old Joseph Henry Vaughn (white, a storekeeper), who was ambushed on the back steps of his home shortly after closing his place of business that day. Motive: attempted robbery. The killer was described as "a hard one to cook," in the words of his hometown newspaper, "three minutes of frying being necessary" to kill him in the electric chair on January 8, 1926. Source: *Winston-Salem Journal*, 8/3/24 (1:8) & 1/9/26 (1:2). See also: 1924 Forsyth Co. death cert. no. 777, and 1926 Wake Co. death cert. no. 15.

Arthur J. Montague (black, age 21). *Rape.* The crime was committed on 4/24/1925 in Burke County. Indecent assault on the person of a 13-year-old white female (name withheld) who was reportedly left in a "mutilated" condition. The rapist was employed as a dining hall porter at the Morganton Institute for the Deaf and Dumb. He forced himself on one of the inmates there and was actually found asleep in her bed when the sun came up. He was executed on January 22, 1926. Source: *Greensboro (NC) Daily Record*, 4/25/25 (1:2), 5/11/25 (1:6) & 1/22/26 (1:1). See also: 1926 Wake Co. death cert. no. 48.

Fred Jones (black, age 24). *Murder.* The crime was committed on 6/14/1925 in Forsyth County. Handgun slaying of 41-year-old Joseph Monroe King (white). Motive: armed robbery. The killer was executed on June 11, 1926. Source: *Winston-Salem Journal*, 3/30/26 (7:1) & 6/12/26 (1:6). See also: World War I draft reg. card (Forsyth Co., NC), no. 858 dated 9/12/18, which notes Mr. King; 1925 Forsyth Co. death cert. no. 467, and 1926 Wake Co. death cert. no. 346.

John Williams (black, age 30). *Murder.* The crime was committed on 7/28/1926 in Halifax County. Shotgun slaying of 66-year-old Alexander Bradley (black). Motive: landlord-tenant dispute. The killer was executed on September 21, 1926. Sources: *Greensboro (NC) Daily Record*, 7/29/26 (12:5); *Gastonia Daily Gazette*, 9/21/26 (5:5). Also: 1926 Wake Co. death cert. no. 548, and 1920 U.S. Census (Halifax Co., NC), which notes Bradley.

1927

Robert Lumpkin (black, age 26). *Murder.* The crime was committed on 12/26/1925 in Robeson County. Cop killer. Executed for the gunshot slaying of 32-year-old Marion Boyd Rogers (the police chief at Rowland), who was deliberately massacred by two shotgun blasts and five pistol shots, including three in the back of the head. Motive: resisting arrest. Lumpkin by then was reportedly fed up with what he perceived to be almost constant police harassment on the part of Rogers, who—he said—had frisked him for concealed weapons on no less than 95 separate occasions. Whether this was true or an exaggeration is now impossible to determine. Lumpkin was executed on March 11, 1927. Source: *The Robesonian* (Lumberton, NC), 2/1/26 (1:1) & 3/14/27 (1:7). See also: 1925 Robeson Co. death cert. no. 130.

Ernest P. Walker (black, age 38). *Murder.* The crime was committed on 7/25/1926 in Durham County. Ax murder of 39-year-old Joseph Cassidy (black) and forcible rape of that man's wife. Motive: aggravated burglary. Walker was described as a 3-way mongrel comprised of white, Negro and Croatoan Indian ethnicity. He was also a 3-way capital offender, having forced a nocturnal entry into the victim's home, murdered that man in his bed and raped his wife all in the same night. He was executed on April 22, 1927. Source: *Winston-Salem Journal*, 8/23/26 (1:2). See also: 1926 Durham Co. death cert. no. 144, and 1927 Wake Co. death cert. no. 223.

Pearl Mitchell (black, age 29). *Murder.* The crime was committed on 1/15/1927 in Chatham County. Handgun slaying of 58-year-old William Larkin Fogleman (white). Motive: serial burglar caught in the act. Mitchell was executed on June 10, 1927. Source: *Greensboro (NC) Daily Record*, 1/17/27 (1:8). See also: 1927 Chatham Co. death cert. no. 14, and Wake Co. death cert. no. 710.

George Frank Bazemore (black, age 25). *Murder.* The crime was committed on 11/5/1926 in Greene County. Gunshot slaying of 16-year-old Gordon Yelverton (white). Motive: highway robbery. The victim was en route to market with a wagonload of tobacco leaves when three men accosted him. They shot the boy dead and stole his wagon. The crop that it contained was later found to have been sold by a tobacco broker, but the culprits failed to appear when it came time to collect their payment. The victim's death certificate says only that he was "shot in the head." A newspaper account says that his body was found "riddled with bullets," suggesting that more than one weapon was used. Bazemore was executed on September 23, 1927. Sources: *Gastonia Daily Gazette*, 11/8/26 (1:5); *Greensboro (NC) Daily Record*, 11/8/26 (2:5) & 3/16/27 (8:2). See also: 1926 Greene County death cert. no. 523.

James Hector Graham (black, age 41). *Murder.* The crime was committed on 8/12/1927 in Hoke County. Handgun slaying of 30-year-old Paul W. Johnson (white), who was knocked down by a bullet fired into his chest at point blank range from a .45 automatic. Motive: because Johnson had reproved the killer for addressing him in an overly familiar manner. Graham was executed on December 9, 1927. Source: *Greensboro (NC) Daily Record*, 8/13/27 (1:8) & 8/25/27 (2:4). See also: 1927 Hoke Co. death cert. no. 163, and Wake Co. death cert. no. 664.

1928

David Devlin (black, age 22). *Murder.* The crime was committed on 6/2/1927 in Rowan County. Cop killer. Handgun slaying of 48-year-old Linzy T. Yarbrough (white), a Rowan County deputy. Motive: resisting arrest. Devlin was executed on February 17, 1928. Source: *Gastonia Daily Gazette*, 6/2/27 (5:2). See also: 1927 Rowan Co. death cert. no. 242, and 1928 Wake Co. death cert. no. 375.

Clarence O. Thomas (black, age 23). *Murder.* The crime was committed on 12/9/1927 in Forsyth County. Cop killer, etc. Executed for the murder of 69-year-old Barnett Branson Graham (white, a night watchman), who was struck on the head with a heavy wrench and died three days later. Motive: burglary. Also indicted (but not tried) for the handgun slaying of 32-year-old Leland Glenn Teague (white, a sergeant in the Winston-Salem Police Dept.), who was shot while attempting to arrest Thomas, and who succumbed to his wound 14 days later. The killer was executed on April 27, 1928. Source: *Greensboro (NC) Daily Record*,

12/13/27 (2:3). See also: 1927 Forsyth Co. death cert. nos. 1067 & 1100, and 1928 Wake Co. death cert. no. 428.

John Webster Clyburn (black, age 22). *Murder.* The crime was committed on 5/28/1927 in Mecklenburg County. Murder of 37-year-old Cyrus M. Fink (white), the victim having been fatally gashed in the gullet with a railroad spike. Motive: mugging. The killer was executed on May 25, 1928. Source: *Greensboro (NC) Daily Record*, 5/30/27 (2:1). See also: 1927 Mecklenburg Co. death cert. no. 434, and 1928 Wake Co. death cert. no. 413.

Larry Newsome (black, age 23). *Murder.* The crime was committed on 12/8/1927 in Wayne County. Child killer. Executed for the murder of 15-year-old Beulah Tedder (white), who was slashed to death with a sharp knife (on her birthday) and her body left lying in a road. Motive: attempted sexual assault. The killer was executed on September 28, 1928. Source: *Greensboro (NC) Daily Record*, 12/10/27 (1:4) & 9/28/28 (1:4). See also: 1927 Wayne Co. death cert. no. 92, and 1928 Wake Co. death cert. no. 588.

1929

Leo McCurry (black, age 28). *Murder.* The crime was committed on 1/24/1929 in Gaston County. Murder of 67-year-old John Neal Dixon (white), who was clubbed to death. Motive: robbery. The killer was executed on April 26, 1929. Source: *The Landmark* (Statesville, NC), 1/28/29 (1:2). See also: 1910 U.S. Census (Gaston Co., NC), which notes Dixon; 1929 Gaston Co. death cert. no. 43, and Wake Co. death cert. no. 268.

Freddie Willey (black, age 16). *Rape.* The crime was committed on 4/1/1929 in Randolph County. Indecent assault on the person of 34-year-old Estelle McKinnon (white), she having been attacked in her own home and beaten to within an inch of her life with a chair and a tree branch. Some 150 stitches were needed to sew up the injuries to her head alone. The rapist was executed on June 28, 1929. Source: *Greensboro (NC) Daily Record*, 4/3/29 (13:4). See also: 1929 Wake Co. death cert. no. 402, 1930 U.S. Census (Randolph Co., NC), which notes Mrs. McKinnon.

Willis Buckner (white, age 32). *Rape.* The crime was committed on 4/18/1929 in Craven County. Indecent assault on the person of 10-year-old Beatrice Eubanks (white). This child rapist was executed on September 12, 1929. Sources: *The Landmark* (Statesville, NC), 6/10/29 (6:2); *Greensboro (NC) Daily Record*, 9/12/29 (1:6). See also: 1920 U.S. Census (Craven Co., NC), which notes the victim as an infant living with her aunt, Nora Stanly.

Ernest Fox (black, age 19). *Murder.* The crime was committed on 5/26/1929 in Edgecombe County. Handgun slaying of 19-year-old Jessie Harvey Taylor (white, a crippled grocer's assistant) who was overpowered in his place of business and shot with his own pistol that had been wrested from him. Motive: robbery. The killer was executed on November 22, 1929. Source: *Greensboro (NC) Daily Record*, 11/22/29 (1:5). See also: 1929 Edgecombe Co. death cert. no. 87, and Wake Co. death cert. no. 726.

1930

Ray Evans (black, age 20). *Murder.* The crime was committed on 6/12/1929 in Richmond County. Cop killer. Handgun slaying of 51-year-old William David Smith (white). Motive: resisting arrest. The killer was executed on March 14, 1930. Source: *Winston-Salem Journal,* 12/12/29 (8:1). See also: 1929 Richmond Co. death cert. no. 238, and 1930 Wake Co. death cert. no. 116.

John Buddy Macon (black, age 33). *Murder.* The crime was committed on 5/3/1929 in Randolph County. Cop killer. Handgun slaying of 35-year-old Samuel Pinnell (white), a special police officer who had been detailed to apprehend Macon on a warrant charging him with having fatally shot another black male in 1912. Motive: resisting arrest. The killer was executed on April 4, 1930. Sources: *Warren (NC) Record,* 5/10/29 (1:7); *Raleigh News & Observer,* 4/5/30 (1:7). See also: 1929 Vance Co. death cert. no. 408, and 1930 Wake Co. death cert. no. 236.

Robert Mangum (black, age 21). *Rape.* The crime was committed on 11/15/1929 in Franklin County. Indecent assault on the person of 46-year-old Leugeney Pearce (white) and near murder of that woman's husband James Pearce (white, age 69), who was dangerously slashed on the neck by the physically overpowering culprit. Mangum was executed on April 17, 1930. Sources: *Greensboro (NC) Daily Record,* 11/16/29 (1:2); *The Landmark* (Statesville, NC), 4/21/30 (2:5); Franklin County Superior Court Minutes (January Term 1930), pg. 99. Also: 1920 U.S. Census (Franklin Co., NC), which notes James and "Lanie" Pearce. Her first name might have really been "Eugenie."

James Broomfield, alias "Brumfield" (black, age 18). *Aggravated Burglary.* The crime was committed on 8/18/1929 in Union County. Executed for a violent break-in at the house of 57-year-old Marcus D. Preslar (white), during which he attempted to abduct that man's daughter Velma Preslar (white, age 18). The girl had a sheet thrown over her head and was dragged from the house kicking and screaming. She managed to break free before reaching a nearby wooded area where the culprit was going to rape her. Broomfield was put to death for this crime on May 9, 1930. Source: *Greensboro (NC) Daily Record,* 10/17/29 (18:2) & 5/9/30 (1:4). See also: 1930 Wake Co. death cert. no. 324.

James Spivey (white, age 25). *Murder.* The crime was committed on 9/21/1929 in Lee County. Ax murder of 19-year-old Betty Spivey (white, his cousin), she having also been raped. Motive: because she had rejected his marriage proposal on the grounds that it was incestuous. The killer was executed on May 23, 1930. Source: *Greensboro (NC) Daily Record,* 10/30/29 (1:1) & 5/23/30 (1:1). See also: 1930 Wake Co. death cert. no. 354.

Aaron Sharp (black, age 22) **and Berry Richardson** (black, age 20). *Murder.* The crime was committed on 4/11/1930 in Wilson County. Murder of 70-year-old Calvin Columbus Williford (white, a reclusive farmer), who was battered to death with an iron poker. Motive: robbery and home invasion. The killers were executed on September 26, 1930. Source: *Greensboro (NC) Record,* 9/26/30 (1:3). See also: 1930 Wilson Co. death cert. no. 21, and Wake Co. death cert. nos. 612 & 613.

Harvey Lawrence (black, age 17). *Aggravated Burglary.* The crime was committed on 3/1/1930 in Hertford County. Executed for a violent break-in at the house of 75-year-old Frank T. Railey (white), the culprit having entered that place in the middle of the night armed with a handgun. Seven shots were fired. Two of these struck the homeowner's wife, Mary Bryant Railey, a woman who was 40 years his junior. She also suffered a broken nose and dental damage when the miscreant allegedly tried to rape her. Harvey Lawrence was executed on October 10, 1930. Source: *Burlington (NC) Daily Times*, 4/24/30 (1:3), 4/26/30 (2:5) & 10/10/30 (1:7). See also: 1930 Wake Co. death cert. no. 635, which notes Lawrence; 1930 U.S. Census (Hertford Co., NC), which notes the Raileys.

Willie Massey (black, age 25). *Murder.* The crime was committed on 3/28/1930 in Durham County. Sororicide, etc. Executed for the murders of 34-year-old Dora Moore and 37-year-old Floyd Moore (blacks, his sister and brother-in-law respectively), who both had their heads knocked in. Motive: tenant-landlord dispute. Massey was a boarder in his sister's home, but to call him a freeloader would be closer to the truth. He was $10 behind in his rent and became violent when asked to pay up. He was executed on November 7, 1930. Source: *Greensboro (NC) Record*, 11/7/30 (1:2). See also: 1930 Durham Co. death cert. nos. 230 & 231, and Wake Co. death cert. no. 695.

Will Sloan, alias "Joe Madison" (black, age 28). *Murder.* The crime was committed on 4/10/1930 in Person County. Suspected serial killer. Executed for the shotgun slaying of 79-year-old Phoebe Yancey Gillis (black), she having been blasted in the back. Motive: sexual assault of the victim's 20-year-old granddaughter. Confirmed to have also murdered 24-year-old Elsa Marshall (white) by the same means at Greenburgh, New York, on 9/26/1929 while working as an itinerant laborer there. Motive: sexual assault. Prime suspect in at least two other murders at Washington, D.C., and Columbia, South Carolina, the latter for which he had been tried and acquitted ten years earlier. He was executed on November 7, 1930. Sources: *The Landmark* (Statesville, NC), 9/30/29 (8:4); *Harrisonburg (VA) Daily News Record*, 8/23/30 (1:3); *Greensboro (NC) Record*, 10/23/30 (1:4) & 11/7/30 (1:2). See also: 1930 Person Co. death cert. no. 293, and Wake Co. death cert. no. 694.

1931

Sidney Gattis (black, age 49). *Murder.* The crime was committed on 9/26/1930 in Durham County. Handgun slaying of 32-year-old Etta Gaston Petty (black), a widowed laundress. Motive: romantic estrangement. Gattis was executed on January 23, 1931. Sources: *Greensboro (NC) Record*, 1/23/31 (1:6); *Raleigh News & Observer*, 1/24/31 (2:1). See also: 1930 Durham Co. death cert. no. 676, and 1931 Wake Co. death cert. no. 43.

David McRae (black, age 24). *Murder.* The crime was committed on 1/3/1930 in Scotland County. Ax murder of 81-year-old Alfred Ellyson (white), a filling station proprietor. Motive: robbery. The killer was executed on February 13, 1931. Source: *Greensboro (NC) Record*, 1/10/30 (1:3) & 2/13/31 (1:4). See also: 1931 Wake Co. death cert. no. 94.

Henry Thomas Barden (black, age 28). *Aggravated Burglary.* The crime was committed on 6/16/1930 in Vance County. Executed for a violent break-in at the house of 79-year-old William A. Mathews (white) during which the homeowner's son Jesse Mathews (white, age 26) was stabbed "a number of times" with an ice pick, to the peril of his life. Barden was executed for this crime on February 13, 1931. Source: *Greensboro (NC) Record*, 1/9/31 (2:6) & 2/13/31 (1:4). See also: 1931 Wake Co. death cert. no. 96; 1930 U.S. Census (Vance Co., NC), which notes the family Mathews.

Woodrow Wilson Autry (black, age 19). *Rape.* The crime was committed on 5/13/1931 in Union County. Indecent assault on the person of 20-year-old Essie Brooks Keziah (white), a young married woman who had recently given birth. The rapist sought to excuse himself by slandering the victim with a tale to the effect that they had had "consensual" relations. This was refuted by the victim's physical condition at the time as well as her good character. Autry was executed on August 10, 1931. Source: *Greensboro (NC) Record*, 5/16/31 (1:3) & 8/10/31 (1:6). See also: 1931 Wake Co. death cert. no. 430, which notes the miscreant, and 1975 Union Co. death cert. no. 22867, which notes Mrs. Keziah.

Ben Golston (black, age 32). *Murder.* The crime was committed on 2/26/1927 in Chatham County. Handgun slaying of 24-year-old John Headen (black), the victim having been shot five times. Motive: personal dispute. Golston had initially shot Headen with a single bullet. This failed to kill him, which was unknown to Golston at that time. Golston heard of this later that day and immediately went to the place where the wounded man was being treated and finished him off with four more bullets. Golston was executed on August 21, 1931. Source: Greensboro (NC) Record, 8/21/31 (1:6). See also: 1927 Chatham Co. death cert. no. 322.

J.W. Ballard, alias "Sus Jackson" (black, age 17) **and Bernice Matthews** (black male, age 18). *Murder.* The crime was committed on 9/7/1931 in Rowan County. Handgun slaying of 44-year-old Albert Franklin Stewart (white), a filling station operator. Motive: armed robbery. The killers were executed on December 11, 1931. Source: *Greensboro (NC) Record*, 9/9/31 (2:1), 9/12/31 (1:3) & 12/11/31 (1:6). See also: 1931 Rowan Co. death cert. no. 168, and Wake Co. death certs. 710 & 711.

Chevis Herring (black, age 23). *Murder.* The crime was committed on 6/28/1930 in Sampson County. Murder of 70-year-old Frederick F. Newton (white, the postmaster at Kerr), who was attacked as he walked home from his place of business and fatally struck on the head. Motive: mugging. The killer was executed on 12/18/1931. Source: *The Robesonian* (Lumberton, NC), 8/18/30 (8:5). See also: 1930 New Hanover Co. death cert. no. 300, and 1931 Wake Co. death cert. no. 731.

1932

Asbury Respus (black, age 56). *Murder.* The crime was committed on 9/30/1931 in Guilford County. Child killer. Serial killer. Recidivist killer. Executed for the murder of 9-year-old Vera DeWitt Leonard (white), who was hit on the head with a blunt instrument and her body "burned to char." Motive: attempted sexual assault. Possibly deranged. Respus said that he had fallen from a barn rafter in his youth, incurring a head injury that left him susceptible to "spells" of homicidal madness. This may have been true due to a noticeable skull indentation that he bore. Seven other murders can be traced to him. The first and second of these were said to have occurred in Northampton Co., North Carolina, during the early 1900s, the victims being Negro women named Lizzie Banks (age about 30) and Zenie Britt. The first was shot and the second was beaten to death with a stick. Number three (according to his own account) was a black female named Becky Storr circa 1910 at Boydton, Virginia. She too was bludgeoned with a stick. The killer's depredations are better documented after that point. In 1912 he gunned down a Northampton County Negro named Ed Wynne and drew a 15-year sentence for manslaughter. He escaped from a road gang in 1916 and took up a roving lifestyle in and around the vicinity of Greensboro, North Carolina. How Respus managed to avoid getting caught for the next 15 years is anybody's guess. On 1/14/1918 he forced his way into the house of a white woman named Jennie Brown Gilbreath (age 56) and killed her with an ax. Her house was then burned down, destroying all evidence of the crime. On 7/22/1920 he came upon a little white boy named Robert Neal Osborne (age 4) who was playing in a field. Respus "viciously slapped" the child again and again before forcing him face down in a stream, standing with his foot firmly planted on the back of the boy's neck, so that he drowned. A verdict of accidental death was recorded at that time. Five years passed ere Respus struck again. Then on 7/17/1925 he forcibly entered the home of an 80-year-old widow woman named Eunice Stephenson (white), knocked her in the head and left her body strung up from a ceiling beam. This time the crime was recognized as murder but remained unsolved for another six years. Respus was executed on January 8, 1932. Source: *Greensboro (NC) Record*, 1/8/32 (1:8). See also: Guilford Co. death cert. no. 49 in 1918, no. 291 in 1920, no. 429 in 1925 and no. 459 in 1931; 1900 U.S. Census (Northampton Co., NC), which notes Lizzie Banks; *Front Page Detective* (magazine) 11/37.

John Robert Myers (black, age 30). *Murder.* The crime was committed on 1/9/1932 in Pitt County. Handgun slaying of 48-year-old Robert Hagan Hodges (white), the postmaster at Pactolus. Motive: mugging. The killer was executed on March 25, 1932. Source: *Greensboro (NC) Record*, 1/18/32 (8:6) & 1/22/32 (2:6). Also: 1932 Wake Co. death cert. no. 190, and Beaufort Co. death cert. no. 11.

Dudley Moore (black, age 18). *Murder.* The crime was committed on 8/15/1931 in Davidson County. Shotgun slaying of 59-year-old Victoria Tussey Berrier (white), she having also been severely battered with the butt of that weapon. Motive: attempted sexual assault and gross perfidy, the victim being his foster mother. Moore was executed on April 29, 1932. Source: *Greensboro (NC) Record*, 8/19/31 (1:6), 8/28/31 (1:4) & 4/29/32 (1:3). See also: 1931 Davidson Co. death cert. no. 37.

Plato Edney (white, age 33). *Murder.* The crime was committed on 8/3/1931 in Henderson County. Uxoricide. Shotgun slaying of 35-year-old Marjorie Alexine Hill Edney (white), irrespective of the fact that she was in the act of dressing a baby at the time. Motive: apparently baseless suspicion of infidelity. The killer was executed on July 15, 1932. Source: *Greensboro (NC) Record*, 8/3/31 (1:8), 10/15/31 (18:7) & 7/15/32 (1:2). See also: 1931 Henderson Co. death cert. no. 329, and 1932 Wake Co. death cert. no. 428.

Nord Donnell (black, age 23). *Murder.* The crime was committed on 11/25/1931 in Guilford County. Handgun slaying of 63-year-old Robert Boston Andrew (white), the postmaster at Sedalia. Motive: attempted armed robbery. The killer was executed on August 26, 1932. Source: *Greensboro (NC) Record*, 11/26/31 (1:8) & 8/26/32 (1:8). See also: 1931 Guilford Co. death cert. no. 329, and 1932 Wake Co. death cert. no. 533.

Leroy Lee (black, age 23). *Murder.* The crime was committed on 11/25/1931 in Guilford County. Accomplice in the handgun slaying of 63-year-old Robert Boston Andrew (white), the postmaster at Sedalia. Motive: attempted armed robbery. Lee was executed on October 14, 1932. Source: *Greensboro (NC) Record*, 10/14/32 (1:1). Also: 1932 Wake Co. death cert. no. 601. See also: DONNELL, Nord (executed 8/26/32), above.

Alec Grier (black, age 21). *Murder.* The crime was committed on 5/1/1932 in Gaston County. Murder of 18-year-old Harold Carter (white, a filling station attendant), who was beaten on the head with heavy glass oil bottles. Motive: robbery. It was the victim's 18th birthday. The killer was executed on December 16, 1932. Source: *Greensboro (NC) Record*, 5/4/32 (2:3) & 5/5/32 (3:7). See also: 1932 Gaston Co. death cert. no. 107, and Wake Co. death cert. no. 727.

Harvey Wallace (black, age 27). *Murder.* The crime was committed on 6/18/1932 in Lee County. Handgun slayings of 61-year-old Norton H. Perry and 66-year-old Thomas Beal (whites). Motive: argument in a country store. The killer was executed on December 16, 1932. Source: *Greensboro (NC) Record*, 7/21/32 (10:5). See also: 1932 Lee Co. death cert. nos. 40 & 50, plus Wake Co. death cert. no. 728.

1933

Hezzie Avant (white, age 29). *Murder.* The crime was committed on 10/6/1931 in Scotland County. Handgun slaying of 19-year-old Smithie Evans Caulder (white female), who was shot multiple times in the back. Motive: immorality. A married man, Avant cohabited with two women on the most intimate of terms. These were his own wife and Smithie Caulder, the latter being the lawful spouse of another man. Avant had two children by his wife and three more by teenage Caulder, who all shared the same hovel. This combination of adultery, bastardy and overcrowding erupted on the above date when alpha male Avant decided that his human herd needed to be thinned. He was executed on January 27, 1933. Source: *The Robesonian* (Lumberton, NC), 12/7/31 (1:6) & 1/30/33 (6:5). See also: 1931 Scotland Co. death cert. no. 11, and 1933 Wake Co. death cert. no. 49.

David McNair (black, age 22). *Murder.* The crime was committed on 11/11/1932 in Guilford County. Handgun slaying of 35-year-old Mary McCown (white), a storekeeper. Motive: attempted armed robbery. The killer was executed on May 19, 1933. Source: *Greensboro (NC) Record*, 11/12/32 (1:8) & 5/19/33 (1:1). See also: 1933 Wake Co. death cert. no. 269; NC Deaths Collection (1908–1967) (NC State Archives), which notes the murdered woman.

Olin Clay Fogleman (white, age 29). *Murder.* The crime was committed on 4/30/1932 in Rockingham County. Cop killer, etc. Executed for the handgun slaying of 61-year-old William J. Carter (white, a service station manager), who was shot seven times. Motive: attempted armed robbery. Also confirmed to have murdered Rockingham County Deputy Sheriff James A. Robertson (white, age 49) nine days later when that lawman came upon him hiding in a schoolhouse. The deputy was also shot multiple times with a handgun. Fogleman was executed on August 4, 1933. Source: *Greensboro (NC) Record*, 5/9/32 (1:3), 5/19/32 (10:3) & 8/4/33 (1:1). See also: 1932 Rockingham Co. death cert. nos. 190 & 205, plus 1933 Wake Co. death cert. no. 438; *Dynamic Detective* (magazine), 3/39.

Bryant Stone (white, age 44). *Murder.* The crime was committed on 6/12/1932 in Wilkes County. Sniper killing of 40-year-old Wayne W. Norman (white, his son-in-law). Motive: parental wrath; the victim had eloped with the killer's daughter despite being forbidden to do so. Bryant Stone was executed on September 8, 1933. Source: *Greensboro (NC) Record*, 5/18/33 (1:8) & 9/8/33 (1:2). See also: 1932 Wilkes Co. death cert. no. 25, and 1933 Wake Co. death cert. no. 494; *Front Page Detective*, 8/47; *Master Detective*, 12/55; *Real Detective*, 4/46.

Johnny Christopher Lee (black, age 21). *Murder.* The crime was committed on 1/15/1933 in Harnett County. Handgun slaying of 44-year-old Jacob Handy Hill (black). Motive: murder-for-hire. Lee was executed on September 15, 1933. Source: *Greensboro (NC) Record*, 6/2/33 (10:3). See also: 1933 Harnett Co. death cert. no. 306, and Wake Co. death cert. no. 510.

1934

Jesse Brooks (black, age 47). *Murder.* The crime was committed on 6/10/1933 in Durham County. Cop killer. Handgun slaying of 36-year-old Roland Anderson Gill (white), who was shot multiple times. Motive: armed robbery gone awry. Brooks was executed on March 16, 1934. Sources: *Greensboro (NC) Record*, 3/16/34 (1:7); *Statesville (NC) Landmark*, 6/13/33 (8:1). Also: 1933 Durham Co. death cert. no. 399, and 1934 Wake Co. death cert. no. 164.

James Johnson (black, age 24). *Murder.* The crime was committed on 7/3/1932 in Hoke County. Shotgun slaying of 19-year-old Virginia Leach (black), who was murdered in her bed. Motive: because she had refused to marry him. The killer was executed on March 16, 1934. Source: Hoke County Superior Court (April Term 1933) case file no. 1158. See also: 1932 Hoke Co. death cert. no. 42, and 1934 Wake Co. death cert. no. 165.

Walter Thaxton (black, age 29). *Murder.* The crime was committed on 11/25/1933 in Person County. Shotgun slaying of 37-year-old Marion Butler Gentry (white). Motive: highway robbery. The killer was executed on March 23, 1934. Source: *Daily Times News* (Burlington, NC), 3/23/34 (1:4). See also: 1933 Durham Co. death cert. no. 791, and 1934 Wake Co. death cert. no. 177.

Theodore Cooper (black, age 28). *Murder.* The crime was committed on 2/25/1933 in Durham County. Shotgun slaying of 42-year-old John Nevious Lassiter (white). Motive: murder-for-hire as part of a larger scheme to defraud an insurance company. Cooper was executed on April 27, 1934. Source: *Greensboro (NC) Record*, 4/27/34 (1:6). See also: 1933 Durham Co. death cert. no. 135, and 1934 Wake Co. death cert. no. 256.

Mike Stefanoff (white, age 44). *Murder.* The crime was committed on 7/29/1933 in Alexander County. Handgun slaying of 45-year-old Thomas Chauncey Barnes (white). Motive: bank robbery. The killer was executed on May 18, 1934. Source: *Greensboro (NC) Record*, 7/31/33 (1:6), 2/23/34 (1:4) & 5/18/34 (1:4). See also: 1933 Alexander Co. death cert. no. 308, and 1934 Wake Co. death cert. no. 304.

James Robert Sheffield (white, age 46). *Murder.* The crime was committed on 8/8/1933 in Haywood County. Rifle slaying of 31-year-old James "Bud" Miller (white), the victim of an ambush. Motive: mistaken identity; the killer was really gunning for someone else. He was executed on May 18, 1934. Source: Haywood County Superior Court Criminal Action Papers (*State vs. Sheffield*, 1933), NC State Archives. Also: 1934 Wake Co. death cert. no. 303; 1930 U.S. Census (Buncombe Co., NC), which notes "Bud" Miller.

Ossie Smith (black, age 20). *Murder.* The crime was committed on 11/11/1933 in Northampton County. Rifle slaying of J. Edward Hedgepeth (white, full name and age not recorded), a farm overseer. Motive: highway robbery. Smith was after a farm payroll carried by the victim. He put a log across the road to inhibit Hedgepeth's route and shot the man dead when he tried to move it. Smith was executed on June 15, 1934. Source: *Roanoke News* (Weldon, NC), 11/16/33 (1:7). See also: 1934 Wake Co. death cert. no. 370.

Joe L. Dalton (white, age 30). *Murder.* The crime was committed on 5/28/1933 in Henderson County. Uxoricide. Handgun slaying of 29-year-old Mabel Zula Brown Dalton (white), who was shot six times. Motive: marital estrangement. The killer was executed on June 22, 1934. Source: *Greensboro (NC) Record*, 6/22/34 (1:2). See also: 1933 Henderson Co. death cert. no. 331, and 1934 Wake Co. death cert. no. 393.

John Lewis Edwards (black, age 16). *Murder.* The crime was committed on 3/11/1933 in Mecklenburg County. Handgun slaying of 62-year-old John W. Brown (white), a trolley motorman. Motive: armed robbery. The killer was executed on July 6, 1934. Source: *Greensboro (NC) Record*, 7/6/34 (1:2). See also: 1933 Mecklenburg Co. death cert. no. 201, and 1934 Wake Co. death cert. no. 426.

Clyde Ferrell (white, age 23). *Murder.* The crime was committed on 3/2/1933 in Durham County. Shotgun slaying of 26-year-old Thaddeus Tilley (white), a filling station attendant. Motive: armed robbery. Ferrell was executed on July 6, 1934. Source: *Greensboro (NC) Record*, 7/6/34 (1:2). See also: 1933 Durham Co.

death cert. no. 484, and 1934 Wake Co. death cert. no. 425.

George Keaton (black, age 26). *Murder.* The crime was committed on 1/19/1933 in Forsyth County. Handgun slaying of 18-year-old Annie Lee Thigpen (black), who was shot three times. Motive: lovers' quarrel. Tertiary syphilis was cited as a mitigating factor. The killer was executed on September 21, 1934. Source: *Daily News Times* (Burlington, NC), 9/21/34 (1:6). Appeals: 172 SE 179 and 175 SE 296. See also: 1933 Forsyth Co. death cert. no. 148, and 1934 Wake Co. death cert. no. 569.

Willie James Crockett (black, age 21). *Murder.* The crime was committed on 8/29/1933 in Forsyth County. Uxoricide. Handgun slaying of 18-year-old Patsy Hilton Crockett (black), who was shot four times. Motive: marital estrangement. She lingered until 11/26/1933. The killer was executed on September 28, 1934. Source: Appeal: 175 SE 91–92. See also: 1933 Forsyth Co. death cert. no. 810, and 1934 Wake Co. death cert. no. 588.

Emanuel Bittings (black, age 41). *Murder.* The crime was committed on 9/7/1933 in Person County. Shotgun slaying of 62-year-old Theophilus Moore Clayton (white). Motive: tenant-landlord dispute. The killer was executed on September 28, 1934. Sources: *Greensboro (NC) Record*, 9/8/33 (7:4) & 9/28/34 (1:6); *Statesville (NC) Landmark*, 9/12/33 (3:3). See also: 1933 Person Co. death cert. no. 121, and 1934 Wake Co. death cert. no. 584.

Johnny Johnson, alias "Tom Johnson" (black, age 27), **Johnny Hart** (black, age 21) **and Preston Howard** (black, age 17). *Murder.* The crime was committed on 12/21/1933 in Sampson County. Handgun slaying of 23-year-old Howard Jernigan (white), a filling station attendant. Motive: armed robbery. The killers were executed on November 16, 1934. Source: *Greensboro (NC) Record*, 11/16/34 (1:2). See also: 1933 Harnett Co. death cert. no. 58, and 1934 Wake Co. death cert. nos. 705, 706 & 707.

Bascom Green (white, age 43), **James Lester Green** (white, age 21) **and Robert Edward Black** (white, age 24). *Murder.* The crime was committed on 7/29/1933 in Alexander County. Accomplices in the handgun slaying of 45-year-old Thomas Chauncey Barnes (white). Motive: bank robbery. Source: *Greensboro (NC) Record*, 12/7/34 (1:1). See also: 1934 Wake Co. death cert. nos. 755, 756 & 757. See also: STEFANOFF, Mike (executed 5/18/34).

Rufus Satterfield (white, age 43). *Murder.* The crime was committed on 10/22/1933 in Wayne County. Shotgun slaying of 32-year-old Herbert Grice (white), who was deliberately lured onto his front porch at night by a sniper. Motive: because the killer coveted the decedent's wife. Satterfield was executed on December 14, 1934. Sources: *Statesville (NC) Record*, 2/13/34 (4:5); *Gastonia Daily Gazette*, 11/20/34 (5:3). See also: 1933 Wayne Co. death cert. no. 267, and 1934 Wake Co. death cert. no. 775; *Crime Detective* (magazine), fall 1944 & 10/52; *Real Detective*, 11/35.

1935

Sidney Etheridge (white, age 43). *Murder.* The crime was committed on

4/10/1934 in Onslow County. Hatchet murder of 69-year-old Mamie Dickerson Moore (white), a reclusive widow. Motive: robbery and home invasion. The killer was executed on March 15, 1935. Source: *Greensboro (NC) Record*, 4/11/34 (5:7), 4/13/34 (1:2), 4/17/34 (2:3) & 3/15/35 (11:3). See also: 1934 Onslow Co. death cert. no. 382, and 1935 Wake Co. death cert. no. 190; *Crime Detective*, 10/43; *Daring Detective*, 1/38.

Louis Sentell (white, age 38). *Murder.* The crime was committed on 2/15/1934 in Cleveland County. Shotgun slaying of 23-year-old Florence Elizabeth Jones Drake (white). Motive: possibly deranged. Sentell was driving around in his automobile when he spotted a group of four young women. He offered to give them a ride, which they demurely declined. Enraged by this, Sentell opened fire on the ladies with a shotgun. He was executed on July 12, 1935. Source: *The Landmark* (Statesville, NC), 2/20/34 (8:7). See also: 1934 Cleveland Co. death cert. no. 30, and 1935 Wake Co. death cert. no. 419.

George Whitfield (black, age 21). *Rape.* The crime was committed on 10/3/1933 in Guilford County. Indecent assault on the person of a pregnant white female identified as "Mrs. R. Bill Douglass," who was attacked in her home at 5:30 a.m. by an assailant who apparently watched as her husband left there to go to his job. Then the culprit (Whitfield) pushed his way in by tearing a screen door from its hinges and beat up the *enceinte* Mrs. Douglass before forcing himself on her. This home invader and rapist was executed on July 12, 1935. Source: *Greensboro (NC) Record*, 10/3/33 (1:5), 10/11/33 (1:5), 10/25/33 (1:7), 10/26/33 (1:5) & 7/12/35 (1:6).

Taft Williams (black, age 24). *Murder.* The crime was committed on or about 9/5/1934 in Columbus County. Uxoricide. Ax murder of 22-year-old Blanche Bennett Williams (black), whose remains were found in woods on the aforesaid date. Motive: uncertain; the killer denied his guilt to the last. He was executed on August 2, 1935. Source: *Daily Times News* (Burlington, NC), 8/2/35 (1:7). See also: 1934 Columbus Co. death cert. no. 15, and 1935 Wake Co. death cert. no. 455.

Dortch Waller (black, age 42). *Murder.* The crime was committed on 12/30/1934 in Granville County. Shotgun slaying of 51-year-old John Harris (white, a storekeeper), who was blasted in the leg but died five days later when that limb was amputated. Motive: attempted armed robbery. Waller was executed on August 2, 1935. Sources: *Oxford (NC) Public Ledger*, 1/1/35 (1:6); *Greensboro (NC) Record*, 2/9/35 (1:1) & 8/2/35 (1:5).

Vander Glover (black, age 38) **and Houston McMillan** (black, age 18). *Murder.* The crime was committed on 4/10/1934 in Cumberland County. Murder of 62-year-old Robert Williams (black, a grocer), who was hit on the head with a bottle and succumbed to a fractured skull. Motive: robbery. The guilty parties were executed on August 9, 1935. Source: *Greensboro (NC) Record*, 8/9/35 (1:5). Appeal: 179 SE 6–7. See also: 1935 Wake Co. death cert. nos. 476 & 477; 1930 U.S. Census (Cumberland Co., NC), which notes Williams.

Caesar Miller (black, age 17). *Murder.* The crime was committed on 12/8/1934 in Craven County. Executed for the murder of 72-year-old Jefferson Davis Gwaltney (white, a physically handicapped storekeeper), who was beaten on the head with a billet of wood. Motive: robbery. The killer rifled the slain man's pockets of $10, which he promptly squandered on whiskey and cigarettes. He was executed on September 6, 1935. Source: *Greensboro (NC) Record*, 9/6/35 (1:6). See also: 1934 Craven Co. death cert. no. 207, and 1935 Wake Co. death cert. no. 526.

Arthur Gosnell (white, age 20), **Oris Gunter** (white, age 19) **and Robert Thomas** (white, age 22). *Murder.* The crime was committed on 2/15/1935 in Madison County. All three executed for the murder of 70-year-old William Thomas (white, a storekeeper and great-uncle of Gunter and Thomas), who was beaten on the head with a monkey wrench and left lying in a mud hole. Motive: highway robbery. The trio lay in wait for the victim on two successive nights because they "wanted money to see the world." The killers got exactly $77 and 100 miles away before lawmen put an end to their world tour. They went to the electric chair on October 4, 1935. Source: *Greensboro (NC) Record*, 10/4/35 (1:2). See also: 1935 Madison Co. death cert. no. 5, and Wake Co. death certs. 569, 570 & 571.

1936

Robert Dunlap (black, age 26). *Murder.* The crime was committed on 2/17/1935 in Buncombe County. Fatal and deliberate poisoning of 26-year-old Ola Pauline McMillan (black) by serving her homemade sausage laced with arsenic. Motive: adultery turned deadly. Dunlap was executed on January 17, 1936. Source: *Greensboro (NC) Record*, 1/17/36 (1:7). See also: 1935 Buncombe Co. death cert. no. 172, and 1936 Wake Co. death cert. no. 34.

Jimmy Lee Foster, alias "Allen Foster" (black, age 19). *Rape.* The crime was committed on 9/28/1935 in Hoke County. Indecent assault on the person of 20-year-old Lillie Capps (white), she having been attacked in her home, beaten on the head with a bottle, robbed of her intrinsic valuables and raped. The miscreant was executed on January 24, 1936. Source: Hoke County Superior Court (November Term 1935) case file no. 1240; NC State Archives. See also: 1936 Wake Co. death cert. no. 53; 1940 U.S. Census (Hoke Co., NC), which notes Mrs. Capps.

Edward L. Jenkins (white, age 48). *Murder.* The crime was committed on 7/4/1935 in Gaston County. Handgun slaying of 35-year-old Paul Hoke Collins (white). Motive: unclear. Both men were seen chatting with each other in a casual manner. Jenkins suddenly pulled out a gun and shot Collins for no apparent reason. He claimed self-defense but there were several witnesses to the contrary. Jenkins was executed on January 31, 1936. Source: *Gastonia Daily Gazette*, 7/6/35 (1:3) & 1/31/36 (1:2). See also: 1935 Gaston Co. death cert. no. 79, and 1936 Wake Co. death cert. no. 66.

William Long (black, age 17). *Murder.* The crime was committed on 1/11/1935 in Alamance County. Executed for the murder of 65-year-old Sam Minor (black, a night watchman at a furniture mill), who was blasted in the back with a shotgun and also battered about the head with the butt of that weapon. Motive: robbery. The killer was executed on February 7, 1936. Source: *Daily News Times*

(Burlington, NC), 1/12/35 (8:1). See also: 1935 Alamance Co. death cert. no. 2, and 1936 Wake Co. death cert. no. 84, which confirms that the killer was 17 days shy of his 18th birthday when he committed the crime.

James T. Sanford (black, age 25) **and Thomas Watson** (black, age 29). *Murder.* The crime was committed on 8/26/1935 in Durham County. Murder of 43-year-old Nathaniel Malone (black, a cabbie), who was battered to death with a hammer. Motive: robbery and carjacking. The killers were executed on February 7, 1936. Source: *Greensboro (NC) Record*, 8/27/35 (1:1) & 2/7/36 (1:8). See also: 1935 Durham Co. death cert. no. 674, and 1936 Wake Co. death cert. nos. 83 & 86; 1920 U.S. Census (Evans Co., GA), which notes Sanford as a minor.

Jake Johnson (black, age 34). *Rape.* The crime was committed on 2/1/1935 in Rockingham County. Probable serial rapist. Executed for an indecent assault on the person of 68-year-old Annie Grogan (white, a maiden woman), who was lured from her home with a contrived story and later found tied up in a ditch. After the assault, the culprit took off to West Virginia with loot plundered from the victim's residence. He was captured in the capital city of that state five months later while attempting to force himself on no less a person than the wife of the state attorney general. He had previously served ten years in prison for sex crimes. Jake Johnson was executed on March 19, 1936. Source: *Greensboro (NC) Record*, 1/20/36 (6:5) & 3/19/36 (1:3).

Edward Hester (white, age 19). *Murder.* The crime was committed on 5/16/1935 in Wake County. Executed for the ax murder of 20-year-old Paul Hunnicutt (white). Motive: prison camp violence. Recidivist killer. Hester came from Gaston County. He was a drunk and a loser while still in his teens. On 2/4/1935 he gunned down his brother-in-law John C. Abernathy (white, age 28) for no reason other than alcoholic turpitude. His own sister (who had been widowed by his misconduct) said that the crime was completely unmitigated. A trial court sentenced Hester to a term of 25 to 30 years at hard labor. He was transferred to the North Carolina State Penitentiary on 3/13/1935 and then assigned to Polk Labor Camp in Wake County. It was there where he murdered fellow prisoner Paul Hunnicutt nine weeks later. Hester was executed on March 20, 1936. Source: *Gastonia Daily Gazette*, 2/8/35 (9:6), 3/13/35 (1:2), 3/20/36 (1:5) & 3/21/36 (1:3). See also: 1920 U.S. Census (Gaston Co., NC), which notes Hester; 1935 Gaston Co. death cert. no. 13, and Wake Co. death cert. no. 286, as well as 1936 Wake Co. death cert. no. 223.

Bright Buffkin, alias "Lenau Buffkin" (white, age 42). *Murder.* The crime was committed on 8/9/1935 in Columbus County. Handgun slaying of 24-year-old Daniel Paul Barefoot (white). Motive: because he felt that the victim had intruded in a private matter. Buffkin was executed on March 27, 1936. Sources: *The Landmark* (Statesville, NC), 9/26/35 (3:1); *Greensboro (NC) Record*, 3/27/36 (1:4). Appeal: 183 SE 543–548. See also: 1930 U.S. Census (Columbus Co., NC), which notes the murdered man.

Lawrence Dingle (black, age 31) **and Germay Williams** (black, age 24). *Murder.* The crime was committed on

4/28/1935 in Forsyth County. Murder of 60-year-old John W. Gant (black), who was hit on the head with an auto jack. Motive: robbery. The killers were executed on May 8, 1936. Source: *Greensboro (NC) Record*, 5/8/36 (1:7). See also: 1935 Forsyth Co. death cert. no. 328, and 1936 Wake Co. death cert. nos. 346 & 347.

Marvin Batten (white, age 29). *Murder.* The crime was committed on 12/13/1935 in Johnston County. Shotgun slaying of 30-year-old Lyda Coffe Daughtry (white). Motive: adultery gone bad. Batten was executed on May 29, 1936. Source: *Greensboro (NC) Record*, 12/16/35 (1:6), 12/20/35 (1:3) & 5/29/36 (1:2). See also: 1935 Johnston Co. death cert. no. 29, and 1936 Wake Co. death cert. no. 392.

John Horne (white, age 37). *Murder.* The crime was committed on 8/14/1935 in Chowan County. Uxoricide. Executed for the murder of 31-year-old Nellie Bennett Horne (white), whose throat was cut. Motive: marital breakdown. The killer was put to death on June 19, 1936. Source: *Greensboro (NC) Record*, 6/19/36 (1:4). See also: 1935 Chowan Co. death cert. no. 37, and 1936 Wake Co. death cert. no. 437.

Henry Grier (black, age 42). *Murder.* The crime was committed on 5/6/1935 in Forsyth County. Handgun slaying of 27-year-old Annie Giles (black), she having been shot in the head. Motive: estranged lover. Grier was executed on July 10, 1936. Source: *Greensboro (NC) Record*, 7/10/36 (1:3). Appeal: 183 SE 272–273. See also: 1935 Forsyth Co. death cert. no. 343, and 1936 Wake Co. death cert. no. 484.

William Abraham Hudgins (black, age 36). *Murder.* The crime was committed on 12/23/1935 in Forsyth County. Hatchet murder of 70-year-old James Herbert Searcy (black), whose body was stuffed into a storage trunk and found five days later. Motive: homosexual matter. The killer was executed on July 17, 1936. Source: *Greensboro (NC) Record*, 6/30/36 (1:8) & 7/17/36 (1:4). See also: 1935 Forsyth Co. death cert. no. 883, and 1936 Wake Co. death cert. no. 497.

Willie Lee Gallman (black, age 21). *Murder.* The crime was committed on 12/13/1935 in Forsyth County. Rifle slaying of 43-year-old John Gaston (black). Motive: gambling dispute for the sake of 75 cents. The killer was executed on August 21, 1936. Source: *The Robesonian* (Lumberton, NC), 8/27/36 (5:3). See also: 1935 Forsyth Co. death cert. no. 863, and 1936 Wake Co. death cert. no. 593.

John Kinyon (black, age 72). *Rape.* The crime was committed on 9/3/1935 in Granville County. Indecent assault on the person of 12-year-old Geraldine Peed (white), the details being too abhorrent for publication. The rapist was executed on August 21, 1936. Sources: *Oxford (NC) Public Ledger*, 9/6/35 (1:7); *Greensboro (NC) Record*, 9/4/35 (1:3) & 8/21/36 (1:3). See also: 1936 Wake Co. death cert. no. 595.

James Buck Carden (white, age 39). *Murder.* The crime was committed on 5/7/1934 in Durham County. Uxoricide. Handgun slaying of 33-year-old Vera Wagoner Carden (white) who was shot five times. Motive: uncertain; the killer insisted that it was an accident. He was executed on September 4, 1936. Source: *Gastonia Daily Gazette*, 9/4/36 (3:3). See also: 1934 Durham Co. death cert. no.

336, and 1936 Wake Co. death cert. no. 630.

George Alston (black, age 23). *Murder.* The crime was committed on 5/6/1935 in Orange County. Handgun slaying of 16-year-old Helen Massey (black). Motive: lovers' quarrel. Alston was executed on September 4, 1936. Source: *Greensboro (NC) Record*, 9/4/36 (1:2). See also: 1935 Orange Co. death cert. no. 348, and 1936 Wake Co. death cert. no. 628, which erroneously noted the killer's ethnicity.

John Pressley, alias "Country John" (black, age 42). *Murder.* The crime was committed on 4/13/1935 in Gaston County. Shotgun slaying of 25-year-old Sylvester Glover (black). Motive: gambling dispute. The killer was executed on November 13, 1936. Source: *Gastonia Daily Gazette*, 4/20/35 (1:6) & 7/25/35 (3:5). See also: 1935 Gaston Co. death cert. no. 212, and 1936 Wake Co. death cert. no. 800.

Evans Snooks Macklin (black, age 19). *Murder.* The crime was committed on 2/16/1936 in Halifax County. Cop killer. Shotgun slaying of 47-year-old Andrew P. Moore (white). Motive: bank robbery gone awry. Macklin was executed on November 20, 1936. Source: *Greensboro (NC) Record*, 2/17/36 (3:7) & 11/20/36 (1:3). See also: 1936 Halifax Co. death cert. no. 207.

Willie Tate (black, age 28). *Murder.* The crime was committed on 2/28/1936 in Pitt County. Handgun slaying of 22-year-old Alexander Warren (white). Motive: sexual assault of the victim's female companion. Tate was executed on November 20, 1936. Source: *Gastonia Daily Gazette*, 2/29/36 (1:8). See also: 1936 Pitt Co. death cert. no. 23, and Wake Co. death cert. no. 821; *Master Detective*, 3/37.

Martin Moore (black, age 22). *Murder.* The crime was committed on 7/16/1936 in Buncombe County. Handgun slaying of 18-year-old Helen Clevenger (white). Motive: thief caught in the act. Moore was a bellboy in a high-class hotel. He attempted to pilfer from one guest room too many. He was executed on December 11, 1936. Source: *Greensboro (NC) Record*, 8/12/36 (1:4) & 8/27/36 (2:1). See also: 1936 Wake Co. death cert. no. 894; *Intimate Detective*, 6/40; *Official Detective*, 10/15/36; *Front Page Detective*, 1/69; *Crime Detective*, 7/52; *Real Detective*, 11/36; *Master Detective*, 1/55, 11/62 & 6/77.

1937

Robert Glenn Brown (black, age 18). *Murder.* The crime was committed on 9/15/1936 in Craven County. Ax murder of 64-year-old Joseph B. Peacock (white), a storekeeper. Motive: robbery. The killer was executed on July 9, 1937. Source: *Greensboro (NC) Record*, 9/16/36 (14:6). See also: 1936 Craven Co. death cert. no. 337, and 1937 Wake Co. death cert. no. 489.

Fred Steele (black, age 23) **and Samuel James Jones** (black, age 20). *Murder.* The crime was committed on 10/1/1936 in Mecklenburg County. Handgun slaying of 21-year-old Thomas Clifford Fowler (white), a cabbie. Motive: robbery. The killers were executed on July 16, 1937. Source: *Gastonia Daily Gazette*, 2/25/37 (1:8). See also: 1936 Mecklenburg Co. death cert. no. 250, and

1937 Wake Co. death cert. nos. 531 & 532.

Fred P. Gray (black, age 26). *Murder.* The crime was committed on 6/6/1936 in Onslow County. Uxoricide. Executed for the murder of 27-year-old Lettuce Hayes Gray (black). Motive: unknown. Neither newspapers nor court records say how or why he did it. Gray was executed on July 23, 1937. Source: 1937 Wake Co. death cert. no. 513. See also: Onslow County Superior Court Files (August Term, 1936) case file no. 1049; Onslow County Negro Marriage Register entry dated 12/29/31, which notes the nuptials of this ill-fated couple (NC State Archives).

Hunter Winchester (black, age 23). *Murder.* The crime was committed on 1/1/1937 in Guilford County. Uxoricide. Handgun slaying of 24-year-old Mabel Teele Winchester (black). Motive: marital estrangement. The killer was executed on July 23, 1937. Sources: *Greensboro (NC) Record*, 1/2/37 (2:8); *Gastonia Daily Gazette*, 7/23/37 (1:2). See also: 1937 Guilford Co. death cert. no. 349, and Wake Co. death cert. no. 525.

Alvin W. Watson (white, age 20). *Murder.* The crime was committed on 11/22/1936 in Martin County. Hammer killing of 24-year-old Thomas S. Holliday (white), a gas station attendant. Motive: robbery. The killer was executed on July 30, 1937. Source: *Gastonia Daily Gazette*, 7/30/37 (1:6). See also: 1936 Martin Co. death cert. no. 151, and 1937 Wake Co. death cert. no. 529; *Front Page Detective, 8/46.*

Thomas Perry (black, age 23). *Rape.* The crime was committed on 12/6/1936 in Wake County. Indecent assault on the person of 40-year-old Pearl Thomas (black), no further details being noted in the record. The rapist was executed on July 30, 1937. Source: Wake County Superior Court Minutes (March Term, 1937), pg. 121; *Greensboro (NC) Record*, 4/8/37 (2:4); *Raleigh News & Observer*, 7/31/37 (1:3).

George Exum (black, age 22). *Murder.* The crime was committed on 11/21/1936 in Wayne County. Executed for the murder of 64-year-old Obelia Fort Exum (black, his aunt) who was beaten and choked to death. Motive: larceny. The killer was put to death on August 6, 1937. Source: *Gastonia Daily Gazette*, 11/23/36 (9:8). See also: 1936 Wayne Co. death cert. no. 350, and 1937 Wake Co. death cert. no. 549.

James McNeil (black, age 21). *Murder.* The crime was committed on 6/12/1935 in Harnett County. Executed for the murder of 20-year-old Suelie Eason (black) who was slashed on the neck so that she bled to death. Motive: adultery turned violent. The killer paid with his own life on August 13, 1937. Source: *Gastonia Daily Gazette*, 8/13/37 (1:3). See also: 1935 Harnett Co. death cert. no. 413, and 1937 Wake Co. death cert. no. 565.

Leroy McNeil (black, age 17). *Murder.* The crime was committed on 2/1/1937 in Robeson County. Fatal and deliberate poisoning of 24-year-old Bernice Cox (white) and near murder of three other people by putting arsenate of lead in their biscuits. Motive: disgruntled employee. The killer was a farmhand employed by the victim's husband. He resented the fact that he had not been provided with his dinner in a timely manner two days before the crime. McNeil was executed on August 13, 1937. Source: *The Robesonian* (Lumberton, NC), 4/14/37 (1:8). See also: North Carolina Death Index (1908–2004), which notes Mrs. Cox, and 1937 Wake Co. death cert. no. 567, which notes 12/17/1919 as the killer's date of birth.

Walter Caldwell (black, age 36). *Rape.* The crime was committed on 7/31/1937 in Iredell County. Executed on his 37th birthday for an indecent assault on the person of 28-year-old Macie Smith (white) who was attacked in her home while minding her two small children. The rapist was put to death on December 10, 1937. Source: *The Landmark* (Statesville, NC), 8/5/37 (1:5). See also: 1937 Wake Co. death cert. no. 801.

William Clifton Perry (black, age 17). *Murder.* The crime was committed on 6/16/1937 in Chatham County. Handgun slaying of 46-year-old Margaret Petty Hammett (white), who was shot three times in her own home. Motive: sexual assault. The killer was executed on December 10, 1937. Source: *Gastonia Daily Gazette*, 6/17/37 (5:4), 6/18/37 (1:5) & 12/10/37 (1:6). See also: 1937 Durham Co. death cert. no. 74, which notes Miss Hamlett [*sic*], and 1937 Wake Co. death cert. no. 802, which notes 1/28/1920 as Perry's date of birth.

1938

James Sermons (black, age 28). *Murder.* The crime was committed on 10/25/1936 in Forsyth County. Handgun slaying of 30-year-old Carlyle Jesse Miller (white). Motive: attempted sexual assault of the victim's female companion. Sermons also confessed to seven other felonies consisting of armed robbery, burglary, carjacking and attempted rape. He was executed on January 21, 1938. Sources: *Greensboro (NC) Record*, 8/6/37 (7:6) & 9/15/37 (10:7); *The Robesonian* (Lumberton, NC), 1/28/38 (1:5). See also: 1936 Forsyth Co. death cert. no. 303, and 1938 Wake Co. death cert. no. 41.

James Marshall (black, age 30). *Aggravated Burglary.* The crime was committed on 8/30/1937 in Wayne County. Executed for breaking into the residence of 40-year-old Robert Smith (white) as the culmination of a week-long crime spree in which several other persons were abducted and robbed. Marshall was executed on February 4, 1938. Sources: *The Landmark* (Statesville, NC), 9/9/37 (8:7); *Greensboro (NC) Record*, 12/7/37 (12:4). See also: 1938 Wake Co. death cert. no. 87.

Milford Harris Exum (white, age 39). *Murder.* The crime was committed on 4/7/1937 in Wayne County. Executed pursuant to the verdict of an all-white jury for the murder of 60-year-old Jim Williams (black), a basket weaver who lived a hermit-like existence. Motive: robbery and home invasion. Several thugs forced their way into the Williams cabin, beat up its lone occupant and made off with his little strongbox containing four dollars. Then one of the culprits (identified as Exum) shot Williams dead, apparently with a handgun. The body was weighted with irons and dumped into a nearby river where it was found 12 days later. Exum was put to death on February 18, 1938. Sources: *The Landmark* (Statesville, NC), 4/26/37 (7:2); *Gastonia Daily Gazette*, 8/27/37 (1:6). See also: 1938 Wake Co. death cert. no. 75.

Edgar Leroy Smoak (white, age 38). *Murder.* The crime was committed on 12/1/1936 in New Hanover County. Filicide. Executed for the fatal and deliberate poisoning of 15-year-old Annie Thelma Smoak (white), his daughter. Motive: insurance fraud. Prime suspect in the untimely deaths of his two wives: Georgia Mae Jones Smoak (white, age 25), who died on 2/10/1922 purportedly of "epileptic convulsions"; and Alice Mason Smoak (white, age 32), who died on 7/8/1935 purportedly of "chronic myocarditis" while pregnant. This stone-cold killer was executed on February 18, 1938. Source: *Daily Times News* (Burlington, NC), 12/17/36 (1:4). See also: New Hanover Co. death cert. nos. 28 (1922), 326 (1935) and 279 (1936). and 1938 Wake Co. death cert. no. 113; *Real Detective,* 9/38; *Master Detective,* 9/46; *Front Page Detective,* 8/37.

Waddell Hadley (black, age 21). *Rape.* The crime was committed on 8/15/1937 in Sampson County. Indecent assault on the person of 53-year-old Mittie Sessoms (white), a maiden woman. The rapist was executed on April 29, 1938. Source: *The Robesonian* (Lumberton, NC), 4/20/38 (2:2). See also: 1957 Sampson Co. death cert. no. 10733, which notes the victim, and 1938 Wake Co. death cert. no. 281, which notes the culprit.

Sylvester Outlaw (black, age 34). *Rape.* The crime was committed on 8/18/1937 in Duplin County. Indecent assault on the person of 18-year-old Clara Coe (white), she and her 22-year-old male companion having been accosted at gunpoint as they sat in a parked automobile. The female victim was abused by three assailants in all. Sylvester Outlaw was executed for his part in this crime on April 29, 1938. Source: *Gastonia Daily Gazette,* 8/20/37 (3:5). See also: 1938 Wake Co. death cert. no. 271.

Empie Baldwin (black, age 23). *Rape.* The crime was committed on 1/16/1938 in Columbus County. Indecent assault on the person of 29-year-old Kathleen Polley (white), she having been forcibly abducted for that purpose. The rapist was executed on June 10, 1938. Source: *The Robesonian* (Lumberton, NC), 6/10/38 (1:3). See also: Columbus County Marriage Register (entry dated 12/19/51), which notes the victim, and 1938 Wake Co. death cert. no. 400, which notes the culprit.

Lonnie Gardner (black, age 26) **and Apsom Outlaw** (black, age 28). *Rape.* The crime was committed on 8/18/1937 in Duplin County. Accomplices and participants in the gang rape of 18-year-old Clara Coe (white), who was accosted at gunpoint along with her 22-year-old male companion as they sat in a parked automobile. Both of these additional culprits were executed on June 17, 1938. Source: *Gastonia Daily Gazette,* 6/17/38 (1:1). See also: OUTLAW, Sylvester (executed 4/29/38).

Wiley Brice (black, age 25). *Murder.* The crime was committed on 4/17/1926 in Alamance County. Handgun slaying of 37-year-old Shellie Lee (black male). Motive: robbery. The killer was executed on July 1, 1938. Source: *Greensboro (NC) Record,* 12/4/37 (3:3) & 7/1/38 (1:8). See also: 1926 Durham Co. death cert. no. 120, and 1938 Wake Co. death cert. no. 448. Appeal: 214 NC 34–35.

William Payne (white, age 40) **and John Washington Turner** (white, age 36). *Murder.* The crime was committed on 8/22/1937 in Buncombe County Cop killers. Executed for the murder of 23-

year-old George Cabell Penn (white), who was shot three times with a high-powered rifle and then deliberately run over by an automobile. Motive: resisting arrest. The killers were executed on July 1, 1938. Sources: *Statesville (NC) Record*, 8/24/37 (1:1); *Daily Times News* (Burlington, NC), 7/1/38 (1:8). See also: 1937 Buncombe Co. death cert. no. 152, and 1938 Wake Co. death cert. nos. 447 & 449.

Thomas J. Jeffries, alias "Tom Jefferson" (black, age 17) **and Tom Linney** (black, age 30). *Murder.* The crime was committed on 4/5/1937 in Forsyth County. Handgun slaying of 25-year-old Herman Walter Fogleman (white, an insurance premium collector), who was going about his daily business. Motive: robbery. The killers were executed on September 23, 1938. Sources: *The Landmark* (Statesville, NC), 5/10/37 (6:4); *The Robesonian* (Lumberton, NC), 9/23/38 (1:8). See also: 1937 Forsyth Co. death cert. no. 271, and 1938 Wake Co. death cert. nos. 594 & 595.

George Ford (black, age 20). *Murder.* The crime was committed on 7/23/1938 in Scotland County. Murder of 44-year-old Eunice R. Munn, a.k.a. "Bill Munn" (white male, a cab driver), who was beaten to death with a piece of timber. Motive: robbery. The killer was executed on September 30, 1938. Source: *The Robesonian* (Lumberton, NC), 7/25/38 (7:5) & 9/30/38 (1:2).

Clyde Bowser, Jr., who was known to some as "Claude Bowser" (black, age 21). *Murder.* The crime was committed on 2/22/1938 in Halifax County. Executed for the murder of 20-year-old Lizzie Bowser (black, kinship uncertain), whose throat was cut "with express malice and fixed purpose to make the deed complete." The killer had forced his middle finger down the victim's throat to more effectively "put his knife under the windpipe and cut it in two." Motive: lovers' quarrel. Bowser was put to death on October 28, 1938. Sources: *Daily Times News* (Burlington, NC), 10/13/38 (1:3); *Gastonia Daily Gazette*, 10/28/38 (2:6). See also: 1938 Halifax Co. death cert. no. 396, and Wake Co. death cert. no. 656.

Ed Robinson (black, age 33). *Rape.* The crime was committed on 5/15/1938 in Iredell County. Indecent assault on the person of 22-year-old Mary Emma Litaker Overcash (white), who was attacked in her home as she lay asleep with her 8-month old baby. She was beaten and then dragged out onto the rear porch of the house, where the culprit forced himself on her. This rapist was executed on November 18, 1938. Sources: *Statesville (NC) Record*, 5/17/38 (1:3); *Daily Times News* (Burlington, NC), 11/18/38 (1:2).

John Ernest Howie (black, age 29). *Rape.* The crime was committed on 11/20/1937 in Forsyth County. Executed for an indecent assault on the person of a 26-year-old white female (name withheld), who was "forced into an automobile under threat of death" and taken to a "secluded" location for that purpose. An additional death sentence was imposed on Howie for the unrelated rape of a woman of his own ethnicity three weeks earlier. He was put to death on December 2, 1938. Sources: *Statesville (NC) Record*, 1/18/38 (1:3); *The Robesonian* (Lumberton, NC), 12/2/38 (1:5).

William Baxter Parnell (white, age 32). *Murder.* The crime was committed on 7/3/1938 in Cabarrus County. Fatal stabbing of 19-year-old Martha Jane Fink (white, his sister-in-law), who was attacked with an ice pick as she knelt praying. Motive: uncertain. The killer claimed that he had been hexed but later repudiated this. He was executed on December 9, 1938. Sources: *Daily Times News* (Burlington, NC), 7/4/38 (1:3), 8/25/38 (2:7) & 12/9/38 (1:5); *Actual Detective,* 9/39; *Front Page Detective,* 4/39; *Real Detective,* 7/47.

1939

King Solomon Stovall (black, age 23). *Murder.* The crime was committed on 4/16/1938 in Granville County. Executed for the murder of 65-year-old Raleigh T. Moore (white, a storekeeper), who was hit on the head with an unknown blunt object. Motive: robbery. Stovall was gassed on January 20, 1939. Source: *Daily Times News* (Burlington, NC), 1/20/39 (1:7). See also: 1938 Granville Co. death cert. no. 310, as well as 1930 U.S. Census (Granville Co., NC), which notes Mr. Moore.

Batt de Journette (black, age 37). *Murder.* The crime was committed on 4/29/1938 in Guilford County. Executed for the murder of 22-year-old Garland Mangum (white), who was clubbed, shot through the head with a handgun, and then dumped into a river with weights attached to his person. Motive: witness removal. The victim was due to testify against the killer in a hit and run case. The latter died in the gas chamber on April 7, 1939. Source: *Gastonia Daily Gazette*, 5/2/38 (9:3) & 5/28/38 (3:3). See also: 1938 Guilford Co. death cert. no. 325, and 1939 Wake Co. death cert. no. 228. Also: 1930 U.S. Census (Cabarrus Co., NC), which notes Mangum as a reform school inmate.

Clarence Bracy, alias "David Jiggetts" (black, age 32). *Murder.* The crime was committed on 9/2/1938 in Vance County. Ax murder of 65-year-old William Hammit Williamson (white), a farmer. Motive: robbery for the sake of three dollars. News accounts say that the victim had been bludgeoned with a wagon standard, but his death certificate specifies "ax" as the murder weapon. Bracy was executed on April 7, 1939. Source: *The Robesonian* (Lumberton, NC), 4/7/39 (1:7). See also: 1938 Vance Co. death cert. no. 363, and 1939 Wake Co. death cert. no. 229.

James Dixon (black, age 30). *Murder.* The crime was committed on 9/9/1938 in Cabarrus County. Uxoricide. Ax murder of 24-year-old Daisy Garland Dixon (black) and destruction of their home by fire. Motive: marital discord. The couple had been wed only four months ere he was accusing her of infidelity. Dixon was executed on May 5, 1939. Source: *Daily Times News* (Burlington, NC), 5/5/39 (1:2). Appeal: 215 NC 438–442. See also: 1938 Cabarrus Co. death cert. no. 104, and 1939 Wake Co. death cert. no. 284.

Edward Lee Mattocks (black, age 20). *Murder.* The crime was committed on 11/29/1938 in Onslow County. Ax murder of 65-year-old Zion Franklin Matthews (white), a filling station operator. Motive: robbery. Mattocks was executed on May 26, 1939. Source: *Daily Times News* (Burlington, NC), 12/1/38 (8:8) & 5/26/39 (1:3). See also: 1938 New Hanover Co. death cert. no. 184.

Dave Burney (black, age 47). *Murder.* The crime was committed on 8/25/1938 in Jones County. Shotgun slaying of 40-year-old Maudie Kinsey (black). Motive: because she had stood against him in a quarrel. Burney was executed on June 9, 1939. Source: *The Robesonian* (Lumberton, NC), 6/9/39 (1:6). Appeal: 215 NC 598–614. See also: 1938 Lenoir Co. death cert. no. 247, and 1939 Wake Co. death cert. no. 350.

Ed Alston (black, age 28). *Murder.* The crime was committed on 12/23/1937 in Durham County. Executed for the murder of 102-year-old Janie Wilkerson (black) who was struck on the head with a club. Motive: robbery and home invasion. The brutality of this crime gave pause to even the most ardent opponents of capital punishment. The killer was gassed on June 16, 1939. Source: *Daily Times News* (Burlington, NC), 5/31/39 (1:2) & 6/16/39 (1:5). See also: 1937 Durham Co. death cert. no. 205, and 1939 Wake Co. death cert. no. 362.

James Henderson (black, age 19). *Murder.* The crime was committed on 11/6/1938 in New Hanover County. Executed on July 7, 1939, for the murder of 42-year-old Stella Cauble Hobbs (white), a widow. Motive: sexual assault. The victim had accidentally run her car off a road during the nighttime. The vehicle was wrecked. Henderson came upon the scene. He did not help the injured woman. He instead pulled her from the wreckage irrespective of her injuries and raped her. Then he beat her to death with a lug wrench. The price he paid was death by cyanide gas. Source: *Daily Times News* (Burlington, NC), 11/9/38 (9:2), 11/16/38 (1:7) & 11/17/38 (1:4). See also: 1938 New Hanover Co. death cert. no. 304, and 1939 Wake Co. death cert. no. 412.

Alfred Capers (black, age 23). *Murder.* The crime was committed on 11/23/1938 in Robeson County. Sniper killing of 27-year-old John C. McNeill (black), who was hit by a rifle shot in the back as he walked on the porch of his house. Motive: presumably a personal vendetta. Capers himself would say nothing about it. He was executed on July 7, 1939. Source: *The Robesonian* (Lumberton, NC), 1/9/39 (1:1), 2/10/39 (1:2) & 7/7/39 (1:8). See also: North Carolina Death Index (Robeson Co.), 11/23/38 at date.

Bricey Hammonds (Native American, age 24). *Murder.* The crime was committed on 2/5/1939 in Robeson County. Prison guard killer. Executed for the handgun slaying of 36-year-old Lacy Brumbles (white), who was shot through the back of the head with his own pistol as he knelt to change a flat tire. Motive: obscure. The killer had only one hand and one leg. He had been released from the Robeson County chain gang that same day, having served four months for making illicit liquor. It is not known in exactly what capacity he met the terms of his incarceration in light of his physical limitations. Whatever the case, Hammonds became chummy enough with "Boss Brumbles" so that the latter agreed to drive him home in his personal automobile on the day of his release. Hammonds took a bus instead. Brumbles then did a highly irregular thing: he drove his car to the ex-convict's home and picked him up there along with that man's father. This made it apparent that Brumbles and Hammonds had made some kind of arrangement with each other even before the latter's release from the work camp.

They took the elder Hammonds to an appointment in a nearby town. Then Brumbles and Bricey Hammonds went to the home of a certain Native American woman (named Lizzie Lowry), purportedly to buy liquor. Whatever the truth, both men were en route back to the Hammonds home (having picked up Papa Hammonds on the return trip) when the car in which they were traveling had a flat tire. The driver (Brumbles) was examining the tire when Bricey Hammonds suddenly came up behind him, snatched his pistol from its holster with his lone hand, and killed Brumbles by firing a shot at him execution style. Bricey Hammonds was executed for this crime on July 7, 1939. Source: *The Robesonian* (Lumberton, NC), 2/6/39 (1:1), 2/10/39 (1:8) & 7/7/39 (1:8).

Arthur Morris, alias "The Gray Mouse," alias "The Eel" (black, age 23). *Aggravated Burglary.* The crime was committed on 12/29/1937 in Wake County. Serial burglar. Executed for breaking into the home of 40-year-old William Banks DeWar (white, a Raleigh physician) while its occupants were asleep and making off with coins to the value of 20 cents. Clemency was refused because the culprit was an incorrigible criminal with several prior convictions and approximately 50 other residential burglaries to his discredit. He was executed on September 1, 1939. Sources: *Gastonia Daily Gazette*, 4/5/39 (7:5) & 9/1/39 (2:3); *Daily Times News* (Burlington, NC), 6/8/39 (11:5), 8/4/39 (4:1) & 8/31/39 (11:2). See also: 1939 Wake Co. death cert. no. 508.

James Godwin (white, age 20). *Murder.* The crime was committed on 10/3/1938 in Guilford County. Executed for the handgun slaying of 30-year-old Donald James Moss (white), a respectable working man who was in the wrong place at the wrong time. Motive: panic. A bad one by any description, Godwin started on his final path to ruin on 7/29/1938 when he and another delinquent broke into his grandfather's house. The old man was mercilessly beaten. Godwin took off to South Carolina with grandpa's cash and a girl purported to be his wife. Arrested there, he was returned to Davidson Co., North Carolina, and charged with aggravated burglary—a capital offense. It was while in the Davidson County jail that Godwin made the acquaintance of the jailer's daughter, a shockingly stupid 22-year-old named Lula Belle Kimel. She gravitated to the good-looking young prisoner and was soon keeping him supplied with such jailhouse luxuries as candy, coffee and cigarettes. Godwin perceived Miss Kimel's vulnerability and resolved to manipulate her for everything he could. So he regaled Lula Belle with a masterful acting performance, saying that he "had found religion" and repented all his sins. He would thenceforth be a better person, a paragon of Christian virtue. The deluded female later claimed that she had taken Godwin at his word. How could she suffer a redeemed sinner (who was also a rakishly handsome one) to face the possibility of a death sentence for aggravated burglary? It was—after all—the devil who had led Jimmy Godwin astray and not poor Jimmy himself. So Lula Belle Kimel arranged for this hustler to escape from the Davidson County jail by giving him the key to his cell. He and his cellmate absconded at once. They carjacked a taxi and forced its driver to take them to a point near the home of Godwin's parents. Once there, they bound the cabbie to a tree with duct tape and stole his money, but left him otherwise unharmed. Next, Godwin and his crony took clothing and a loaded handgun from his parents' home. They fled in the stolen taxi, robbing pedestrians and roadside vendors along the way. Eventually they came to a Guilford County gas station and paused to refuel their vehicle. The attendant there was in the act of pumping gas for them when another car pulled into the station. This was driven by Donald James Moss, a textile man then on his way home from work. Moss got out of his car. In doing so he spooked the nervous-fingered Godwin, who shot him twice in the chest. The killer then jumped back into the stolen taxi and ordered his accomplice (who was driving) to get out of there pronto. The taxi spun rubber in doing so. The attendant was left standing there with the gasoline nozzle in one hand and the taxi's gas cap in the other. The culprits were caught a short time later. James Godwin was executed on September 22, 1939. Source: *Daily Times News* (Burlington, NC), 10/4/38 (1:1), 10/5/38 (1:2) & 10/7/38 (1:2). See also: 1938 Guilford Co. death cert. no. 306, and 1939 Wake Co. death cert. no. 546; *Actual Detective,* 1/39; *Front Page Detective,* 5/43.

Charles Fain (black, age 26). *Rape.* The crime was committed on 1/29/1939 in Cherokee County. Fain was a former hospital employee at Murphy. He broke into that place shortly before dawn on the above date, masked and armed with a knife. His knowledge of the building facilitated his actions. Fain terrorized the maternity ward. He found two women in one of the rooms there (both white females), a nurse and a patient who had given birth some hours earlier. Fain tied up the nurse (name withheld) with medical tape and raped her. Then he turned to the newly delivered mother (name withheld), who lay helpless in her hospital bed and threatened her with death if she did not give up her valuables. Fain took the rings from her fingers. He fled the scene with the lady's pocketbook as well. It contained $90. Fain was caught less than a week later, having squandered all but 30 cents of what he had stolen. He was gassed on October 6, 1939. Source: *Daily Times News* (Burlington, NC), 2/4/39 (1:2), 4/6/39 (16:8), 8/30/39 (1:7) & 10/6/39 (1:4).

Willie Richardson (black, age 19). *Aggravated Burglary.* The crime was committed on 2/10/1939 in Nash County. Executed for a violent break-in at the house of 33-year-old Frank Edwards Butler (white), during which that man's wife, Mrs. Alice Lindsey Butler (white, age 28), was severely beaten and dragged outdoors. The culprit fled from the scene with an empty pocketbook and a pack of cigarettes. He was gassed on October 27, 1939. Sources: *Daily Times News* (Burlington, NC), 2/11/39 (5:1); *Gastonia Daily Gazette,* 10/12/39 (4:3) & 10/27/39 (9:1). See also: 1940 draft registration card no. 382 (Nash Co., NC), and North Carolina Death Register (NC State Archives), entry dated 2/11/1977, which note Mr. and Mrs. Butler; 1939 Wake Co. death cert. no. 641.

Raymond Williams (black, age 19). *Murder.* The crime was committed on 11/24/1938 in Sampson County. Ax murder of 53-year-old Nathan Reif (white, a traveling salesman), who was lured to his doom on the pretense of sampling his wares. Motive: robbery. The killer was executed on November 24, 1939. Source: *Gastonia Daily Gazette,* 11/25/38 (7:3). See also: 1939 Wake Co. death cert. no. 709.

1940

Glenn Maxwell (black, age 48). *Murder.* The crime was committed on 4/14/1938 in Alleghany County. Shotgun slaying of 37-year-old Charlie Burgess Shepherd (white). Motive: the victim had ejected the killer's son from his place of business. Maxwell wound up in the gas chamber on January 19, 1940. Sources: *Greensboro (NC) Record*, 4/19/38 (9:1); *Daily Times News* (Burlington, NC), 1/19/40 (2:2). See also: 1938 Alleghany Co. death cert. no. 57, and 1940 Wake Co. death cert. no. 46.

Clarence Rogers (black, age 26). *Murder.* The crime was committed on 11/17/1938 in Durham County. Murder of 17-year-old Howard Moore (white, a newsboy), who was found among roadside bushes with his throat cut and his head caved in. Motive: presumed robbery of his newspaper receipts. The killer was gassed on January 19, 1940. Sources: *Gastonia Daily Gazette*, 11/21/38 (11:3); *Daily Times News* (Burlington, NC), 2/11/39 (1:5) & 1/19/40 (1:2). See also: 1938 Durham Co. death cert. no. 94, and 1940 Wake Co. death cert. no. 37.

Nathaniel Bryant (black, age 17) **and William Young** (black, age 22). *Murder.* The crime was committed on 3/23/1939 in Hoke County. Rifle slaying of 33-year-old Thomas R. Moore (white), the victim having been murdered in his bed. Motive: burglary. The killers were executed on February 16, 1940. Source: *Gastonia Daily Gazette*, 2/16/40 (1:5). See also: 1939 Hoke Co. death cert. no. 109, and 1940 Wake Co. death cert. nos. 111 & 112, which respectively note the culprits' dates of birth as 9/23/21 and 8/21/16.

Robert Williams, alias "McNair" (black, age 17). *Rape.* The crime was committed on 7/19/1938 in Cumberland county. Indecent assault on the person of 53-year-old Lela Bullard (white), who was attacked in the backyard of her home while gathering wood chips. The culprit had previously done odd jobs for her husband, a merchant of that locale. The rapist was executed on March 15, 1940. Source: *The Robesonian* (Lumberton, NC), 7/22/38 (1:3) & 3/15/40 (1:6). See also: 1930 U.S. Census (Cumberland Co., NC), which notes Mrs. Bullard; 1940 Wake Co. death cert. no. 188, which notes that Williams had been born on 12/17/1920.

Zebulon Page (black, age 28). *Rape.* The crime was committed on 10/29/1939 in Johnston County. Indecent assault on the person of about 40-year-old Elizabeth Phillingame Stancil (white, a widow), who was attacked in her own home at between 3 and 4 o'clock in the morning. Her three young children were terrorized in the same incident. The rapist was executed on April 5, 1940. Sources: *The Landmark* (Statesville, NC), 11/2/39 (4:1); *Gastonia Daily Gazette*, 4/5/40 (2:4). See also: Johnston County Marriages Female Index, which notes the nuptials of Elizabeth "Philligan" and Dewey Fletcher Stancil on 1/24/1928. He was murdered on 12/7/1935 per his death certificate. See also: 1928 Johnston County Birth Index, which notes the arrival of the couple's first child on July 18 of that year and "Filigan" as the maiden name of its mother. One wonders if even she knew the correct spelling of her name.

Simon Gibson, alias "Coochie Gibson" (black, age 22). *Rape.* The crime was committed on 7/23/1939 in New Hanover County. Indecent assault on the person of 49-year-old Gladys Barnes (white), she having been attacked in her own home. The rapist was executed on May 24, 1940. Sources: *Wilmington (NC) Morning Star*, 8/25/39 (1:1) & 5/25/40 (3:4); New Hanover County Superior Court Minutes (Sept. Term, 1939), pg. 50. See also: 1940 Wake Co. death cert. no. 316; 1940 U.S. Census (Wilmington, NC), which notes the female party.

Charlie Hopkins (black, age 62). *Murder.* The crime was committed on 10/7/1939 in Rutherford County. Cop killer. Shotgun slaying of 29-year-old Roy Eugene Watkins (white). Motive: resisting arrest. Hopkins was executed on June 14, 1940. Source: *Daily Times News* (Burlington, NC), 6/14/40 (11:2). See also: 1939 Rutherford Co. death cert. no. 61.

Lee Flynn (white, age 43). *Murder.* The crime was committed on 10/9/1939 in McDowell County. Uxoricide. Handgun slaying of 37-year-old Mae Davis Flynn (white). Motive: heated argument. He is reported to have dragged the woman out of their house to a point in the yard thereof, where he ordered their 7-year-old-child to kiss its mother good-bye before shooting her. Flynn was executed on June 28, 1940. Source: *Gastonia Daily Gazette*, 6/28/40 (2:4). See also: 1939 McDowell Co. death cert. no. 182, and 1940 Wake Co. death cert. no. 398.

Zedekiel Smith (black, age 29). *Murder.* The crime was committed on 10/29/1939 in Sampson County. Murder of 62-year-old William R. Daniel (white, a reclusive farmer), who was bludgeoned with "a deadly weapon" because the killer thought that he had a miser's hoard hidden in his house. Motive: home invasion. The killer was executed on December 6, 1940. Source: *The Robesonian* (Lumberton, NC), 12/6/40 (2:5). See also: 1939 Sampson Co. death cert. no. 108, and 1940 Wake Co. death cert. no. 714.

1941

Dollie Lee Hudson (black, age 25). *Murder.* The crime was committed on 11/15/1939 in Northampton County. Rifle slaying of 50-year-old Hampton Wilfred Elliott (white), who was battered about the head and face with the butt of that weapon before being finished off by a shot through the neck. Motive: tenant-landlord dispute. Hudson was executed on April 18, 1941. Source: *Daily Times News* (Burlington, NC), 4/17/41 (2:4) & 4/18/41 (2:1). See also: 1939 Northampton Co. death cert. no. 351, and 1941 Wake Co. death cert. no. 255.

Sylvester Woodward (black, age 33). *Murder.* The crime was committed on 5/24/1940 in Wayne County. Handgun slaying of 24-year-old Lillie O. Townsend (black). Motive: because she had sought to end their romantic entanglement. Woodward was executed on May 2, 1941. Source: *The Landmark* (Statesville, NC), 12/12/40 (8:3). See also: 1940 Wayne Co. death cert. no. 344, and 1941 Wake Co. death cert. no. 281.

Jesse James Shaw (black, age 21). *Murder.* The crime was committed on 1/21/1941 in Columbus County. Shotgun slaying of 28-year-old James Oliver Freeman (black). Motive: brawling. The killer claimed self-defense on the grounds that the victim had come at him with a knife. He admitted that this was a lie moments before entering the gas chamber on May 23, 1941. Sources: *Daily Times News* (Burlington, NC), 1/31/41 (3:3); *The Robesonian* (Lumberton, NC), 5/22/41 (2:5); *Gastonia Daily Gazette*, 5/23/41 (5:4). See also: 1941 Columbus Co. death cert. no. 180.

Jack Fleet Wall (black, age 33). *Murder.* The crime was committed on 3/9/1940 in Anson County. Uxoricide. Fatal beating of 27-year-old Laura Mae Ingram Wall (black), she having been battered with a splintered railroad tie. Motive: drunkenness and suspected infidelity. The killer was executed on June 6, 1941. Source: *Daily Times News* (Burlington, NC), 6/6/41 (1:5). See also: 1940 Anson Co. death cert. no. 34, and 1941 Wake Co. death cert. no. 352.

Noah Cureton (black, age 59). *Murder.* The crime was committed on 6/23/1940 in Mecklenburg County. Handgun slaying of 30-year-old John William Henniken, alias "Johnnie Williams" (black). Motive: gambling dispute. Cureton was executed on June 13, 1941. Source: *The Robesonian* (Lumberton, NC), 6/16/41 (6:5). Appeal: 218 NC 491–496. See also: 1940 Mecklenburg Co. death cert. no. 585, and 1941 Wake Co. death cert. no. 358.

Hubert Y. Cash (white, age 40). *Murder.* The crime was committed on 9/17/1940 in Durham County. Uxoricide. Handgun slaying of 30-year-old Mary Ruth Copley Cash (white), she having been shot three times as she ran down a street in fear for her life. Motive: obnoxious drunk. The killer was executed on August 22, 1941. Source: *Daily Times News* (Burlington, NC), 8/22/41 (1:1). See also: 1940 Durham Co. death cert. no. 87, and 1941 Wake Co. death cert. no. 498.

Tom Melvin (black, age 40). *Murder.* The crime was committed on 12/31/1939 in Wayne County. Hatchet killing of 42-year-old Gilbert Irby Holmes (white). Motive: murder-for-hire at the behest of the victim's wife. She received a sentence of life imprisonment. Melvin the hatchet man was executed on September 5, 1941. Source: *The Landmark* (Statesville, NC), 1/27/41 (7:6). See also: 1939 Wayne Co. death cert. no. 388, and 1941 Wake Co. death cert. no. 526; *Actual Detective*, 4/41; *TRUE* (magazine), 6/41.

George Peele (black, age 20). *Murder.* The crime was committed on 1/31/1941 in Bertie County. Executed for the murder of 77-year-old Edward Watson Gray (white), the victim having been battered to death with the butt of a rifle. Motive: thief caught in the act. The killer was gassed on October 10, 1941. Source: *Daily Times News* (Burlington, NC), 2/18/41 (9:1) & 10/10/41 (16:2). See also: 1941 Bertie Co. death cert. no. 106.

Luther Morrow (black, age 25). *Murder.* The crime was committed on 8/3/1941 in Union County. Uxoricide. Shotgun slaying of 27-year-old Lottie Belle Morrow, alias "Sassafras" (black). Motive: because she had dared to have him arrested on a charge of spousal abuse. The killer was executed on December 12, 1941. Sources: *Charlotte Observer*, 8/4/41 (Sec. 2)(7:4); *High Point (NC) Enterprise*, 12/13/41 (2:4). See also: 1941 Union Co. death cert. no. 210.

1942

Roland Paul Wescott (white, age 20). *Murder.* The crime was committed on 4/12/1941 in New Hanover County. Executed for the murder of 17-year-old Mildred Frances Lee (white, his fiancé), she having been attacked with a club and finished off with a handgun. Motive: "a fit of jealousy." Wescott paid with his life for this on January 9, 1942. Sources: *Greensboro (NC) Record*, 1/9/42 (1:5); *Daily Times News* (Burlington, NC), 1/9/42 (1:2). See also: 1941 New Hanover Co. death cert. no. 371.

Robert Sturdivant (black, age 28). *Murder.* The crime was committed on 2/25/1941 in Bladen County. Uxoricide. Ax murder of 26-year-old Ollie Mae Sturdivant (black). Motive: suspicion of infidelity. The killer was gassed on February 13, 1942. Sources: *High Point (NC) Enterprise*, 2/13/42 (1:5); *The Robesonian* (Lumberton, NC), 2/27/41 (1:6) & 2/16/42 (6:3).

Arthur Gibson (black, age 31). *Rape.* The crime was committed on 1/4/1942 in Buncombe County. Indecent assault on the person of 6-year-old Jean Ann Robinson (black), the details being too obscene for publication. This pervert was put to death on August 7, 1942. Source: Buncombe County Superior Court Minutes (January Term, 1942), pg. 412. See also: 1942 Wake Co. death cert. no. 632.

Walter Smith (white, age 63). *Murder.* The crime was committed on 11/24/1941 in Wayne County. Shotgun slaying of 47-year-old Alfonso P. Price (white). Motive: disgruntled employee. Smith worked on the farm of a North Carolina state senator. Price was the overseer there. The killer was executed on August 21, 1942. Source: *High Point (NC) Enterprise*, 11/25/41 (9:1). See also: 1941 Wayne Co. death cert. no. 332, and 1942 Wake Co. death cert. no. 640.

Herman Allen (white, age 33). *Murder.* The crime was committed on 1/15/1942 in Johnston County. Uxoricide, etc. Executed for the shotgun slayings of 26-year-old Ruth Mae Lee Allen, 28-year-old Grady Lee and 35-year-old William "Cap" Raynor (whites), they respectively being his wife, his brother-in-law and his imaginary rival in love. Motive: obsessive male jealousy. Recidivist killer. On 8/5/1930 this same Herman Allen murdered a boarder in his home named Handy Minson Hodges (white, age 50) with a shotgun because he suspected him of undue intimacy with his first wife. The killer claimed that he had caught the pair actually in bed together, but this was (in light of subsequent events) likely a ploy to justify himself based on "the unwritten law." A trial jury convicted Allen of manslaughter and he was sentenced to 20 years' imprisonment. Paroled after only eight years, Allen returned to Johnston County and (bad reputation notwithstanding) became affianced to the widow Ruth Mae Lee Massengill, whose husband had committed suicide in 1935. The couple wed, and ever-manic Herman Allen promptly convinced himself that every man in the county was angling to bed down with his wife. The situation re-exploded on the above date. Allen armed himself with a shotgun. He went to the home of "Cap" Raynor at 3 o'clock in the morning and pounded on the door. One blast killed Raynor instantly as he opened his door. Allen then stomped back to his own home, where he found his wife and brother-in-law together. Both were shot dead. Allen once again pled extenuating circumstances based on purported adultery—this time between his second wife and Raynor. The brother-in-law also had to die, said Allen, because he was a lazy freeloader who had opposed his sister's marriage from the start. Allen's injured cuckold story didn't save him this time. He was gassed on October 30, 1942. Source: *The Landmark* (Statesville, NC), 8/11/30 (3:3). See also: 1930 U.S. Census (Johnston Co., NC), which notes Hodges; 1935 Johnston Co. death cert. no. 201, plus 1942 Johnston Co. death cert. nos. 82, 84 & 112; *Intimate Detective*, 5/42; *Master Detective*, 6/43, 6/55 & 1/58; *Crime Detective*, 7/42 & 2/49; *Dynamic Detective*, 6/42; *Official Detective*, 9/72 & 1/84; *Real Detective*, 3/72 & 9/77; *TRUE* (magazine) 6/42.

Otis Harris (black, age 16). *Rape.* The crime was committed on 4/7/1942 in Bertie County. Indecent assault on the person of 26-year-old Arlene Warren (white), she having been severely beaten and left to crawl 700 yards across a tobacco field (with a fractured skull) in search of help. The rapist was put to death on October 30, 1942. Sources: *Gastonia Daily Gazette*, 4/8/42 (6:6); *The Robesonian* (Lumberton, NC), 5/11/42 (10:8). See also: 1942 Wake Co. death cert. no. 770 noting 8/24/1925 as Harris's birth date.

William Lang (black, age 31). *Murder.* The crime was committed on 8/8/1942 in Pitt County. Uxoricide, etc. Shotgun slayings of 25-year-old Nannie Pearl Lang and 44-year-old Nannie Powell (blacks), they being his wife and her aunt. Motive: irate cuckold. Lang was executed on November 13, 1942. Source: *Daily Times News* (Burlington, NC), 11/11/42 (10:8) & 11/13/42 (10:8). See also: 1942 Pitt Co. death cert. nos. 259 & 267.

1943

Daniel Phillips (black, age 29) **and Rosanna Lightner Phillips** (black female, age 25). *Murder.* The crime was committed on 8/3/1942 in Durham County. Ax murder of 64-year-old Harry F. Watkins (white), who was struck down from behind and nearly decapitated "in his own yard not far from the bedside of his invalid and helpless wife." The killers eloped with Watkins's money and used part of it to get married two days later. The mutilated remains of the victim were carted 25 miles to another farm that he owned (in Orange Co.) and there thrown into an abandoned well where they lay for 47 days. Motive: robbery and gross perfidy. Both of the culprits were gassed on January 1, 1943. Sources: *The Robesonian* (Lumberton, NC), 9/28/42 (6:5); *Daily Times News* (Burlington, NC), 1/1/43 (1:2).

Sam Hairston (black, age 21). *Rape.* The crime was committed on 11/30/1941 in Forsyth County. Indecent assault on the person of a 52-year-old semi-invalid white female (name withheld), she having been attacked by a burglar as she lay asleep in her bed and struck on the head with a hammer. The rapist was executed on January 29, 1943. Source: *Greensboro (NC) Daily News*, 12/2/41 (2:2). Appeal: 222 NC 454–463. See also: 1943 Wake Co. death cert. no. 56.

Palmer Mears (white, age 34). *Murder.* The crime was committed on 5/20/1942 in Robeson County. Shotgun slaying of 63-year-old George E. Allen (white), the victim having been struck with five loads of buckshot. Motive: because Mears thought that Allen had reported him to the authorities for operating an illegal still. The killer was executed on February 19, 1943. Source: *The Robesonian* (Lumberton, NC), 6/9/42 (1:4). See also: 1942 Robeson Co. death cert. no. 338, and 1943 Wake Co. death cert. no. 116.

John Henry Lee (black, age 19). *Rape.* The crime was committed on 9/26/1942 in Camden County. Indecent assault on the person of 20-year-old Doris Turner McPherson (white), who was attacked in her home and choked into insensibility. The culprit had watched until her husband left for work that day. This rapist was executed on April 16, 1943. Source: *Greensboro (NC) Record*, 4/16/43 (8:3). Also: 1943 Wake Co. death cert. no. 220; Camden Co. World War II draft registration card no. 122.

Lewis Moody (black, age 28). *Murder.* The crime was committed on 6/7/1942 in Northampton County. Fatal stabbing of 30-year-old John Arthur Kee (black), the victim having been jumped on a country road, "cut 23 times" by being hit on the head with a hoe and his body left under a pile of burning pine needles. Motive: indiscernible. The killer was executed on May 21, 1943. Source: *Roanoke News* (Weldon, NC), 6/11/42 (1:1). See also: 1942 Northampton Co. death cert. no. 244, and 1943 Wake Co. death cert. no. 312.

Bill Bryant (white, age 39). *Murder.* The crime was committed on 8/23/1942 in McDowell County. Murder of 75-year-old Joseph Reid McNeeley (white), who was bludgeoned with a brick. Motive: tenant-landlord dispute. Bryant was executed on June 4, 1943. Source: *The Robesonian* (Lumberton, NC), 6/4/43 (1:6). See also: 1942 McDowell Co. death cert. no. 175, and 1943 Wake Co. death cert. no. 346; *Official Detective,* 8/45; *Real Detective,* 3/43.

Harvey Hunt (Native American, age 21) **and Purcell Smith** (Native American, age 22). *Rape.* The crime was committed on 10/27/1942 in Robeson County. Indecent assault on the person of 27-year-old Eldora Hinson Eason (white), who was abducted at gunpoint and driven in a stolen car to a remote site where the "gross looking" culprits took turns forcing themselves on her. The victim's younger sister (age 19) was also pulled into the same vehicle with the same intent, but managed to break free. The perpetrators were also guilty of slander and perjury, having insisted that the sex act was consensual despite positive proof to the contrary. Both of them were gassed on June 4, 1943. Source: *The Robesonian* (Lumberton, NC), 11/16/42 (1:1), 12/1/42 (6:1) & 6/4/43 (1:6).

James Utley (black, age 24). *Murder.* The crime was committed on 7/24/1942 in Montgomery County. Uxoricide, etc. Executed for the butcher knife killings of 24-year-old Carrie Lee Collins Utley and 22-year-old J.T. Collins (full name not recorded in any known record) (blacks), they being his wife and brother-in-law. Motive: estranged husband gone berserk. Utley was executed on June 18, 1943. Source: *Daily Times News* (Burlington, NC), 4/16/43 (8:5). See also: 1930 U.S. Census (Hoke Co., NC), which notes the victims; 1942 Montgomery Co. death cert. no. 135, and 1943 Wake Co. death cert. no. 368.

William Henry Poole (black, age 29). *Murder.* The crime was committed on 1/1/1943 in Pasquotank County. Shotgun slaying of 19-year-old Andrew Jackson Sawyer (white). Motive: street brawl with a group of young sailors. Poole was executed on October 8, 1943. Source: *Daily Times News* (Burlington, NC), 10/8/43 (6:3). See also: 1943 Pasquotank Co. death cert. no. 360 and Wake Co. death cert. no. 624.

Willie Smith (black, age 37). *Murder.* The crime was committed on 12/31/1942 in Warren County. Ax murder of 50-year-old Spencer Vernon Powell (white, a storekeeper), who had previously paid the killer to do odd jobs around his place of business. Motive: robbery and gross perfidy. Smith was put to death on October 29, 1943. Source: *The Robesonian* (Lumberton, NC), 11/1/43 (6:6). See also: 1942 Warren Co. death cert. no . 281, and 1943 Wake Co. death cert. no. 665.

John Willie Redfern (black, age 39). *Murder.* The crime was committed on 5/14/1943 in Wake County. Shotgun slaying of 28-year-old Zedrick Sturdivant (black). Motive: tavern brawl. Redfern was executed on November 26, 1943. Sources: *Daily Times News* (Burlington, NC), 11/25/43 (2:8); *Statesville (NC) Daily Record*, 11/26/43 (1:5). See also: 1943 Wake Co. death cert. nos. 227 & 698.

Clyde Grass (white, age 30). *Murder.* The crime was committed on 10/1/1942 in Cabarrus County. Shotgun slayings of 52-year-old William Alexander Godwin and 18-year-old Annie Lee Godwin Stafford (whites, his father-in-law and sister-in-law), the latter being murdered in her bed. Motive: family problems. The killer was executed on December 10, 1943. Source: *Statesville (NC) Landmark*, 10/5/42 (7:6). See also: 1942 Cabarrus Co. death cert. nos. 383 & 384, and 1943 Wake Co. death cert. no. 736.

1944

Alex Harris, alias "W.A. Harris," alias "Alec Harris" (white, age 47). *Murder.* The crime was committed on 8/27/1942 in Hoke County. Handgun slayings of 52-year-old Nellie Thrower Bill, 35-year-old Estelle Bill Wilson, and 24-year-old Eugene Bill (whites, a mother and her two grown children). Motive: revenge. The killer's son (John H. Harris, age 22) had been fatally shot by Eugene Bill four days earlier in an altercation at the latter's place of business, a combination country store and gas station. The trouble stemmed from Bill's refusal to sell beer to young Harris on a Sunday. Harris became irate and was shot when he tried to take the beer by force. His father (Alex Harris) waited till "Johnny" had been laid to rest in Raiford Cemetery. Then he went to the family-owned site of his son's demise and slaughtered everybody he found there. Alex Harris was executed on January 28, 1944. Source: *The Robesonian* (Lumberton, NC), 8/28/42 (1:2). See also: 1930 U.S. Census (Surry Co., NC), which notes the Harris family; 1942 Cumberland Co. death cert. no. 210, which notes the younger Harris; 1942 Hoke Co. death cert. nos. 129, 130 & 131, which note the Bills; and 1944 Wake Co. death cert. no. 92, which notes "Alec Harris."

Andrew Wilson Farrell (white, age 24). *Rape.* The crime was committed on 3/23/1943 in Durham County. Indecent assault on the person of an 8-year-old white female (his stepdaughter, name withheld), she having been lured from school on the pretense of visiting her mother and then forced to drink whiskey. This child rapist was executed on February 18, 1944. Source: *The Robesonian* (Lumberton, NC), 2/21/44 (6:7). Appeal: 223 NC 321–331. See also: 1944 Wake Co. death cert. no. 159.

Wayman Grainger (black, age 31). *Murder.* The crime was committed on

1/13/1943 in Columbus County. Handgun slaying of 26-year-old Harry Vance Fipps (white). Motive: random violence. The victim was walking along with two family members at the time when he was shot for no apparent reason. The killer was executed on February 25, 1944. Source: *The Robesonian* (Lumberton, NC), 1/14/43 (6:7) & 2/28/44 (4:4). See also: 1943 Columbus Co. death cert. no. 125, and 1944 Wake Co. death cert. no. 165.

James Taylor (black, age 47). *Murder.* The crime was committed on 5/30/1944 in Wake County. Cop killer. Handgun slaying of 58-year-old John Leco Taylor (white), who was shot twice in the chest. Motive: resisting arrest for the sexual molestation of a young black girl. James Taylor was executed on November 3, 1944. Source: *Gastonia Daily Gazette*, 11/3/44 (8:7). See also: 1944 Wake Co. death cert. nos. 703 & 13655.

Charles Alexander (black, age 24). *Rape.* The crime was committed on 7/31/1944 in Halifax County. Indecent assault on the person of a 9-year-old black female (name withheld), the details being too obscene for publication. This child rapist was executed on November 17, 1944. Source: *Roanoke (NC) News*, 8/24/44 (1:7) & 11/23/44 (10:4). See also: 1944 Wake Co. death cert. no. 718.

George Walter Brooks (black, age 19) **and James Wallace Buchanan** (black, age 18). *Rape.* The crime was committed on 5/29/1944 in Mecklenburg County. Indecent assault on the person of a 33-year-old white female (name withheld), she having been forcibly dragged from her home and raped in a ditch. The culprits had escaped from a road gang earlier that day. They were gassed on November 24, 1944. Sources: *Statesville (NC) Landmark*, 6/1/44 (3:6); *Daily Times News* (Burlington, NC), 11/24/44 (1:6). Also: 1944 Wake Co. death cert. nos. 754 & 756.

Melvin Wade (black, age 22). *Rape.* The crime was committed on 6/13/1944 in Scotland County. Indecent assault on the person of 9-year-old Annie Mae Terry (black), a "blame the victim" defense not availing. This child rapist was executed on December 29, 1944. Source: *Daily Times News* (Burlington, NC), 12/29/44 (1:2). Appeal: 224 NC 760–762. See also: 1944 Wake Co. death cert. no. 834.

Ralph Thompson (black, age 18) **and Bessie Mae Williams** (black female, age 19). *Murder.* The crime was committed on 4/28/1944 in Mecklenburg County. Fatal stabbing of 42-year-old Mack Minyard (white, a cabbie) who was knifed multiple times by four assailants. Motive: robbery. Two of the killers (Thompson and Williams) were gassed on December 29, 1944. Source: *Daily Times News* (Burlington, NC), 12/29/44 (1:2). Appeal: 32 SE (2nd) 24. See also: 1944 Mecklenburg Co. death cert. no. 8236, and Wake Co. death cert. nos. 817 & 818.

1945

John Edgar Messer (white, age 18), **Elmer Hardy Biggs** (white, age 18) **and William Dalton Biggs** (white, age 18). *Murder.* The crime was committed on 2/19/1943 in Guilford County. All three executed for the handgun slaying of 67-year-old Ernest J. Swanson (white, a storekeeper), who was shot in the head and chest. Motive: armed robbery. The killers met their own ends on March 9, 1945. Source: *Daily Times News* (Burlington, NC), 3/9/45 (1:7). See also: 1943 Guilford Co. death cert. no. 273, and 1945 Wake Co. death cert. nos. 149, 150 & 151; *Crime Detective,* 2/46; *Master Detective,* 11/48.

Horris Hill (black, age 22). *Murder.* The crime was committed on 12/15/1944 in Jones County. Shotgun slayings of 19-year-old Lillie Mae Horton and 42-year-old Lula Wilson (blacks). Motive: outburst by angry lover. Hill was executed on May 25, 1945. Source: *The Robesonian* (Lumberton, NC), 5/29/45 (2:1). See also: 1944 Jones Co. death cert. nos. 26516 & 26517, and 1945 Wake Co. death cert.no. 315.

Lacy Alexander McDaniels (black, age 33). *Rape.* The crime was committed on 7/17/1944 in Guilford County. Indecent assault on the person of 26-year-old Beatrice Collins Harris (white), she having been stalked "for about a week" prior to the actual felony, then accosted on a footpath, choked, stabbed, raped and left naked at the scene, her clothes carried off by the culprit. McDaniels was executed for this on June 8, 1945. Sources: *Daily Times News* (Burlington, NC), 6/8/45 (5:4); *The Robesonian* (Lumberton, NC), 7/19/44 (2:4). See also: 1974 Durham Co. death cert. no. 1085, which notes the victim's husband, and North Carolina Dept. of Health Death Index (1993–1996), which notes the death of the victim herself on 6/13/1995.

Henry French (black, age 35). *Murder.* The crime was committed on 9/3/1944 in Montgomery County. Rifle slayings of 42-year-old Nathaniel LeGrand and 55-year-old Odessa Ingram LeGrand (blacks, a married couple). The man was shot twice (in the neck and chest) and the woman was shot once in the back when she tried to flee. Motive: because the killer blamed the victims for damage to his car. He was executed on June 22, 1945. Source: *Statesville (NC) Daily Record,* 6/22/45 (1:4). See also: 1944 Montgomery Co. death cert. nos. 21978 & 21979, as well as 1945 Wake Co. death cert. no. 406.

William H. Jones (black, age 53). *Murder.* The crime was committed on 10/31/1944 in Wake County. Uxoricide. Executed for the murder of 40-year-old Annabelle Banks Jones (black), she having been thrown to her kitchen floor in the presence of their 12-year-old daughter and her throat cut with a carving knife. Motive: atavistic male brutality. The killer was gassed on June 22, 1945. Source: *Gastonia Daily Gazette,* 6/22/45 (1:2). See also: 1944 Wake Co. death cert. no. 22598, and 1945 Wake Co. death cert. no. 402.

Burnett Williams (black, age 24). *Rape.* The crime was committed on 3/4/1945 in Lee County. Indecent assault on the person of 20-year-old Kathleen Hall (white), she and her male companion having been attacked as they sat in a parked car. Both were also robbed of their intrinsic valuables. The male victim was then locked in the trunk of the car. The female victim was raped on the front seat and left tied to the steering wheel. Lover's lane marauder Williams was put to death on October 26, 1945. Source: *Daily Times News* (Burlington, NC), 10/17/45 (2:3), 3/31/45 (9:3) & 10/26/45 (1:2). See also: 1940 U.S. Census (Lee Co., NC), which notes the female party.

Edward Mays (black, age 54). *Murder.* The crime was committed on 6/17/1945 in Lee County. Murder of 75-year-old

Mattie L. Salmon (white, a maiden woman), who was attacked in her home and suffocated by a dress that was firmly and forcibly held over her face. Motive: sexual assault. The killer was gassed on November 2, 1945. Source: *Daily Times News* (Burlington, NC), 10/17/45 (2:3). See also: 1945 Lee Co. death cert. no. 23161, and Wake Co. death cert. no. 702.

1946

Walter Hightower (black, age 38). *Murder.* The crime was committed on 4/1/1945 in Wilkes County. Fatal stabbing of 20-year-old Willie Bunker (black). Motive: dispute among jail inmates. Hightower was executed on February 15, 1946. Source: *Statesville (NC) Daily Record*, 2/1/46 (8:1) & 2/15/46 (1:2). See also: North Carolina Death Index (1908–1967), and 1946 Wake Co. death cert. no. 142.

Thomas B. Hart (black, age 22). *Murder.* The crime was committed on 8/1/1945 in Halifax County. Executed for the shotgun slaying of pregnant 24-year-old Marjorie Blackman, and also convicted in a lesser degree for the concomitant murder of that woman's 19-year-old brother Algernon Preston Blackman (blacks). Motive: because the killer felt that the victims had treated him disdainfully. Hart was executed on April 5, 1946. Sources: *Statesville (NC) Daily Record*, 8/3/45 (1:2); *Gastonia Daily Gazette*, 4/5/46 (8:4). See also: 1946 Wake Co. death cert. no. 255. Appeal: 226 NC 200–204, which gives "Blackwood" as the victims' surname.

Alligood King (black, age 32). *Murder.* The crime was committed on 9/9/1945 in Lenoir County. Murder of 32-year-old Jemmie Margarot Hardy (white), whose throat was cut by a knife-wielding burglar in the bedroom of her own home. Motive: sexual assault. The killer was executed on April 26, 1946. Source: *Daily Times News* (Burlington, NC), 4/26/46 (1:5). See also: 1945 Lenoir Co. death cert. no. 18523, and 1946 Wake Co. death cert. no. 296.

Gurney Herring (black, age 24). *Rape.* The crime was committed on 6/15/1945 in Wayne County. Indecent assault on the person of 44-year-old Clarinette Brock (black), she having been "forced from her home and raped." The attacker was executed on May 24, 1946. Source: *Gastonia Daily Gazette*, 5/24/46 (3:1). Appeal: 226 NC 213–216. See also: 1946 Wake Co. death cert. no. 358; 1930 U.S. Census (Wayne Co., NC), which notes the female party.

George Walker (black, age 39). *Rape.* The crime was committed on 7/22/1945 in Harnett County. Indecent assault on the person of a 13-year-old white female (name withheld), who was accosted and dragged into the woods as she walked homeward with a pail of freshly picked grapes. Her pail, torn clothing and spilled fruit were found at the scene of the crime. The rapist was executed on June 21, 1946. Source: Appeal: 226 NC 458–461. See also: 1946 Wake Co. death cert. no. 444.

Fred Deaton (white, age 38). *Murder.* The crime was committed on 9/17/1945 in Gaston County. Handgun slaying of 40-year-old Walter A. Clark (white), who was shot three times in a pub. Motive: ill feeling from some prior conflict. The killer was executed on June 28, 1946. Source: *Gastonia Daily Gazette*, 5/9/46

(13:7). See also: 1946 Wake Co. death cert. no. 434.

Fab Stewart (black, age 45). *Murder.* The crime was committed on 12/15/1945 in Wake County. Handgun slaying of 22-year-old Ernest Jones, Jr. (black). Motive: heated argument. The killer was executed on June 28, 1946. Source: *Daily Times News* (Burlington, NC), 6/28/46 (1:2). Appeal: 226 NC 299–303. See also: 1945 Wake Co. death cert. no. 26894, and 1946 Wake Co. death cert. no. 438.

Edward W. Floyd (white, age 39). *Murder.* The crime was committed on 11/10/1945 in Northampton County. Rifle slayings of 61-year-old Wade A. Cook (his father-in-law) and 29-year-old Rosa Lee Cook (his sister-in-law) (whites). Motive: family flare up. Floyd was executed on October 25, 1946. Source: *Daily Times News* (Burlington, NC), 10/22/46 (1:2). See also: 1945 Halifax Co. death cert. no. 22958, Northampton Co. death cert. no. 26257, and 1946 Wake Co. death cert. no. 703.

Robert L. Nash (white, age 42). *Murder.* The crime was committed on 1/14/1946 in Wake County. Handgun slaying of 22-year-old Margie L. Parker (white) who was shot four times "at Raleigh's busiest intersection." Motive: frustrated lover. The victim was a married woman whose husband had gone to war. Nash had sought to supplant that young man while he was absent. Whether he actually succeeded in doing so is not a matter of public record. Whatever the case, Nash could not bear to see the object of his ardor reunited with her husband at the war's end. So he brooded until the above date and then lost all self-control. He was executed on November 1, 1946. Sources: *The Landmark* (Statesville, NC), 1/17/46 (3:1) & 5/13/46 (6:2); *Statesville (NC) Daily Record*, 11/1/46 (1:5).

Wilbert Johnson (black, age 22) **and Charles Primus, Jr.** (black, age 24). *Rape.* The crime was committed on 7/19/1945 in Wake County. Indecent assault on the person of 23-year-old Virginia Lipscomb (white), she and her male companion having been carjacked, driven to a wooded area, robbed of their money and sexually assaulted. The culprits were executed on November 22, 1946. Source: *Statesville (NC) Daily Record*, 9/14/45 (1:6), 11/7/46 (1:3) & 11/22/46 (1:3).

Herman Mathews (black, age 18) **and Calvin Coolidge Williams** (black, age 17). *Murder.* The crime was committed on 11/9/1945 in Sampson County. Both executed for the murder of 53-year-old John Addison (black), who was lured to a wooded area under the pretense of buying whiskey and once there, battered to death with the stock of a shotgun. Motive: robbery. The killers were gassed on December 13, 1946. Sources: *Burlington (NC) Daily Times News*, 11/1/46 (4:1); *The Robesonian* (Lumberton, NC), 12/13/46 (6:1). See also: 1945 Sampson Co. death cert. no. 26673, and 1946 Wake Co. death cert. nos. 824 & 826.

1947

Otis Ragland (black, age 30). *Rape.* The crime was committed on 11/8/1946 in Martin County. Indecent assault on the person of 41-year-old Florence Williams Moore (white), she having been attacked in her home by a work camp escapee. Eight desperate men had fled the

Martin County Prison Farm that day. Ragland was one of them. He was gassed on March 14, 1947. Source: *Gastonia Daily Gazette*, 11/9/46 (1:4) & 3/14/47 (1:6). See also: World War II draft reg. card (Martin Co., NC), which notes Mr. and Mrs. Moore. They both died in 1988, per the Social Security Death Index.

Bennie Montgomery (black, age 23). *Murder.* The crime was committed on 6/1/1946 in Union County. Fatal stabbing of 60-year-old William Marvin Mangum (white). Motive: tenant-landlord dispute. The killer was executed on March 28, 1947. Source: *Burlington (NC) Daily Times News*, 3/25/47 (2:6). See also: 1946 Union Co. death cert. no. 13125, and 1947 Wake Co. death cert. no. 236.

Richard Horton (black, age 23). *Murder.* The crime was committed on 10/27/1946 in Wilkes County. Shotgun slaying of 26-year-old Francis M. Baker (white), a cabbie. Motive: robbery and carjacking. The killer was executed on April 4, 1947. Source: *Statesville (NC) Daily Record*, 10/30/46 (1:6). See also: 1946 Wilkes Co. death cert. no. 22421, and 1947 Wake Co. death cert. no. 264.

Eunice Martin (black male, age 29). *Murder.* The crime was committed on 3/8/1946 in Forsyth County. Uxoricide. Handgun slaying of 26-year-old Bernice Patterson Martin (black), she having been shot in the head. Motive: obnoxious drunk. The killer was put to death on April 11, 1947. Source: *Greensboro (NC) Record*, 3/11/46 (1:2). See also: 1946 Forsyth Co. death cert. no. 4854, and 1947 Wake Co. death cert. no. 282.

Benjamin Franklin McCleod (black, age 26). *Murder.* The crime was committed on 7/1/1946 in Scotland County. Baby killer, etc. Executed for the murders of 18-month-old William Kenneth Lowry (Native American), who perished in his blazing house together with his parents, Henry Thomas Lowry (age 39) and Fannie Revels Lowry (age 34), plus their overnight guest Edward Clifton Koonce (white, age 17). All were shot with a .22 caliber rifle before the house was fired. Forensic evidence indicated that one or more of the victims were still alive as the flames consumed them. Motive: because the killer felt threatened, or so he said. He died in the gas chamber on May 23, 1947. Sources: *Greensboro (NC) Record*, 7/4/46 (14:6) & 7/12/46 (2:4); *The Robesonian* (Lumberton, NC), 7/3/46 (1:4) & 7/11/46 (1:2). See also: 1946 Scotland Co. death cert. nos. 15291, 15292, 15293 and 45294, as well as 1947 Wake Co. death cert. no. 392.

Albert Sanders (black, age 20) **and James Marvin Farmer** (black, age 19). *Murder.* The crime was committed on 9/7/1946 in Johnston County. Both executed for the murder of 26-year-old Robert Thomas Mitchell (white), a serviceman lately returned from overseas. The victim was struck down from behind with a wooden pole and then beaten to death. Motive: mugging. The killers thought that Mitchell was flush with military severance pay. The fact that they owed him a debt of gratitude for the defense of their country in wartime did not even occur to them. They were gassed on June 6, 1947. Source: *Statesville (NC) Daily Record*, 6/6/47 (1:5). See also: 1946 Johnston Co. death cert. no. 19012, and 1947 Wake Co. death cert. nos. 405 & 406.

Moses Artis (black, age 42). *Murder.* The crime was committed on 5/31/1946 in Duplin County. Shotgun slaying of 46-year-old George Graham Houston (white). Motive: tenant-landlord dispute. The killer was put to death on June 27, 1947. Source: *Gastonia Gazette*, 6/27/47 (6:7). See also: 1946 Duplin Co. death cert. no. 27829, and 1947 Wake Co. death cert. no. 470.

Woodrow Brown (black, age 26). *Rape.* The crime was committed on 7/11/1946 in Wake County. Indecent assault on the person of 59-year-old Stella Edwards (white, a maiden woman), who was dragged from her home (after the culprit had broken into the place) to a wooded area 100 yards distant and there mistreated in an even worse way. The rapist was executed on June 27, 1947. Sources: *Burlington (NC) Daily Times News*, 4/30/47 (2:7); *The Robesonian* (Lumberton, NC), 6/30/47 (2:5). See also: 1947 Wake Co. death cert. no. 456.

Roy Kirksey (black, age 24). *Murder.* The crime was committed on 7/5/1945 in Columbus County. Uxoricide. Handgun slaying of 25-year-old Agnes Eloise Walker Kirksey (black), she having been shot in the back. Motive: marital estrangement. The woman had just returned home from a hospital where she had been treated for injuries suffered in a prior spat with her husband. He was executed on June 27, 1947. Source: *Gastonia Gazette*, 6/27/47 (6:7). Appeal: 227 NC 445–449. See also: 1945 Columbus Co. death cert. no. 15495, and 1947 Wake Co. death cert. no. 449.

Jethro Lampkin (black, age 20) **and Richard McCain** (black, age 21). *Murder.* The crime was committed on 1/2/1947 in Mecklenburg County. Fatal stabbing of 67-year-old Thomas Franklin McClure (white), who was "punctured 18 times." Motive: armed robbery. The killers were gassed on October 3, 1947. Sources: *Burlington (NC) Daily Times News*, 1/3/47 (2:5); *The Robesonian* (Lumberton, NC), 2/5/47 (4:5). See also: 1947 Mecklenburg Co. death cert. no. 893, and Wake Co. death cert. nos. 678 & 679.

Robert Messer (white, age 20) **and Earl O'Dear** (white, age 23). *Murder.* Their crime was committed on 4/21/1947 in Jackson County. Both executed for the murders of 39-year-old Jack W. Hall and 20-year-old Margie Lee Maples Hall (whites, a married couple), who were carjacked and battered to death with a hammer. Motive: robbery. The killers were gassed on October 3, 1947. Source: *Burlington (NC) Daily Times News*, 4/22/47 (10:7). See also: 1930 U.S. Census (Jackson Co., NC), which notes the male victim; 1947 Jackson Co. death cert. no. 7929, which notes the female victim; 1947 Wake Co. death cert. nos. 675 & 676; *Front Page Detective,* 9/47; *Master Detective,* 1/48; *Real Detective,* 10/47.

Willie Cherry (black, age 27). *Rape.* The crime was committed on 4/25/1947 in Northampton County. Indecent assault on the person of 39-year-old Rachel Edwards Tarrant (white), she having been attacked by two men who forced their way into her home. One rummaged for valuables while the other (Cherry) raped her. The lesser offender (James Boone, black, age 21) drew a life sentence for aggravated burglary. Willie Cherry was put to death on October 3, 1947. Sources: *Statesville (NC) Daily Record*, 6/21/47 (3:2) & 6/26/47 (2:2); *The Robesonian* (Lumberton, NC), 6/30/47 (2:5). See also: 1947 Wake Co. death cert. no. 680; Cumberland Co. (NC) World War II draft re. card no. 1568, which notes the female party. She died in 1994.

Oscar Douglas, alias "Jack Peed" (black, age 36). *Rape.* The crime was committed on 10/22/1946 in Davie County. Indecent assault on the person of 19-year-old Hazel Swicegood Foster (white), she having been dragged into a thicket and outraged three times. The culprit had been a sawyer employed by the victim's spouse. He feigned discussing business with that man just before Mr. Foster left his home for a drive into town. The woman was attacked as soon as her husband left the scene. The rapist was executed on October 10, 1947. Source: *Statesville (NC) Daily Record*, 10/23/46 (1:4). See also the victim's gravestone in Concord Methodist Church Cemetery, Cooleemee, North Carolina. She died in 1989. The culprit's death certificate is missing. His name appears on the official list of executed criminals of the North Carolina Dept. of Corrections.

Lester Stanley (black, age 27). *Murder.* The crime was committed on 3/10/1947 in Edgecombe County. Uxoricide. Executed for the murder of 26-year-old Shirley Ruffin Stanley (black), whose throat was cut with a razor as she lay in her bed. Motive: because she did not meet her husband's sexual demands. He was put to death on October 31, 1947. Sources: *Burlington (NC) Daily Times News*, 5/3/47 (2:5); *Statesville (NC) Daily Record*, 10/10/47 (1:8). See also: 1947 Edgecombe Co. death cert. no. 4559, and Wake Co. death cert. no. 736.

Grady Brown (black, age 27), **James Charles Brooks** (black, age 27) **and Thurman Jefferson Munn** (black, age 27). *Murder.* Their crime was committed on 3/3/1947 in Henderson County. Prison guard killers. All executed for the rifle slaying of 53-year-old George S. Bowman (white). Motive: work camp breakout. They were put to death on October 31, 1947. Source: *Statesville (NC) Daily Record*, 6/5/47 (2:2). See also: 1947 Henderson Co. death cert. no. 5005, and Wake Co. death cert. nos. 733, 735 & 737.

William Little, alias "James Harrington" (black, age 42). *Rape.* The crime was committed on 11/25/1946 in Wake County. Indecent assault on the person of 52-year-old Nannie Rook (white), she having been attacked in her own home. The miscreant had fled from a prison work camp. He forced his way into the first house he saw and mistreated its female occupant in a vile manner. He was gassed on November 14, 1947. Source: *Gastonia Gazette*, 4/22/47 (1:1). See also: 1947 Wake Co. death cert. no. 780; 1930 U.S. Census (Wake Co., NC), which notes the victim of this outrage.

Marion Claude Bell (white, age 23) **and Vernon J. Litteral** (white, age 34). *Rape.* Their crime was committed on 8/23/1946 in Wilkes County. Indecent assault on the person of 15-year-old Peggy Ruth Shore (white), who was forcibly abducted from a point in Surry County and taken on a harrowing night ride through the mountains to Tennessee. The kidnappers and rapists were put to death on November 14, 1947. Source: *Gastonia Daily Gazette*, 1/17/47 (6:6). See also: 1947 Wake Co. death cert. nos. 762 & 763.

1948

Frank Black (black, age 20). *Murder.* The crime was committed on 10/5/1947 in Lenoir County. Ax murder of 37-year-old William Lester Corey (white), a cab driver. Motive: robbery. The killer was executed on January 2, 1948. Source: *The Landmark* (Statesville, NC), 1/5/48 (5:6). See also: 1947 Lenoir Co. death cert. no. 22501, and 1948 Wake Co. death cert. no. 13.

John Henry Breeze (black, age 32). *Murder.* The crime was committed on 2/19/1947 in Orange County. Fatal beating of 73-year-old Agnes Wilkerson (white), she having been "severely mauled" with a stick and left semi-conscious on a burning bed. She died on 3/11/1947. Motive: home invasion. The killer made off with $16 that the old lady had saved in a jar. He was executed on January 16, 1948. Source: *Burlington (NC) Daily Times News*, 2/22/47 (9:4). See also: 1947 Alamance Co. death cert. no. 3791, and 1948 Wake Co. death cert. no. 42.

Booker T. Anderson (black, age 28). *Murder.* The crime was committed on 5/16/1947 in Pitt County. Baby killer. Child killer, etc. Executed for the arson deaths of 23-year-old Willie Belle Moore Cratch, 6-year-old Bobby Jean Moore, and 11-month-old Jessie Juanita Cratch (blacks), a mother and her two children. Motive: frustrated suitor. The killer had wanted Willie Belle to leave her mother's house and take up residence with him. She refused. So Anderson set the place ablaze and later said, "I figured that if she didn't have a house to live in, she would live with me instead." His logic was shockingly puerile. He was executed on April 23, 1948. Source: *Statesville (NC) Daily Record*, 5/20/47 (1:8). See also: 1947 Pitt Co. death cert. nos. 11054, 11055 & 11056, and 1948 Wake Co. death cert. no. 303.

Buster Hooks (black, age 27). *Rape.* The crime was committed on 8/16/1947 in Randolph County. Indecent assault on the person of 38-year-old Ora Belle Hughes Bouldin (white) during the course of a residential burglary. The presence of the victim's two children did not deter him. The rapist was executed on April 23, 1948. Source: *Statesville (NC) Daily Record*, 4/7/48 (8:2) & 4/23/48 (1:6). See also: 1948 Wake Co. death cert. no. 292; 1930 U.S. Census (Randolph Co., NC), which notes the victim as a newlywed.

James Leroy Jackson (black, age 42). *Murder.* The crime was committed on 11/18/1947 in Burke County. Shotgun slaying of 59-year-old David L. Francum (white), a refreshment stand proprietor. Motive: armed robbery. The killer came away with $2 at the cost of two lives including his own. He was gassed on May 7, 1948. Source: *Gastonia Gazette*, 11/21/47 (6:4). See also: 1947 Burke Co. death cert. no. 26097, and 1948 Wake Co. death cert. no. 322.

George Hammond (black, age 30) **and Henderson Wilson** (black, age 26). *Murder.* The crime was committed on October 31, 1947, in Davidson County. Both executed for the murder of 66-year-old Robert B. Hayes (black, a filling station operator), who was battered to death with an auto jack handle and very nearly decapitated. Motive: robbery. The killers were executed on June 4, 1948. Source: *Gastonia Gazette*, 6/4/48 (1:5). See also: 1947 Davidson Co. death cert. no. 26536, and 1948 Wake Co. death cert. nos. 408 & 409.

James Pete West (black, age 20). *Murder.* The crime was committed on 1/22/1948 in Duplin County. Ax murder of 63-year-old Walter J. Johnson (white), a small store owner. Motive: robbery. The killer was executed on November 19, 1948. Source: *Statesville (NC) Daily Record*, 11/19/48 (8:4). See also: 1948 Duplin Co. death cert. no. 1335, and Wake Co. death cert. no. 817.

1949

James Creech (white, age 36). *Murder.* The crime was committed on 7/28/1948 in Johnston County. Uxoricide. Shotgun slaying of 28-year-old Mattie Woodall Creech (white). Motive: marital estrangement. The killer was executed on January 28, 1949. Source: *Gastonia Gazette*, 8/3/48 (8:6). See also: 1948 Johnston Co. death cert. no. 17935, and 1949 Wake Co. death cert. no. 77.

Emmett Garner (white, age 35). *Murder.* The crime was committed on 7/23/1947 in Harnett County. Uxoricide. Executed for the murder of 33-year-old Dessie Woodall Garner (white), who was beaten almost beyond recognition with a singletree and her body dragged into a swamp, where the assault was repeated. Motive: because she had dared to walk out on their abusive marriage. The killer was executed on March 18, 1949. Source: *Statesville (NC) Daily Record*, 7/24/47 (1:2) & 3/18/49 (1:2). See also: 1947 Harnett Co. death cert. no. 19752, and 1949 Wake Co. death cert. no. 198.

Roy Thomas Cockrell (white, age 42). *Murder.* The crime was committed on 11/2/1948 in Nash County. Uxoricide. Shotgun slaying of 40-year-old Geneva Batts Cockrell (white), she having been dragged from her home and killed in a field. Motive: suspected infidelity. The wrathful husband was gassed on March 25, 1949. Source: *Statesville (NC) Daily Record*, 11/5/48 (5:2) & 3/11/49 (4:6). See also: 1949 Wake Co. death cert. no. 230, as well as the victim's gravestone in Mt. Herman Missionary Baptist Church Cemetery, Rocky Mount, North Carolina.

James Edward Lewis (black, age 26). *Murder.* The crime was committed on 5/29/1948 in Robeson County. Uxoricide. Executed for the murder of 31-year-old Jadie McMillan Lewis (black), she having been felled by a shotgun blast fired through a window, stomped, beaten and cut twice across the throat, each time from ear to ear. Motive: marital estrangement. He was a wife beater and she had dared to walk out on him. This killer was executed on June 17, 1949. Source: *The Robesonian* (Lumberton, NC), 6/1/48 (1:5). See also: 1948 Robeson Co. death cert. no. 16167, and 1949 Wake Co. death cert. no. 13978.

Allen T. Reid (black, age 29). *Aggravated Burglary.* The crime was committed on 9/2/1948 in Wilson County. Executed for a violent break-in at the house of 67-year-old James Barnes (white), during which that man's 63-year-old wife was terrorized with intent to commit sodomy. The miscreant was put to death on December 9, 1949. Source: Appeal: 230 NC 561–566. See also: 1949 Wake Co. death cert. no. 29620; 1940 U.S. Census (Wilson Co., NC), which notes the victims of this outrage.

Audie Lee Brown (black, age 25). *Murder.* The crime was committed on 1/1/1949 in Randolph County. Shotgun slaying of 37-year-old Edgar Melvin Cain (white, a cattle dealer), who was forcibly abducted, brought to a wooded area and blasted from behind. Motive: robbery. The killer was put to death on December 9, 1949. Source: *Gastonia Gazette*, 12/9/49 (1:6). See also: 1949 Randolph Co. death cert. no. 3582, and Wake Co. death cert. no. 29619.

Monroe Medlin (black, age 23). *Murder.* The crime was committed on 8/1/1949 in Mecklenburg County. Shotgun slaying of 68-year-old Virginia Shober Anderson (white). Motive: house robbery. The victim was a society matron. The killer had previously been a manservant in her home. He resented having been fired from that position and sought to get even by stealing from his former jobsite. Mrs. Anderson caught him in the act, so he shot her dead on the spot. Another manservant who had been hired to replace Medlin was also assaulted with murderous intent (his throat being slashed with a razor), but survived. Monroe Medlin died in the gas chamber on December 9, 1949. Source: *Statesville (NC) Daily Record*, 8/9/49 (8:4) & 12/9/49 (1:7). See also: 1949 Mecklenburg Co. death cert. no. 18304.

Uzelle Jones (black male, age 35). *Murder.* The crime was committed on 12/10/1948 in Hoke County. Handgun slaying of 30-year-old Flora Belle Smith Anderson (black), she having been shot in the head at close range. Motive: adultery gone sour. The killer was executed on December 16, 1949. Source: *Statesville (NC) Daily Record*, 12/15/49 (1:5). See also: 1948 Hoke Co. death cert. no. 27556, and 1949 Wake Co. death cert. no. 29638.

Hector Chavis (Native American, age 29) **and Leander Jacobs** (Native American, age 27). *Murder.* Their crime was committed on 4/5/1949 in Robeson County. Both executed for the hatchet killing of 79-year-old Martin L. Blackwell (white), a grocer. Motive: armed robbery and gross perfidy. They met their ends in the gas chamber on December 30, 1949. Source: *The Robesonian* (Lumberton, NC), 4/6/49 (1:5) & 4/7/49 (1:8). See also: 1949 Robeson Co. death cert. no. 8644, and Wake Co. death cert. nos. 30620 & 30621; *Real Detective,* 2/50.

1950

Lee Heller (black, age 48). *Murder.* The crime was committed on 10/10/1948 in Catawba County. Uxoricide. Executed for the handgun slaying of 43-year-old Nettie Simmons Heller (black). Motive: brutish male jealousy. Recidivist killer. Heller had previously drawn a 5-year sentence for fatally knifing another black man named Robert Hall in an incident eight years earlier. He was gassed on January 6, 1950. Sources: *Statesville (NC) Landmark*, 2/10/49 (1:3); *Statesville (NC) Daily Record*, 1/6/50 (1:5). See also: 1948 Catawba Co. death cert. no. 24139, and 1950 Wake Co. death cert. no. 1662.

John Robert Bridges (white, age 21). *Murder.* The crime was committed on 2/7/1949 in Wake County. Executed for the murder of 21-year-old Kreston Norris Privett (white), who was knocked on the head with a rifle butt and then buried alive in a grave that the killer had dug in advance. Motive: wife stealing. Bridges was put to death on May 19, 1950. Source: *Statesville (NC) Daily Record*, 2/16/49 (8:6). See also: 1949 Wake Co. death cert. no. 4020, and 1950 Wake Co. death cert. no. 12011.

Claude Shackleford (white, age 33). *Rape.* The crime was committed on 8/11/1949 in Guilford County. Indecent assault on the person of 10-year-old Shirley Ann Hunt (white). He was then on federal parole from a prison sentence that had been imposed on him for "shooting a Frenchman" when on military duty in Europe. His previous rap sheet also included two arrests for manslaughter. This child rapist was gassed on July 21, 1950. Source: *Statesville (NC) Daily Record,* 8/18/49 (8:5) & 6/30/50 (1:4). See also: 1950 Wake Co. death cert. no. 17044.

Covey Connor Lamm (white, age 47). *Murder.* The crime was committed on 2/27/1950 in Wilson County. Uxoricide. Handgun slaying of 41-year-old Mettie Eatman Lamm (white), she having been shot three times in the chest. Motive: unclear. The woman was described as an "invalid" but the killer stubbornly refused to say why he did it. He was gassed on November 10, 1950. Source: *High Point (NC) Enterprise,* 11/10/50 (1:5). See also: 1950 Wilson Co. death cert. no. 4146, and Wake Co. death cert. no. 26736.

Ernest Lyles (black, age 33). *Rape.* The crime was committed on 3/9/1950 in Franklin County. Indecent assault on the person of 63-year-old Daisy Etheridge (white, a physically handicapped maiden woman), who was attacked in her "small country home" by a midnight assailant. This happened "just a few hours after" Lyles had been released from a detention facility where he had served five years for attempted rape. He was gassed on November 24, 1950. Source: *Statesville (NC) Daily Record,* 11/24/50 (1:6). See also: 1950 Wake Co. death cert. no. 29542, which notes the pervert, and 1958 Franklin Co. death cert. no. 30914, which notes the object of his malice.

1951

Curtis Shedd (white, age 30). *Murder.* The crime was committed on 8/3/1950 in Macon County. Child killer, etc. Executed for the strangulation murders (by means of a leather belt) of 14-year-old Johnnie Mae Boyter and 8-year-old Jo Ann Boyter (whites, sisters) who were lured to their doom under false pretenses. Motive: sexual assault. All parties came from Walhalla, South Carolina. The killer had for some time been obsessed with the thought of deflowering the elder of these girls. So seeing a means to an end, Shedd inveigled their father John Boyter (white, age 38) into going for a ride in his newly refurbished automobile. The two men motored to a point in nearby Rabun County, Georgia, where Shedd treacherously killed Boyter with a shotgun blast. Then Shedd doubled back to his starting point, where he fetched the two girls, saying that he had been sent for them by their father. They wound up just across the state line in Macon County, North Carolina, and it was there where the last atrocity took place. Curtis Shedd was himself put to death on March 23, 1951. Source: *Crime Detective,* 12/50; *Front Page Detective,* 1/51; *Master Detective,* 7/56. See also: 1951 Wake Co. death cert. no. 7059.

James Richard Hall (white, age 26). *Murder.* The crime was committed on 6/14/1950 in Jackson County. Manual strangulation of 32-year-old Lura Ellen Taylor (white, his sister-in-law), she having also been stripped of her jewelry and her body stashed under a pile of rocks. Motive: sexual assault. Hall was executed on March 23, 1951. Source: *Greensboro (NC) Record*, 3/23/51 (1:4). See also: 1950 Jackson Co. death cert. no. 13592, and 1951 Wake Co. death cert. no. 7060; *Master Detective*, 7/56.

John Henry Rogers (black, age 25). *Murder.* The crime was committed on 6/15/1950 in Sampson County. Fatal beating of 48-year-old Eunice S. Kornegay (white), whose body was found in a thicket across the street from the small country store that she owned. Motive: sexual assault. The killer was executed on April 27, 1951. Sources: *Statesville (NC) Daily Record*, 6/17/50 (1:7); *Daily Times News* (Burlington, NC), 6/23/50 (1:6). See also: 1930 U.S. Census (Sampson Co., NC), which notes the victim; 1951 Wake Co. death cert. no. 9746 which notes the transgressor.

1952

John Andrew Roman (black, age 29). *Murder.* The crime was committed on 8/12/1951 in Davidson County. Fatal beating and stabbing of 65-year-old Beulah Miller Hinshaw (white). Motive: home invasion. The trial jury was comprised of 8 whites and 4 blacks. The killer was executed on June 6, 1952. Source: *Daily Times News* (Burlington, NC), 6/6/52 (1:5). See also: 1951 Davidson Co. death cert. no. 20512, and 1952 Wake Co. death cert. no. 15257; *Official Detective*, 9/52.

1953

Lafayette Miller (black, age 19). *Murder.* The crime was committed on 11/21/1951 in Beaufort County. Shotgun slaying of 21-year-old Harvey C. Boyd (white), who was fired upon by a sniper standing outside his bedroom window. Motive: carjacking. The killer also abducted the victim's wife and forced her to drive him away in the dead man's automobile. He left her locked in its trunk without regard to freezing weather. The trial jury was comprised of 9 whites and 3 blacks. Miller was put to death on May 1, 1953. Source: *Statesville (NC) Daily Record*, 11/23/51 (1:3) & 4/7/53 (1:7). See also: 1951 Beaufort Co. death cert. no. 25033, and 1953 Wake Co. death cert. no. 12917.

Raleigh Speller (black, age 45). *Rape.* The crime was committed on 7/18/1947 in Bertie County. Indecent assault on the person of 52-year-old Bessie Holoman Davis (white), she having been attacked on the rear porch of her house while her deaf 68-year-old husband (who was inside at the time) was unable to hear her screams. This rapist was executed on May 29, 1953. Source: *Statesville (NC) Daily Record*, 7/19/49 (5:4) & 3/8/50 (17:3). See also: 1953 Wake Co. death cert. no. 12964, and 1957 Bertie Co. death cert. no. 111; 1930 U.S. Census (Bertie Co., NC), which notes Mr. and Mrs. Davis.

Clyde Brown (black, age 19). *Rape.* The crime was committed on 6/16/1950 in Forsyth County. Indecent assault on the person of 17-year-old Betty Jane Clifton (white), she having been beaten and otherwise violated while minding her father's store. Clyde Brown the rapist was put to death on May 29, 1953. Source: *Statesville (NC) Daily Record*, 11/9/50 (12:1). See also: 1953 Wake Co. death cert. no. 12965; *Official Detective*, 9/50.

Bennie Daniels (black, age 17) **and Floyd Ray Daniels** (black, age 17).

Murder. Their crime was committed on 2/5/1949 in Pitt County. Both executed for the murder of 28-year-old William Benjamin O'Neal Jr. (white, a cabbie) who was beaten with sticks, bludgeoned with a brick and stabbed multiple times. Motive: robbery. The killers were gassed on November 6, 1953. Sources: *Statesville (NC) Daily Record,* 6/4/49 (1:1); *Official Detective,* 10/49. Also: 1949 Pitt Co. death cert. no. 3550, and 1953 Wake Co. death cert. nos. 27898 & 27899; Pitt County Births Index, which notes that the killers (cousins) were respectively born on 11/1/31 and 9/25/31.

1955

Richard Scales (black, age 29). *Murder.* The crime was committed on 1/19/1955 in Guilford County. Child killer, etc. Executed for the fatal stabbings of 30-year-old Bertha Marie Reynolds Cook and 6-year-old Betty Marie Cook (blacks, a mother and daughter), by means of a butcher knife in their home. Motive: sexual assault. Scales was executed on July 15, 1955. Source: *Evening Telegram* (Rocky Mount, NC), 7/1/55 (1:6). See also: 1955 Guilford Co. death cert. nos. 3700 & 3701, plus 1955 Wake Co. death cert. no. 17978; *Official Detective,* 5/55.

1956

Robert S. Conner (black, age 28). *Murder.* The crime was committed on 5/24/1954 in Forsyth County. Executed for the handgun slaying of 44-year-old Langston B. Roberts (black), the superintendent of the Winston-Salem Negro Juvenile Detention Home, who was shot during a grocery store robbery. The killer was gassed on July 13, 1956. Source: *The Robesonian* (Lumberton, NC), 9/16/55 (8:8). See also: 1954 Forsyth Co. death cert. no. 10850, and 1956 Wake Co. death cert. no. 18963.

1957

Ross McAfee, alias "J.C. Adams" (black, age 41). *Aggravated Burglary.* The crime was committed on 1/31/1957 in Alexander County. Executed for a violent break-in at the house of 24-year-old Walter Glenn Waugh (white), during which that man's 17-year-old wife (name withheld) was attacked and cut with a knife for the purpose of attempted rape. McAfee is also confirmed to have murdered 76-year-old Willie M. Milam (white, a maiden woman), whose body was found in a well at Fairburn, Georgia, on 10/21/56. The trial jury in the burglary case was comprised of 10 whites and 2 blacks. Ross McAfee was gassed on November 22, 1957. Sources: *Gastonia Gazette,* 2/13/57 (16:7); *Statesboro (NC) Record & Landmark,* 3/13/57 (1:7). See also: 1957 Wake Co. death cert. no. 31266; 1900 U.S. Census (Campbell Co., GA), which notes young Willie Milam.

1958

Julius Bunton (black, age 21). *Murder.* The crime was committed on 1/5/1957 in Guilford County. Handgun slaying of 26-year-old Clifford Whitt Phillips (white), a cabbie. Motive: robbery. Bunton was executed on February 28, 1958. Source: *Burlington (NC) Daily Times News,* 1/8/57 (12:4) & 2/5/57 (10:1).

See also: 1957 Guilford Co. death cert. no. 1161, and 1958 Wake Co. death cert. no. 5801.

Matthew Philip Bass (black, age 43). *Rape.* The crime was committed on 6/12/1958 in Wake County. Indecent assault on the person of 35-year-old Sarah K. Mahler (white), who was forced into a janitor closet at the Occidental Life Insurance Building in Raleigh and slashed with a knife to more effectively subdue her. The rapist was put to death on December 5, 1958. Sources: *Statesville (NC) Record & Landmark*, 6/18/58 (13:4); *Daily Times News* (Burlington, NC), 12/5/58 (1:5).

1961

Theodore Boykin (black, age 31). *Murder.* The crime was committed on 12/24/1960 in Duplin County. Handgun slaying of 57-year-old Lena T. Barnes (white), she having been attacked in her own home. Motive: sexual assault. Boykin also stole articles of clothing, a wallet and a wristwatch from the crime scene. He gave those items to four young black women the following day as Christmas gifts. All of those women testified against Boykin because they were disgusted by what he had done. Boykin was gassed on October 27, 1961. Sources: *The Bee* (Danville, VA), 4/6/61 (7B:3); *Rocky Mount (NC) Evening Telegram*, 10/27/61 (1:4).

Part Two
Persons Executed in South Carolina
(Listed Chronologically)

1866

Lewis J. Harrell (white, age 53). *Murder.* The crime was committed on 2/13/1866 in Marion County. Executed for the handgun slaying of 61-year-old James H. Jarrott (white, a physician), who was shot in the knee and died in agony. Motive: obnoxious drunk. Harrell was the overseer on a farm that Jarrott owned. Florence National Cemetery now occupies the site. This killer was hanged at Marion on June 1, 1866. Source: *Daily Phoenix* (Columbia, SC), 2/20/66 (2:1) & 6/7/66 (2:5). See also: 1860 U.S. Census (Marion Co., SC), which notes Harrell and "J.H. Jarrot." Also: Letters of Gov. James Lawrence Orr (Box 2, Folder 32), SC State Archives.

Henry Cheatham (black, age about 22). *Murder.* The crime was committed on 1/13/1866 in Anderson County. Executed for the murder of 20-year-old Samuel Albert Geer (white), who was fatally pistol-whipped. The killer had shot a hog belonging to the victim's father. His reason for doing so was criminal mischief. The younger Geer caught Cheatham in the act and ordered him to carry the dead animal to an abattoir lest the pork get left to the buzzards. Cheatham feared further consequences of what he had done. So he made matters worse by firing a shot at Samuel Geer. The bullet missed, whereupon Cheatham pulled Geer off his horse and beat him on the head with the hammer end of his pistol, making four holes in his skull. Motive: vandalism; willful destruction of private property. The killer was hanged at Anderson on November 23, 1866. Source: *Anderson (SC) Intelligencer*, 10/18/66 (2:2) & 11/29/66 (2:1). See also: 1860 U.S. Census (Anderson Co., SC), which notes Geer, and also the 1860 Slave Schedule for the same census which notes Daniel Brown, the killer's former owner, along with his human chattel.

London Jones, alias "Adams" (black, age 24). *Murder.* The crime was committed on 7/22/1866 in Chester County. Executed for the handgun slaying of 38-year-old Alexander D. Walker (white). Motive: robbery and home invasion. Incipient serial killer. Jones ran with a gang of bandits whose members had no regard for anything save their own aggrandizement. He admitted to having murdered two other white men: a traveler named John Cureton near Columbia, South Carolina, in April 1864 and a Newberry County cotton grower named Lemuel Lane (age 51) three days after the Walker killing. The latter was butchered with an ax as he dozed on his veranda. His house was then plundered and $9,000 in gold (the proceeds of his cotton sales) stolen. London Jones was hanged at Chester on November 30, 1866. Sources: *Augusta (GA) Constitutionalist*, 8/2/66 (1:3); *Daily Phoenix* (Columbia, SC), 8/17/66 (2:5), 8/25/66 (3:4) & 12/9/66 (2:1); *Charleston (SC) Mercury*, 12/8/66 (4:5). See also: 1860 U.S. Census (Newberry Co., SC), which notes Mr. Lane. Also: the broken gravestone of Mr. Walker in Liberty Baptist Church Cemetery, Chester, South Carolina.

1867

Horace Greeley, alias "Johnson" (black, age 19). *Murder.* The crime was committed on 7/3/1866 at Charleston. Shotgun slaying of 68-year-old Benjamin Smith Rhett (white), who was struck by the blasts of two barrels fired from ambush. Motive: attempted highway robbery. The killer was hanged at Charleston on March 1, 1867. Sources: *Charleston Daily News*, 7/4/66 (5:1); *Charleston Daily Courier*, 1/21/67 (4:1), 1/22/67 (1:3) & 3/2/67 (2:3). See also: Charleston Municipal Death Register entry dated 3/1/67, as well as Mr. Rhett's gravestone in St. Peter's Episcopal Church Cemetery, Charleston, South Carolina.

Samuel D. Hodge, alias "Henry Thomas" (white, age not recorded). *Murder.* The crime was committed on 4/8/1866 in Richland County. Executed for the murder of 33-year-old Charles F. van Eaton (white), a traveling peddler from Davie County, North Carolina. The victim was found in a creek three months later. His body was decapitated and wrapped in his own saddle quilt. Motive: highway robbery. The killer was hanged at Columbia on June 7, 1867. Source: *Daily Phoenix* (Columbia, SC), 7/26/66 (2:6) & 6/8/67 (2:6). See also: 1860 U.S. Census (Davie Co., NC), which notes the murdered man.

1868

No legal executions have been confirmed in South Carolina this year.

1869

Cyrus Coachman (black, age not recorded). *Murder.* The crime was committed on 1/10/1869 in Darlington County. Shotgun slaying of Robert P. Suggs (white, age not recorded), a storekeeper. Motive: plunder. The killer was hanged at Darlington on June 18, 1869. Sources: *Daily Phoenix* (Columbia, SC), 6/22/69 (3:1) & (3:3); *Charleston Daily News*, 6/19/69 (1:1) wrongly reported that Suggs was a black man, but corrected itself on 6/21/69 (1:1).

Toby Lybrand (black, age not recorded). *Murder.* The crime was committed on 7/9/1869 in Lexington County. Executed for the murder of Louisa Long (black, age not recorded), his lover, she having been struck on the head with a club and then dragged into a stream where the killer forcibly held her underwater till she drowned. Motive: abusive relationship. Toby Lybrand was hanged at Lexington on October 8, 1869. Sources: *Charleston Courier*, 8/21/69 (2:3); *Daily Phoenix* (Columbia, SC), 10/10/69 (2:5). See also the original case file (Lexington General Sessions August Term, 1869), SC State Archives.

1870

Paul Brown (black, age about 20). *Murder.* The crime was committed on 12/4/1869 in Darlington County. Executed for the murder of 65-year-old John LeGrand Dickson (white), who was beaten and clubbed as he walked home from town. Motive: mugging. The loot consisted of "an old knife," a ball of yarn and $1.85 in money. Brown was hanged at Darlington on May 6, 1870. Sources: *Darlington (SC) Democrat*, 12/8/69 (3:1); *Charleston Daily News*, 5/14/70 (1:4). See also: 1860 U.S. Census (Darlington, SC), which notes "J.L. Dickson." The killer was described as a "youth" but his exact age is unknown.

John William Sweedenburg (black, age not recorded). *Murder.* The crime was committed sometime during the year 1870 in Newberry County. Baby killer. This case is sparsely documented because most of its original records have not survived. One newspaper says that the little victim was drowned. The motive was probably unwanted paternity. Sweedenburg was hanged at Newberry on November 8, 1870. Sources: *Anderson (SC) Intelligencer*, 11/17/70 (1:3); *Charleston Daily News*, 11/11/70 (1:6).

Lewis Berry (black, age 39). *Murder.* The crime was committed on 12/7/1869 in Newberry County. Mutilation murder of 48-year-old Samuel H. Dunwoody (white), the night watchman at the Newberry railroad station. Motive: safecracking. The victim was found with the skin peeled from half of his head and half of his face. The killer was hanged at Newberry on November 8, 1870. Sources: *Daily Phoenix* (Columbia, SC), 12/11/69 (2:6); *Charleston Daily News*, 12/17/69 (1:5) & 11/11/70 (1:6). See also: 1870 U.S. Census (Newberry Co., SC), which notes the killer; 1860 U.S. Census (Newberry, SC), which notes Mr. Dunwoody.

Ezekiel McAbee (white, age 21). *Murder.* The crime was committed on 6/15/1870 in Spartanburg County. Musket slaying of Simon Latham (black, age not recorded), the victim having been deliberately blasted in the crotch. Motive: workplace dispute. Both parties were laborers at Cherokee Ironworks. McAbee was hanged at Spartanburg on November 18, 1870. Sources: *Charleston News & Courier*, 6/24/70 (1:1) & 6/27/70 (1:5); *Daily Phoenix* (Columbia, SC), 11/24/70 (2:4). See also: 1870 U.S. Census (Spartanburg, SC), which notes the killer. See also the original trial record (Spartanburg General Sessions, July Term 1870), SC State Archives.

Andy Hill (black, age not recorded). *Murder.* The crime was committed on 5/1/1870 in Greenville County. Ax murder of 33-year-old Thomas A. Holtzclaw (white), who was attacked on a highway seven miles east of Greenville for no apparent reason. The murdered man had previously served with distinction in defense of his homeland during the War for Southern Independence, being the captain in command of Co. H (Palmetto Battalion) SC Light Artillery. His killer was hanged at Greenville on November 25, 1870. Sources: *Anderson (SC) Intelligencer*, 5/12/70 (4:5); *Charleston Daily News*, 11/28/70 (1:5). See also: 1860 U.S. Census (Anderson Co., SC), which notes young Holtzclaw.

1871

Andrew Brown (black, age not recorded). *Murder.* The crime was committed on 11/22/1870 in Barnwell County. Shotgun slaying of Jacob Barton (black, age not recorded), who caught two barrels in the back. Motive: umbrage for having been worsted by the victim in a fistfight. The killer was hanged at Barnwell Courthouse on February 24, 1871. Sources: *Charleston Daily News*, 2/28/71 (3:3); *New York Herald*, 3/3/71 (5:6).

Henry Cannon (black, age 26) **and Taylor Palmer** (black, age not recorded). *Murder.* The crime was committed on 12/31/1870 in Union County. Executed for the murder of George Mattison Stevens (white, age not recorded), who died in a fusillade fired from Winchester rifles. Motive: misuse of authority. This case exemplifies the agony of its time. The victim (Stevens) was a handicapped veteran who had lost an arm in the War for Southern Independence. He had gone grocery shopping on the above date and was returning home with his purchases in his wagon when a group of between 25 and 40 so-called "Negro Militiamen" barred his way. Henry Cannon and Taylor Palmer were among them. All were armed. There being a newly bought keg of whiskey among the contents of Stevens's wagon, the men demanded that they be allowed to drink freely from it. Stevens knew better than to refuse. The level of intimidation steadily mounted until Mr. Stevens decided to make a run for it. A rifle volley cut him down as he did so. The murder weapons were all found to be state issue, a fact that enraged local citizenry almost as much as the homicide itself. The root cause for this was the political situation throughout the South at that time, or more specifically the misrule of the military-backed puppet regimes that then controlled every state of the former Confederacy. The problem was especially egregious in South Carolina due to that state having been made into a political scapegoat for the war. Its "Radical Republican" governor had an official policy of organizing companies of so-called "Negro Militia" throughout the State for the ostensible purpose of "keeping order" and protecting the "civil rights" of emancipated blacks. In reality, however, these same militias were little or nothing more than government goon squads which took particular delight in humiliating anyone—black or white—who disagreed with them. The result was a statewide crime wave not seen in South Carolina at any time before or since. The state's newspapers were filled with bloodcurdling accounts of murders, rapes and other acts of violence committed by brutish freedmen who could not comprehend the difference between freedom under the 14th Amendment and a license to do as they pleased. This was further aggravated by gross abuse of the pardoning power by "carpetbag" governors (themselves the products of rigged elections) whose prime political directive was to ingratiate themselves to newly enrolled black voters. It was a recipe for disaster. It was racial politics at its worst. It spawned a pernicious system of revolving-door justice for African American lawbreakers in particular. Indeed, the situation became so bad that it destroyed public confidence in the rule of law. The persecuted citizenry (whose appeals to reason had been arrogantly brushed aside by the state governments imposed on them) had recourse to its inherent right of self-defense. Hence the true explanation for what gave rise to the "lynching epidemic" that held sway in the Southern states during the next six decades. It was one of the uglier aspects of American history and one that could have been avoided had the law been allowed to take its course as intended. The murderers of George Mattison Stevens learned this firsthand. Twelve of them were rounded up and charged with capital felony. A night of horror followed. More than 500 masked men stormed the Union County jail. Ten of the aforesaid prisoners were found dangling from tree limbs early the next morning. Only Henry Cannon and Taylor Palmer were left to have their day in court. A trial jury of six whites and six blacks refused to recommend mercy. Cannon and Palmer were legally hanged at Union Courthouse on April 21, 1871. Sources: *Charleston Daily News*, 2/8/70 (1:2), 1/5/71 (1:4), 4/24/71 (3:2) & 4/29/71 (1:2); *Savannah Morning News*, 2/16/71 (1:3) & 6/22/71 (2:3); *Charleston News & Courier*, 1/16/74 (1:2); *New York Herald*, 3/19/71 (10:2) & 5/4/71 (4:4). See also: 1870 U.S. Census (Union Co., SC), which notes Henry Cannon; *Charleston Daily Courier*, 9/17/69 (1:5); *Daily Phoenix* (Columbia, SC), 11/23/70 (1:1).

Edom Hammond (black, age 40). *Murder.* The crime was committed on 12/17/1870 in Lancaster County. Shotgun slaying of 54-year-old David Kirkpatrick (white), the victim having been lured to his own doorway by a sniper. Motive: vengeful ex-employee, or so it was alleged. Hammond said that Kirkpatrick's wife had put him up to it. The murder weapon belonged to the victim. The case raises as many questions as it does answers. Edom Hammond was hanged at Lancaster Courthouse on May 19, 1871. Source: *Charleston Daily News*, 12/28/70 (1:4) & 5/27/71 (1:5). See also: 1870 U.S. Census (Lancaster Co., SC), which notes Hammond, and 1860 U.S. Census (Lancaster Co., SC), which notes the murdered man.

Henry Houston (black, age 24). *Murder.* The crime was committed on 12/17/1870 in Fairfield County. Executed for the murder and illegal burial of William Powell (black, age not recorded), a wayfarer from North Carolina. Motive: highway robbery. A search party found the victim seven weeks after the crime. The killer was hanged at Winnsboro on May 26, 1871. Sources: *Keowee Courier* (Pickens, SC), 2/10/71 (2:4); *Charleston Daily News*, 5/25/71 (1:2) & 5/29/71 (1:2). See also: 1870 U.S. Census (Fairfield Co., SC), which notes the killer.

Shadrach Webster (black, age not recorded). *Murder.* The crime was committed on 5/14/1871 in Anderson County. Fatal stabbing of 21-year-old Adeline Agnew (black), his paramour. Motive: adultery turned deadly. The killer was hanged at Anderson on July 21, 1871. Source: *Anderson (SC) Intelligencer*, 5/18/71 (2:1) & 7/27/71 (2:2). See also: 1870 U.S. Census (Anderson, SC), which notes the female party. Webster was described as a rover from Abbeville, South Carolina.

Andrew Doyle (black, age not recorded) **and Charles Mechanick** (black, age 18). Murder. The crime was committed on 1/27/1871 in Colleton County. Mutilation murder of about 40-

year-old Daniel F. Driggers (white). Motive: highway robbery. The victim was a provisions trader who transported rice and pork products in a wagon. His head was shattered by two shotgun blasts fired from ambush. An undetermined number of pistol bullets were also fired into him. The body was then stripped and thrown into a roadside ditch. A dog was eating the remains when it was noticed by passersby. The trial jury was comprised of 9 blacks and 3 whites. The killers were hanged at Walterboro on August 18, 1871. Source: *Charleston Daily News*, 1/31/71 (3:3), 2/20/71 (3:2), 2/22/71 (3:2) & 8/23/71 (1:3).

1872

Samuel White (black, age 25). *Murder.* The crime was committed on 10/7/1871 at Charleston. Executed for the murder of 52-year-old William B. Fiddia (white, a storekeeper), who was smitten on the head and neck with an artillery saber, commonly called a short sword. Motive: robbery. The aforesaid weapon was probably the property of the victim, he having served in the 3rd Battalion South Carolina Light Artillery (CSA) during the War for Southern Independence. The killer was hanged at Charleston on February 2, 1872. Sources: *Charleston Daily Courier*, 2/3/72 (1:3); *Charleston Daily News*, 10/12/71 (3:2), 10/13/71 (3:2), 10/19/71 (3:2) & 2/3/72 (3:2). See also: Charleston, SC, Burial Register entry dated 2/2/72, line 33; 1860 U.S. Census (St. Johns Berkeley, SC), which notes Mr. Fiddia.

Peter Culp (black, age 23). *Murder.* The crime was committed on 5/1/1871 in York County. Uxoricide. Executed for the murder of 24-year-old Lucinda Culp (black), who was hacked to death with the blade of a hoe. Motive: unclear. The killer was hanged at York on March 8, 1872. Sources: *Charleston Daily News*, 5/6/71 (3:1); *Daily Phoenix* (Columbia, SC), 3/15/72 (3:5). See also: 1870 U.S. Census (York Co., SC), which notes both parties.

Taylor Wilson (black, age 21). *Murder.* The crime was committed on or about 11/15/1871 in Sumter County. Executed for the murder and illegal burial of 76-year-old Thomas Keith (black). Motive: unknown. Surviving records provide no further details. The killer was hanged at Sumter on April 5, 1872. Source: *Charleston Daily News*, 4/9/72 (1:4). See also: 1870 U.S. Census (Sumter Co., SC), which notes both parties.

Eli Chavis (white, age 26). *Murder.* The crime was committed on 12/23/1871 in Barnwell County. Fatal stabbing of 40-year-old Adam Jackson (black). Motive: road rage. The victim and his three sons were transporting a wagonload of cotton to market. Adam Jackson walked beside the wagon while his lads rode atop, the eldest one driving. They encountered a wagon containing five white men coming in the opposite direction. Papa Jackson ordered his own wagon to pull to the side of the road so the other party could have the right of way. Hearing this, Eli Chavis (who was reportedly a hothead by nature) became enraged, having leapt to the conclusion that Jackson had said something snide. Jackson stood next to his wagon and respectfully doffed his hat as the other wagon passed. It was at that point that Chavis jumped upon him, knife in hand. He was hanged for this senseless murder at Barnwell Courthouse on August 2, 1872. Sources: *Daily Phoenix* (Columbia, SC), 1/6/72 (3:5); *Charleston Daily News*, 8/5/72 (1:6). See also: 1870 U.S. Census (Barnwell Co., SC), which notes both parties.

Edward Harris, known to some as "Ned Harris" (black, age 44). *Murder.* The crime was committed on 12/18/1871 in Richland County. Executed for the hatchet murder of 65-year-old Patrick Murphy (white). Motive: home invasion. Harris the hatchet man was hanged at Columbia on August 30, 1872. Source: *Daily Phoenix* (Columbia, SC), 12/20/71 (2:7) & 8/31/72 (2:5). See also: 1870 U.S. Census (Richland Co., SC), which notes both parties.

William Lucas (black, age about 35). *Murder.* The crime was committed on 3/16/1872 in Richland County. Fatal stabbing of John Simpson (white, age not recorded), who was run through the groin with a butcher knife or "cut across the thigh with a small pocket knife," depending on which published account is more accurate. Motive: obnoxious drunk. The killer was hanged at Columbia on August 30, 1872. Sources: *Daily Phoenix* (Columbia, SC), 3/17/72 (2:6), 3/19/72 (2:6) & 8/31/72 (2:5); *New York Herald*, 8/31/72 (5:1).

1873

Samuel Brown (black, age 39). *Murder.* The crime was committed on 7/30/1872 in Marion County. Fatal stabbing of 49-year-old Ebb West (black), his father-in-law. Motive: drunken row. The killer was hanged at Marion on January 24, 1873. Sources: *Daily Phoenix* (Columbia, SC), 8/8/72 (2:4); *Charleston Daily News*, 1/27/73 (1:6). See also: 1870 U.S. Census (Marion Co., SC), which notes both parties.

Levi Souls (white, age 22). *Murder.* The crime was committed on 2/3/1873 in Marion County. Gunshot slaying of 25-year-old Noah Sutton (white) while aboard a flatboat on the Little Peedee River. Motive: drunken row. The killer was hanged at Marion on May 23, 1873. Sources: *Charleston Daily News*, 2/15/73 (1:4); *Charleston News & Courier*, 5/24/73 (1:7) & 5/28/73 (1:2). See also: 1870 U.S. Census (Horry Co., SC), which notes Sutton.

1874

Samuel Vinson, alias "Vincent" (black, age not recorded) **and Aaron Furman** (black, age 44). *Murder.* Their crime was committed on 2/11/1874 in Sumter County. Hatchet murder of 29-year-old Henry Widekind (white). Motive: mugging. An all-black jury found that Furman had held the victim in a wrestling hold while Vinson struck him eleven times on the head with the murder weapon. The killers were hanged at Sumter on March 27, 1874. Sources: *Charleston News & Courier*, 3/28/74 (1:1); *New York Herald*, 3/28/74 (4:1). See also: 1870 U.S. Census (Sumter Co., SC), which notes Widekind and Furman.

Samuel Banks (white, age 23). *Murder.* The crime was committed on 11/15/1873 in Abbeville County. Handgun slaying of 40-year-old Thomas Shedd (white). Motive: obnoxious drunk. Both men were gold miners. They were drinking at their camp commissary when Banks heard Shedd say that he had $15 with which to buy a cow. Banks asked Shedd how it was that he had that kind of money. "None of your damned business!" came the reply. Irked by Shedd's abrupt manner, Banks pulled out a pistol and shot him. Banks was hanged for this at Abbeville on March 27, 1874. Source: *Charleston News & Courier*, 3/28/74 (1:1) & 3/30/74 (1:5). See also: 1860 U.S. Census (Pickens Co., SC), and 1870 U.S. Census (Edgefield Co., SC), which note Thomas "Shed" [*sic*].

Cambyses Hunter (black, age about 30). *Murder.* The crime was committed on 10/9/1873 in Darlington County. Executed for the murder of Cornelius Robinson (black, age not recorded), who was cracked on the head with a billet of wood and died exactly 30 days later. Motive: because the victim had accused the killer of stealing an ox. Hunter was hanged at Darlington to April 10, 1874. Sources: *Charleston News & Courier*, 4/14/74 (1:7); *New York Herald*, 4/11/74 (3:3).

Daniel DeSaussure (black, age 24). *Murder.* The crime was committed on 10/6/1873 in Colleton County. Executed for the murder of 16-year-old Annie Black (black), whose throat and neck were cut all the way around three times. Motive: because the murdered girl had tried to blackmail him. She had already borne the reputation of a field slut. DeSaussure said that he would give her some money with which to buy new clothes. He failed to make good on this. Irritated, the girl then threatened to report DeSaussure for forcing himself on her. She knew that he had a prior conviction for that kind of felony and tried to misuse that knowledge as leverage to get over on him. Dreading this, DeSaussure intercepted Annie on her way to the local magistrate and killed her. He was hanged at Walterboro on May 15, 1874. Sources: *Daily Phoenix* (Columbia, SC), 10/12/73 (4:5); *Charleston News & Courier* 5/21/74 (1:5). See also: 1870 U.S. Census (Colleton Co., SC), which notes Annie Black.

1875

William Auld (black, age 18). *Murder.* The crime was committed on 11/22/1874 in Orangeburg County. Handgun slaying of Butler Goldson (black, age not recorded). Motive: because the victim had confronted him for not keeping a respectful distance from his wife. This young killer was hanged at Orangeburg on April 2, 1875. Source: *Charleston News & Courier*, 11/27/74 (1:3) & 4/3/75 (1:2).

Scipio Bryan (black, age 40) **and Elijah Atkinson** (black, age not recorded). Murder. Their crime was committed on 6/11/1874 in Beaufort County. Both executed for the murder of 65-year-old Thomas S. Behn (white, a store clerk), whose charred remains were found in the ruins of his place of business, his body having been set upon a barrel of kerosene and then a torch applied. Motive: plunder. The killers were hanged at Beaufort on April 16, 1875. Sources: *Macon (GA) Weekly Telegraph*, 6/23/74 (4:5); *Charleston News & Courier*, 4/17/75 (1:1). See also: 1870 U.S. Census (Beaufort Co., SC), which notes Behn and Bryan.

John Richardson (black, age 22). *Murder.* The crime was committed on 2/27/1874 in Colleton County. Shotgun slaying of Constantine Bass (white, age not recorded), a storekeeper. Motive: robbery. The victim was a Greek. The killer admitted to being present at the crime scene but insisted to his last breath that an accomplice named Carolina Deas (black) had wielded the murder weapon. Deas was acquitted at trial but shot dead on 9/24/1875 by a vigilant homeowner during the course of a residential burglary. Richardson was hanged at Walterboro on April 30, 1875. Sources: *Daily Phoenix* (Columbia, SC), 3/7/74 (2:5) & 3/27/74 (3:6); *Charleston News & Courier*, 5/5/75 (5:1) & 10/2/75 (3:1). See also: 1870 U.S. Census (Colleton Co., SC), which notes Richardson.

Joshua Frazer (black, age 32). *Murder.* The crime was committed on 12/27/1874 in Kershaw County. Shotgun slaying of Benjamin Cooper (black, age not recorded) by means of a blast fired into his cabin. Motive: meanspiritedness. The victim had asked Frazer for a small amount of money that was owed him. Frazer replied in a cocky manner, saying that he had the coins in his pocket, sure enough, but that he would "see Cooper in hell" before he parted with them. A "mixed jury" found this sufficient to hang the killer at Camden on May 14, 1875. Sources: *Charleston News & Courier*, 5/15/75 (1:1); *New York Herald*, 5/15/75 (5:5).

Kelly McDolan (black, age 34). *Murder.* The crime was committed on or about 12/15/1874 in Darlington County. Executed for the murder of Jack Johnson (black, age not recorded), who was beaten on the head with a stick. Motive: big attitude. The victim had tried to quell an argument between the killer and another field hand, they all being thus employed. McDolan then turned on Johnson and killed him for having dared to interfere. McDolan was hanged for this at Darlington on June 18, 1875. Source: *Charleston News & Courier*, 4/20/75 (3:1) & 6/22/75 (1:6). See also: 1870 U.S. Census (Darlington Co., SC), which notes McDolan as "McDole" [*sic*].

Oliver Spencer (black, age 29). *Murder.* The crime was committed on 10/30/1874 in Darlington County. Shotgun slaying of 39-year-old Mack Thomas (black), who was killed while sitting in his own cabin. Motive: because the victim had given information that resulted in the recovery of stolen goods. Spencer was hanged at Darlington on June 18, 1875. Source: *Charleston News & Courier*, 11/3/74 (1:2), 4/20/75 (3:1) & 6/22/75 (1:6). See also: 1870 U.S. Census (Darlington Co., SC), which notes both parties.

George Hardee (black, age not recorded). *Murder.* The crime was committed on 7/4/1874 at Charleston. Shotgun slaying of Staten Lanier (black, age not recorded). Motive: dance hall fracas. The killer was hanged at Charleston on June 25, 1875. Source: *Charleston News & Courier*, 2/18/75 (4:2), 6/25/75 (4:2) & 6/26/75 (1:4).

Dennis R. Bunch (black, age 31). *Murder.* The crime was committed on 12/18/1874 at Charleston. Cop killer. Handgun slaying of 43-year-old John Donahue (white). Motive: obnoxious drunk. Both men were police officers on duty at the time. Bunch had been assigned to patrol King Street in Charleston. Somebody reported him for being intoxicated while on the job. Patrolman Donahue was sent to escort Patrolman Bunch to the police station for possible discipline. Enraged by this, Bunch opened fire with his service revolver, fatally wounding his fellow officer. Five shots were fired in all. The killer felt no contrition after he had sobered up. His only comment was that "he had killed one Irish bastard." He was hanged at Charleston on June 25, 1875. Source: *Charleston Daily News & Courier*, 12/19/74 (1:5), 6/25/75 (4:2) & 6/26/75 (1:4). See also: 1874 Charleston death cert. no. 866, and also 1875 Charleston death cert. no. 16, which notes that Donahue succumbed on 1/4/75.

John Smith (black, age 24). *Murder.* The crime was committed on 2/24/1875 at Charleston. Executed for the murder of 34-year-old James Garaty (white, an Edisto Island grocer), who was beaten on the head with a hickory stick. Motive: taking goods without paying for them. Smith was convicted by an all-black jury. He was hanged at Charleston on July 30, 1875. Sources: *Charleston News & Courier*, 7/31/75 (1:4); *New York Herald*, 7/31/75 (3:6). See also: 1875 Charleston death cert. nos. 262 & 1151; 1870 U.S. Census (Charleston, SC), which notes James "Gerrity," no doubt the correct spelling.

Alfred Walker (black, age 35). *Murder.* The crime was committed on 4/3/1875 in Union County. Handgun slaying of 66-year-old J. Claudius Miller (white, full name not specified in any known record), a circuit-riding Methodist minister who was shot twice in the chest as he knelt to pray. Motive: highway robbery. The killer took the reverend gentleman's watch, wallet, overcoat and hat, all of which were found in his possession. He was hanged at Union Courthouse on August 6, 1875. Sources: *Charleston News & Courier*, 4/12/75 (1:6), 4/14/75 (1:4) & 8/7/75 (1:2); *New York Herald*, 8/7/75 (10:1). See also: 1870 U.S. Census (Union Co., SC), which notes Walker, and 1850 U.S. Census (Charleston, SC), which notes Miller.

1876

Stephen Young (black, age 28). *Murder.* The crime was committed on 12/27/1875 in Chester county. Fatal stabbing of 50+-year-old George Mercer (black). Motive: obnoxious drunk. The trial jury was comprised of 8 blacks and 4 whites. The killer was hanged at Chester on January 28, 1876. Sources: *Charleston News & Courier*, 1/29/76 (1:2); *New York Herald*, 1/29/76 (3:3). See also: 1870 U.S. Census (Chester Co., SC), which notes "Stephens Yongue" [*sic*].

W.R. Thompson (black, full name not recorded, age 33). *Murder.* The crime was committed on 12/24/1875 in Newberry County. Executed pursuant to the verdict of an all-black jury for the murder of 35-year-old Hayne D. Reid (white), a storekeeper, who was shot in the back with a handgun and then finished off by multiple shotgun blasts. His place of business was torched, but forensics revealed evidence of foul play. Motive: robbery. The killer was hanged at Newberry on March 10, 1876. Sources: *Augusta (GA) Chronicle*, 12/29/75 (1:2); *Charleston News & Courier*, 3/13/76 (3:1); *New York Herald*, 3/11/76 (6:4). See also: 1870 U.S. Census (Newberry Co., SC), which notes Mr. Reid.

William Alexander Lowry, known to some as "Aleck Lowry" (black, age 21). *Murder.* The crime was committed on 3/15/1876 in Sumter County. Ax murder of 60+-year-old John Murphy (white), a storekeeper who was slain in his place of business and the premises burnt in an effort to cover up the crime. Motive: plunder. The trial jury was comprised of 11 blacks and one white man. The killer was hanged at Sumter on June 16, 1876. Sources: *Charleston News & Courier*, 4/19/76 (1:3) & 6/17/76 (1:8); *New York Herald*, 6/17/76 (10:2).

Wesley Brooks (black, age 25). *Murder.* The crime was committed sometime during the summer of 1875 in Barnwell County. He was condemned by an all-black jury for the murder of another black man. Further details are unobtainable because the original trial papers perished long ago. Brooks was hanged at Barnwell Courthouse on July 14, 1876. Sources: *Augusta (GA) Chronicle*, 5/26/76 (4:5) & 7/15/76 (1:6); *Charleston News & Courier*, 7/17/76 (1:5). See also: 1870 U.S. Census (Barnwell Co., NC), which notes this killer.

John Snipes (black, age 24). *Murder.* The crime was committed on 4/15/1876 in Beaufort County. Shotgun slaying of 74-year-old John H. Howard (white), a retired general who had served in the Mexican War. Motive: highway robbery. The killer found only 50 cents in the victim's pockets. He was hanged at Beaufort on August 11, 1876. Source: *Charleston News & Courier*, 4/18/76 (1:6), 4/19/76 (1:3), 4/29/76 (1:6) & 8/12/76 (1:8). See also: 1850 & 1870 U.S. Census (Beaufort Co., SC), which note Howard.

Jerry Coleman (black, age 36). *Murder.* The crime was committed on 4/13/1873 in Abbeville County. Executed pursuant to the verdict of an all-black jury for the murder of Adam Hackett (black, age not recorded), who was whacked upside the head with a heavy sassafras stick. Motive: personal grudge. The two men had previously butted heads at a social gathering. Coleman was hanged at Abbeville on August 18, 1876. Source: *Charleston News & Courier*, 8/19/76 (1:3).

1877

Adam Johnson (black, age 43), **Nelson Brown** (black, age about 38), **John Henry Dennis** (black, age about 30) **and Lucius Thomas** (black, age about 22). *Murder.* Their crime was committed on 11/2/1876 in Aiken County. All executed pursuant to the verdict of an all-black jury for the ax murders of about 60-year-old Rudolph Hausmann and about 25-year-old Fritz Portmann (whites), two German immigrants described as "Republicans" and "Great Friends of the Negroes." Motive: robbery and home invasion. The victims had reportedly come to Aiken County for the climate, they having a medical condition of some kind. They supported themselves through the operation of a gristmill and granary that they had built. They took an active part in local "Radical Republican" politics, motivated either by idealism or European naiveté. Whatever the case, an all-black bandit gang (led by Adam Johnson) showed its appreciation for these two white men by bursting into their home, hacking them to death with axes, robbing the place and burning it to the ground. The above-named quartet died on a specially constructed gallows at Aiken on March 16, 1877. They were not the first to take cruel advantage of white progressives. Nor would they be the last. Sources: *Charleston News & Courier*, 3/16/77 (1:7) & 3/17/77 (1:3); *New York Herald*, 3/17/77 (2:5).

See also: 1870 U.S. Census (Aiken-Barnwell, SC), which notes Adam Johnson.

Steve Anderson (black, age about 21). *Murder.* The crime was committed on 11/2/1876 in Aiken County. Accomplice in the ax murders of about 60-year-old Rudolph Hausmann and about 25-year-old Fritz Portmann (whites), together with the looting and burning of their house. Anderson was hanged at Aiken on April 20, 1877. He had been tried together with Adam Johnson, et al., but was reprieved for the space of five weeks. Sources: *Charleston News & Courier*, 4/21/77 (1:2); *New York Herald*, 4/21/77 (3:2). See: JOHNSON, et al. (executed 3/16/77).

John Allen (black, age 20), **Wightman Allen** (black, age not recorded) **and Jenkins Whitner** (black, age not recorded). *Murder.* Their crime was committed on 12/4/1876 in Abbeville County. All three executed for the musket slaying of 28-year-old Clayton Allen (white), who was ambushed on the highway by an armed gang intent on freeing a man who was then in his custody. In all, ten defendants were convicted by a trial jury comprised of 4 whites and 8 blacks. All were sentenced to death, but seven got off the hook through various legal maneuvers. The man who had been under escort had been pronounced an undesirable because of his own obnoxious behavior. The fact that he was black and his two escorts white was all the justification the all-black gang needed to explain its intervention. The prisoner—in actuality—was merely being brought to a Savannah River ferry with the understanding that he thereafter abide on the Georgia side. The killers had probably assumed that he was headed for a worse fate and intervened on this false assumption. The above-named trio was legally hanged at Abbeville on May 4, 1877. Sources: *Charleston News & Courier*, 5/5/77 (1:6); *New York Herald*, 5/5/77 (3:1). See also: 1870 U.S. Census (Abbeville Co., SC), which notes the Allens.

Jack Burgoyne (black, age about 30). *Murder.* The crime was committed on 11/6/1876 in Marion County. Executed for the murder of 45-year-old Alexander Gregg (white), who was shot three times with a handgun, battered with a persimmon club and his body dumped in a swamp. Motive: an argument over the price of cotton. The killer was hanged at Marion on May 18, 1877. Sources: *Charleston News & Courier*, 5/19/77 (1:7); *New York Herald*, 5/19/77 (6:6). See also the victim's gravestone in Hopewell Presbyterian Cemetery, Florence, South Carolina.

William Bradley (black, age 22). *Murder.* The crime was committed sometime during the summer of 1875 in Barnwell County. This offender was executed pursuant to the verdict of an all-black jury for killing another black man named Hampton Ronken. Motive: fracas at a turpentine camp. Further details are unobtainable because the original trial papers perished long ago. The killer was hanged at Barnwell Courthouse on July 13, 1877. Sources: *Augusta (GA) Chronicle*, 5/26/76 (4:5); *Savannah (GA) Morning News*, 11/17/76 (1:2); *Charleston News & Courier*, 7/16/77 (3:1). See also: 1870 U.S. Census (Barnwell Co., SC), which notes Bradley.

David Pierce (black, age 28) **and George Stevens** (black, age 23). *Murder.* Their crime was committed on 5/11/1877 at Charleston. Shotgun slaying of 18-year-old Joseph Evans Edings, Jr. (white, a payroll messenger), who was ambushed while transporting a shipment of coins. Motive: highway robbery. The killers were hanged at Charleston on July 13, 1877. Sources: *Charleston News & Courier*, 7/14/77 (1:3); *New York Herald*, 7/14/77 (3:5). See also: 1877 Charleston death cert. no. 590.

Cush Harris (black, age not recorded). *Murder.* The crime was committed on or about 1/6/1877 in Edgefield County. Executed for the murder of 56-year-old Lewis Holloway (white), whose throat was cut and house burned down around him. Motive: home invasion. Harris was one member of a 5-man gang who attacked Mr. Holloway because they thought that he was a miser with a monetary stash. Cush Harris was hanged at Edgefield on August 31, 1877. Sources: *Augusta (GA) Chronicle*, 9/4/77 (1:1) & 9/9/77 (1:1); *Cleveland (OH) Plain Dealer*, 9/4/77 (2:3). See also: 1870 U.S. Census (Edgefield Co., SC), which notes Holloway.

1878

John Smith, alias "Lew Mooring" (black, age not recorded). *Murder.* The crime was committed on 12/28/1877 in Chester County. Executed for the murder of 28-year-old Bergen Conger (white), who was struck on the head with some heavy object and his body laid upon railroad tracks with the intention that it be run over by a train. Motive: mugging and gross perfidy. The killer was a vagrant. The victim was an itinerant brick mason from New Jersey. Would-be rescuers revived Conger so that he was able to describe and identify the culprit. Then he lapsed into a coma and died. The killer was hanged at Chester on February 1, 1878. Sources: *Charleston News & Courier*, 1/4/78 (1:6); *New York Herald*, 2/2/78 (6:2).

Fortune Bush (black, age not recorded) **and Dexter McCreary** (black, age not recorded). *Murder.* Mass killers and baby killers. The crime was committed on 1/4/1878 in Barnwell county. Both executed for the deliberate slaughter of 24-year-old Stephen Enicks, about 22-year-old Mary Enicks (blacks, a married couple), and their two small children, ages 3 years and 18 months. The adults were hacked to death with an ax, the woman regardless of the fact that she was holding her baby in her arms at the time. Their cabin was burnt so that the two little ones (names not recorded) perished in the flames. Motive: home invasion. Enicks was described as a hard-working thrifty type who had a fat purse full of silver. The killers were ne'er-do-wells who thought that they could make better use of that money. They were hanged at Barnwell Courthouse on March 22, 1878. Sources: *Charleston News & Courier*, 3/25/78 (1:6); *New York Herald*, 3/26/78 (4:3). See also: 1870 U.S. Census (Barnwell Co., SC), which notes Stephen "Enix" [*sic*].

Robert McEvoy (black, age 22). *Murder.* The crime was committed on 4/19/1876 in Aiken County. Handgun slaying of 41-year-old James Jones Gregg (white), a factory superintendent. Motive: revenge. The victim had previously employed the killer as an errand boy when he was a teenager. The lad had only one leg and one eye so it was primarily human kindness that got him the job. Alas, the company's board of directors saw no further need for an errand boy, so Mr. Gregg (known to some as "Major

Gregg") broke the news to McEvoy as gently as possible. McEvoy brooded over this for seven years. He regarded his dismissal as a grave injustice. Then on the above date he went to Gregg's office and shot the man multiple times. A trial jury of 9 blacks and 3 whites condemned McEvoy to the gallows. He was hanged at Aiken on April 19, 1878. Sources: *Charleston News & Courier*, 4/22/76 (1:6), 4/24/76 (1:3), 5/8/76 (1:6) & 4/20/78 (1:1); *New York Herald*, 4/20/78 (9:5). See also: 1850 U.S. Census (Charleston, SC), which notes the victim, son of William Gregg, founder of the Graniteville Mills.

Anthony McKay (black, age not recorded). *Murder.* The crime was committed on 1/10/1869 in Darlington County. Accomplice in the shotgun slaying of Robert P. Suggs (white, age not recorded), a store clerk who was attacked by a five-member gang while on the job. Motive: armed robbery. McKay was hanged at Darlington on May 3, 1878. Source: *New York Herald*, 5/12/78 (7:6), copied from the *Charleston (SC) Journal of Commerce*, 5/8/78. See: COACHMAN, Cyrus (executed 6/18/69).

Henry M. Wise (white, age about 30). *Murder.* The crime was committed on 11/3/1877 in Colleton County. Handgun slaying of 22-year-old Fletcher Brown (white). Motive: an argument about an intercepted lover letter. The killer was hanged at Walterboro on July 12, 1878. Sources: *Charleston News & Courier*, 11/5/77 (1:6) & 11/6/77 (1:7); *New York Herald*, 7/14/78 (5:5).

Alexander DeWitt (black, age not recorded). *Murder.* The crime was committed on 7/26/1871 in Darlington County. Executed for the ax murder of William Warren (white, age not recorded), the victim having succumbed to his wounds three weeks later. Motive: gross perfidy. Both parties had argued a month earlier. The killer feigned a conciliatory manner and invited Warren to take a "fine watermelon" from his field as a goodwill gesture. Warren went into the field as bidden, accompanied by DeWitt. The latter had evidently concealed an ax under the melon leaves there. He used it to basely strike down the unsuspecting man from behind. DeWitt was hanged at Darlington on August 9, 1878. Sources: *Charleston Daily News*, 8/25/71 (1:4); *New York Herald*, 8/16/78 (7:6).

John Locklear (Native American, age 32), **Neil Locklear** (Native American, age 26) **and Pompey Easterling** (black, age not recorded). *Murder.* Their crime was committed on 2/25/1878 in Marlboro County. All executed for the murder of Frank Bryce (white, age not recorded), an "Irish peddler" who was blasted by a shotgun, then shot again with his own pistol, stripped naked, bludgeoned repeatedly and buried. Motive: robbery and gross perfidy. Their trial jury was comprised of 8 blacks and 4 whites. They were all hanged at Bennettsville on August 23, 1878. Sources: *Charleston News & Courier*, 8/24/78 (1:3); *New York Herald*, 8/24/78 (2:6).

1879

Neil W. Blair (black, age not recorded). *Murder.* The crime was committed on 8/9/1879 in Kershaw County. Fatal stabbing of 54-year-old William Adamson (black). Motive: obnoxious drunk. The killer was hanged at Camden on October 17, 1879. Sources: *Charleston News &*

Courier, 8/13/79 (1:8); *Ft. Wayne (IN) Weekly Sentinel*, 10/22/79 (5:3). See also: 1870 U.S. Census (Kershaw Co., SC), which notes Adamson.

Edward Holmes (black, age 16). *Rape.* The crime was committed on 7/23/1879 in Union County. Indecent assault on the person of 6-year-old Mary Humphries (white), she having been "roughly handled" in her own home and found in a "semi-conscious" condition. The rapist was hanged at Union Courthouse on November 21, 1879. Sources: *Charleston News & Courier*, 11/22/79 (1:4); *New York Herald*, 11/22/79 (4:1). See also: 1880 U.S. Census (Union Co., SC), which notes the victim.

George Gary (black, age 22). *Murder.* The crime was committed on 3/9/1879 in Beaufort County. Murder of 34-year-old Cyrus Brown (black), who was hit on the head with a wooden rice roller. Motive: because 50 cents had been withheld from his pay. The trial jury was comprised of 2 whites and 10 blacks. The killer was hanged at Beaufort on November 21, 1879. Sources: *Charleston News & Courier*, 11/22/79 (1:4); *New York Herald*, 11/22/79 (4:1). See also: 1870 U.S. Census (Beaufort Co., SC), which notes both parties.

1880

Amos Wooten (black, age not recorded). *Arson.* The crime was committed on 10/10/1879 in Marlboro County. Executed for deliberately setting fire to the granary and cotton ginning mill of 51-year-old James B. Breeden (white), both of which burned to the ground along with all of their contents. Motive: to cover up the theft of four bales of cotton. The trial jury was comprised of six whites and six blacks. The incendiary was hanged at Bennettsville on April 9, 1880. Sources: *Charleston News & Courier*, 4/10/80 (1:3); *New York Herald*, 4/10/80 (8:1).

William S. Bates (white, age 27). *Murder.* The crime was committed on 12/24/1879 in Barnwell County. Handgun slaying of Stephen W. Bush (white, age not recorded). Motive: obnoxious drunk. The killer was hanged at Barnwell Courthouse on April 16, 1880. Source: *Charleston News & Courier*, 12/27/79 (1:4) & 4/17/80 (1:3). See also: 1870 U.S. Census (Barnwell Co., SC), which notes Bates.

Alexander Williams (black, age not recorded). *Murder.* The crime was committed on 2/25/1876 in Lexington County. Fatal stabbing of Smith Fields (black, age not recorded), who was run through the chest with a bayonet. Motive: because he thought that the victim had gossiped about his woman. The killer was hanged at Lexington on April 23, 1880. Sources: *Charleston News & Courier*, 4/24/80 (1:3); *New York Herald*, 4/24/80 (5:1).

Thomas White (white, age about 28). *Murder.* The crime was committed on 11/15/1879 in Spartanburg County. Handgun slaying of about 19-year-old "Pet" Hawkins (black), a porter. Motive: obnoxious drunk. The killer was hanged at Spartanburg on May 14, 1880. Source: *Charleston News & Courier*, 5/15/80 (1:3); *New York Herald*, 5/15/80 (5:1).

Daniel Washington (black, age 37). *Murder.* The crime was committed on 9/11/1877 at Charleston. Shotgun slaying of 31-year-old Allen Collins (black), who succumbed to gangrene twelve days after the shooting. Motive: gangland assassination. The killer had headed up a gaggle of horse thieves called the "Ten Mile Gang." The victim had been active in law enforcement efforts to thwart them. Daniel Washington was hanged at Charleston on July 9, 1880. Source: *Charleston News & Courier*, 9/13/77 (4:1) & 7/10/80 (1:7). See also: 1877 Charleston City death cert. no. 1334, and 1880 death cert. no. 996.

1881

Frank Magrath (black, age 27). *Murder.* The crime was committed on 7/12/1880 in Georgetown County. Executed for the fatal stabbing of about 25-year-old Josie Smalls (black, male). Motive: apparent jealousy. The killer disliked the fact that Smalls had gone to his house and asked his wife for the return of a borrowed padlock when he himself wasn't there. Smalls was run through the heart with a butcher knife and his head beaten in with a tree branch. Frank Magrath was hanged at Georgetown on January 28, 1881. Sources: *Charleston News & Courier*, 1/29/81 (1:1) & 1/31/81 (1:5); *New York Herald*, 1/29/81(4:2).

James Black (black, age 21). *Murder.* The crime was committed on 2/9/1880 in Marion County. Handgun slaying of 20-year-old Eli Wilcox (black). Motive: an argument over who was a better brick maker. The killer was hanged at Marion on March 18, 1881. Source: *Charleston News & Courier*, 2/12/80 (1:4), 10/5/80 (1:8) & 3/19/81 (1:3). See also: 1870 U.S. Census (Marion Co., SC), which notes Wilcox.

Abraham Martin (black, age 47). *Murder.* The crime was committed on 7/15/1880 in Abbeville County. Uxoricide. Ax murder of 48-year-old Lucinda Martin (black). Motive: none apparent. The crime was a spontaneous one and without explanation. The killer was described as a "half idiot." He was hanged at Abbeville on April 22, 1881. Sources: *Charleston News & Courier*, 4/23/81 (1:4); *New York Herald*, 4/23/81 (8:2). See also: 1880 U.S. Census (Abbeville Co., SC), which notes both parties.

Joseph Stevens (black, age 48). *Murder.* The crime was committed on 1/12/1878 in Edgefield County. Fatal stabbing of 41-year-old Andrew Mobley, alias "Richardson" (black), who was attacked during a church service. Motive: voodoo. The trial jury was comprised of 8 whites and 4 blacks. The killer was hanged at Edgefield on May 20, 1881. Source: *Charleston News & Courier*, 5/21/81 (1:3); *New York Herald*, 5/21/81 (8:1).

Benjamin James (black, age 22). *Murder.* The crime was committed on 8/9/1880 in Marion County. Hatchet murder of 34-year-old David Merriwether Harrell (white). Motive: mugging. The trial jury was comprised of 9 whites and 3 blacks. The killer was hanged at Marion on June 3, 1881. Sources: *Charleston News & Courier*, 6/4/81 (1:3); *New York Herald*, 6/4/81 (8:1). See also: 1870 U.S. Census (Marion Co., SC), which notes James, and 1880 U.S. Census (Marion Co., SC), which notes Harrell.

Josh Munday (black, age 26). *Murder.* The crime was committed on 6/16/1881 in Edgefield County. Uxoricide. Handgun slaying of 26-year-old Julia Munday (black). Motive: suspicion of infidelity. The killer was hanged at Edgefield on August 26, 1881. Sources: *Charleston News & Courier*, 8/27/81 (1:7); *New York Herald*, 8/27/81 (8:1). See also: 1880 U.S. Census (Edgefield Co., SC), which notes both parties.

Berryman Whitney Hicks (white, age 33). *Murder.* The crime was committed on 5/9/1881 in Spartanburg County. Uxoricide. Executed for the murder of 34-year-old Mary Ann Clement Hicks (white), she having been wounded by a shotgun blast and then finished off when her throat was cut with a razor. Motive: paranoid male jealousy. The killer was hanged at Spartanburg on September 30, 1881. Sources: *Charleston News & Courier*, 10/1/81 (1:3); *New York Herald*, 10/1/81 (5:2). See also: 1870 U.S. Census (Cherokee, SC), which notes the victim by her maiden name.

Henry Johnson, alias "Johnston" (black, age 29). *Murder.* The crime was committed on 2/5/1881 in Sumter County. Shotgun slaying of 51-year-old John Davis (black), the victim having been stalked and then gunned down from behind. Motive: wife stealing. The killer was hanged at Sumter on November 25, 1881. Sources: *Charleston News & Courier*, 11/26/81 (1:5); *New York Herald*, 11/26/81 (5:1). See also: 1880 U.S. Census (Sumter Co., SC), which notes Davis.

Richard James (black, age 31). *Murder.* The crime was committed on 8/9/1880 in Marion County. Accomplice in the hatchet murder of 34-year-old David Merriwether Harrell (white). Motive: mugging. This offender was hanged at Marion on November 25, 1881. Sources: *Charleston New & Courier*, 11/26/81 (1:5); *New York Herald*, 11/26/81 (5:1). See: JAMES, Benjamin (executed 6/3/81).

Gabriel White (black, age 25). Murder. The crime was committed on 1/30/1880 in Colleton County. Executed for the murder of 26-year-old Frederick Bellinger (black), the victim having been slashed to death with a razor. Motive: rivalry for a female. The killer was hanged at Walterboro on December 30, 1881. Sources: *Charleston News & Courier*, 12/31/81 (1:2); *New York Herald*, 12/31/81 (9:4). See also: 1870 & 1880 U.S. Census (Colleton Co., SC), which note the victim and the killer.

1882

Jesse Barber (black, age 30). *Murder.* The crime was committed on 7/31/1881 in Fairfield County. Handgun slaying of 57-year-old Mack Perry (black), the victim having been shot in the back. Motive: because the murdered man had accused the killer of stealing watermelons. The trial jury was comprised of 10 whites and 2 blacks. Jesse Barber was hanged at Winnsboro on February 10, 1882. Sources: *Charleston News & Courier*, 2/11/82 (1:1); *New York Herald*, 2/11/82 (6:1). See also: 1880 U.S. Census (Chester Co., SC), which notes Barber, and (Fairfield Co., SC), which notes Perry.

Pleasant Adams (black, age 18), **Richard Bates** (black, age 19) **and Joseph Burton** (black, age 24). *Arson.* Their crime was committed on 12/7/1879 in Greenville County. All executed for setting fire to and totally destroying the Greenville Academy of Music or "Opera House" (as it was otherwise known), described as one of the grandest buildings in the state of South Carolina. Total loss: $50,000, a fantastic sum of money in those days. Motive: to cover up the burglary of three retail stores on the Academy's ground floor. The trial jury was comprised of six whites and six blacks. The three incendiaries were hanged at Greenville on April 28, 1882. Sources: *Charleston News & Courier*, 4/29/82 (1:1); *New York Herald*, 4/29/82 (9:4). See also: 1880 U.S. Census (Greenville, SC), which notes the culprits as prisoners.

Abram Anderson (black, age 32) **and Boston Singletary** (black, age 17). *Arson.* Their crime was committed on 3/26/1882 in Williamsburg County. Both executed for maliciously firing the barn and stables of 29-year-old Thomas D. Brockington (white), together with that man's storehouse, which they had previously plundered. Motive: spitefulness; the property owner had been parsimonious as a provisioner. These incendiaries were hanged at Kingstree on June 23, 1882. Source: *Charleston Daily News & Courier*, 6/24/82 (1:1). See also: 1880 U.S. Census (Williamsburg Co., SC), which notes the executed pair.

Lucinda Tisdale (black female, age 23) **and Anderson Singleton** (black, age 24). *Murder.* Their crime was committed on 1/21/1882 in Williamsburg County. Sororicide. Both executed for the murder of 19-year-old Phoebe Tisdale (black), who was battered to death with a hammer. Motive: love triangle. The killers were hanged at Kingstree on June 23, 1882. Sources: *Charleston Daily News & Observer*, 6/24/82 (1:1); *New York Herald*, 6/24/82 (5:1). See also: 1870 U.S. Census (Williamsburg Co., SC), which notes the daughters of Joe Tisdale.

Robert Parker (white, age 22). *Murder.* The crime was committed on 12/22/1881 in Aiken County. Uxoricide. Fatal and deliberate poisoning (strychnine) of 39-year-old Caroline Parker (white), who was served the lethal substance in a toddy. Motive: desire for a younger mate. One wonders why they got married in the first place. Whatever the case, this dissatisfied young husband was hanged at Aiken on August 25, 1882. Sources: *Charleston Daily News & Courier*, 8/26/82 (1:3); *New York Herald*, 8/26/82 (9:5). See also: 1880 U.S. Census (Aiken Co., SC), which notes both parties.

Moses Lockhart (black, age 23). *Murder.* The crime was committed on 5/19/1882 in Edgefield County. Shotgun slaying of 32-year-old Mose Blalock (black). Motive: rivalry for a female. The killer was hanged at Edgefield on December 1, 1882. Sources: *Edgefield (SC) Chronicle*, 5/24/82 (3:4); *Charleston News & Courier*, 12/2/82 (1:2); *Macon (GA) Telegraph*, 12/2/82 (1:5). See also: 1880 U.S. Census (Edgefield Co., SC), which notes Blalock.

1883

Oliver Bristow (black, age not recorded). *Murder.* The crime was committed on 11/30/1882 in Kershaw County. Accomplice in the ax murder of Frank M. McDowall (white, age not recorded). Motive: unclear. The actual killer (Joe Wilson) fled and is not known to have ever been caught. Another accomplice (Joe Ross) was killed when he tried to run a roadblock. Bristow had helped to conceal the murdered man's body. He was hanged at Camden on March 30, 1883. Sources: *Charleston News & Courier*, 3/31/83 (1:3); New York Herald, 3/31/83 (3:3).

Frazier Copeland (black, age 42). *Murder.* The crime was committed on 12/2/1882 in Oconee County. Executed for the murder of 50-year-old William John Hunnicutt (white) and near murder of that man's 10-year-old son. Both were punched in their temples (probably with brass knuckles) as they rode their wagon home from market. Motive: highway robbery. The killer was hanged at Walhalla on April 27, 1883. Sources: *Charleston News & Courier*, 4/28/83 (1:6); *New York Herald*, 4/28/83 (4:2). See also: 1880 U.S. Census (Oconee Co., SC), which notes Copeland, and 1850 U.S. Census (Pickens Co., SC), which notes Mr. Hunnicutt.

Willie Hardee (black, age about 24) **and Solomon Hewitt** (black, age 28). *Murder.* Their crime was committed on 10/26/1882 in Horry County. Both executed for the murder of 64-year-old Jeremiah Stalvey (white, a storekeeper), who was beaten on the head with a piece of iron stolen from a turpentine still. Motive: robbery. The killers were hanged at Conway on June 15, 1883. Sources: *Charleston News & Courier*, 6/16/83 (1:3); *New York Herald*, 6/16/83 (4:6). See also: 1870 and 1880 U.S. Census (Horry Co., SC), which respectively note "Hewett" [*sic*] and Stalvey.

Benjamin Perry, alias "Perry Cely" (black, age 33). *Murder.* The crime was committed on 4/22/1883 in Greenville County. Handgun slaying of 33-year-old Perry Anderson (black). Motive: because the murdered man had objected to Cely's flirting with his wife. The killer was hanged at Greenville on August 17, 1883. Sources: *Charleston News & Courier*, 8/18/83 (1:6); *New York Herald*, 8/18/83 (9:5). See also: 1880 U.S. Census (Greenville Co., SC), which notes both parties.

Jerry Cox (black, age about 30). *Murder.* The crime was committed on 6/6/1883 in Georgetown County. Executed for the murder of 24-year-old Herbert H. Rembert (white), a butcher by trade. Motive: highway robbery and gross perfidy. The victim had employed Cox to assist him in transporting some beef. Cox returned to town alone, saying that Mr. Rembert had been drowned in a river crossing. The body was recovered two days later. It was found to have a traumatic head injury but no water in the lungs. Cox the killer was hanged at Georgetown on December 21, 1883. Source: *Charleston News & Courier*, 12/22/83 (1:8). See also: 1880 U.S. Census (Georgetown Co., SC), which notes Mr. Rembert.

1884

Isaac Anderson (black, age not recorded). *Murder.* The crime was committed on 9/12/1883 in Barnwell County. Shotgun slaying of 38-year-old Owen Williams (white). Motive: because Williams had killed Anderson's sheep killing dog after numerous warnings to control the animal. Anderson was hanged for this homicide at Barnwell on January 11, 1884. Sources: *Charleston News & Courier*, 1/12/84 (1:5); *Columbia (SC) Daily Register*, 1/12/84 (1:3). See also: 1880 U.S. Census (Barnwell Co., SC), which notes Mr. Williams.

Joseph Howard (black, age 35). *Murder.* The crime was committed on 3/20/1883 in Sumter County. Shotgun slaying of Simon Gaskins (black, age not recorded). Motive: because Gaskins had married the killer's stepdaughter. Howard regarded the girl as his concubine and therefore off limits to other males. He was hanged at Sumter on March 28, 1884. Sources: *Charleston News & Courier*, 3/29/84 (1:5); *Columbia (SC) Daily Register*, 3/29/84 (1:3). See also: 1880 U.S. Census (Sumter Co., SC), which notes Howard.

James S. Coleman (black, age 26). *Murder.* The crime was committed on 12/27/1882 in Richland County. Hatchet killing of 23-year-old Sarah Willis (black) and forcible rape of 23-year-old Mattie Faust (black), his sisters-in-law. Motive: sexual assault. The trial jury was comprised of 10 whites and 2 blacks. All-black mobs made two attempts to lynch this killer. He was legally hanged at Columbia on May 9, 1884. Source: *Charleston News & Courier*, 5/10/84 (1:3). See also: 1880 U.S. Census (Columbia, SC), which notes the murdered women.

Alfred McCullough (black, age about 45) **and James McCullough** (black, age 22). *Murder.* Father and son. Their crime was committed on 2/10/1884 in Greenville County. Handgun slaying of 19-year-old Ephraim Saxon (black). Motive: revenge. Saxon had publicly humiliated the McCulloughs at a social function by worsting them in a brawl and triumphantly claiming as his own a young woman who had been in their company. The incident was especially galling because the female had hitherto been the younger McCullough's girlfriend. The killers were hanged at Greenville on May 16, 1884. Sources: *Charleston News & Courier*, 5/17/84 (1:5); *New York Herald*, 5/17/84 (7:4). See also: 1880 U.S. Census (Greenville Co., SC), which notes Saxon.

William Trezevant (black, age 31). *Murder.* The crime was committed on 3/17/1883 in Orangeburg County. Executed for the murder of 20-year-old Frank Mitchell (black), who was bludgeoned with a spade and buried alive face down in a shallow grave. Motive: rivalry for a female. The killer was hanged at Orangeburg on June 6, 1884. Sources: *Charleston News & Courier*, 6/7/84 (1:6); *New York Herald*, 3/20/83 (3:4) & 6/7/84 (5:6).

William Stevens (black, age 18). *Murder.* The crime was committed on 11/14/1883 in Edgefield County. Executed for the murder of 50+ year old Henry S. Steifer (white), described as a "German peddler." Motive: robbery and gross perfidy. Stevens had treacherously hired himself out as the victim's guide. The pair made camp on a roadside. Stevens bludgeoned Steifer with a "lightwood knot" as the latter lay sleeping. Then he plundered the dead man's trade goods and fled. He was hanged at Edgefield on August 1, 1884. Sources: *Charleston News & Courier*, 8/2/84 (1:3); *New York Herald*, 8/2/84 (2:6).

John Scott, alias "Jack Nesmith" (black, age 24). *Murder.* The crime was committed on 6/24/1884 in Berkeley County. Cop killer. Handgun slaying of 36-year-old James J. Schipmann (white), a special magistrate's deputy, who was shot six times. Motive: resisting arrest. The killer was hanged at Mount Pleasant on December 5, 1884. Source: *Charleston News & Courier*, 7/7/84 (4:6), 10/24/84 (10:3), 12/5/84 (8:2) & 12/6/84 (1:6). See also: 1880 U.S. Census (Charleston Co., SC), which notes the murdered man.

1885

Richard Fraser (black, age 25). *Murder.* The crime was committed on 7/17/1884 at Charleston. Ax murder of Jack Githers (black, age not recorded). Motive: theft of stores. Both parties were crewmen aboard a sloop then moored in the Ashley River. Githers had been left in charge during the skipper's absence. Fraser butchered Githers in his bunk and went ashore in a boat laden with stolen provisions. He didn't get far. He was hanged at Charleston on April 10, 1885. Sources: *Charleston News & Courier*, 4/11/85 (1:6); *New York Herald*, 4/11/85 (9:3). See also: 1880 U.S. Census (Charleston, SC), which notes Fraser.

Columbus Crawford (black, age 49). Murder. The crime was committed on 10/5/1884 in York County. Shotgun slaying of 22-year-old Ellison Sanders (black). Motive: because Sanders had reported him for stealing. Crawford was hanged at York on April 10, 1885. Sources: *Charleston News & Courier*, 4/11/85 (2:2); *New York Herald*, 4/11/85 (9:3). See also: 1880 U.S. Census (York Co., SC), which notes both parties.

Hamp Nethers (black, age 35). *Murder.* The crime was committed on 1/24/1885 in Union County. Handgun slaying of 17-year-old Adolphus "Dolph" Abrams (black). Motive: because the killer's sister (who bore the reputation of a public slut) said that Abrams had talked dirty to her. Nethers was hanged at Union Courthouse on April 24, 1885. Sources: *Columbia (SC) Register*, 4/25/85 (1:2); *Charleston News & Courier*, 4/25/85 (1:4); *New York Herald*, 4/25/85 (3:3). See also: 1870 U.S. Census (Newberry Co., SC), which notes "Dolphus" Abrams.

John Terry (black, age 26). *Murder.* The crime was committed on 5/22/1884 in Barnwell County. Executed for the murder of 40-year-old John G. Sessions (white), who was bludgeoned with a railroad coupling pin and buried in a shallow grave. Motive: alleged murder-for-hire. The killer was hanged at Barnwell on May 29, 1885. Sources: *Charleston News & Courier*, 5/27/85 (1:3); *Augusta (GA) Chronicle*, 5/30/85 (1:2). See also: 1850 U.S. Census (Fairfield Co., SC), which notes the murdered man as a minor.

1886

Jenkins Wright (black, age 23). *Murder.* The crime was committed on 10/28/1885 in Hampton County. Uxoricide. Executed for the murder of 25-year-old Charlotte Wright (black), who was beaten with a billy club and shoved head-first into their fireplace so that her head was roasted. Motive: spousal abuse. The killer was hanged at Hampton Courthouse on July 2, 1886. Sources: *Macon (GA) Telegraph*, 11/11/85 (7:1); *Charleston News & Courier*, 5/8/86 (6:1) & 7/3/86 (1:4). See also: 1880 U.S. Census (Hampton Co., SC), which notes both parties.

George Edward Bundy (black, age 22). *Murder.* The crime was committed on 3/5/1885 in Spartanburg County. Handgun slaying of about 40-year-old Mary Annie Isabella Shiver, alias "Annie Heckman" (white), a notorious prostitute who was shot dead in her doorway. Motive: because the killer feared the social ramifications of their miscegenation and also because he felt trapped by it. Bundy was hanged at Spartanburg on August 6, 1886. Source: *Charleston News & Courier*, 3/7/85 (8:1) & 8/7/86 (1:6).

Wright Weldon (black, age about 31). *Murder.* The crime was committed on

11/24/1874 in Edgefield County. Shotgun slaying of 35-year-old John W. Lagrone (white). Motive: highway robbery. This killer was hanged at Edgefield on October 8, 1886. Sources: *Augusta (GA) Chronicle*, 11/26/74 (4:2); *Charleston News & Courier*, 10/9/86 (1:4); *New York Herald*, 10/9/86 (5:3). See also: 1870 U.S. Census (Edgefield Co., SC), which notes the murdered man.

Bob Butler, alias "Jeter" (black, age 17). *Murder.* The crime was committed on 8/24/1886 in Spartanburg County. Executed for the murder of Hampton Littlefield (white, age not recorded), a blacksmith who died at his forge. Motive: personal grudge. The victim had intervened when he saw the killer bullying a younger boy. Butler (a.k.a. Jeter) threw a rock at Littlefield, which hit him square on the head and killed him. Butler was hanged for this at Spartanburg on December 17, 1886. Sources: *Carolina Spartan*, 9/1/86 (3:2) & 12/22/86 (3:1); *Charleston News & Courier*, 12/18/86 (3:4).

1887

Lewis Stewart (black, age 33). *Murder.* The crime was committed on 5/7/1883 in Laurens County. Uxoricide. Shotgun slaying of 26-year-old Frances Stewart (black). Motive: marital estrangement and adultery on her part. The killer was hanged at Laurens on April 1, 1887. Sources: *Charleston News & Courier*, 4/2/87 (1:6); *New York Herald*, 4/2/87 (4:2). See also: 1880 U.S. Census (Newberry Co., SC), which notes both parties.

Solomon Conyers (black, age about 30). *Murder.* The crime was committed on or about 5/1/1887 in Hampton County. Shotgun slaying of 32-year-old Jordan Robinson (black). Motive: rivalry for a female. Conyers was hanged at Hampton Courthouse on August 12, 1887. Sources: *Charleston News & Courier*, 8/13/87 (1:4); *Augusta (GA) Chronicle*, 8/13/87 (3:1); *Columbia (SC) Daily Register*, 8/13/87 (1:7). See also: 1880 U.S. Census (Edgefield Co., SC), which notes Robinson.

Talton Danzy (black, age 38). *Murder.* The crime was committed on 4/1/1887 in Kershaw County. Fatal stabbing of 18-year-old Noel Perkins (black). Motive: an argument about an ox that had strayed onto the victim's land. Perkins demanded a dollar before he would relinquish the animal. A fight erupted over the matter and Danzy fought dirty. He was hanged at Camden on August 26, 1887. Source: *Charleston News & Courier*, 8/27/87 (1:3). See also: 1870 U.S. Census (Kershaw Co., SC), which notes both parties.

Jake Nimmons (black, age not recorded). *Murder.* The crime was committed on 2/23/1887 in Berkeley County. Handgun slaying of about 25-year-old Michael Plotkin (white), a storekeeper. Motive: argument over merchandise. The trial jury was comprised of eleven blacks and one white man. Nimmons was hanged at Mount Pleasant on December 2, 1887. Source: *Charleston News & Courier*, 2/25/87 (8:5), 10/23/87 (8:2), 10/26/87 (8:3) & 12/3/87 (8:1).

John Strickland (white, age about 20). *Murder.* The crime was committed on 7/2/1887 in Horry County. Shotgun slaying of Adeline D. Strickland (white, age not recorded), his stepmother. Motive: family problems. She had accused him of bestiality and traducing his wife's honor in so doing. He was hanged at Conway on December 30, 1887. Source: *Charleston News & Courier*, 10/26/87 (6:2) & 12/31/87 (1:4). See also: Commutation Petitions of Gov. J.P. Richardson (Box 1, Folder 38), SC State Archives.

1888

Prophet Fraser (black, age not recorded). *Murder.* The crime was committed on 10/2/1887 in Colleton County. Uxoricide. Executed for the murder of pregnant Viney Fraser (black, age not recorded), who was severely beaten with an iron poker in the presence of their 6-year-old son. One of her arms thus being broken, she was then finished off by a shotgun blast. Next, the battered corpse of the woman was slung over the back of a horse and carried into some woods where the killer dumped it. He was hanged at Walterboro on April 6, 1888. Source: *Charleston News & Courier*, 10/8/87 (6:2), 2/25/88 (2:3) & 4/7/88 (1:6).

Jack Prater (black, age about 32). *Murder.* The crime was committed on 7/16/1885 in Orangeburg County. Shotgun slaying of Andrew Jackson (black, age not recorded), his brother-in-law. Motive: because the victim had turned state's evidence in a case involving the theft of a white man's cotton. As a result, Prater and some other black men had served jail time. Jackson was thereafter a marked man despised by his fellow blacks who called him "traitor" instead of honest citizen. Jack Prater was also the prime suspect in the laudanum overdose death of his stepchild, but a trial court acquitted him on that charge. He was hanged at Orangeburg on April 27, 1888. Sources: *Charleston News & Courier*, 7/18/85 (1:6), 7/22/85 (1:4) & 4/28/88 (1:3); *New York Herald*, 4/28/88 (5:2).

Thomas Jasper Davis (white, age 44). *Murder.* The crime was committed on 9/25/1886 in Anderson County. Uxoricide. Executed for the shotgun slaying of 42-year-old Mary Moore Davis (white), who was ambushed on a road with a weapon that had been loaded with shrapnel for maximum killing effect. Motive: marital estrangement. The killer was hanged at Anderson on April 27, 1888. Source: *Charleston News & Courier*, 10/9/86 (1:4) & 4/28/88 (1:3). See also: 1880 U.S. Census (Anderson Co., SC), which notes both parties.

Dock Dargan (black, age 16). *Murder.* The crime was committed on 4/28/1888 in Marlboro County. Shotgun slaying of 18-year-old William N. Coxe (white). Motive: escalated argument. Coxe had gone to town that day to enroll in the local militia. He encountered Dargan while on the way home. One of them said something to the other and the results proved fatal for both. Dargan was hanged at Bennettsville on September 14, 1888. Source: *Charleston News & Courier*, 9/15/88 (2:2). See also: 1880 U.S. Census (Marlboro Co., SC), which notes the killer as "Doctor" Dargan, the son of Essex Dargan.

Ephraim Mays (black, age about 19). *Murder.* The crime was committed on 12/4/1887 in Edgefield County. Ax murder of 37-year-old Jake Burt (black, a deaf-mute), whom he then buried in his potato patch. Motive: adultery and wife stealing. Mays was hanged for this at Edgefield on October 26, 1888. Sources: *Edgefield (SC) Chronicle*, 12/14/87 (3:2);

Charleston News & Courier, 8/10/88 (3:2) & 10/27/88 (1:1). See also: 1880 U.S. Census (Edgefield Co., SC), which notes Burt.

James Woods (black, age not recorded). Murder. The crime was committed on 7/8/1888 in Aiken County. Handgun slaying of 37-year-old Robert Ollie (black). Motive: adultery and wife stealing. Woods was hanged at Aiken on November 30, 1888. Sources: *Charleston News & Courier*, 12/1/88 (1:6); *Columbia (SC) Daily Register*, 12/1/88 (1:7). See also: original case file (*State vs. Woods*), Aiken County General Sessions (Indictments bundle no. 86), SC State Archives; 1880 U.S. Census (Columbia Co., GA), which notes "Robert Olley" before he came to Aiken County.

Adolphus Wheeler (black, age 29). *Murder.* The crime was committed on 7/27/1888 in York County. Handgun slaying of 23-year-old George Beckham (black). Motive: adultery. Beckham had been in prison for 18 months. He returned home to find Wheeler cohabiting with his wife. Friction flared between the two men with fatal results for both. Wheeler was hanged at York on December 7, 1888. Source: *Charleston News & Courier*, 12/8/88 (2:6). See also: 1880 U.S. Census (York Co., SC), which notes Beckham, and (Laurens Co., SC), which notes Wheeler.

Samuel Phifer (black, age about 28). *Murder.* The crime was committed on 10/8/1888 in York County. Handgun slaying of 19-year-old Lucy Smith (black, his stepdaughter), who he ambushed on a road. Motive: brutish male passion. The killer had regarded the victim as his concubine ever since he had married her mother. He had even warned every other black male in their vicinity to steer clear of her on pain of death. One young man broke this prohibition. Phifer then went on the warpath. He killed the girl for daring to receive the attentions of someone else. This wrathful man was hanged at York on December 7, 1888. Sources: *Yorkville (SC) Enquirer*, 11/7/88 (2:2) & 12/12/88 (2:6); *Charleston News & Courier*, 12/8/88 (2:6).

1889

Emanuel Gaskins (black, age 23). *Murder.* The crime was committed on 12/1/1888 in Kershaw County. Executed for the murder of Betsy Clark (black, age not recorded), she having been slashed with a knife and her head dashed in with a pine knot. Motive: attempted sexual assault. The killer was hanged at Camden on March 8, 1889. Sources: *Charleston News & Courier*, 2/9/89 (6:1) & 3/9/89 (1:4); *Camden (SC) Journal*, 3/15/89 (1:3).

Jack Givens (black, age not recorded). *Murder.* The crime was committed on an unknown date in Colleton County. Uxoricide. Executed for the murder of Della Givens (black, age not recorded), whose throat was cut from ear to ear. Motive: indiscernible. The killer was hanged at Walterboro on April 5, 1889. The trial record in this case is presently inaccessible. Source: *Charleston News & Courier*, 4/6/89 (1:2).

James R. McLaurin (black, age 16). *Rape.* The crime was committed on 1/13/1889 in Marlboro County. Indecent assault on the person of 15-year-old Annie Jane McLaurin (white) under circumstances that were deemed heinous enough to warrant his execution pursuant to law. The rapist was hanged at Bennettsville on April 26, 1889. The shared surname probably stems from the time of emancipation. Sources: *Columbia (SC) Daily Register*, 1/15/89 (1:3); *Charleston News & Courier*, 4/27/89 (1:6). See also: 1880 U.S. Census (Marlboro Co., SC), which notes the female party.

Caesar Fraser (black, age 22). *Murder.* The crime was committed on 2/9/1889 at Charleston. Handgun slaying of 60-year-old Eide Henry Oldenburg (white), a storekeeper. Motive: armed robbery. The killer was hanged at Charleston on April 26, 1889. Source: *Charleston News & Courier*, 2/11/89 (8:1) & 4/27/89 (1:5). See also the victim's gravestone in Bethany Cemetery, Charleston, South Carolina; 1861 Charleston Municipal Census, which notes Oldenburg by his full name.

Charles Colston (black, age not recorded) **and John Henry Williams**, alias "John C. Feaster" (black, age 34). *Murder.* The crime was committed on 1/25/1889 in York County. Both executed for the murder of 39-year-old William Calhoun Abernathy (white), a storekeeper. The victim's skull was fractured when he was hit on the head with a singletree as he sat dozing in his place of business. Motive: burglary. The killers were hanged at York on June 7, 1889. Sources: *Charleston News & Courier*, 2/2/89 (1:3) & 6/8/89 (2:1); *Yorkville (SC) Enquirer*, 4/10/89 (2:4) & 6/12/89 (2:4). See also: 1870 U.S. Census (York Co., SC), which notes "Henry" Williams, son of Joshua Williams.

1890

Charles Simmons (black, age 18). *Murder.* The crime was committed on 10/16/1889 in Berkeley County. Shotgun slaying of 50+-year-old Otto Fischang (white, a storekeeper), who was killed by a sniper who deliberately lay in wait for him when he came outdoors to feed his chickens. Motive: attempted robbery. The culprit was hanged at Mount Pleasant on April 11, 1890. Source: *Charleston News & Courier*, 10/18/89 (8:1), 10/21/89 (8:3), 4/11/909 (1:5) & 4/12/90 (8:1).

William Davis (black, age 28). *Murder.* The crime was committed on 1/9/1890 in Union County. Executed for the murder of Susie Fernandez (black), a known prostitute. She was choked after being lured to an assignation in a cemetery receiving vault and her throat cut with a barlow knife. Motive: robbery of $18 that she had concealed in her brassiere. The killer was hanged at Union Courthouse on May 9, 1890. Sources: *Weekly Union (SC) Times*, 1/24/90 (2:2); *Charleston News & Courier*, 5/10/90 (1:5).

Armistead Jones (black, age 17). *Murder.* The crime was committed on 12/4/1889 in Orangeburg County. Executed for the murder of Margaret Jones (black, age not recorded), his stepmother. The victim was struck in the head with duck shot fired from a small bore shotgun. Then she was finished off by having her skull stove in by a rock and the butt of the firearm that had been used to wound her. Motive: a spoiled, self-indulgent brat. The killer had had a mind to go duck hunting and revolted when his stepmother bade him carry grain to a gristmill instead. The boy was hanged at

Orangeburg on July 11, 1890. Source: *Charleston News & Courier*, 5/8/90 (5:2) & 7/13/90 (2:3).

Rochel Catoe (black male, age 27) **and William Clyburn** (black, age 19). *Murder.* Their crime was committed on 3/23/1890 in Lancaster County. Both executed for the mutilation murder of Gustavus "August" Hennis (white, age not recorded), a recent New York City transplant and ethnic German. He was lured from his home with a contrived story and set upon. His mouth was stuffed with mud to stifle his screams. He was slashed repeatedly about the head and face, being completely scalped. His body was found in a roadside ditch covered with brush and brambles. Motive: adultery and miscegenation. Catoe, himself the offspring of a white mother, had met that woman's equal in the person of Roxy Hennis, wife of the murdered man. Catoe then teamed up with Billy Clyburn to get rid of the cuckold. Both of the actual killers were hanged at Lancaster Courthouse on August 1, 1890. Sources: *Columbia (SC) Daily Register*, 4/1/90 (1:6) & 8/2/90 (1:3); *Charleston News & Courier*, 6/21/90 (2:1); *New York Herald*, 8/2/90 (4:2); *Wheeling (WV) Register*, 8/3/90 (4:3). See also: 1880 U.S. Census (Lancaster Co., SC), which notes the culprits.

Robert Shelton (black, age about 45). *Murder.* The crime was committed on 2/25/1890 in Laurens County. Ax murder of William Rayford (black, age not recorded) and illegal disposal of his corpse by dumping it down a well. Motive: rivalry for a female. Shelton was hanged at Laurens on September 5, 1890. Source: *Columbia (SC) Daily Register*, 3/4/90 (1:2) & 9/7/90 (1:4).

Adam Mongin (black, age 21). *Murder.* The crime was committed on 5/31/1890 in Berkeley County. Handgun slaying of 27-year-old Simon Jackson (black), the victim having been shot in the back. Motive: gambling dispute for the sake of 20 cents. The killer was hanged at Mount Pleasant on December 19, 1890. Source: *Charleston News & Courier*, 12/15/90 (8:3) & 12/20/90 (9:1). See also: Charleston death cert. no. 986 dated 6/7/90, which notes Jackson as having died in a hospital there; 1870 U.S. Census (Savannah, GA), which notes the killer as a baby.

1891

Sentry Butler (black, age 26) **and Hampton Nelson** (black, age 32). *Murder.* Their crime was committed on 1/19/1891 in Sumter County. Both executed for the shotgun slaying of John Maxcy (white, age not recorded), who was ambushed as he drove his wagon along a road near his home. The wagon overturned and the mortally wounded man lay in agony beneath it for many hours before he was discovered. Motive: disgruntled employees. The killers were hanged at Sumter on April 10, 1891. Sources: *The Watchman & Southron* (Sumter, SC), 3/11/91 (5:3); *The State* (Columbia, SC), 4/10/91 (5:2); *Charleston News & Courier*, 1/21/91 (1:3), 1/29/91 (1:6) & 4/11/91 (1:4). See also: 1880 U.S. Census (Sumter Co., SC), which notes Nelson.

Walker Brown (black, age 21). *Murder.* The crime was committed on 10/16/1890 in Laurens County. Handgun slaying of 24-year-old Noah Ramage (black). Motive: gambling dispute. The killer was hanged at Laurens on April 17, 1891. Sources: *The State* (Columbia, SC),

2/22/91 (5:3); *Laurens (SC) Advertiser*, 4/21/91 (3:2); *Charleston News & Courier*, 4/18/91 (1:2), which misreported the victim's ethnicity. See also: 1880 U.S. Census (Laurens Co., SC), which notes Ramage.

Edmund Holladay (black, age 37). *Murder.* The crime was committed on 11/24/1890 in Clarendon County. Handgun slaying of 44-year-old John W. du-Bose (white), who succumbed to his wound exactly three weeks later. Motive: escalated argument. The killer had picked an argument with the victim for no apparent reason and then came back to the scene armed an hour later to renew it. He was hanged at Manning on April 24, 1891. Source: *Charleston News & Courier*, 12/18/90 (1:6) & 4/26/91 (1:4). See also: 1880 U.S. Census (Clarendon Co., SC), which notes the miscreant, and 1850 U.S. Census (Sumter Co., SC), which notes duBose as a small child.

Bill Miles (black, age not recorded). *Murder.* The crime was committed on 10/19/1890 in Pickens County. Handgun slaying of 42-year-old Jacob Griffin (black), who was shot three times. Motive: gambling dispute for the sake of a nickel. The killer was hanged at Pickens on April 24, 1891. Sources: *Pickens (SC) Sentinel*, 10/23/90 (3:2) & 4/30/91 (3:2); *Columbia (SC) Daily Register*, 4/25/91 (1:5). See also: 1880 U.S. Census (Pickens Co., SC), which notes Griffin.

Waites Martin (black, age not recorded). *Murder.* The crime was committed on 1/23/1891 in Richland County. Executed for the murder of about 30-year-old Alice McLeod (white, his alleged paramour), she having been beaten, choked and dumped in a river, her person weighted with stones. Motive: jealous rage. The victim came from the sub-basement of society. She lived in a shack with a brood of illegitimate children fathered by any male opportunist who happened to come along. Martin objected when this "lady" sold vegetables to some railroad men, no doubt thinking that she would include herself in the bargain. So he tracked her down that very same night and rid the world of her. He was hanged for this at Columbia on April 24, 1891. Sources: *The State* (Columbia, SC), 4/1/91 (8:1) & 4/25/91 (8:1); *Charleston News & Courier*, 1/26/91 (2:1).

Isaac Kinard (black, age 30). *Murder.* The crime was committed on 6/13/1891 in Newberry County. Musket slaying of 26-year-old Lemuel G. Oxner (white), his landlord. Motive: workplace dispute. Venue changed from Newberry County to Laurens County. The killer was hanged at Laurens on October 16, 1891. Sources: *The State* (Columbia, SC), 10/17/91 (5:1); *Charleston News & Courier*, 6/15/91 (1:1) & 10/17/91 (1:3). See also: Oxner's gravestone in Sharon Cemetery, Kinards, South Carolina; 1870 U.S. Census (Newberry Co., SC), which notes the killer.

William Somerset (black, age 28). *Murder.* The crime was committed on 1/19/1885 in Marion County. Executed for the murder of 35-year-old Edward M. Fore (white), who was struck on the head with the flat side of an ax and his body positioned to make it look like he had been run over by a heavy farm wagon. Motive: a sordid tale of interracial adultery. The killer was hanged at Marion on November 13, 1891. Sources: *Charleston News & Courier*, 10/20/91 (5:1); *The State* (Columbia, SC), 11/14/91 (5:1). See also: 1880 U.S. Census (Marion Co., SC), which notes both parties.

John W. Patterson (black, age not recorded). *Murder.* The crime was committed on 6/22/ 1891 in Horry County. Cop killer. Shotgun slaying of 34-year-old Henry Cornelius Hardee (white), a magistrate's constable in Simpson Creek Township. Motive: resisting arrest. Patterson was hanged at Conway on November 20, 1891. Sources: *Horry (SC) Herald*, 6/25/91 (3:1); *Charleston News & Courier*, 6/24/91 (1:4) & 11/23/91 (6:1).

1892

Van Thomas, alias "Thomason" (black, age 32). *Murder.* The crime was committed on or about 5/15/1890 in Abbeville County. Executed for the ax murder of John Brackett (black, age not recorded). Motive: robbery and gross perfidy. Thomas confessed that he had also murdered another black man named Ephraim Laddis at Chester, South Carolina, on 12/22/1889, having smashed his head with a rock in order to get his pay packet. This killer was hanged at Abbeville on March 4, 1892. Sources: *Abbeville (SC) Press & Banner*, 3/9/92 (5:2); *The State* (Columbia, SC), 3/5/92 (3:1); *Charleston News & Courier*, 3/5/92 (1:4).

Thomas Hamilton, alias "Hammond" (black, age 25). *Murder.* The crime was committed on 1/2/1892 at Charleston. Executed for the murder of 41-year-old Thomas Henry Massalon (white, a night watchman at a fertilizer plant), who was bludgeoned with a crowbar and slashed about the head and neck. Motive: burglary. The killer was hanged at Charleston on April 22, 1892. Sources: *Charleston News & Courier*, 1/5/92 (8:2), 1/13/92 (8:1) & 4/22/92 (8:1); *The State* (Columbia, SC), 4/23/92 (4:4). See also: Mr. Massalon's gravestone in Bethany Cemetery, Charleston, South Carolina.

Julius Wyse (black, age 36). *Murder.* The crime was committed on 2/23/1889 in Lexington County. Executed for the murder of Willis Stark (black, age not recorded), who was slashed with a knife across the left side of his face with such severity that he died on March 5. Motive: because Stark owed him money. Wyse was hanged at Lexington Courthouse on July 29, 1892. Sources: *The State* (Columbia, SC), 7/30/92 (5:1); *Charleston News & Courier*, 6/15/90 (1:5); *Lexington (SC) Dispatch*, 8/3/92 (4:2). See also: 1880 U.S. Census (Lexington Co., SC), which notes Wyse; original case file (Lexington General Sessions, June Term, 1892), SC State Archives.

Charles Williams (black, age not recorded). *Murder.* The crime was committed on 10/31/1891 in Hampton County. Executed for the shotgun slaying of Silas Bryant (black, age not recorded), who was lured from his home with deliberate intent. Motive: because the killer coveted the victim's wife. Williams was hanged at Hampton Courthouse on August 5, 1892. Source: *Charleston News & Courier*, 8/6/92 (1:5); *Savannah (GA) Morning News*, 8/6/92 (1:3).

Andrew Jeffries (black, age 23). *Murder.* The crime was committed on 7/16/1892 in Spartanburg County. Executed for the murder of William Atkins (white, age not recorded), who was slashed to death with "a large hawk bill knife" as he stood on a public sidewalk. Motive: racial hostility. The killer resented the sight of a white man (Atkins) being propositioned by a black prostitute. So he went on the attack. He was hanged at Spartanburg on

September 9, 1892. Sources: *Columbia (SC) Daily Register*, 9/10/92 (1:1); *Carolina Spartan*, 7/20/92 (3:2); *The State* (Columbia, SC), 7/17/92 (1:5), 7/18/92 (1:3) & 9/10/92 (1:5).

Adam Foster (black, age 24). *Murder.* The crime was committed on 11/17/1891 in Spartanburg County. Executed for the shotgun slaying of Mayberry Sanders (black, age not recorded). Motive: rivalry for a white whore. Foster was hanged at Spartanburg on September 9, 1892. Sources: *The State* (Columbia, SC), 9/10/92 (1:5); *Charleston News & Courier*, 9/10/92 (1:6). See also: 1880 U.S. Census (Spartanburg Co., SC), which notes the killer.

Thomas Brock (black, age 18). *Murder.* The crime was committed on 6/23/1892 in Pickens County. Cop killer. Executed for the shotgun slaying of 38-year-old Jeremiah Hughes (white), the town marshal of Easley. Motive: mistaken identity. The killer had quarreled with another black man for the affection of a young woman of their own race. Brock stomped out of the female's house, muttering threats as he did so. Expecting further trouble, the occupants of that abode called the marshal. The latter was standing in the doorway of that place when Brock returned as predicted. Brock was toting a shotgun. He mistook a silhouette of the marshal for that of his rival. The gun roared and the marshal was hit in the back. Brock was hanged at Pickens Courthouse on October 7, 1892. Sources: *The State* (Columbia, SC), 6/25/92 (1:5) & 10/8/92 (5:1); *Charleston News & Courier*, 10/8/92 (1:1). See also: 1880 U.S. Census (Pickens Co., SC), which notes Brock, and 1850 U.S. Census (Anderson Co., SC), which notes Hughes as a minor.

William Wilson (white, age 34). *Murder.* The crime was committed on 5/10/1892 in Anderson County. Uxoricide. Executed for the murder of 29-year-old Laura Garrett Wilson (white), who was slashed to death with a razor despite the proximity of their infant child, who got soaked in its mother's blood. Motive: brutality, jealousy and pending separation. The killer was hanged at Anderson on October 7, 1892. Sources: *Anderson (SC) Intelligencer*, 5/19/92 (3:3) & 10/12/92 (3:3); *The State* (Columbia, SC), 10/8/92 (5:1).

Anna Tribble (black female, age 23). *Murder.* The crime was committed on 2/23/1892 in Newberry County. Infanticide. Executed for the murder of her unnamed baby (black, gender not specified), which she birthed outdoors by the side of a brook and threw alive into the water. She was hanged at Newberry on October 7, 1892. Source: *The State* (Columbia, SC), 10/8/92 (5:1). See also: 1870 U.S. Census (Newberry Co., SC), which notes the killer as a minor.

Milbry Brown (black female, age 14). *Murder.* The crime was committed on 6/27/1892 in Spartanburg County. Baby killer. Executed for the murder of 11-month old Geraldine Carpenter (white, the daughter of William C. Carpenter and Carrie Brown Carpenter of Gaffney, South Carolina) by putting carbolic acid in the child's mouth as it lay asleep in its cradle. Motive: an act of spite aimed at the victim's mother. This poisoner was hanged at Spartanburg on October 7, 1892. Source: original case file (*State vs. Brown, alias Smith*), Spartanburg General Sessions, July Term 1892; South Carolina State Archives; *Charleston News & Courier*, 6/30/92 (1:4); *The State* (Columbia, SC), 6/29/92 (1:3) & 10/8/92 (1:2).

John L. Williams (black, age not recorded). *Murder.* The crime was committed on 9/27/1891 in Spartanburg County. Handgun slaying of 55-year-old John Adam Henneman (white, the mayor of Spartanburg), who was shot in the back. Motive: resisting arrest. His Honor had happened to walk by the Williams residence at a time when its occupant was beating up his female lover. The mayor ordered the bully to stop what he was doing. A scuffle ensued. The results were fatal to both parties. The assassin was hanged at Spartanburg on October 7, 1892. Source: *The State* (Columbia, SC), 9/29/91 (1:1), 9/29/91 (1:5) & 10/7/92 (1:1). See also: 1880 U.S. Census (Spartanburg, SC), which notes Henneman.

Joseph Jenkins (black, age about 20). *Murder.* The crime was committed on 3/6/1892 in Berkeley County. Ax murder of 62-year-old John Morgan (white), the victim having also been robbed of $1.73 in money, a razor, a pistol and the shoes off his feet. Motive: mugging. Jenkins was wearing the victim's shoes when he was arrested. He was hanged at Mount Pleasant on December 16, 1892. Sources: *The State* (Columbia, SC), 3/8/92 (5:6); *Charleston News & Courier*, 3/8/92 (8:1) & 12/17/92 (12:1).

Toby Jackson (black, age 59). *Murder.* The crime was committed on 12/13/1890 in Orangeburg County. Shotgun slaying of 29-year-old Nelson Hook (black), the musician at a Negro dance. Motive: because the victim had dared to reproach the killer for spoiling the party. Jackson was hanged at Orangeburg on December 30, 1892. Sources: *Charleston News & Courier*, 12/31/92 (1:3); *Savannah (GA) Morning News*, 1/2/93 (6:3). See also: 1880 U.S. Census (Orangeburg Co., SC), which notes both men.

1893

Henry Perry, alias "Jack Bradley," alias "Bigoty Jack" (black, age 21). *Murder.* The crime was committed on 8/6/1892 in Marlboro County. Executed for the handgun slaying of L.D. Taylor (white, age and full name not recorded), the victim having been shot in the back. Motive: rivalry for the services of a prostitute. Taylor was a railroad man from Pennsylvania. He was also described as a drunk and a whoremonger. The killer had escaped from the South Carolina State Prison on 12/27/1891, where he had been serving a life sentence for an undisclosed felony committed in Kershaw County. He was hanged at Bennettsville on April 14, 1893. Sources: *Marlboro (SC) Democrat*, 8/10/92 (3:3); *The State* (Columbia, SC), 8/8/92 (1:4) & 4/15/93 (1:4); *Charleston News & Courier*, 5/12/89 (1:5), 12/28/91 (1:3) & 4/15/93 (1:4).

Wade Haynes (black, age 15). *Murder.* The crime was committed on 11/1/1890 in Richland County. Executed for the fatal stabbing of 16-year-old Florence Hornsby (white), who was attacked as she washed clothes at an outdoor spring. Motive: attempted sexual assault. The killer was hanged at Columbia on May 5, 1893. Source: *The State* (Columbia, SC), 4/3/91 (8:1) & 5/6/93 (8:1). See also: 1880 U.S. Census (Richland Co., SC), which notes Miss Hornsby.

Joe Brannon, alias "Joe Williams" (black, age about 25). *Murder.* The crime was committed on 8/31/1892 in Chester County. Handgun slaying of 72-year-old Stephen Kearney (white), the victim having been shot four times. Motive: wage dispute. The killer was hanged at Chester on May 12, 1893. Source: *Charleston News & Courier*, 9/23/92 (5:2); *The State* (Columbia, SC), 9/21/92 (4:4) & 5/13/93 (1:4). See also: 1870 U.S. Census (Chester Co., SC), which notes the murdered man.

Jerry Hennegan (black, age 27). *Arson.* The crime was committed on 4/2/1893 in Marlboro County. Executed for maliciously and willfully firing the barn, stable and granary of 32-year-old Elisha D. Graham (white, a "highly respected" farmer), with the resultant loss of that man's provender, vehicles and five horses, in addition to the buildings themselves. Motive: vindictiveness. The culprit had already been fired from Mr. Graham's employ. He was hanged at Bennettsville on July 7, 1893. Source: *The State* (Columbia, SC), 7/8/93 (3:1). See also: 1900 & 1910 U.S. Census (Marlboro Co., SC), which note farmer Graham.

Adam Hiers (black, age not recorded). *Murder.* The crime was committed on or about 6/5/1893 in Colleton County. Executed for the murder of another black man named "Walker," who was reported to be his brother-in-law. Motive: family feud. The killer's father, Riley Hiers, was also sentenced to death in this case but wrangled a commutation. Adam Hiers was hanged at Walterboro on July 28, 1893. The original court papers being inaccessible, no further details can be found. Source: *Charleston News & Courier*, 7/29/93 (2:5) & 10/17/93 (2:3).

Oscar Johnson (black, age 29). *Murder.* The crime was committed on 3/4/1893 in Berkeley County. Executed for the ax murders of 29-year-old Heinrich Wilhelm Tweitmann and 34-year-old Anna Rebecca Catherine Ronner Tweitmann (whites), a married couple. Motive: robbery. Recidivist killer. This offender had previously been sentenced to a term of life imprisonment for a Georgia murder. It was committed on 7/11/1890 in Richmond County. The victim was an 18-year-old black female named Lucinda Sims. She was raped, her throat was cut from ear to ear with a razor, and her body was dumped in the Savannah River. Johnson's life was spared upon conviction for that crime because some doubts were raised about his sanity. He was sent to the Dade County mines but soon was transferred to the Negro Insane Asylum at Milledgeville, from whence he escaped on 12/17/1892. The governor of South Carolina refused to commute Johnson's death sentence on the grounds that, crazy or not, he was too dangerous to live. He was hanged at Mount Pleasant on September 1, 1893. Sources: *Augusta (GA) Chronicle*, 7/15/90 (3:3), 7/17/90 (5:1) & 3/8/91 (5:3); *The State* (Columbia, SC), 3/7/93 (5:1); *Charleston News & Courier*, 1/14/93 (5:1), 3/10/93 (8:1) & 9/2/93 (8:1). See also the gravestone of Mr. and Mrs. Tweitmann in Bethany Cemetery, Charleston, South Carolina, as well as their marriage certificate (same city) dated 9/8/87, on which the bride lied about her age; 1870 U.S. Census (Augusta, GA), which notes Oscar Johnson as a minor.

Henry Ewing (black, age about 30). *Murder.* The crime was committed on 2/20/1893 in Berkeley County. Shotgun slaying of 35-year-old Tony Fickling (black). Motive: rivalry for a "black prostitute." Ewing was hanged at Mount

Pleasant on September 1, 1893. Source: *Charleston News & Courier*, 2/25/93 (2:2), 9/1/93 (8:4) & 9/2/93 (8:1). See also: 1880 U.S. Census (Haywood Co., TN), which notes Fickling.

George Bowers (black, age 22) **and Wade Cannon** (black, age 22). Their crime was committed on 7/14/1893 in Laurens County. *Arson of an Inhabited Dwelling House.* Both executed for burning down the residence of 42-year-old John Dorrah Hairston (white) in order to cover up the theft of "several containers of milk" from that man's kitchen. They were hanged at Laurens on September 1, 1893. Source: *The State* (Columbia, SC), 9/2/93 (4:3). See also: 1860 & 1870 U.S. Census (Laurens Co., SC), which note Mr. Hairston, as well as his broken gravestone in Hopewell United Methodist Church Cemetery, Joanna, South Carolina.

John Ferguson (black, age 24). *Murder.* The crime was committed on 3/12/1893 in Laurens County. Uxoricide. Executed for the murder of Emma Ferguson (black, age not recorded), her throat being cut. Motive: marital estrangement. The victim had attempted to defend herself with a razor, but the killer got the better of her with a knife. He was hanged at Laurens on September 1, 1893. Sources: *Charleston News & Courier*, 3/13/93 (1:2); *The State* (Columbia, SC), 9/2/93 (4:3); *Laurens (SC) Advertiser*, 9/4/93 (3:3). See also: 1880 U.S. Census (Laurens Co., SC), which notes the miscreant.

George S. Turner (white, age 39). *Murder.* The crime was committed on 3/7/1890 in Spartanburg County. Executed for the handgun slaying of 28-year-old Edgar Finger (white), his brother-in-law. Motive: mutual antagonism. Turner had previously disgraced their families by sexually molesting his wife's younger sister, Clara Finger. The story was that he had lured the girl to a hotel where she was drugged and made the mother of a bastard child. Recidivist killer. Turner was a man of substantial means both materially and financially. He had ridden with the KKK during the years 1867–1870, but went on to become a successful merchant-farmer. It was on 6/24/1887 that he murdered one of his farmhands (Julius Metzkia, a German) by blowing off the top of that man's head with a shotgun blast. Reason: because he was too stingy to pay $1.03 disputed wages. Turner was subsequently represented by "the finest legal talent that money could buy." He drew a 5-year term for manslaughter, which was then thrown out on appeal. A retrial followed which ended in acquittal. He had gotten away with murder but overplayed his hand when he tried to do it again. He was hanged at Spartanburg on September 1, 1893. Sources: *Augusta (GA) Chronicle*, 6/29/87 (2:3); *The State* (Columbia, SC), 9/2/93 (1:1). See also: 1880 U.S. Census (Spartanburg Co., SC), which notes the family Finger.

1894

Gabriel Graves (black, age about 32). *Murder.* The crime was committed on 9/5/1893 in Colleton County. Child killer. Executed for the handgun slaying of 13-year-old Frank Thompson (white) and the burning of the house in which he dwelt. Motive: plunder. The killer was hanged at Walterboro on January 26, 1894. Source: *Charleston News & Courier*, 9/14/93 (8:1), 11/4/93 (8:2) & 2/3/94

(2:2). See also: *The State* (Columbia, SC), 5/9/1908 (1:5) in retro.

Jerry Horlbeck (black, age 35). *Murder.* The crime was committed on 2/10/1893 in Berkeley County. Cop killer. Shotgun slaying of Robert Hasell (black, age not recorded), a magistrate's deputy, or "constable," as he was called. Motive: resisting arrest. The scene was the Magnolia Phosphate Mines, fifteen miles from Charleston. The killer was hanged at Mount Pleasant on March 16, 1894. Source: *Charleston News & Courier*, 2/12/93 (2:3), 3/26/93 (2:2) & 3/17/94 (8:1).

Alexander Edwards (black, age 33). *Murder.* The crime was committed on 12/23/1893 in Marlboro County. Ax murder of James Burnett (black, age not recorded), the victim having lingered in agony for several days before he was found. Motive: robbery and gross perfidy. The killer was hanged at Bennettsville on April 20, 1894. Source: *Charleston News & Courier*, 4/21/94 (1:3).

Moses Fair (black, age 27). *Murder.* The crime was committed on or about 6/15/1889 in Chester County. Executed for the murder of Isaac Wilson (black, age not recorded), who was beaten up by at least four men and his comatose person laid across railroad tracks so that he was mangled by a train. Motive: gambling dispute. Moses Fair was hanged at Chester on May 4, 1894. Source: *The State* (Columbia, SC), 3/24/93 (5:3) & 5/5/94 (5:1). See also: 1880 U.S. Census (Chester Co., SC), which notes the miscreant.

James Morgan (white, age 35). *Murder.* The crime was committed on 6/18/1892 in Greenville County. Shotgun slaying of 62-year-old LeRoy Washington Hipp (white, his father-in-law), who was struck in the back with 53 pieces of shrapnel. Motive: family row. The killer had impregnated more than just one of the victim's daughters. He was hanged at Greenville on June 1, 1894. Source: *Charleston News & Courier*, 6/2/94 (3:1). See also: 1870 U.S. Census (Greenville Co., SC), which notes both parties.

Dick Green (black, age about 48). *Murder.* The crime was committed on 4/18/1894 in Berkeley County. Fatal stabbing of about 40-year-old Nancy Drayton (black), she having been attacked on a public road and her body thrown into a ditch. Motive: estranged lover. Dick Green was hanged at Mount Pleasant on July 27, 1894. Source: *Charleston News & Courier*, 4/20/94 (8:4), 6/8/94 (8:2) & 7/28/94 (8:1).

Jasper Atkinson (white, age 22) **and John Atkinson** (white, age 50+). Murder. Their crime was committed on 1/28/1893 in Fairfield County. Shotgun slaying of 32-year-old John H. Clamp (white), the victim having been blasted from ambush and his brains scattered on a road. Motive: tenant-landlord dispute. The killers were hanged at Winnsboro on September 21, 1894. Source: *The State* (Columbia, SC), 1/30/93 (1:7), 3/1/93 (1:7) & 9/22/94 (1:1); *Charleston News & Courier*, 1/31/93 (2:2) & 9/22/94 (1:1). See also: 1880 U.S. Census (Richland & Lexington Co., SC), which note the younger assassin and the homicide victim.

1895

Sloan Hearst (black, age 37). *Murder.* The crime was committed on 12/3/1894 in Abbeville County. Handgun slaying of 34-year-old Lemmie Rapley (black female), who was shot three times. Motive: adultery turned deadly. The killer was hanged at Abbeville on April 26, 1895. Source: *The State* (Columbia, SC), 12/4/94 (10:3) & 4/27/95 (1:3). See also: 1880 U.S. Census (Abbeville Co., SC), which notes both parties.

Robert Poole (black, age not recorded). *Murder.* The crime was committed on 11/2/1890 in Spartanburg County. Handgun slaying of William Long (black, age not recorded). Motive: because the victim had assisted law enforcement in a way that was detrimental to the killer. Robert Poole was hanged at Spartanburg on September 20, 1895. Sources: original case file (*State vs. Poole*) Spartanburg General Sessions, July Term 1895; SC State Archives; *Charleston News & Courier*, 11/3/90 (1:2); *The State* (Columbia, SC), 9/21/95 (1:3).

Prince Graves (black, age 25), **Jason Blake** (black, age about 20) **and William Frazier** (black, age about 20). *Murder.* Their crime was committed on 8/9/1895 in Hampton County. Murder of 72-year-old Eldred Raymond Mears (white, a storekeeper and rural postmaster), who was beaten with "a heavy gum club about 3' long" and stabbed multiple times. Motive: attempted robbery. The three killers were hanged at Hampton Courthouse on December 6, 1895. Source: *The State* (Columbia, SC), 8/15/95 (3:1) & 12/7/95 (1:2). See also: 1860 U.S. Census (Beaufort Co., SC), which notes Mears, and 1880 U.S. Census (Hampton Co., SC), which notes Mears and Graves.

Charles Lloyd (black, age not recorded). *Murder.* The crime was committed on 8/24/1895 in Lancaster County. Handgun slaying of 17-year-old William B. Welsh (white), who was first shot in the side and then finished off when the killer "deliberately put the muzzle of the pistol to his temple and fired." Motive: rowdy conduct at a "negro frolic." The victim had happened to walk by at the wrong time. The sight of him triggered canine-like aggression. Venue changed from Lancaster County to Chester County. The killer was hanged at Chester on December 6, 1895. Source: *The State* (Columbia, SC), 8/26/95 (1:3) & 12/7/95 (1:1).

Thomas Peterson (black, age 30). *Murder.* The crime was committed on 10/13/1895 in Abbeville County. Cop killer. Handgun slaying of 47-year-old Johnson J. Moseley (white), a so-called "whiskey constable" or state prohibition agent. Motive: because the murdered man had intercepted a shipment of illegal liquor. The killer was hanged at Abbeville on December 6, 1895. Source: *Abbeville (SC) Press & Banner*, 10/16/95 (4:2), 10/23/95 (4:2), 10/30/95 (4:3) & 12/11/95 (4:3). See also: 1880 U.S. Census (Lowndesville, SC), which notes Moseley as a civilian.

Walker Derrick (black, age not recorded). *Murder.* The crime was committed on or about 8/15/1894 in Abbeville County. Shotgun slaying of Sam Robertson (black, age not recorded), a newlywed of two days' duration. The victim was killed as he sat eating dinner with his bride. Motive: jealous suitor for the same woman. The killer was hanged at Abbeville on December 13, 1895. Sources: *Abbeville Press & Banner*, 12/18/95 (9:1); *Abbeville (SC) Medium*, 12/19/95 (7:3).

1896

James Sanders (black, age 16). *Murder.* The crime was committed on 10/17/1895 in Barnwell County. Executed for the murder of 62-year-old Simon Riley (black, his wife's stepfather), whom he beat to death with a hickory club. Motive: undisclosed, but not difficult to imagine. The killer was hanged at Barnwell on January 3, 1896. Sources: *Barnwell (SC) People*, 10/24/95 (3:2); *Charleston News & Courier*, 1/4/96 (1:2). See also: 1880 U.S. Census (Barnwell Co., SC), which notes both parties, the killer as a baby.

Richard Washington (black, age 28). *Murder.* The crime was committed on 11/23/1895 in Abbeville County. Handgun slaying and illegal cremation of 32-year-old Narcissa Bagwell (white), a known harlot who had formed a design to run off with him. Motive: robbery and gross perfidy. The pair were huddled around a roadside campfire. The killer shot the female in the back of the head and stole her money. Then he dragged the body into a barn that was loaded with hay and burned the place down. He was hanged at Abbeville on March 27, 1896. Sources: *Abbeville (SC) Medium*, 11/28/95 (8:5); *Abbeville (SC) Press & Banner*, 1/29/96 (5:2) & 4/1/96 (4:3). See also: 1880 U.S. Census (Abbeville Co., SC), which notes the murdered woman.

Aaron Duffy (black, age not recorded). *Murder.* The crime was committed on 3/26/1896 in Newberry County. Prison guard killer. Executed for the murder of 20-year-old James Solomon Hargrove (white, a guard assigned to the Newberry county chain gang), who was hit from behind (on the back of the head and right shoulder) with the flat end of a pickaxe. Motive: jailbreak. The killer was hanged at Newberry on September 4, 1896. Sources: *Newberry (SC) Observer*, 4/1/96 (3:3) & 9/9/96 (3:3); *Newberry Herald & News*, 4/1/96 (3:3) & 9/9/96 (2:2); *The State* (Columbia, SC), 3/29/96 (1:3) & 9/5/96 (1:4). See also Hargrove's broken gravestone in Mount Tabor Cemetery, Newberry, South Carolina.

1897

Tourney Lyles (black, age 18). *Rape.* The crime was committed on 3/15/1897 in Newberry County. Indecent assault on the person of 65-year-old Jane Willard (white, a maiden woman), she having been pounced on as she walked along a rural road and dragged into woods where the attacker accomplished his purpose. Lyles was hanged for this at Newberry on August 20, 1897. Sources: *Charleston News & Courier*, 3/20/97 (6:1); *The State* (Columbia, SC), 8/21/97 (1:4). See also: 1880 U.S. Census (Santuck, SC), which notes Jane Willard.

George Green (black, age not recorded). *Murder.* The crime was committed on 7/20/1897 in Beaufort County. Fatal stabbing of Sam Deas (black, age not recorded). Motive: dispute over the ownership of a pickaxe, they both being phosphate diggers. Green was hanged for this homicide at Beaufort on October 15, 1897. Source: *Charleston News & Courier*, 10/16/97 (3:1).

John Wright (black, age 33). *Murder.* The crime was committed on 8/3/1897 in Darlington County. Shotgun slaying of 20-year-old Clarence L. Byrd (white). Motive: obnoxious drunk. The killer was hanged at Darlington on December 10, 1897. Source: *The State* (Columbia, SC), 8/4/97 (1:1) & 12/11/97 (1:3). See also: 1880 U.S. Census (Darlington Co., SC), which notes Wright; Byrd's gravestone in Antioch Baptist Church Cemetery, Antioch, South Carolina.

1898

John Butler, alias "Washington" (black, age 22). *Murder.* The crime was committed on 9/13/1897 in Orangeburg County. Cop killer. Handgun slaying of 52-year-old Christian J.D. Wolfe (white), the police chief of Orangeburg. Motive: resisting arrest. The killer was hanged at Orangeburg on February 11, 1898. Source: *The State* (Columbia, SC), 9/14/97 (1:3), 9/18/97 (8:2), 9/23/97 (5:3) & 2/12/98 (1:5).

Rion William Johnson (black, age not recorded). *Murder.* The crime was committed on 12/26/1897 in Beaufort County. Executed for the gunshot slaying of another black man named "Robertson," who was killed in his own doorway. Motive: rivalry for a female. Johnson was hanged at Beaufort on February 25, 1898. Sources: *Evening Post* (Charleston, SC), 2/25/98 (1:4); *Charleston News & Courier*, 2/26/98 (3:3). Most of this county's pre–World War II Court of General Sessions records are missing and no one seems to know what happened to them.

Jefferson Habersham (black, age not recorded). *Murder.* The crime was committed on 12/25/1897 in Beaufort County. Executed for the murder of Laura Williams (black, age not recorded), a woman whom he had previously lured away from her husband. She was beaten down with a rake and stabbed as she lay hurting on the ground. Motive: an argument over how they should divide a crop that they had raised. The killer was hanged at Beaufort on February 25, 1898. Source: Ibid.

Nathan Willis (black, age 24). *Murder.* The crime was committed on 11/15/1897 in Horry County. Shotgun slaying of 20-year-old Samuel J. Stevens (white). Motive: highway robbery. The murdered man was driving an ox cart at the time. Buckshot struck him in the back of the head, he being attacked from behind. The killer stripped him of everything (even the shoes off his feet) and dragged the body into some woods. Then he tried to sell both ox and cart, saying that he had purchased them from the decedent. He was hanged at Conway on April 1, 1898. Source: *The State* (Columbia, SC), 11/26/97 (4:3), 11/28/97 (2:5:1) & 4/2/98 (2:2). See also: 1880 U.S. Census (Horry Co., SC), which notes Samuel Stevens as a minor.

Jim Anderson (black, age about 25). *Murder.* The crime was committed on 2/7/1898 in Chester County. Cop killer. Handgun slaying of 54-year-old James K. Marshall (white), the policeman for the town of Chester. Motive: because he was about to be exposed as a check forger. This killer was hanged at Chester on April 15, 1898. Source: *The State* (Columbia, SC), 2/8/98 (1:3), 3/26/98 (1:4) & 4/16/98 (3:1). See also Marshall's gravestone in Old Purity Presbyterian Church Cemetery, Chester, South Carolina.

Christopher Cannon (black, age 17). *Murder.* The crime was committed on 8/16/1896 in Spartanburg County.

Handgun slaying of 64-year-old John H. Blassingame (white), who was shot twice through the heart. Motive: house robber caught in the act. Cannon was hanged for this murder at Spartanburg on August 19, 1898. Source: *The State* (Columbia, SC), 8/17/96 (1:3) & 8/22/98 (6:1). See also: 1880 U.S. Census (Spartanburg Co., SC), which notes both parties.

Jesse Hill (black, age 21). *Murder.* The crime was committed on 7/9/1898 in Lexington County. Shotgun slaying of 60+-year-old Mary Lybrand (white), she having been killed on a road near her home. Motive: apparent highway robbery. Jesse Hill was hanged at Lexington Courthouse on November 18, 1898. Sources: *The State* (Columbia, SC), 7/16/98 (8:2) & 11/19/98 (2:1); *Charleston News & Courier*, 7/21/98 (6:1) & 11/19/98 (1:7).

Matthew Moseley (black, age 24). *Murder.* The crime was committed on 6/26/1898 in Orangeburg County. Handgun slaying of Andrew McMillan (black, age not recorded), the victim having been shot in the back. Motive: fracas at a church picnic. The killer was hanged at Orangeburg on December 2, 1898. Sources: *Times & Democrat* (Orangeburg, SC), 7/6/98 (8:3) & 12/7/98 (8:4); *Charleston News & Courier*, 9/27/98 (6:1) & 12/5/98 (2:1).

John Harper (black, age 30). *Murder.* The crime was committed on 5/28/1898 in Chesterfield County. Handgun slaying of 66-year-old John Alexander Campbell (white, known to some as "Sandy Campbell"), the bullet having missed its intended target and struck him instead. Motive: drunken brawl. The killer was hanged at Chesterfield on December 16, 1898. Source: original case file (*State vs. Harper*), Chesterfield General Sessions, June Term, 1898; South Carolina State Archives. *The State* (Columbia, SC), 12/17/98 (3:2). See also: 1880 U.S. Census (Chesterfield Co., VA), which notes Harper before he came to South Carolina. Also: 1870 & 1880 U.S. Census (Chesterfield Co., SC), which note Mr. Campbell.

1899

Frank Castles (black, age 32) **and Amzi Dunnovant** (black, age about 35). *Murder.* Their crime was committed on 6/13/1898 in York County. Both executed for the murder of 50+-year-old Ben Goore (black), who was strangled in his cabin by means of a long cord put around his neck and pulled by both assailants at each end. They then looped the murder weapon around the decedent's entire length, inserted a fence rail therein, and carried the corpse away like a side of beef until coming to a dry well, where it was stashed beneath a layer of debris. Motive: fear of witchcraft. The killers were hanged at York on January 6, 1899. Sources: *The State* (Columbia, SC), 11/16/98 (7:1) & 1/9/99 (6:1); *Yorkville (SC) Enquirer*, 1/7/99 (2:6).

Scipio Rhame (black, age 26). *Murder.* The crime was committed on 10/28/1898 in Clarendon County. Executed for the murder of Ellerson Butler (black, age not recorded), who had his head cracked open by a wooden fence rail. Motive: drunken brawl. The killer was hanged at Manning on May 5, 1899. Sources: *Charleston News & Courier*, 11/4/98 (1:5) & 5/8/99 (6:2); *Manning (SC) Times*, 5/10/99 (3:3). See also: 1880 U.S. Census (Clarendon Co., SC), which notes the killer as a minor.

Sam Bailey (black, age not recorded). *Murder.* The crime was committed on 4/16/1899 at Charleston. Executed for the shotgun slaying of Arthur Duncan (black, age not recorded), who was emasculated by a blast fired at his groin. Motive: gambling dispute. The killer was hanged at Charleston on August 4, 1899. Source: *Charleston News & Courier*, 4/18/99 (3:1), 4/24/99 (8:3) & 8/5/99 (8:1).

James Phelps (black, age 30). *Murder.* The crime was committed on 4/20/1899 at Charleston. Cop killer. Handgun slaying of 25-year-old John Joseph Bean (white), who was deliberately shot in the back of the head. Motive: obnoxious drunk. The killer was hanged at Charleston on August 4, 1899. Source: *Charleston Evening Post*, 4/21/99 (5:1), 4/22/99 (5:5) & 8/4/99 (5:1). See also 1899 City of Charleston death cert. no. 1549.

Ed Luckey (black, age about 20) **and Tom Mitchell** (black, age about 20). *Rape.* Their crime was committed on 10/8/1899 in Darlington County. Indecent assault on the person of about 23-year-old Josephine Lafferty (white), she having been pounced on while walking to church, dragged into woods where she was "choked into insensibility" and raped by at least two assailants. The two who were identified were hanged for this at Darlington on November 24, 1899. Sources: *Charleston Evening Post*, 11/24/99 (1:3); *Charleston News & Courier*, 10/10/99 (2:3), 10/13/99 (6:3) & 11/25/99 (1:6).

1900

Charlie Wilson (black, age about 21). *Murder.* The crime was committed on 9/6/1898 at Charleston. Handgun slaying of 28-year-old Theodore P. Godfrey (white), a soldier at arms. Motive: drunken confrontation. Wilson was one of several drunks who were behaving in an openly vulgar manner on a public sidewalk. Female passersby had to make a detour to avoid them. Seeing this, Godfrey and some of his buddies asked the inebriates to tone it down. Wilson's response to this was to pull out a pistol and start shooting. The state's response was to legally hang Charlie Wilson at Charleston on January 5, 1900. Sources: *Charleston News & Courier*, 9/11/98 (8:1), 10/1/98 (3:4) & 1/6/00 (8:1); *Charleston Evening Post*, 9/10/98 (8:4) & 1/5/00 (5:1).

Zachariah Singleton (black, age 20). *Murder.* The crime was committed on 11/3/1899 at Charleston. Handgun slaying of 19-year-old Christopher Bennett (black). Motive: gambling dispute. The killer was hanged at Charleston on January 5, 1900. Source: *Charleston Evening Post*, 1/5/00 (5:1). See also: 1899 Charleston death cert. no. 2024, and 1900 Charleston death cert. no. 124.

Hamilton McGill (black, age 22). *Rape.* The crime was committed on 5/10/1900 in Williamsburg County. Indecent assault on the person of 9-year-old Colee Eaddy (white), she having been forced despite the culprit's claims to the contrary. The question of consent was a moot point anyway, because state law did not draw such a distinction in cases involving persons less than ten years old. This child rapist was hanged at Kingstree on June 15, 1900. Source: *The State* (Columbia, SC), 6/16/00 (1:7). See also: 1900 U.S. Census (Williamsburg Co., SC), which notes the female party.

Warby Wine (black, age 28). *Murder.* The crime was committed on 12/17/1898 in Orangeburg County. Handgun slaying of 24-year-old Hamp H. Paulling (white), the victim having been set upon by four attackers as he staggered home drunk. Motive: mugging. One of these attackers (Wine) was hanged at Orangeburg on October 26, 1900. Source: *Charleston News & Courier*, 12/21/98 (6:1), 1/15/99 (2:4) & 10/27/00 (5:2). See also: 1900 U.S. Census (Columbia, SC), which notes this killer as a prisoner.

1901

James Kelly (black, age 16). *Murder.* The crime was committed on 8/2/1900 at Charleston. Ax murder of 60-year-old Willis Bonneau (black). Motive: robbery and gross perfidy. The killer was hanged at Charleston on January 4, 1901. Source: *Charleston News & Courier*, 11/16/00 (3:1) & 1/5/01 (8:1). See also: 1900 U.S. Census (Charleston, SC), which notes both parties.

George Thomas (black, age about 50). *Rape.* The crime was committed on 4/15/1900 in Beaufort County. Indecent assault on the person of 17-year-old Rosa Brabham Douberly (white), she having been pounced on as she was walking toward her father's house and ravished at gunpoint. The rapist was hanged at Beaufort on February 15, 1901. Source: *Charleston News & Courier*, 4/16/00 (2:5), 4/17/00 (5:2) & 2/16/01 (1:6). See also: 1900 U.S. Census (Savannah, GA), which notes the female party.

Alfred Jacobs, alias "Suss Jacobs" (black, age 18). *Murder.* The crime was committed on 5/28/1900 in Darlington County. Shotgun slaying of about 40-year-old John L. Byrd (white), who took a load of buckshot in the chest as he sat soaking his feet. A sniper (Jacobs) got him through his bedroom window. Motive: umbrage. The killer had previously been insolent to the murdered man and gotten slapped across the face for it. He was hanged at Darlington on April 26, 1901. Source: *The State* (Columbia, SC), 5/30/00 (1:3) & 4/27/01 (1:1). See also: 1900 U.S. Census (Darlington, SC), which notes the prisoner.

Jim Harris (black, age 22). *Murder.* The crime was committed on 2/20/1900 in Marlboro County. Prison guard killer. Executed for the ax murder of 63-year-old Amos Carter (white), the superintendent of the Marlboro County chain gang. Motive: jailbreak. The killer was hanged at Bennettsville on August 9, 1901. Sources: *Charleston News & Courier*, 8/10/01 (5:2); *Charlotte (NC) Observer*, 6/29/01 (8:1) & 8/10/01 (7:1). See also: 1850 U.S. Census (Fayetteville, NC), which notes Mr. Carter as a youngster.

1902

Oliver Greer (black, age 17). *Rape.* The crime was committed on 12/7/1901 in Anderson County. Indecent assault on the person of 65-year-old Rebecca Ann Kelly (white, a maiden woman), she having been cruelly beaten "and a piece of flesh almost severed from her arm by the negro's teeth." This rapist was hanged at Anderson on March 14, 1902. Sources: *Augusta (GA) Chronicle*, 12/9/01 (1:2); *The State* (Columbia, SC), 2/13/02 (5:5) & 3/15/02 (1:7). See also: 1850 U.S. Census (Anderson Co., SC), which notes the victim as a teenager, and 1900 U.S. Census (Anderson Co., SC), which notes Greer.

Julius Gibbes (black, age 41). *Rape.* The crime was committed on 3/5/1902 in Florence County. Indecent assault on the person of 15-year-old Daisy Lee Haynes (white), a farmer's child bride. The rapist was hanged at Florence on April 25, 1902. Source: *Charleston News & Courier*, 4/2/02 (8:1) & 4/26/02 (3:3). See also: 1900 U.S. Census (Florence Co., SC), which notes the culprit, and 1910 U.S. Census (Florence Co., SC), which notes the victim as the 23-year-old mother of an 8-year-old daughter.

1903

Joseph Keenan (black, age 42). *Murder.* The crime was committed on 11/15/1902 in Greenville County. Handgun slaying of 48-year-old Samuel Willimon (white). Motive: burglar caught in the act. The killer was hanged at Greenville on February 27, 1903. Source: *The State* (Columbia, SC), 11/16/02 (9:5), 11/20/92 (1:5), 11/21/02 (8:2) & 2/28/03 (1:5). See also: 1880 U.S. Census (Union Co., SC), which notes the killer, and 1900 U.S. Census (Greenville Co., SC), which notes Mr. Willimon.

Winter Cantey (black, age about 53). *Murder.* The crime was committed on 10/25/1902 in Richland County. Executed for the murder of 23-year-old Eliza Kershaw (black), she having been slashed to death with a razor and her body dumped along a roadside. Motive: disappointed suitor. The killer was hanged at Columbia on May 29, 1903. Source: *The State* (Columbia, SC), 10/27/02 (8:1), 4/11/03 (8:3) & 5/30/03 (5:3). See also: 1880 U.S. Census (Columbia, SC), which notes Eliza Kershaw as a baby.

Brown Rodgers (black, age not recorded). *Murder.* The crime was committed on 4/5/1903 in Union County. Handgun slaying of 30-year-old John Roger Fant (white), the victim having been apparently lured into a Negro shack while in the pursuit of unwholesome pleasure. The killer was hanged at Union Courthouse on November 13, 1903. Source: *Charleston News & Courier*, 6/13/03 (1:2) & 11/15/03 (6:2). See also: Fant's gravestone in Forest Lawn Cemetery, Union, South Carolina.

1904

Henry Jones (black, age not recorded). *Murder.* The crime was committed on 7/7/1904 in Pickens County. Cop killer. Handgun slaying of 24-year-old Columbus T. Jones (white), a magistrate's constable at Easley. Motive: resisting arrest. The killer was hanged at Pickens Courthouse on August 26, 1904. Sources: *Charleston News & Courier*, 7/10/04 (1:7); *The State* (Columbia, SC), 8/27/04 (1:7). See also: 1900 U.S. Census (Pickens Co., SC), which notes C.T. Jones.

Will Hardin (black, age 28). *Murder.* The crime was committed on 9/7/1904 in Chester County. Shotgun slaying of 69-year-old Henry Sanders (black, his father-in-law), the victim's head having also been dashed in with the butt of that weapon. Motive: because the murdered man had dared to object when Hardin was beating his wife. Hardin was hanged at Chester on December 16, 1904. Source: *The State* (Columbia, SC), 12/17/04 (1:6). See also: 1900 U.S. Census (Chester Co., SC), which notes both parties.

1905

Marion Parr (white, age 28). *Murder.* The crime was committed on 8/26/1904 in Richland County. Child killer. Executed for the murder of 15-year-old Clarence Lafayette Shealy (white), whose head and face were hacked to ribbons by the blade of a hoe. Motive: theft of a shotgun. The killer was hanged at Columbia on April 14, 1905. Source: *The State* (Columbia, SC), 8/31/04 (8:3) & 4/15/05 (1:1). See also: 1900 U.S. Census (Aiken Co., SC), which notes the killer, and (Lexington Co., SC), which notes Shealy.

Edward Mackey, alias "Ned Mack" (black, age 24). *Murder.* The crime was committed on 12/3/1904 in Clarendon County. Shotgun slaying of 51-year-old Dave Connors (black), his wife's stepfather. Motive: because the murdered man had exposed Mack as an adulterer. The latter was hanged at Manning on April 28, 1905. Sources: *Charleston News & Courier*, 12/10/04 (3:2); *The State* (Columbia, SC), 4/29/05 (1:5). See also: 1900 U.S. Census (Clarendon Co., SC), which notes both parties in the same household.

William Johnson (black, age 22). *Rape.* The crime was committed on 3/9/1905 in Orangeburg County. Indecent assault on the person of 8-year-old Geneva H. Howell (white), she having also been infected with a particularly virulent STD that left her paralyzed from the waist down. This rapist and knowing spreader of infectious disease was hanged at Orangeburg on June 16, 1905. Source: *The State* (Columbia, SC), 6/17/05 (3:1). See also: 1900 U.S. Census (Orangeburg Co., SC), which notes both parties in the same household.

Fletcher Byrd (black, age not recorded). *Murder.* The crime was committed on 5/14/1904 in Greenville County. Cop killer. Handgun slaying of 47-year-old William J. Cox (white), a local magistrate who was acting in an official capacity together with a police constable. Motive: resisting arrest. The murdered man had observed "Bird" transporting two barrels of whiskey in a wagon. Suspecting illegal activity, he halted the wagon with the assistance of his assigned constable. A gunfight then erupted. The killer was hanged at Greenville on November 10, 1905. Source: *The State* (Columbia, SC), 5/16/04 (4:4) & 11/11/05 (1:5). See also: 1900 U.S. Census (Greenville Co., SC), which notes Cox.

1906

Jenkins Burrows (black, age not recorded) **and Arthur Williams** (black, age 19). *Murder.* Their crime was committed on 10/13/1905 in Williamsburg County. Both executed for the murder of 57-year-old Julian Wilson (white, a storekeeper), who was beaten on the head with a wooden wagon jack. Motive: robbery. These killers were hanged at Kingstree on January 12, 1906. Sources: *The State* (Columbia, SC), 10/15/05 (1:4), 12/10/05 (1:1) & 1/13/06 (1:4); *County Record* (Kingstree, SC), 10/19/05 (1:1); *Charleston News & Courier*, 10/15/05 (1:6) & 10/17/05 (1:5). See also: 1900 U.S. Census (Williamsburg Co., SC), which notes Wilson and Williams.

Robert Scott (black, age not recorded). *Murder.* The crime was committed on

10/13/1905 in Williamsburg County. Accomplice in the murder of 57-year-old Julian Wilson (white, a storekeeper), who was beaten on the head with a wooden wagon jack. Motive: robbery. He was hanged at Kingstree on February 16, 1906. Source: *The State* (Columbia, SC), 2/17/06 (3:3). See also: BURROWS, Jenkins (executed 1/12/06).

Andrew Thompson (black, age 38). *Rape.* The crime was committed on 12/17/1905 in Greenville County. Indecent assault on the person of 21-year-old Lilly Duncan James (white), she having been choked into insensitivity by her attacker. The rapist was hanged at Greenville on March 2, 1906. Source: *The State* (Columbia, SC), 12/20/05 (1:4), 2/24/06 (1:3) & 3/3/06 (1:5). See also: 1900 U.S. Census (Greenville Co., SC), which notes the culprit and the victim by her maiden name, and 1910 U.S. Census (Greenville, SC), which notes her by her married name.

Colclough Stukes (black, age 26). *Murder.* The crime was committed on 5/12/1905 in Sumter County. Fatal stabbing of 42-year-old David E. Wells (white), a plantation owner by whom he was employed as a laborer. The victim was knifed at least 20 times and his throat cut from ear to ear. Motive: disgruntled employee. A local family man, Stukes had wound up on the chain gang for some nonviolent offense. He was deemed docile enough to be bonded out as cheap labor under the convict lease system. This penal practice was harshly criticized as a thinly veiled form of slavery, but it was legal in those days. David Wells became bondholder for Colclough Stukes and put him to work at a nominal salary. Stukes was horrified when Mr. Wells expressed second thoughts about their arrangement. He then went berserk and slashed the planter to death. He was hanged at Sumter on May 18, 1906. Sources: *Charleston News & Courier*, 5/13/05 (1:6); *The State* (Columbia, SC), 5/14/05 (2:3) & 5/19/06 (1:3). See also: 1900 U.S. Census (Sumter Co., SC), which notes both parties.

Arthur McFadden (black, age 25). *Murder.* The crime was committed on 9/25/1905 in Williamsburg County. Shotgun slaying of 22-year-old George Burgess (black), the victim having been blasted from behind by a concealed sniper. Motive: personal grudge stemming from a fight in which the killer had been cut with a knife. McFadden was hanged at Kingstree on May 25, 1906. Source: *The State* (Columbia, SC), 5/26/06 (6:1). See also: 1900 U.S. Census (Williamsburg Co., SC), which notes both parties.

Epps Snowden (black, age 22). *Murder.* The crime was committed on 6/3/1905 in Williamsburg County. Fatal stabbing of 37-year-old Bob W. Brown (black, a storekeeper), who had tried to eject the killer from his place of business. Motive: escalated argument. Snowden had made a bet in the amount of 40 cents. Some other young black men had challenged him to drink eight bottles of soda pop with the understanding that they would pay him five cents each if he succeeded. Snowden won his wager but became enraged when not immediately paid in full. The storeowner (Brown) would have no brawling there but got knifed four times instead. Snowden was hanged at Kingstree on May 25, 1906. Sources: *County Record* (Kingstree, SC), 6/8/05 (1:3); *The State* (Columbia, SC), 11/21/05 (2:1) & 5/26/06 (6:1). See also: 1900 U.S. Census (Williamsburg Co., SC), which notes Snowden.

William A. Marcus (white, age 41). *Murder.* The crime was committed on 4/14/1906 at Charleston. Uxoricide. Executed for the murder of 48-year-old Maggie Stone Marcus (white, his bigamous wife), who was stabbed 14 times with an ice pick. Motive: suspicion of infidelity. The killer had no moral reservations against deserting his lawful spouse in Ohio, but woe to any woman who played similar games with him. Marcus was hanged at Charleston on August 3, 1906. Source: *The State* (Columbia, SC), 4/16/06 (1:1) & 8/4/06 (1:7). See also: 1906 Charleston death certs. nos. 355 & 857.

Luke Gray (black, age 23). *Murder.* The crime was committed on 2/2/1906 in Aiken County. Shotgun slaying of 27-year-old Clifford Woodward (white), a storekeeper. Motive: because the murdered man had insulted the killer's wife, or so the latter claimed. Woodward died of his wound on 3/4/1906. Luke Gray was hanged at Aiken on August 31, 1906. Sources: *Charleston News & Courier*, 2/4/06 (1:7); *The State* (Columbia, SC), 4/3/06 (10:1) & 9/1/06 (1:7). See also Mr. Woodward's gravestone in First Baptist Church Cemetery, Montmorenci, South Carolina.

Richard Dargan (black, age 21). *Rape.* The crime was committed on 9/16/1906 in Marlboro County. Indecent assault on the person of 32-year-old Lucy Ann Patterson (white). The victim and her two small children had fled from their home in the middle of the night when Dargan broke down their door. He tackled the woman in a cotton field and "accomplished his purpose" while the kids escaped unharmed. He was hanged at Bennettsville on October 19, 1906. Source: *Charleston News & Courier*, 9/19/06 (1:7) & 10/20/06 (1:4). See also: 1900 U.S. Census (Sumter Co., SC), which notes the culprit, and 1910 U.S. Census (Marlboro Co., SC), which notes the female party.

Commander Johnson (white, age 26). *Murder.* The crime was committed on 6/23/1905 in Horry County. Shotgun slaying of 52-year-old Harmon D. Grainger (white, a Baptist minister), who was blasted in the back with two barrels' worth. Motive: because the victim had denounced him for immorality. Johnson was hanged for this atrocity at Conway on October 19, 1906. Source: *The State* (Columbia, SC), 6/25/05 (1:1) & 10/20/06 (1:7). See also: 1900 U.S. Census (Horry Co., SC), which notes Johnson.

Isaac Knight (black, age 24). *Rape.* The crime was committed on 7/9/1906 in Aiken County. Indecent assault on the person of 56-year-old Ellen S. Chapin (white), she having been raped on her kitchen floor. The victim was made into a public laughingstock. Her name was published in the newspapers for all to see, as were implied statements to the effect that she had gotten what she had coming to her. One self-explanatory example thereof is as follows: "Mrs. Chapin is a Northern lady and before her misfortune did not understand the nature of the Negro. She had put every trust in Knight and had even considered him the equal of the average white man. She had treated him as well as she could have treated any white person, thinking that he was a gentleman. Knight was always respectful to Mrs. Chapin but it could be seen by his actions among other Negroes that the treatment that he was receiving was giving him a false idea of his importance. On Monday morning the nature of the Negro asserted itself; it could be held back no longer. Mrs. Chapin was originally from Manchester, Vermont but she has made her home near Aiken for a number of years. White people had warned her several times that she should not stay alone with no one near her except Negroes but she would pay no attention to them, thinking that the Negro was worthy of trust. She came South with the New Englander's usual idea of Negro character and no argument that could be put forth could shake the Negro from the pedestal on which she had placed him." Isaac Knight was legally hanged at Aiken on October 26, 1906. Sources: *The State* (Columbia, SC), 7/12/06 (1:3) & 10/30/06 (1:3); *Charleston News & Courier*, 10/27/06 (1:5). See also: 1900 U.S. Census (Aiken Co., SC), which notes the female party.

William Bennett (black, age not recorded). *Murder.* The crime was committed on 8/26/1906 in Beaufort County. Handgun slaying of 72-year-old George M. Harvey (white). Motive: to avoid the repayment of a 40-cent loan. This penurious killer was hanged at Beaufort on November 2, 1906. Sources: *Beaufort (SC) Gazette*, 10/8/06 (1:1); *Savannah (GA) Morning News*, 8/28/06 (9:5) & 11/3/06 (1:6); *The State* (Columbia, SC), 8/28/06 (1:4) & 11/3/06 (1:6).

1907

Thomas Harris (white, age 28). *Murder.* The crime was committed on 11/20/1906 in Cherokee County. Executed for the murder of 62-year-old Hortensia Morgan (white), whose throat was cut in her own home and her money belt stolen. Motive: robbery. The killer was hanged at Gaffney on March 29, 1907. Sources: *The State* (Columbia, SC), 3/30/07 (1:5); *Spartanburg Weekly Herald*, 4/2/07 (2:1). See also: 1900 U.S. Census (Cherokee Co., SC), which notes the murdered woman.

Joe Evans (black, age 30). *Murder.* The crime was committed on 12/2/1906 in Greenwood County. Handgun slaying of 30-year-old William Hughey (black, his brother-in-law) who was shot three times. Motive: because Hughey had gone to the law with a story about sexual assault, his wife reportedly having been molested by Evans. The latter was hanged at Greenwood on April 12, 1907. Source: original case file (*State vs. Evans*), Greenwood County Courthouse. See also: *The State* (Columbia, SC), 12/6/06 (6:1) & 4/13/07 (1:4); 1900 U.S. Census (Greenwood Co., SC), which notes both parties.

John Shelton (black, age 24). *Murder.* The crime was committed on 11/10/1905 in Spartanburg County. Handgun slaying of Alfred Briggs (black), his father-in-law. Motive: because the murdered man had given refuge to his daughter when she fled to him for protection from the brutality of her husband. John Shelton was hanged at Spartanburg on May 3, 1907. Source: original case file (*State vs. Shelton*), Spartanburg General Sessions, April Term 1907; South Carolina State Archives; *Spartanburg Herald*, 5/4/07 (1:7). See also: 1900 U.S. Census (Spartanburg, SC), which notes the killer.

1908

George Kenny (black, age about 23). *Murder.* The crime was committed on

8/16/1906 at Charleston. Prison guard killer. Executed for the murder of 56-year-old Herman G. Stello (white), who was slashed to death with a butcher knife and a razor. Motive: jailbreak. George Kenny was hanged at Charleston on January 17, 1908. Source: *Charleston Evening Post*, 8/17/06 (1:7), 8/20/06 (5:3) & 1/17/08 (1:7). See also: 1906 Charleston death cert. no. 652.

Jack Blake (black, age about 28). *Murder.* The crime was committed on 8/18/1906 in Georgetown County. Cop killer. Handgun slaying of 41-year-old James Green (black), a police constable for Santee Magistrate's Court. Motive: resisting arrest. The killer was hanged at Georgetown on March 27, 1908. Sources: *Georgetown (SC) Times*, 8/22/06 (1:2); *Charleston News & Courier*, 3/26/08 (1:6); *Macon (GA) Daily Telegraph*, 3/28/08 (1:8). See also: 1900 U.S. Census (Santee, SC), which notes the murdered man.

Ned Toland (black, age 20) **and Brack Toland** (black, age 17). *Murder.* Their crime was committed on 2/26/1908 in Lexington County. Both executed for the ax murder of 52-year-old Frances M. Ellisor (white, the wife of Paul W. Ellisor), who was attacked in her own home and her body hidden beneath a pile of clothes. Motive: robbery. The culprits had gone around to the woman's kitchen door (pursuant to protocol) and made a pretense of purchasing bread. They knew in advance that the lady's husband had gone to town that day. They were hanged at Lexington on May 1, 1908. Source: *The State* (Columbia, SC), 2/28/08 (12:1), 2/29/08 (1:1) & 5/2/08 (1:1). See also: 1900 U.S. Census (Lexington Co., SC), which notes Mrs. Ellisor.

Gaddy Graham (black, age about 35). *Murder.* The crime was committed on 11/18/1907 in Darlington County. Handgun slaying of 36-year-old Furman Moody (white), a farm manager. Motive: thief caught in the act; the victim had found the killer pilfering from his cornfield. Graham was hanged at Darlington on May 1, 1908. Source: *The State* (Columbia, SC), 11/20/07 (11:2) & 5/2/08 (1:2). See also: 1900 U.S. Census (Darlington Co., SC), which notes Graham.

Thomas Washington (black, age 27). *Murder.* The crime was committed on 8/11/1907 in Colleton County. Shotgun slaying of 34-year-old Frank Richardson (black). Motive: rivalry for a female. The killer was hanged at Walterboro on May 8, 1908. Sources: *The Press & Standard* (Walterboro, SC), 8/14/07 (1:2) & 5/13/08 (1:5); *The State* (Columbia, SC), 5/9/08 (1:5). See also: 1900 U.S. Census (Colleton Co., SC), which notes Richardson.

Jim Malloy (black, age about 30). *Murder.* The crime was committed on 4/26/1907 in Marlboro County. Uxoricide. Executed for the murder of 19-year-old Minnie Malloy (black), who was slashed to death with a razor. Motive: obsessive jealousy and spousal abuse. The killer was hanged at Bennettsville on May 22, 1908. Source: *The State* (Columbia, SC), 4/27/07 (8:1) & 5/23/08 (1:3).

John Wesley Shedd (black, age not recorded). *Murder.* The crime was committed on 5/15/1908 in Fairfield County. Shotgun slayings of 20-year-old George Lawhone (black) and a black female (age not recorded) named Alice White. Motive: jealousy in romance. Shedd was hanged at Winnsboro on July 17, 1908.

Source: *The State* (Columbia, SC), 5/19/08 (1:7) & 7/18/08 (3:1). See also: 1900 U.S. Census (Fairfield Co., SC), which notes Lawhone.

Lawrence Hampton (black, age about 21). *Murder.* The crime was committed on 6/18/1906 in Greenwood County. Shotgun slaying of 19-year-old Robert White (black). Motive: brawl at a church picnic. The killer was hanged at Greenwood on October 16, 1908. Sources: *The State* (Columbia, SC), 8/21/06 (8:1); *Charleston News & Courier*, 10/17/08 (2:1). Appeal: 79 SC 179–187. See also: 1900 U.S. Census (Greenwood Co., SC), which notes Robert White; Pardons & Commutations Files of Gov. Martin Ansell (Box 5), which contains a complete trial transcript; South Carolina State Archives.

Elliot Greene (black, age 21). *Murder.* The crime was committed on 4/4/1908 in Barnwell County. Murder of 21-year-old Oliver Smalls (black), who had his head smashed in with a clothes iron and his cabin burnt with him in it. Motive: gambling dispute. The killer was hanged at Barnwell on October 16, 1908. Source: *Charleston News & Courier*, 4/6/08 (1:6) & 10/17/08 (2:2). See also: 1900 U.S. Census (Barnwell Co., SC), which notes both parties.

Robert Starke Means (black, age 18). *Murder.* The crime was committed on 3/13/1907 in Fairfield County. Shotgun slaying of 22-year-old Anna Belle Russell (black). Motive: scorned lover. The killer was hanged at Winnsboro on October 23, 1908. Source: *The State* (Columbia, SC), 3/18/07 (10:4) & 10/24/08 (6:3). See also: 1900 U.S. Census (Fairfield Co., SC), which notes both parties.

Will Herrin (black, age about 30). *Murder.* The crime was committed on 9/14/1908 in Saluda County. Shotgun slaying of 30-year-old Emanuel Carver (white), who also had the wooden stock of the murder weapon smashed over his head. Motive: possibly deranged. The killer was hanged at Saluda on November 27, 1908. Sources: *The State* (Columbia, SC), 9/15/08 (1:3); *Charleston News & Courier*, 10/21/08 (2:3) & 11/28/08 (1:6). See also: 1900 U.S. Census (Saluda Co., SC), which notes Mr. Carver.

1909

Jeff Clarke, alias "Mulatto Jeff" (black, age 21). *Murder.* The crime was committed on 8/13/1908 in Berkeley County. Patricide. Executed for the murder of 67-year-old Calvin W. Clarke, his white father. The killer began by putting concentrated lye in his dad's coffee. Then when that failed to produce death in a timely manner, a shotgun was used to finish off the victim in his bed. The corpse (with its face blown away) was loaded onto a farm wagon and carted some distance before finally being thrown onto a compost heap with rotten hay and offal. Motive: theft of that month's mortgage money. The killer was hanged at Monck's Corner on January 15, 1909. Sources: *Charleston News & Courier*, 8/16/08 (2:3); *The State* (Columbia, SC), 1/16/09 (10:3).

Will Foster (black, age not recorded). *Murder.* The crime was committed on 11/25/1907 in Spartanburg County. Executed for the murder of 52-year-old John Young (white, a teamster), who had his head smashed in for the sake of 15 cents. The murder weapon was a pipe with an elbow joint. Motive: highway robbery. The killer was hanged at Spartanburg on February 5, 1909. Sources: *The State* (Columbia, SC), 11/26/07 (4:5), 11/27/07 (8:4), 12/11/07 (5:3), 1/10/08 (1:4) & 2/6/09 (1:3); *Spartanburg Weekly Herald*, 11/28/07 (1:3); *Spartanburg Herald*, 2/6/09 (1:1). See also: 1900 U.S. Census (Campobello, SC), which notes Mr. Young.

Dan Robertson (black, age not recorded). *Murder.* The crime was committed on 2/7/1909 in Hampton County. Murder of Eliza Hunter (black), who was slashed and stabbed to death on a railroad depot platform. Her throat was cut from ear to ear. She was knifed multiple times. The blade of the murder weapon broke off after penetrating her skull. Motive: wrathful lover. The killer was hanged at Hampton Courthouse on April 23, 1909. Source: *The State* (Columbia, SC), 2/22/09 (3:4) & 4/24/09 (2:4).

Lawson Addison (black, age 22). *Murder.* The crime was committed on 9/3/1906 in Chester County. Handgun slayings of 31-year-old Matilda McMaster (black) and her sister Mamie Halsell (black, age not recorded), who were gunned down as they walked home from church. Motive: estranged lover. The killer was hanged at Chester on April 23, 1909. Sources: *The State* (Columbia, SC), 9/5/06 (1:1) & 4/24/09 (8:2); *The Lantern* (Chester, SC), 4/23/09 (3:3). See also: 1900 U.S. Census (Chester Co., SC), which notes Addison and McMaster.

Willie Carter (black, age about 30). *Murder.* The crime was committed on 3/15/1908 in Bamberg County. Executed for the mutilation murder of 27-year-old Shellie Raysor (black female), who was slashed to ribbons by her knife wielding lover. Motive: adultery turned deadly. Carter was a married man who had no qualms about cheating on his wife. But he went berserk when he caught his paramour treating him in a like manner. He was hanged at Bamberg on April 30, 1909. Sources: *The State* (Columbia, SC), 5/1/09 (1:2); *Charleston News & Courier*, 5/1/09 (1:6). See also: 1900 U.S. Census (Bamberg Co., SC), which notes the victim as "Sallie Raysor."

Love Robinson (black, age 15). *Murder.* The crime was committed on 4/26/1908 in York County. Child killer. Shotgun slaying of 13-year-old Lena Watson (black). Motive: because she refused to have sex with him. This juvenile murderer was hanged at York on May 14, 1909. Source: *The State* (Columbia, SC), 5/8/09 (10:2) & 5/15/09 (4:5). See also: 1900 U.S. Census (York Co., SC), which notes that the killer was born in May of 1892.

Marshall Washington (black, age 24). *Murder.* The crime was committed on 6/1/1908 in Greenwood County. Shotgun slaying of 20-year-old Ola Williams (black), described as his "paramour," she having been attacked while at work in the fields. Motive: love turned to hate. *Malice prepense* was fully evident in that Washington had purchased shotgun shells that morning and invited several acquaintances to come and watch him "kill a nigger," in his own words. Then when he had actually carried out that boast the next thing he did was walk up to a policeman, surrender his weapon and say: "I just killed me a nigger!" He was hanged at Greenwood on July 30, 1909. Source: *Charleston News & Courier*, 6/3/08 (1:6); *The State* (Columbia, SC), 7/31/09 (2:3). See also: 1900 U.S. Census (Anderson Co., SC), which notes the killer, and

(Greenwood Co., SC), which notes the victim.

John Jenkins, alias "Slippery Jim" (black, age 52). *Attempted Rape.* The crime was committed on 6/18/1909 in Georgetown County. Felonious assault on the person of an 18-year-old white female (name withheld) with intent to commit rape. The culprit was described as a "notorious villain" in the black community. The victim was a rookie schoolmarm. She was traveling homeward in a buggy at the time together with a smaller girl. Jenkins halted the buggy and pulled the 18-year-old down out of the driver's seat. He threw her onto the ground and began tearing off her clothes. She was left "horribly scarred and bruised" but still *virgo intacta.* "Slippery Jim" was hanged for this at Georgetown on August 13, 1909. Source: *The State* (Columbia, SC), 6/20/09 (1:1) & 8/14/09 (1:4). See also: 1900 U.S. Census (Georgetown Co., SC), which notes Jenkins.

Melvin Watson (black, age about 25). *Murder.* The crime was committed on 6/2/1909 in Horry County. Shotgun slaying of 21-year-old John B. Watson (white), an acting plantation foreman. Motive: personal grudge. The victim had reprimanded the killer for using foul language in the presence of small children. Resenting this, Melvin (who had only one arm) lay in ambush for John B. He used the corner of a fence upon which to position the end of his shotgun barrel while aiming and pulling the trigger. He was hanged for this at Conway on November 12, 1909. Sources: *Charleston News & Courier*, 6/4/09 (6:4) & 6/6/09 (1:2); *The State* (Columbia, SC), 6/5/09 (8:3) & 11/13/09 (1:7). See also: 1900 U.S. Census (Horry Co., SC), which notes John Watson.

1910

John Rose (black, age 19). *Attempted Rape.* The crime was committed on 12/6/1909 in Williamsburg County. Felonious assault on the person of a 14-year-old white female (name withheld) with intent to commit rape. She had been attacked as she walked to school that morning. The attacker was hanged at Kingstree on February 4, 1910. Source: *County Record* (Kingstree, SC), 12/9/09 (1:1) & 2/10/10 (1:1).

Coot Lever (black, age about 27). *Attempted Rape.* The crime was committed on 11/1/1909 in Lexington County. Felonious assault on the person of a white female (name and age not disclosed) with intent to commit rape. The victim was the wife of a farmer. She was in her private yard with her 2-year-old child engaged in the act of hanging out laundry to dry. Her husband was at work in a distant field. Lever threw the woman to the ground and tore away nearly all of her clothes. He also throttled her with his hands in so brutal a manner that she suffered fingernail lacerations on her neck which bled freely. This attacker was hanged at Lexington on February 25, 1910. Source: *The State* (Columbia, SC), 11/2/09 (1:2), 11/3/09 (1:5) & 2/26/10 (3:1).

Haas Butler (black, age not recorded). *Attempted Rape.* The crime was committed on 4/28/1909 in Pickens County. Felonious assault on the person of a 21-year-old white female (name withheld) with intent to commit rape. She was menaced in her bedroom by a prowler (Butler), whom she recognized as one of her father's farmhands. He jumped out a window upon discovering that his intended victim had the whooping cough. He was hanged at Pickens for this felony on April 8, 1910. Sources: *Keowee (SC) Courier*, 6/16/09 (3:2); *The State* (Columbia, SC), 4/10/10 (1:4).

Allen Davis (black, age 22). *Murder.* The crime was committed on 1/30/1910 in Orangeburg County. Uxoricide. Handgun slaying of Leila Davis (black, age not recorded), she having been shot five times as she exited a church service. Motive: marital estrangement. The killer was a roving type who liked to sleep around. His wife left him for that reason and refused to be reconciled, no doubt fearful of what disease she might catch. This was more than the fickle husband would tolerate. He was hanged at Orangeburg on July 1, 1910. Sources: *Times & Democrat* (Orangeburg, SC), 2/1/10 (4:1) & 7/2/10 (4:1); *The State* (Columbia, SC), 5/6/10 (9:1) & 7/2/10 (1:1).

Walter Sherrard, alias "Bunk Sherrard" (black, age 24). *Murder.* The crime was committed on 6/25/1910 at Greenville. Cop killer. Shotgun slaying of 24-year-old Edgar Cleveland Waldrop (white), a special police officer. Motive: gambling raid turned deadly. The killer was hanged at Greenville on October 7, 1910. Sources: *The State* (Columbia, SC), 6/27/10 (1:3), 6/28/10 (3:2) & 10/8/10 (1:5); *Daily Record* (Columbia, SC), 10/7/10 (7:7). See also: Waldrop's gravestone in Rose Hill Cemetery, Piedmont, South Carolina. 1910 U.S. Census (Anderson, SC), which notes the killer.

Clarence Ham (black, age 25). *Murder.* The crime was committed on 10/28/1910 in Florence County. Shotgun slaying of 53-year-old Elihu M. Moye (white), who was killed by three blasts fired in his own house. Motive: robbery. The killer was hanged at Florence on December 16, 1910. Source: *The State* (Columbia, SC), 10/30/10 (1:5), 11/2/10 (6:1) & 12/17/10 (3:1). See also: 1910 U.S. Census (Florence Co., SC), which notes both parties.

William Kelley (black, age 30). *Murder.* The crime was committed on 4/15/1910 in Berkeley County. Executed for the murder of 20-year-old Archie Smalls (black), the victim having been fatally slashed with a butcher knife. Motive: indiscernible. The killer was hanged at Monck's Corner on December 23, 1910. Source: *Charleston News & Courier*, 12/24/10 (1:1). See also: 1900 U.S. Census (Dorchester Co., SC), which notes Smalls, and 1910 U.S. Census (Berkeley Co., SC), which notes "Kelly."

James Edwards (black, age 24). *Murder.* The crime was committed on or about 5/15/1901 in Berkeley County. Uxoricide. Handgun slaying of 19-year-old Rebecca Edwards (black). Motive: obnoxious drunk. On the day of the crime, Edwards was already in a foul mood because his cow had wandered onto railroad tracks and been killed by a train. Nor was there any food in his cabin to feed his wife and child. An elderly neighbor gave him half a dollar so he could procure victuals for his family. Edwards squandered the money on liquor instead. He came home to find his wife stir frying some rice that had been given to her by the same neighbor. Enraged at this, Edwards shot his wife dead as she stood at her hearth. The woman fell head first into the cooking fire. Edwards fled from the scene and remained at large for eight years. Then the long arm of the law overtook him. He was hanged at Monck's Corner on December 23, 1910. Source: *The State* (Columbia, SC), 12/29/09 (9:1) & 12/24/10 (1:1). See also: 1900 U.S. Census (Berkeley Co., SC), which notes this ill-fated couple.

Minus Hightower (black, age 19). *Rape.* The crime was committed on 10/18/1910 in Richland County. Indecent assault on the person of 27-year-old Meta P. McDonald (white), who was raped at gunpoint in her own home despite the presence of two small children. The details were "too horrible to be printed," according to the local newspaper. This pervert was hanged at Columbia on December 23, 1910. Sources: *Daily Record* (Columbia, SC), 10/19/10 (8:1) & 12/23/10 (3:1); *The State* (Columbia, SC), 10/19/10 (1:5) & 12/24/10 (1:3). See also: the original trial record, Special Term, Fall 1910, case no. 4907 (Richland County Court of General Sessions); South Carolina State Archives.

1911

Milton Kiser, alias "Henry Huntley" (black, age not recorded). *Murder.* The crime was committed on 9/8/1910 in Kershaw County. Executed for the murder of 42-year-old John Cook (white, the superintendent of the Kershaw County jail), who was beaten on the head with a heavy iron cuspidor. Motive: jailbreak. The killer was hanged at Camden on January 6, 1911. Sources: *The State* (Columbia, SC), 10/17/10 (7:1) & 1/7/11 (1:4); *Camden (SC) Chronicle*, 1/6/10 (1:2).

Gary Gist (black, age 19). *Attempted Rape.* The crime was committed on 2/25/1911 in Spartanburg County. Felonious assault on the person of 27-year-old Annie West Anderson (white) with intent to commit rape. The woman was attacked in her own home while tending her two small children ages 3 years and 3 months. The toddler was "badly cut about the face" by the knife-wielding marauder. The mother was choked "until the blood gushed from her nose." Gist had gotten into big trouble the previous year for trying to burn down a warehouse. He was executed at Spartanburg on May 26, 1911. Sources: *Charleston Evening Post*, 2/27/11 (5:4); *The State* (Columbia, SC), 4/3/10 (1:1) & 5/27/11 (1:3); *Spartanburg Herald*, 2/26/11 (1:6) & 5/27/11 (8:3); original trial record (*State vs. Gist*), Spartanburg General Sessions (April Term, 1911), South Carolina State Archives. See also: Spartanburg County Death Register entry dated 5/26/11, and 1910 U.S. Census (Spartanburg Co., SC), which notes Mrs. Anderson.

Daniel Duncan (black, age 22). *Murder.* The crime was committed on 6/21/1910 at Charleston. Executed for the murder of 35-year-old Max Lubelsky (white, a clothier), who was battered to death with a 2 × 4 and his place of business ransacked. Motive: robbery. The killer was caught 12 days later when he returned to the scene of the crime and assaulted the victim's widow. He was hanged at Charleston on July 7, 1911. Source: *Charleston Evening Post*, 7/7/11 (1:7). See also: 1910 Charleston death cert. no. 992, and 1911 death cert. no. 1152.

Wade Hood, alias "Mack Hood" (black, age 26). *Murder.* The crime was committed on 9/16/1911 in Lancaster County. Executed for the murder of 19-year-old Walker Dunlap (black) by cutting his throat. Motive: personal grudge. The two parties had had a prior disagreement over some personal matter. They were riding together in a wagon on the above date along with two other persons when harsh words were exchanged. Hood then pulled out a knife and attacked Dunlap. The stabber was hanged at Lancaster on December 20, 1911. Sources: *Charlotte (NC) Daily Observer*, 9/17/11 (9:5); *The State* (Columbia, SC), 12/21/11 (1:5). See also: 1910 U.S. Census (Lancaster Co., SC), which notes "Mack" Hood, and (York Co., SC), which notes Dunlap.

Henry Kee (black, age 29). *Murder.* The crime was committed on 8/21/1911 in Lancaster County. Handgun slaying of 48-year-old Sam Dye (black), who was shot multiple times. Motive: an argument over who should smoke a pipe. The killer was hanged at Lancaster on December 20, 1911. Source: *The State* (Columbia, SC), 8/22/11 (6:4) & 12/21/11 (1:5). See also: 1900 & 1910 U.S. Census (Lancaster Co., SC), which note both parties; original trial record (*State vs. Kee*) Lancaster Court of General Sessions (Fall Term, 1911), South Carolina State Archives.

1912

William Reed (black, age 24). *Attempted Rape.* The crime was committed on 2/26/1912 in Anderson County. Felonious assault on the person of a 26-year-old white female (name withheld) with intent to commit rape. He admitted to having entered the victim's home for the purpose of burglary but claimed to have tripped over a chair in the dark and thereby fallen across the bed in which she lay sleeping. Reed was executed by high voltage at the South Carolina State Penitentiary on August 6, 1912. Sources: *The State* (Columbia, SC), 3/2/12 (1:3), 4/2/12 (11:1) & 8/7/12 (16:1); *Keowee (SC) Courier*, 3/6/12 (3:3).

Alex Weldon (black, age 53). *Murder.* The crime was committed on 10/28/1910 in Florence County. Accomplice in the shotgun slaying of 53-year-old Elihu M. Moye (white), who was blasted three times in his own house. Motive: robbery. Weldon was executed on August 13, 1912. Source: *The State* (Columbia, SC), 8/14/12 (12:1). See: HAM, Clarence (executed 12/16/10).

John Cole (black, age 39). *Murder.* The crime was committed on 10/2/1911 at Charleston. Handgun slaying of 22-year-old Sam Fraser (black, a night porter in a mercantile establishment), who was shot in the neck and died two days later. Motive: burglary. The killer was executed on August 22, 1912. Source: *Charleston Evening Post*, 10/3/11 (9:1), 10/5/11 (9:3), 10/24/11 (9:2) & 8/22/12 (9:3). See also: 1911 Charleston death cert. no. 291.

Edward Alexander (black, age 23). *Attempted Rape.* The crime was committed on 6/24/1912 in Fairfield County. Felonious assault on the person of a white female (name withheld and age not specified) with intent to commit rape. Alexander snuck into the victim's house determined to force himself on her but fled when she screamed too loud. A posse ran him down later that day. He was executed on September 20, 1912. Source: *The State* (Columbia, SC), 6/25/12 (1:7) & 9/21/12 (10:2). See also: 1910 U.S. Census (Fairfield Co., SC), which notes the culprit.

Samuel N. Hyde (white, age 27). *Murder.* The crime was committed on 7/17/1911 in Anderson County. Uxoricide, etc. Handgun slayings of 22-year-old

Emma Beasley Hyde and 54-year-old William V. Beasley (whites), his wife and father-in-law. Motive: marital estrangement. The young woman had moved back to her father's house because "Sam" mistreated her. This did not sit well with "Sam." So he broke into the place with a loaded revolver and fired three bullets into his fugitive spouse as she lay in her bed. The flash from the gun even set the bedclothes afire. The male victim was slain with one shot when he tried to save his daughter. The killer was executed on October 1, 1912. Source: *The State* (Columbia, SC), 7/20/11 (1:5) & 10/2/12 (11:1). See also: the gravestone of the murdered pair in Silver Brook Cemetery, Anderson, South Carolina.

Clinton Glover (black, age 19). *Attempted Rape.* The crime was committed on 8/15/1911 in Dorchester County. Felonious assault on the person of a white female (name withheld and age not specified) with intent to commit rape. The victim was attacked in her home but Glover fled out a window when she started screaming. Bloodhounds were very effectively put on his trail. It was determined that he had sneaked into the lady's bedroom as she lay asleep. He grabbed her by the throat and punched her in the face. He was executed on November 12, 1912. Sources: *Charleston Evening Post*, 8/16/11 (1:7); *Charleston News & Courier*, 8/16/11 (1:7); *The State* (Columbia, SC), 8/17/11 (1:3) & 11/13/12 (14:3). See also: 1910 U.S. Census (Orangeburg Co., SC), which notes the culprit.

1913

Sam Boozer (black, age 49). *Murder.* The crime was committed on 3/3/1911 in Newberry County. Shotgun slaying of 43-year-old James S. Gilliam (white), overseer on the plantation that he sharecropped. Motive: a convoluted one. The murder victim had reportedly threatened Boozer's wife and daughter with a knife, even slashing them by some accounts. He was concerned lest the women foul a well with dirty laundry (or so the story went) and the situation turned violent. The plantation owner himself was tried (and acquitted) as an accessory because it was thought for a while that he had put Boozer up to the shooting. Gossip had it that that man was carrying on with the overseer's wife and had passed a shotgun to Boozer shortly before the homicide. The case against the owner fell apart when it was proven in court that Boozer had used a different gun. Whatever the truth of this matter, Sam Boozer was executed for the murder of James Gilliam on January 2, 1913. Source: *The State* (Columbia, SC), 3/4/11 (1:6), 3/5/11 (1:3), 6/15/11 (2:3) & 1/3/13 (11:3). Appeal: 92 SC 495–501. See also: 1870 & 1880 U.S. Census (Newberry Co., SC), which note young Sam Boozer.

Frank Green (black, age 18). *Attempted Rape.* The crime was committed on or about 10/6/1912 in Marlboro County. Felonious assault on the person of a 14-year-old white female (name withheld) with intent to commit rape. The victim was attacked while picking cotton and left "severely injured" at the scene. The attacker was executed on April 4, 1913. Sources: *The State* (Columbia, SC), 10/17/12 (3:4) & 3/17/13 (11:1); *Charleston Evening Post*, 4/4/13 (15:1).

Charles P. Rushing (white, age 40). *Murder.* The crime was committed on 1/27/1913 in Chesterfield County. Uxoricide. Handgun slaying and savage beating of 40-year-old Sue Rushing (white), she having up to then suffered mistreatment that was more animalistic than human. Motive: spousal abuse. Eight children were orphaned by this tragedy. The wife abuser turned killer was executed on April 18, 1913. Sources: *The State* (Columbia, SC), 1/31/13 (12:3) & 3/7/13 (9:1); *Charleston Evening Post*, 4/18/13 (9:4). See also: 1910 U.S. Census (Chesterfield Co., SC), which notes the family Rushing.

Sam Dukes (black, age 22). *Murder.* The crime was committed on 2/10/1913 in Sumter County. Cop killer. Handgun slaying of 24-year-old Isadore Barwick (white), policeman for the town of Pinewood. Motive: escalated confrontation. The officer had walked up to Dukes on a public sidewalk and asked him to identify himself. Dukes answered by pulling a pistol out of his pants and opening fire with it. He was executed on July 1, 1913. Sources: *The State* (Columbia, SC), 2/11/13 (1:5), 2/14/13 (6:4) & 6/4/13 (3:5); *Augusta (GA) Chronicle*, 7/2/13 (7:5). See also: 1900 & 1910 U.S. Census (Sumter Co., SC), which note Barwick.

Manning L. Garrett (white, age 48). *Murder.* The crime was committed on 5/18/1913 in Lee County. Shotgun slayings of 19-year-old Aaron Campbell and 52-year-old John H. Campbell (whites), they respectively being his son-in-law and that boy's father. Motive: incestuous obsession. The younger Campbell had married Garrett's 19-year-old daughter (Gertrude, a.k.a. "Gertie"), two or three days before the tragedy, apparently without her father's consent. Papa Garrett had *reportedly* been using the girl as a sex slave up until that time. He was furious when told that "Gertie" had eloped. The irate father (and "degenerate," as he was called) stomped over to the Campbell cabin and blasted every male he saw with a shotgun. Then he forcibly abducted his daughter (she being there at the time) and fled into the swamps. Papa Garrett was executed on July 14, 1913. Source: *The State* (Columbia, SC), 5/20/13 (1:5), 6/13/13 (3:6) & 7/15/13 (11:2). See also: 1910 U.S. Census (Kershaw Co., SC), which notes the Campbells, and 1900 U.S. Census (Sumter Co., SC), which notes the Garretts.

Herman Kelly (black, age 23.). *Attempted Rape.* The crime was committed on 4/19/1913 in Florence County. Felonious assault on the person of a white female (name withheld and age not specified) with intent to commit rape. Kelly had gone to the woman's house under the pretense of fetching a pail of milk. Then he attacked her with a metal wrench that he had hidden up his sleeve, seriously wounding both the lady herself and her 12-year-old son. He was executed on August 8, 1913. Source: *The State* (Columbia, SC), 4/21/13 (1:1) & 8/9/13 (10:2).

Ernest Mulwee (black, age 21). *Murder.* The crime was committed on 10/24/1911 in Oconee County. Executed for the murder of 27-year-old Samuel Hyde (white, the foreman of the farm on which he worked), who was hit on the back of the head with "a heavy garden paling." Motive: payday dispute. Mulwee paid for this in the electric chair on August 18, 1913. Source: *The State* (Columbia, SC), 10/26/11 (6:4), 3/13/12 (1:2) & 8/19/13 (12:5). See also: 1910 U.S. Census (Oconee Co., SC), which notes both parties.

Jasper Green (black, age 40) **and Davis Reynolds** (black, age not recorded). Murder. Their crime was committed on

3/29/1913 in Beaufort County. Cop killers. Shotgun slaying of 37-year-old James Rollin Cooler (white, a liquor enforcement constable), who caught a load of buckshot in his face as he walked along a rural road with one of his assistants. It was never determined exactly who fired the fatal blast. It was done from ambush a short distance from the Reynolds cabin. Davis Reynolds was found to be the owner of the murder weapon and to have purchased ammo for it shortly before the homicide. He and Jasper Green were dispensers of illegal liquor who had allegedly taken part in a conspiracy by persons of that ilk to rid themselves of the all too efficient lawman. Green and Reynolds were executed on September 4, 1913. Sources: *Beaufort (SC) Gazette*, 4/4/13 (1:7) & 8/1/13 (1:1); *The State* (Columbia, SC), 9/5/13 (12:1). See also: 1910 U.S. Census (Beaufort Co., SC), which notes Green and Cooler.

Scott Madison (black, age 24). *Murder.* The crime was committed on 12/3/1913 in Barnwell County. Handgun slaying of 35-year-old Edward Peyton Best (white), the victim having been shot in the back. Motive: short-tempered escalation of a minor encounter. The shooting followed a bumping incident as Mr. Best walked out of a restaurant where he had just eaten his supper. The killer was executed exactly 19 days later on December 22, 1913. Sources: *The State* (Columbia, SC), 12/5/13 (1:3), 12/11/13 (3:4) & 12/23/13 (16:5); *Columbia (SC) Record*, 12/22/13 (2:4). See also: 1910 U.S. Census (Barnwell Co., SC), which notes "E.P. Best."

1914

Albert Canty (black, age 27) **and Harry Thompson** (black, age 17). *Murder.* Their crime was committed on 3/2/1913 at Charleston. Handgun slaying of 48-year-old Alfred W. Steeger (white), who was found dead on the road. Motive: highway robbery. The killers were executed on January 3, 1914. Source: *Charleston Evening Post*, 3/3/13 (9:3), 3/4/13 (14:1), 8/8/13 (12:3) & 1/3/14 (1:3). See also: 1910 U.S. Census (Charleston, SC), which notes all parties.

Buck Hill, alias "McLeod" (black, age 25). *Rape.* The crime was committed on 12/23/1913 in Richland County. Indecent assault on the person of a 35-year-old white female (name withheld), she having been attacked in her home and severely beaten. The rapist was executed on February 9, 1914. Sources: *The State* (Columbia, SC), 12/24/13 (12:4); *Augusta (GA) Chronicle*, 2/10/14 (5:3). See also: 1910 U.S. Census (Union Co., SC), which notes Hill.

1915

Floyd McCullum (black, age 24). *Murder.* The crime was committed on 6/29/1914 in Pickens County. Executed for the murder of 55-year-old James L. Hendricks (white, who was clubbed to death), and the forcible rape of that man's 54-year-old wife. It is unclear whether the miscreant was tried on two separate indictments, one for murder and the other for rape. He died in the electric chair on February 6, 1915, Sources: *Augusta (GA) Chronicle*, 7/1/14 (10:3); *The State* (Columbia, SC), 2/7/15 (24:6). See also: 1915 Richland Co. death cert. no. 24249; 1910 U.S. Census (Pickens Co., SC), which notes the victims.

Durant Haile (black, age 26). *Murder.* The crime was committed on 5/7/1914 in Kershaw County. Uxoricide. Handgun slaying of 23-year-old Lucille Haile (black), she having been shot in the back of the head as they were working the fields. Motive: suspected infidelity. The killer was executed on March 17, 1915. Source: *The State* (Columbia, SC), 7/11/14 (3:1) & 3/18/15 (9:1). See also: 1910 U.S. Census (Lee Co., SC), which notes both parties.

Tonnie Grice (black, age 17). *Rape.* The crime was committed on or about 8/15/1914 in Florence County. Indecent assault on the person of a white female (name withheld and age not specified) who was attacked in her own bedroom. The victim's testimony was deemed to be so disgusting that the courtroom had to be cleared. This rapist was executed on August 4, 1915. Source: *The State* (Columbia, SC), 10/14/14 (1:5), 8/4/15 (10:1) & 8/5/15 (6:3). See also: 1915 Richland Co. death cert. no. 16630; 1910 U.S. Census (Florence Co., SC), which notes that "Tony" Grice had been born in 1897.

Jesse McNeal (black, age 26). *Murder.* The crime was committed on or about 2/20/1915 in Marlboro County. Uxoricide. Executed for the murder of about 25-year-old Ida McNeal (black), whose throat was cut and her nearly nude body dumped in a pond where it was found three weeks later. Motive: marital discord. The killer was executed on September 3, 1915. Source: *The State* (Columbia, SC), 3/11/15 (9:1). See also: 1915 Richland Co. death cert. no. 24250.

Melton Brice (black, age 20), **John Cosby** (black, age about 33), **Meeks Griffin** (black, age 25) **and Tom Griffin** (black, age 27). *Murder.* Their crime was committed on 4/24/1913 in Chester County. All executed for the shotgun slaying of 73-year-old John Q. Lewis (white), a wealthy farmer. Motive: robbery and home invasion. The South Carolina electric chair ended the lives of this quartet on September 29, 1915. Source: *The State* (Columbia, SC), 4/26/13 (1:7) & 9/30/15 (14:2). See also: 1915 Richland Co. death cert. nos. 18618 thru 18621. In 2009 posthumous pardons were granted to the Griffins, based on what may have been little or nothing more than hearsay.

Joe Malloy (black, age 45). *Murder.* The crime was committed on 11/24/1910 in Marlboro County. Child killer. Shotgun slayings of 11-year-old Prentiss Moore and 15-year-old Guy Rogers (whites). Motive: because these boys went hunting on his land in direct disobedience of his orders not to do so. Malloy was also the prime suspect in the untimely death of his wife who died "under mysterious circumstances" several weeks later, allegedly because he feared that she might expose what he had done. Malloy was executed on September 29, 1915. Source: *The State* (Columbia, SC), 11/27/10 (1:3), 12/22/11 (1:4), 1/1/12 (10:1) & 9/30/15 (14:2).

Charles Logan (black, age 17). *Murder.* The crime was committed on 3/16/1915 in Abbeville County. Executed for the murder of 80-year-old Frances Helmina Boles Scott (white), who was struck on the head with a hammer. Motive: burglary and attempted sexual assault of the victim's 14-year-old granddaughter. Logan was executed on October 15, 1915. Source: *The State* (Columbia, SC), 3/18/15 (1:6) & 10/16/15 (6:1). See also: 1915 Abbeville Co. death cert. no. 3662, and Richland Co. death cert. no. 24248.

1916

Peter Hamilton (black, age 25). *Attempted Rape.* The crime was committed on 11/27/1915 in Pickens County. Felonious assault on the person of a "young" white female (name withheld and age not specified) with intent to commit rape. The victim was attacked in her own bedroom but the culprit failed to accomplish his purpose. Hamilton made a full confession. He had crept into the open window of the *boudoir* wherein two white females lay sleeping shortly before midnight. They fought him off so that he fled back out of the same window. He was executed for this ill-intentioned felony on February 4, 1916. Sources: *Keowee (SC) Courier*, 12/1/15 (1:3); *Pickens (SC) Sentinel*, 12/2/15 (5:1); *The State* (Columbia, SC), 12/28/15 (3:1) & 12/29/15 (3:3). See also: 1916 Richland Co. death cert. no. 27815.

Israel Good (black, age 17). *Rape.* The crime was committed on 12/29/1915 in York County. Indecent assault on the person of a 6-year-old white female (name withheld), she and another "little white girl" having been lured into a cotton house for no good purpose. One examining physician testified that he thought the culprit to be innocent because he was free of venereal disease. The prisoner himself debunked that theory by confessing his guilt. He was executed on February 25, 1916. Source: *The State* (Columbia, SC), 2/1/16 (3:1) & 2/26/16 (9:1).

Stobo Bailey (black, age 25). *Murder.* The crime was committed on 2/11/1916 in Laurens County. Shotgun slaying of 36-year-old Sallie Barksdale (black) who was blasted to pieces by five successive volleys fired from the killer's weapon, he having paused to carefully reload it each time. Angry blacks hunted Bailey like an animal in the aftermath of this crime. Motive: because the victim's husband (Ran Barksdale) had taken a hog that Bailey owned. The latter was executed on April 28, 1916. Source: *Laurens (SC) Advertiser*, 2/16/16 (5:3), 3/22/16 (1:1) & 5/3/16 (1:4). See also: 1900 U.S. Census (Laurens Co., SC), which notes Bailey, and 1910 U.S. Census (Laurens Co., SC), which notes Barksdale.

James Monroe Collins (black, age 22). *Attempted Rape.* The crime was committed on 1/30/1916 in Greenville County. Felonious assault on the person of a white female (name withheld and age not specified) with intent to commit rape. The victim and her 8-year-old daughter were terrorized by the culprit but saved from further harm when their loyal dog tore into him. Collins was put to death for this on May 5, 1916. Source: *The State* (Columbia, SC), 2/3/16 (3:4) & 5/6/16 (8:6). See also: 1916 Richland Co. death cert. no. 33217.

Joe Grant (black, age 47). *Murder.* The crime was committed on April 14, 1906, in Edgefield County. Handgun slaying of 36-year-old Jesse T. Durst (white). Motive: tenant-landlord dispute. The killer was a barber by trade. His rent was in arrears. Rather than pay and be done with it, he pulled a gun on his landlord and shot him in the gut. The wounded man died after four days in agony. Eight years later the killer was caught in Pennsylvania by a Negro detective. Joe Grant was executed on May 15, 1916. Sources: *Augusta (GA) Chronicle*, 4/15/06 (4:3), 4/19/06 (7:1) & 5/16/16 (4:2); *Columbia (SC) Record*, 5/15/16 (1:6). See also: 1880 U.S. Census (Edgefield Co., SC), which notes Mr. Durst as a minor.

Ellis Jonathan (black, age 38). *Attempted Rape.* The crime was committed on 6/21/1916 in Edgefield County. Felonious assault on the person of a white female (name withheld and age not disclosed) who was terrorized by a home intruder (Jonathan) and only rescued from further harm by a neighbor who heard her screams. This offender was executed on September 15, 1916. Source: *The State* (Columbia, SC), 6/22/16 (9:1) & 8/16/16 (5:3). See also: State Penitentiary Execution Roster entry at date (handwritten ledger, since microfilmed), South Carolina State Archives; 1880 U.S. Census (Edgefield, SC), which notes Ellis Jonathan as a young child.

1917

John Johnson (black, age 23). *Murder.* The crime was committed on 11/21/1916 in Dillon County. Executed for the killing of 67-year-old Hugh Harrelson (white, the owner of a country store), who was struck on the head with a metal plow point by two assailants who then went on to rape his wife. Motive: a previous disagreement, or so the killers claimed. John Johnson was executed on March 23, 1917. The fate of his accomplice is unknown. Source: *The State* (Columbia, SC), 11/23/16 (1:3), 12/17/16 (7:7) & 3/24/17 (10:4). See also: 1917 Richland Co. death cert. no. 19251; 1910 U.S. Census (Dillon Co., SC), which notes Harrelson.

Mackey Palmer (black, age 20). *Murder.* The crime was committed on 3/9/1917 in Orangeburg County. Cop killer. Handgun slaying of 60-year-old Howard H. Franklin (white). Motive: resisting arrest. Palmer was executed on October 11, 1917. Sources: *Augusta (GA) Chronicle*, 3/10/17 (2:3); *Keowee (SC) Courier*, 10/17/17 (1:1). See also: 1917 Richland Co. death cert. no. 19333.

1918

John Gardner (black, age 21). *Murder.* The crime was committed on 12/1/1917 in Beaufort County. Handgun slaying of 42-year-old Samuel Hirsch Schein (white), a grocer. Motive: some kind of smoldering resentment. Gardner had been "adopted by Mr. Schein when but a small child and had been taken care of by him for a number of years." No further details are discernible. Gardner was executed on January 25, 1918. Sources: *Beaufort (SC) Gazette*, 12/7/17 (1:6); *Augusta (GA) Chronicle*, 1/26/18 (3:6). See also: 1910 U.S. Census (Beaufort Co., SC), which notes the murdered man; the victim's gravestone in Beth Israel Cemetery, Beaufort, South Carolina.

Will Ferguson (black, age 18). *Attempted Rape.* The crime was committed on 4/14/1918 in Barnwell County. Felonious assault on the person of a white female (name withheld and age not specified) with intent to commit rape. Details of this case were toned down by the local press—presumably to minimize the risk of lynching—but those same details were sufficiently heinous to bring about Ferguson's death through legal means less than a month later. He was executed on May 10, 1918. Sources: *Barnwell (SC) People*, 5/16/18 (3:2); *The State* (Columbia, SC), 5/11/18 (2:3).

Sam Hallman (black, age 37). *Attempted Rape.* The crime was committed on 5/10/1918 in Colleton County. Felonious assault on the person of a white female (name withheld, age not specified) with intent to commit rape. Hallman was a "trusty" on the Colleton County chain gang. He was serving a three-year sentence for larceny and was classified as a minimum risk prisoner. He went to a lady's house on the pretense of borrowing a buggy for use by the chain gang boss. The woman opened the door of the carriage barn for him and he rolled the buggy out into the driveway. Then he suddenly grabbed the female party and tried to force himself on her. Screams brought rescuers running to the scene. Hallman was executed for this on July 19, 1918. Source: *The Press & Standard* (Walterboro, SC), 5/15/18 (1:3), 6/12/18 (1:5) & 7/24/18 (1:1).

1919

Samuel Johnson (black, age 18). *Attempted Rape.* The crime was committed on 11/30/1918 in York County. Felonious assault on the person of a "young" white female (name withheld) with intent to commit rape. The victim had been accosted on a public road. Further details were not divulged to the public. Johnson was executed on January 10, 1919. Sources: *Yorkville (SC) Enquirer*, 12/3/18 (2:5); *Columbia (SC) Record*, 1/10/19 (16:2); *Augusta (GA) Chronicle*, 1/11/19 (10:3).

Aaron Walker (black, age 25). *Attempted Rape.* The crime was committed on 12/3/1918 in Greenwood County. Felonious assault on the person of a white female named Eliza Hill (age not recorded) with intent to commit rape. Walker was a "trusty" on the Greenwood County chain gang. He entered the victim's house without her knowledge and hid beneath her bed. He later emerged from that place of concealment as the lady was undressing herself for the night and grabbed her by the throat. The screaming of a small child saved her from further violence. Walker was executed on March 8, 1919. Sources: original trial record (*State vs. Walker*), Greenwood County Courthouse; *Columbia (SC) Record*, 3/8/19 (2:3); *The State* (Columbia, SC), 3/2/19 (18:1) & 3/9/19 (16:1).

George Johnson (black, age 19). *Attempted Rape.* The crime was committed on 4/6/1919 in Aiken County. Felonious assault on the person of a "young" white female (name withheld) with intent to commit rape. The victim was walking along a public road minding her own business when Johnson sprang out of some bushes and threw her to the ground. He throttled her with his bare hands but was driven off when law-abiding black folks came to the rescue. A posse ran Johnson into the swamps and caught him when he climbed a tree. He was executed on July 11, 1919. Sources: *Aiken (SC) Journal & Review*, 4/9/19 (4:3) & 5/14/19 (4:4); *The State* (Columbia, SC), 7/12/19 (12:1).

Moses Witherspoon (black, age 27). *Murder.* The crime was committed on 5/23/1919 in Lancaster County. Handgun slaying of 41-year-old Luther Horton (white), who was shot three times in the head. Motive: gross ingratitude. The killer was a tenant farmer who tilled shares for the victim's father, Henry E. Horton. The elder Horton had previously been instrumental in securing a verdict of acquittal when Witherspoon was tried for an unrelated homicide. The two men somehow had words with each other on the above date. Witherspoon then repaid the elder Horton's favor to him by murdering his son. The ingrate was himself put to death (albeit legally) on November 14, 1919. Source: *The State* (Columbia, SC), 5/24/19 (9:4) & 11/5/19 (14:3). See also: 1919 Richland Co. death cert. no. 20517; 1910 U.S. Census (Lancaster Co., SC), which notes the Hortons.

1920

John Maxwell (black, age 20). *Murder.* The crime was committed on 3/2/1920 at Charleston. Executed for the hatchet murder of 55-year-old George S. Douan (white), who was chopped five times on the head and shot once in the arm with a handgun. Motive: belligerent attitude. The victim was a bill collector. Maxwell resented this. He attacked the man as he was going about his business, but not before first berating him with foul language. He was executed on August 6, 1920. Source: *Charleston (SC) Evening Courier*, 3/4/20 (3:4), 7/6/20 (1:5) & 8/6/20 (18:4). See also: 1920 Charleston Co. death cert. no. 4490, and Richland Co. death cert. no. 23808.

James Washington (black, age 22). *Rape.* The crime was committed on 7/12/1920 in Greenville County. Indecent assault on the person of a 14-year-old white female (name withheld) under circumstances that no newspaper would dare to describe. This rapist was executed on September 24, 1920. Source: *The State* (Columbia, SC), 7/14/20 (1:1) & 9/25/20 (10:5).

Grover Butler (black, age 24). *Attempted Rape.* The crime was committed on 9/15/1919 in Spartanburg County. Felonious assault on the person of 29-year-old Emily Mabry (white), who was accosted on a "public highway" with intent to commit rape. Butler had walked up to the woman and asked her if she could make change for a five-dollar bill. Then he grabbed her by the belt with enough force to break it. He was executed on December 14, 1920. Sources: original trial record (Spartanburg General Sessions, Oct. Term 1919, case no. 39), South Carolina State Archives; *Spartanburg Herald*, 9/16/19 (2:1:7); *The State* (Columbia, SC), 9/24/19 (5:3) & 12/15/20 (7:4). Appeal: 114 SC 433–444. See also: 1920 Richland Co. death cert. no. 23812.

1921

Ivey Littlejohn (black, age 25). *Murder.* The crime was committed on 3/20/1919 in Spartanburg County. Prison guard killer. Executed for the murder of 48-year-old Joseph S. Holbert (white), a foreman on the Spartanburg County chain gang. Motive: a grudge, apparently. A mason by trade, Holbert had been given authority over a group of convicts engaged in building bridge buttresses. One of these shackled laborers was Ivey Littlejohn. The killer snuck up behind Mr. Holbert and bludgeoned him with a rock. Then he finished him off by shooting the man with his own service pistol. Littlejohn was executed on February 18, 1921. Source: *The State* (Columbia, SC), 3/21/19 (1:3). See also: 1919 Spartanburg Co. death cert. no. 7003, and 1921 Richland Co. death cert. no. 12840. Also: 1910 U.S. Census (Henderson Co., NC), which notes Mr. Holbert.

Adam Griffin (black, age 27). *Murder.* The crime was committed on 4/22/1920 in Sumter County. Prison guard killer. Executed for the murder of 41-year-old Archie M. Sox (white, a guard on the DeSaussure Convict Farm), who was struck on the head with a shovel. Motive: attempted breakout. Fourteen prisoners were left unsupervised by this incident. Eleven of them were smart enough to return to the stockade of their own accord. Three of them (including Griffin) fled into the swamps despite being shackled. Two were caught. The third was presumed lost in the quicksand. Adam Griffin was executed on March 4, 1921. Source: *The State* (Columbia, SC), 4/23/20 (1:4) & 3/5/21 (5:2). See also: 1920 U.S. Census (Sumter Co., SC), which notes Sox, and (Richland Co., SC), which notes Griffin as a prisoner.

Richard Fogle, alias "Feetie Fogle" (black, age 14). *Murder.* The crime was committed on 1/12/1921 in Calhoun County. Executed for the shotgun slaying of 23-year-old Earle Wadford and concomitant maiming of 23-year-old Corbett Zeigler (whites), the latter of whom lost a leg. Motive: ramifications of larceny. Fogle had stolen meats from Wadford's smokehouse. He got caught and was then goaded into killing Mr. Wadford by an older cousin (Harvey Whaley) who had put him up to committing the theft in the first place and feared that the matter would be traced back to him. Fogle went to Wadford's house with a loaded shotgun and blasted away at anything that moved. Shots were fired through doorways and windows alike. These proved fatal to Mr. Wadford and crippling to Mr. Zeigler. The slain man's wife and 4-month old baby were also struck by buckshot but survived. "Feetie" Fogle was executed on March 25, 1921. Harvey Whaley met the same fate later that year. Source: *The State* (Columbia, SC), 1/14/21 (1:7), 1/15/21 (1:7), 1/19/21 (2:4) & 3/26/21 (10:4). See also: 1921 Calhoun Co. death cert. no. 206; 1920 U.S. Census (Calhoun Co., SC), which notes Fogle, Whaley and Zeigler. The official list of state prison executions (since microfilmed by the South Carolina State Archives) says Fogle was aged 16. The census record proves this to be incorrect.

Albert Wilson (black, age 24). *Murder.* The crime was committed on 3/20/1920 in Richland County. Handgun slaying of 23-year-old Bryan E. Butler (white), who was shot as he boarded a trolley car. Motive: none apparent. Wilson was riding the back end of a crowded trolley car in downtown Columbia. Butler and his wife boarded the same trolley, whereupon Wilson (without saying a word) pulled out a revolver and shot the young white man once in the chest. He never did say why he did it. He was executed on May 3, 1921. Source: *The State* (Columbia, SC), 3/21/20 (13:1) & 5/4/21 (10:1). See also: 1921 Richland Co. death cert. no. 7692.

Pink Griffin (black, age 24). *Murder.* The crime was committed on 7/5/1921 in Greenwood County. Handgun slaying of 60-year-old Lawton C. Lipscomb (white, formerly the official pharmacist for the South Carolina State Penitentiary), who was shot six times. Motive: personal resentment. Lipscomb had scolded Griffin for beating a mule. Annoyed at being lectured on how to treat his own animal, Griffin then pulled a fully loaded pistol on Lipscomb and emptied its contents into him. This killer was executed on September 2, 1921. Source: *The State* (Columbia, SC), 7/6/21 (1:1) & 9/3/21 (8:4). See also: 1921 Greenwood Co. death cert. no. 10731, and Richland Co. death cert. no. 14715.

Harvey Whaley (black, age 40). *Murder.* The crime was committed on 1/12/1921 in Calhoun County. Catalyst in the shotgun slaying of 23-year-old Earle Wadford and concomitant maiming of 23-year-old Corbett Zeigler (whites), the latter of whom lost a leg. Motive: ramifications of larceny. This offender was executed on November 4, 1921. Source: *The State* (Columbia, SC), 11/5/21 (5:5). Also: 1921 Richland Co. death cert. no. 18002. See: FOGLE, Richard (executed 3/25/21).

Tillman Choice (black, age 21). *Rape.* The crime was committed on 10/4/1921 in Spartanburg County. Indecent assault on the person of 37-year-old Mollie Ivey (white) under circumstances that were deemed egregious enough to secure a capital verdict. The rapist was executed on December 2, 1921. Sources: original trial record (*State vs. Choice*) Spartanburg General Sessions, Oct. Term 1921, South Carolina State Archives; *Spartanburg Journal*, 10/5/21 (7:1) & 10/6/21 (11:1); *The State* (Columbia, SC), 12/3/21 (10:4). See also: 1920 U.S. Census (Spartanburg Co., SC), which notes both parties.

1922

Curtis Franklin (black, age 33). *Rape.* The crime was committed on 11/26/1921 in Aiken County. Indecent assault on the person of a "young" white female (name withheld), she having also been beaten, her face mangled by the culprit's teeth and one of her arms broken. This criminal was legally executed on February 3, 1922. Source: *The State* (Columbia, SC), 11/28/21 (1:3) & 2/4/22 (8:4).

Will Hood (black, age 19). *Murder.* The crime was committed on 9/30/1921 in Greenville County. Handgun slaying of 65-year-old George W. Smith (white, a watchman at a lumber mill), who was shot four times. Motive: burglary. The killer was executed on April 7, 1922. Source: *The State* (Columbia, SC), 10/29/21 (1:5) & 4/8/22 (6:1). See also: 1921 Greenville Co. death cert. no. 14163, and 1922 Richland Co. death cert. no. 6016; 1920 U.S. Census (Greenville Co., SC), which notes Mr. Smith.

Casey O. Fox (white, age 31), **Jesse J. Gappins** (white, age 21) **and Samuel J. Kirby** (white, age 35). *Murder.* Their crime was committed on 8/7/1921 in Lexington County. All three executed for the murder of 19-year-old Willie C. Brazell (white, a taxi driver), who was blackjacked, stabbed multiple times, and his body dumped in a wooded area. Motive: robbery and carjacking. The killers died in the electric chair on June 16, 1922. Source: *The State* (Columbia, SC), 8/9/21 (1:1) & 6/17/22 (8:1). See also: 1921 Lexington Co. death cert. no. 14415; 1922 Richland Co. death cert. nos. 9305, 9383 and 9384; 1920 U.S. Census (Richland Co., SC), which notes Brazell, Gappins and Kirby.

Frank M. Jeffords (white, age 29). *Murder.* The crime was committed on 5/9/1922 in Richland County. Catalyst in the murder of 45-year-old John C. Arnette (white, his business partner), who was battered to death with an iron automobile axle. Motive: insurance fraud. Jeffords was executed on December 22, 1922. Source: *The State* (Columbia, SC),

5/18/22 (1:8) & 11/28/22 (7:1). See also: 1922 Richland Co. death cert. nos. 7727 & 19876.

1923

Thomas Johnson (black, age 16). *Murder.* The crime was committed on 1/9/1923 in Bamberg County. Executed for the mutilation murder of 63-year-old Laura Riley Lancaster (white), she having been attacked in a ginnery, battered about the face and head with a heavy iron pin, and her body stuffed down the hole of a cotton press. Motive: sexual assault. This juvenile offender was legally put to death on February 2, 1923. Sources: *Augusta (GA) Chronicle*, 1/11/23 (1:4) & 1/23/23 (3:1); *The State* (Columbia, SC), 2/3/23 (6:1). See also: 1923 Bamberg Co. death cert. no. 217, and Richland Co. death cert. no. 3139.

Ira Harrison (white, age 21). *Murder.* The crime was committed on 5/9/1922 in Richland County. Accomplice in the murder of 45-year-old John C. Arnette (white, a filling station owner), who was battered to death with a heavy iron automobile axle. Motive: insurance fraud. Harrison was executed on February 16, 1923. Source: *The State* (Columbia, SC), 5/18/22 (1:8). See also: 1922 Richland Co. death cert. no. 7727, and 1923 Richland Co. death cert. no. 3152. See: JEFFORDS, Frank (executed 12/22/22).

Jake Terry (black, age 25). *Murder.* The crime was committed on 4/9/1922 in Hampton County. Handgun slaying of 29-year-old Thaddeus Fulton (black), who was gunned down during a church service. Motive: rivalry for a female. The killer was executed on March 16, 1923. Source: *The State* (Columbia, SC), 4/11/22 (10:4), 2/12/23 (10:3) & 3/17/23 (12:5). See also: 1923 Richland Co. death cert. no. 4832; Fulton's World War I draft registration card (Hampton Co., SC), which notes that he was born on 1/3/1893.

Eugene Adams (black, age 20). *Murder.* The crime was committed on 2/9/1923 in Orangeburg County. Shotgun slaying of 61-year-old. J. Attaway Brown (white), a storekeeper. Motive: robbery. The killer was executed on June 22, 1923. Sources: *The State* (Columbia, SC), 2/17/23 (1:8) & 6/23/23 (10:1); *Times & Democrat* (Orangeburg, SC), 2/15/23 (1:8) & 2/17/23 (1:8). See also Mr. Brown's gravestone in Trinity United Methodist Church Cemetery, North, South Carolina. His full name is not found in any known record.

Frank Gaines (black, age 26) **and Julius Garvin** (black, age 28). *Murder.* Their crime was committed on 7/3/1923 in Beaufort County. Both executed for the willful killings of 68-year-old William D. Brown and 54-year-old Lulia Bradley Brown (whites, a married couple) who were burned alive. Motive: robbery and home invasion. The killers went to the electric chair on December 21, 1923. Source: *Augusta (GA) Chronicle*, 12/16/23 (2:7:3). See also: 1923 Beaufort Co. death cert. nos. 10623 & 10624, plus Richland Co. death cert. nos. 20040 & 20041.

1924

Thomas Jefferson Chandler (white, age 34). *Murder.* The crime was committed on 2/25/1922 in Greenville County. Uxoricide, etc. Handgun slayings of 32-

year-old Theodus Bramlett Chandler and 68-year-old Rosie McDaniel Bramlett (whites), his wife and mother-in-law. Motive: family tension. Six shots were fired, all of which found their mark. The presence of the couple's terrified children (ages 4 and 6) did not deter the killer. He was tried only in the death of Mrs. Bramlett. The other indictment was held in abeyance. Chandler was executed on February 1, 1924. Sources: *The State* (Columbia, SC), 2/26/22 (19:4); *Augusta (GA) Chronicle*, 2/2/24 (1:1). See also: 1922 Greenville Co. death cert. nos. 2339 & 2340, plus 1924 Richland Co. death cert. no. 3151.

Charlie Simuel (black, age 24). *Murder.* The crime was committed on or about 11/16/1923 in Spartanburg County. Shotgun slaying of 60-year-old Lemick Long (black), a farmer whose body was not found until several days later. Motive: robbery. The killer was executed on June 20, 1924. Sources: *Augusta (GA) Chronicle*, 1/18/24 (2:1:7); *Greensboro (NC) Record*, 6/20/24 (5:2); *Columbia (SC) Record*, 6/20/24 (1:2); *The State* (Columbia, SC), 6/21/24 (8:4). See also: 1923 Spartanburg Co. death cert. no. 18239, and 1924 Richland Co. death cert. no. 15316.

Reuben Robinson (black, age 17). *Attempted Rape.* The crime was committed on 9/22/1924 in Chester County. Felonious assault on the person of an 18-year-old white female (name withheld) with intent to commit rape. The victim was accosted on the Chester to Great Falls highway as she sat by the roadside awaiting the delivery of her mail. The culprit severely beat her (while holding rocks in his fists) and finding her knocked out cold, tumbled her into a culvert. He was executed on November 7, 1924. Source: *The State* (Columbia, SC), 9/23/24 (1:3), 10/7/24 (1:2) & 11/8/24 (10:5). See also: 1924 Richland Co. death cert. no. 21121.

Mortimer King (white, age 24) **and Sherd Harrell** (white, age 22). *Murder.* Their crime was committed on 7/2/1924 in Chesterfield County. Handgun slaying of 43-year-old Samuel H. McLeary (white), a major in the United States Army. Motive: robbery and carjacking. The killers were executed on December 5, 1924. Sources: *Greensboro (NC) Daily Record*, 7/17/24 (1:7) & 7/17/24 (5:1); *Greensboro (NC) Daily News*, 12/6/24 (1:4). See also: 1924 Chesterfield Co. death cert. no. 12508, and Richland Co. death cert. nos. 23112 & 23113.

1925

Carroll Orr (black, age 54). *Murder.* The crime was committed on 12/7/1923 in Berkeley County. Shotgun slaying of 79-year-old John Madison Heape (white). Motive: argument in a country store. Venue changed from Berkeley County to Charleston County. The killer was executed on June 5, 1925. Source: *Augusta (GA) Chronicle*, 1/21/24 (2:5) & 6/7/25 (3:1:5). See also: 1923 Berkeley Co. death cert. no. 18629, and 1925 Richland Co. death cert. no. 10527.

Draper Jeffries (black, age 30). *Murder.* The crime was committed on 9/1/1924 in Spartanburg County. Handgun slaying of 25-year-old Essie Mitchell (black), she having been chased through the streets prior to being shot in the back. Motive: obnoxious drunk. The killer was executed on August 28, 1925. Sources: *Spartanburg Herald*, 9/2/24 (1:5); *The State* (Columbia, SC), 8/29/25 (10:1); *Florence (SC)*

Morning News, 8/28/25 (1:6); *Augusta (GA) Chronicle*, 8/29/25 (7:5). See also: 1924 Spartanburg Co. death cert. no. 17174, and 1925 Richland Co. death cert. no. 15441.

1926

John Cooper (black, age 42). *Murder.* The crime was committed on 5/23/1926 at Charleston. Executed for the murders of 29-year-old Spiro Constan and 22-year-old Louie L. Smith (whites), they being a storekeeper and his clerk. Motive: armed robbery. Cooper and an accomplice named Elijah Benson (black, age 31) had gone into the aforesaid place of business pretending to look at its wares. Benson engaged Constan in conversation about a pair of socks, at which point Cooper fatally struck him on the head with a hammer. Seeing this, the storekeeper's assistant (Smith) emerged from the back room firing a handgun. Benson was hit by at least one bullet that killed him. Cooper somehow got the better of Smith and stunned him with a blackjack. The latter staggered out onto the sidewalk where he was then finished off by the angry Cooper, who crushed his skull with an iron fishplate (an implement used by railroad track repairmen) that happened to be lying close by. Cooper was executed on August 27, 1926. Source: *Florence (SC) Morning News*, 6/1/26 (1:7). See also: 1926 Charleston Co. death cert. nos. 8108, 8186 and 8187, plus Richland Co. death cert. no. 15441.

1927

McKinley Thomasson (black, age 18). *Murder.* The crime was committed on 6/25/1927 in York County. Executed for the murder of 78-year-old Frances Cowan Thomasson (white), her throat being cut. Motive: house robbery. The killer was executed on August 12, 1927. Source: *The State* (Columbia, SC), 6/26/27 (1:5) & 8/13/27 (1:7). See also: 1927 York Co. death cert. no. 10427, and Richland Co. death cert. no. 13862.

1928

South Carolina did not execute any criminals this year.

1929

John Brown (black, age 21) **and George Palmer** (black, age 21). *Murder.* Their crime was committed on 8/6/1928 at Charleston. Both executed for the murder of 58-year-old Chu Yuan Fat, also known as "Charlie Loy" (the proprietor of a Chinese laundry establishment), whose throat was cut with a razor. Motive: robbery. The killers died in the electric chair on January 4, 1929. Source: *Greensboro (NC) Daily News*, 1/5/29 (3:4). See also: 1928 Charleston Co. death cert. no. 14034, and 1929 Richland Co. death cert. nos. 5248 & 5249.

Charlie Robinson (black, age 22). *Murder.* The crime was committed on 4/10/1928 at Charleston. Executed for the murder of 18-year-old Mamie Hutchinson Smith (black, a reputed prostitute), whose "clothes were maliciously set on fire" after he had splashed her with lamp oil. Motive: lovers' spat. Robinson paid with his life for this on April 19, 1929. Source: *The State* (Columbia, SC), 4/20/29 (1:4). Appeal: 149 SC 439–445. See also: 1928 Charleston Co. death cert. no. 6003, and 1929 Richland Co. death cert. no. 7069.

1930

Eli Truesdale (black, age 29). *Murder.* The crime was committed on 12/5/1929 in Lee County. Ax murders of 54-year-old Willie Bristow and 46-year-old Lillian Burris Bristow (blacks), a married couple. Motive: home invasion. The killer was executed on April 29, 1930. Source: *The State* (Columbia, SC), 4/20/30 (16:1). See also: 1929 Lee Co. death cert. nos. 21909 & 21910, plus 1930 Richland Co. death cert. no. 12737.

Ossie Moore (black, age 24) **and George Washington** (black, age 22). *Murder.* Their crime was committed on 1/20/1930 in Allendale County. Both executed for the handgun slaying of 43-year-old Elliott "Shan" Bates (black), whose body was then dumped in the Savannah River. Also indicted (but not tried) for the concomitant slaying of 48-year-old Frank Harley (white), who was blasted in the head by a shotgun and his body disposed of in the same manner. Motive: bootleggers' quarrel. The killers died in the electric chair on May 16, 1930. Source: *Augusta (GA) Chronicle*, 1/23/30 (9:8), 1/27/30 (1:1), 2/2/30 (1:1) & 5/15/30 (2:1). See also: 1930 Allendale Co. death cert. no. 1685, and Richland Co. death cert. nos. 8733 & 8741.

Ray Coleman (white, age 29) **and Paul Johnson** (white, age 29). *Murder.* Their crime was committed on 12/14/1928 in Spartanburg County. Handgun slaying of 28-year-old Earle Belue (white), a payroll clerk. Motive: highway robbery. These killers were executed on June 24, 1930. Sources: *Greensboro (NC) Daily News*, 12/15/28 (1:3); *Florence (SC) Morning News*, 6/25/30 (1:8). See also: 1928 Spartanburg Co. death cert. no. 23563, plus 1930 Richland Co. death cert. nos. 10738 & 10741.

1931

George Byrd (black, age 21), **Lindsey Cantrell**, alias "John Ackwright" (black, age 26), **Robert Eldridge** (black, age 26), **James Hickman** (black, age 26) **and Ernest Thompson** (black, age 23). *Murder.* Their crime was committed on 1/6/1931 in Lexington County. All executed for the rifle slaying of 41-year-old Bob Wilbur Hendrix (white, a storekeeper), who was fired upon through his display window without even being accosted first. Motive: armed robbery. The killers comprised a notorious gang of bandits that cut a swath from central South Carolina all the way to Asheville, North Carolina. They were put to death on February 27, 1931. Source: *Florence (SC) Morning News*, 1/15/31 (1:5) & 2/28/31 (1:2). See also: 1931 Lexington Co. death cert. no. 965, and Richland Co. death cert. nos. 2865, 2893, 2894, 2895 & 2896.

Tillman Poozer (black, age 32). *Murder.* The crime was committed on 1/3/1931 in Lexington County. Ax murder of 52-year-old Clarence D. Mills (white, a night watchman at a lumberyard), who was struck down from behind and robbed of the money in his pockets. The killer was executed on February 27, 1931. Source: *Florence (SC) Morning News*, 2/28/31 (1:2). See also: 1931 Lexington Co. death cert. no. 957, and Richland Co. death cert. no. 2903.

Norman Blakely (black, age 16). *Murder.* The crime was committed on 9/19/1929 in Greenville County. Prison guard killer. Executed for the murder of 55-year-old Dock M. Garrett (white, a convict guard on the Greenville County chain gang), who was struck down from behind with a shovel. Motive: insubordination. The killer was executed on May 26, 1931. Source: *Florence (SC) Morning News*, 3/27/31 (2:3). See also: 1929 Greenville Co. death cert. no. 15805, and 1931 Richland Co. death cert. no. 8535; 1920 & 1930 U.S. Census (Greenville Co., SC), which note both parties.

John P. Moore (black, age 20). *Attempted Rape.* The crime was committed on 4/13/1931 in Cherokee County. Felonious assault on the person of a "young" white female (name withheld) with intent to commit rape. The victim was waiting on a roadside for the delivery of her mail. Moore came along and had the impudence to make indecent proposals to her. The lady warned him to watch his saucy mouth, whereupon he grabbed her by the throat and attempted to force himself on her. The culprit fled when screams attracted the attention of others. He was executed for this on June 12, 1931. Source: *Gaffney (SC) Ledger*, 4/14/31 (1:4), 5/14/31 (1:1) & 6/13/31 (1:6).

Albert Floyd (white, age 34). *Murder.* The crime was committed on 9/29/1930 in Aiken County. Executed for the murder of 34-year-old Howard Bell (white), who was bludgeoned with a pipe and fatally choked when he came home to find his wife in the arms of the killer. His corpse was then propped up in the driver's seat of his own car, which was then run into a ditch to fake an accident scene. Motive: adultery turned deadly. Floyd met his end in the electric chair on July 10, 1931. Source: *Aiken (SC) Standard*, 7/10/31 (1:1). See also: 1930 Aiken Co. death cert. no. 14940, and 1931 Richland Co. death cert. no. 12275.

1932

Richard Dean (black, age 17) **and David King** (black, age 21). *Murder.* Their crime was committed on 3/27/1931 in Spartanburg County. Both executed for the murder of 24-year-old Haskell Hill (white, a filling station attendant), who was bludgeoned with an iron bar. Motive: robbery. The killers went to the electric chair on January 8, 1932. Sources: *Florence (SC) Morning News*, 3/29/31 (6:7) & 1/9/32 (1:4); *Spartanburg Herald*, 3/28/31 (1:8), 3/30/31 (1:7) & 1/9/32 (1:2). See also: 1931 Spartanburg Co. death cert. no. 5059.

James L. Sturdevant (black, age 27). *Rape.* The crime was committed on 11/14/1931 in Horry County. Indecent assault on the person of a 48-year-old white female (name withheld) while he was a "trusty" on the Horry County chain gang. The victim was pounced on while puttering in her yard. The rapist was executed on January 8, 1932. Sources: *The State* (Columbia, SC), 12/15/31 (2:3); *Greensboro (NC) Record*, 12/15/31 (14:6); *Florence (SC) Morning News*, 1/9/32 (1:4). See also: 1932 Richland Co. death cert. no. 1024.

Roy Jones (black, age 23). *Murder.* The crime was committed on 12/2/1931 in Spartanburg County. Fatal stabbing of 21-year-old Annie Mae Young (black). Motive: lovers' quarrel. Jones was executed on April 29, 1932. Source: *Augusta (GA) Chronicle*, 4/30/32 (1:6). See also:

1932 Spartanburg Co. death cert. no. 20586; 1930 U.S. Census (Spartanburg Co., SC), which notes the killer.

Hilton Williams (black, age 28). *Murder.* The crime was committed on 9/14/1930 in Marlboro County. Executed for the murder of 52-year-old John L. James (white), whose body was found in his parked automobile with its throat cut. Motive: robbery. Williams had gone to a Negro shack at an odd hour of the night. There were women there. A blood trail was found leading from that place to the victim's car, showing that James had been slain in the shack and his body purposely dragged from there and put in the car. All of his money was missing. News accounts were too discreet to say why he had gone to that shack, but the facts speak for themselves. The murderer in this case (Hilton Williams) was put to death on July 15, 1932. Source: *Greensboro (NC) Record*, 9/15/30 (1:2), 9/23/30 (1:4) & 7/15/32 (2:4). See also: 1930 Marlboro Co. death cert. no. 15948, and 1932 Richland Co. death cert. no. 11187.

Booker T. Copeland (black, age 35) **and Buster Tucker** (black, age 19). *Murder.* Their crime was committed on 4/16/1932 in Colleton County. Both executed for the murder of 55-year-old Henry Creech McMillan (white), who was clubbed on the head and then finished off with a handgun. Motive: obnoxious drunks. The murdered man was a farmer who had gone to check on a disturbance in one of his tenant cabins. He found Copeland and Tucker in the act of abusing the wife of another tenant. They then turned on McMillan and attacked him with deadly force. They wound up in the electric chair on July 29, 1932. Source: *Florence (SC) Morning News*, 4/18/32 (1:2), 4/19/32 (1:3) & 7/30/32 (1:7). See also: 1932 Richland Co. death cert. nos. 11159 & 11160.

Evans Wood (black, age 32). *Murder.* The crime was committed on 1/20/1932 in Darlington County. Fatal stabbing of 28-year-old Hattie Chambers Samuel (black). Motive: adultery turned deadly. The killer was executed on July 29, 1932. Source: *Florence (SC) Morning News*, 7/30/32 (1:7). See also: 1932 Darlington Co. death cert. no. 444, and Richland Co. death cert. no. 11145.

Edward O. Howell (white, age 40). *Murder.* The crime was committed on 6/18/1930 in Sumter County. Handgun slaying of 33-year-old Ernest Hart Williams (white), who was shot five times. Motive: "the unwritten law." Howell was a controlling husband who had somehow formed the idea that his wife was being sexually molested by someone other than himself. Mrs. Carrie Howell later said that "E.O." had beaten her into agreeing to ride around town with him for the purpose of pointing out the man—*any man*—who had done her wrong. Terrified, the woman indicated a filling station attendant (Williams) as they happened to pass by his place of business. Howell then got out of his car, walked up to Williams and shot him five times. The killer based his defense on the "the unwritten law," i.e. that he had acted on a point of honor and should therefore be let off with a verdict of justifiable homicide. It was a ruse that availed him not. He was executed on December 16, 1932. Sources: *Greensboro (NC) Record*, 6/19/30 (2:3) & 12/16/32 (1:4); *Augusta (GA) Chronicle*, 6/24/30 (1:7). See also: 1930 U.S. Census (Sumter Co., SC), which notes all parties.

1933

James Arthur Dicks (black, age 27) **and James Jones** (black, age 23). *Murder.* Their crime was committed on 12/20/1932 in Aiken County. Fatal beating of 68-year-old Charles Green (white). Motive: highway robbery. The killers were executed on March 3, 1933. Sources: *Journal and Review* (Aiken, SC), 1/4/33 (1:2); *Aiken (SC) Standard*, 12/23/32 (1:5); *Florence (SC) Morning News*, 12/31/32 (1:7) & 3/4/33 (1:4). See also: 1932 Aiken Co. death cert. no. 17625, and 1933 Richland Co. death cert. nos. 116 & 117.

William Sanders (black, age 18). *Murder.* The crime was committed on 1/2/1933 in York County. Executed for the murder of 59-year-old Zula Stephenson (white, a maiden woman), who was beaten to death with an ax handle. Motive: because he didn't like something she said, or so he himself explained it. The victim lived with her bachelor brother. The killer's grandmother was their laundress. He had gone to the Stephenson home to pick up a batch of laundry, presumably at his grandmother's behest. Sanders set the laundry parcel down on the ground as he was homeward bound with it and then deliberately returned to the Stephenson residence with murderous intent. He was executed on March 3, 1933. Source: *Florence (SC) Morning News*, 1/3/33 (1:7) & 1/4/33 (1:3). See also: 1933 York Co. death cert. no. 1410, and Richland Co. death cert. no. 118.

Barnett Smith (black, age 21). *Rape.* The crime was committed on 3/7/1933 in Laurens County. Indecent assault on the person of a "young married" white female (name withheld) during the course of a drunken spree. Smith confessed that he had deliberately waited until the victim's husband had left home to go to work that day, leaving her alone with their baby. He then forced his way into the house. The rapist had already been roving for three days. He had attacked two other women with an ax during that time and fired a shotgun at at least two others. He was executed on July 21, 1933. Sources: *Laurens (SC) Advertiser*, 3/9/33 (1:6); *The State* (Columbia, SC), 3/9/33 (10:5) & 7/22/33 (6:8).

Tom Wardlaw (black, age 52). *Murder.* The crime was committed on 4/8/1932 in Abbeville County. Executed for the murder of 62-year-old Andrew J. Ferguson (white), who was slashed to death with a knife, his throat being reportedly "cut to shreds." Motive: workplace violence. The killer worked on a farm belonging to the victim. An argument flared over the way a field had been plowed and one man pulled a knife on the other. Venue changed from Abbeville County to Newberry County. The electric chair made short work of Wardlaw on December 4, 1933. Source: *Florence (SC) Morning News*, 4/9/32 (1:4), 4/13/32 (2:5), 9/9/32 (1:4) & 12/5/33 (6:7).

James Holmes (black, age 25). *Murder.* The crime was committed on 11/17/1932 in Sumter County. Strangulation of 39-year-old Nora Franklin (black), his aunt. Motive: insurance fraud. The strangler was executed on December 4, 1933. Source: *Florence (SC) Morning News*, 10/10/33 (1:5) & 12/5/33 (6:7). See also: 1932 Sumter Co. death cert. no. 17452.

1934

Robert H. Wiles (white, age 49). *Murder.* The crime was committed on

12/23/1933 in Richland County. Child killer. Executed for the murder of 15-year-old Hubbard H. Harris Jr. (white), who was lured to a vacant house and there battered to death with an iron bar. Motive: kidnapping for ransom. The lad's body was found on Christmas Day. The killer was caught before he could send an extortionate demand, but he did make it a point to seek out the boy's distraught father in the aftermath of the crime, shake his hand and wish him a Merry Christmas. The snide aspect of that gesture outraged criminals and law abiding citizens alike. Robert Wiles was executed on March 12, 1934. Harris Sr. succumbed to heart failure nine years later at the age of 51. The loss of his beloved son was almost certainly the reason for his overall decline. Source: *Greensboro (NC) Record*, 12/26/33 (1:1), 1/9/34 (13:6) & 3/12/34 (1:1). See also: 1933 Richland Co. death cert. no. 18699, and 1934 Richland Co. death cert. no. 4541.

John Watkins (black, age 24). *Murder.* The crime was committed on 11/3/1933 in Fairfield County. Cop killer. Handgun slaying of 44-year-old Raymond A. Feaster (white, the sheriff of Fairfield County), who was shot four times with his own pistol. Motive: escape from custody. Watkins was executed on April 13, 1934. Source: *Florence (SC) Morning News*, 11/4/33 (1:5), 11/9/33 (1:4). See also: 1933 Fairfield Co. death cert. no. 17723, and 1934 Richland Co. death cert. no. 222.

John Ellis (black, age 18) **and James Kinlaw** (black, age 20). *Murder.* Their crime was committed on 12/22/1933 at Charleston. Mutilation murder of 41-year-old George C. Garrett (white, a grocer), the victim having been savaged with a hatchet and a pump handle. Motive: attempted robbery. The killers were executed on April 27, 1934. Source: *Greensboro (NC) Record*, 4/27/34 (14:7). See also: 1933 Charleston Co. death cert. no. 17376.

Thomas Richardson (black, age 17) **and Eddie Lee** (black, age 19). *Murder.* Their crime was committed on 3/7/1934 in Georgetown County. Ax murder of 37-year-old John Milton (black), a taxi driver. Motive: carjacking. The killers were executed on June 6, 1934. Source: *Columbia (SC) Record*, 6/6/34 (1:5). See also: 1934 Charleston Co. death cert. no. 3357 (Milton having died in the "Colored" hospital there), plus 1934 Richland Co. death cert. nos. 224 and 9712, which show that the crime was committed ten days before Richardson attained the age of 18.

Peyton Brown (white, age 22). *Murder.* The crime was committed on 1/22/1934 in Darlington County. Uxoricide. Handgun slaying of 25-year-old Gertrude Melton Brown (white). Motive: "because she liked to run around," or so he said, despite being a suspected bigamist himself. Brown was executed on July 13, 1934. Source: *Florence (SC) Morning News*, 7/14/34 (1:7). See also: 1934 Darlington Co. death cert. no. 511.

Reuben Jones (black, age 18). *Murder.* The crime was committed on 3/23/1934 in Lancaster County. Executed for the murder of 17-year-old Bernard McCullens (white, a filling station attendant), who was bludgeoned with a tire iron, his body doused with gasoline and then set ablaze. Motive: robbery. Jones was put to death for this atrocity on July 20, 1934. Source: *Florence (SC) Morning News*,

7/21/34 (1:4). See also: 1934 Lancaster Co. death cert. no. 4144, and Richland Co. death cert. no. 13165.

Evan Pugh (black, age 24). *Murder.* The crime was committed on 7/9/1934 in Sumter County. Ax murder of 57-year-old James W. Grooms (white), a farmer. Motive: revenge. The killer had served three years on a chain gang for stealing $1,100 from Mr. Grooms. It was a substantial amount of money at that time. Pugh had also been tried and acquitted for the ax murder of an aged Negro man named "Brunson" prior to the Grooms affair. He later admitted that he was guilty of that crime as well. He was put to death on October 12, 1934. Source: *Greensboro (NC) Record*, 10/12/34 (13:4). See also: 1934 Sumter Co. death cert. no. 14938.

Joe Cunningham (black, age 19). *Murder.* The crime was committed on 7/2/1934 in Richland County. Executed for the murder of 76-year-old Samuel C. Moore (white, a filling station operator), who was struck on the head with a crowbar. Motive: robbery. The killer paid with his life for this on November 30, 1934. Source: *Florence (SC) Morning News*, 7/6/34 (8:6) & 11/30/34 (1:4). See also: 1934 Richland Co. death cert. nos. 11497 and 21316.

1935

Clarence Floyd (black, age 20). *Rape.* The crime was committed on 8/5/1933 in Lexington County. Serial Rapist. Executed for an indecent assault on the person of a 20-year-old white female (name withheld) while her male escort was held at bay by means of a loaded handgun. Floyd had reportedly "made a racket of" stalking young Caucasian couples as they sat in parked automobiles. He would always rob them at gunpoint and then force himself on the female party. He is confirmed to have perpetrated seven such attacks on the outskirts of Columbia. He was put down on January 4, 1935. Source: *Greensboro (NC) Record*, 9/16/33 (4:7) & 1/4/35 (9:3). Appeal: 174 SC 288–338.

Curtis Williams (black, age 24). *Murder.* The crime was committed on 2/13/1935 in Greenville County. Handgun slaying of 21-year-old Ansel Gary Drummond (white), a taxi driver. Motive: robbery. Williams was executed on May 24, 1935. Sources: *Florence (SC) Morning News*, 2/25/35 (8:4) & 5/25/35 (1:7); *The State* (Columbia, SC), 5/25/35 (2:4). See also: 1935 Greenville Co. death cert. no. 2401.

Thurmond Harris (black, age 24). *Attempted Rape.* The crime was committed on 3/3/1935 in Barnwell County. Felonious assault on the person of a 68-year-old white female (name withheld) with intent to commit rape. The culprit had called at a Williston funeral parlor that same day to view the body of his deceased father. He then went out and attacked the white lady as she was walking home from church. She was later found semiconscious in an oat field. Harris had a strange way of showing his filial grief. He was executed on June 7, 1935. Source: *Columbia (SC) Record*, 3/4/35 (1:5) & 6/7/35 (1:5).

Ransome Emanuel (black, age 50). *Murder.* The crime was committed on 3/24/1935 in Florence County. Fatal beating and traumatic rape of 90-year-old Jane Calcutt Haines (white), who succumbed after five days in agony. Motive: robbery and sexual assault. So thoroughly did the killer ransack the old woman's abode that he even stole three one-dollar bills that she had concealed between the pages of her Bible. He was executed on July 26, 1935. Source: *Florence (SC) Morning News*, 3/28/35 (1:7), 3/29/35 (1:8), 4/4/35 (1:7) & 7/27/35 (1:4). See also: 1935 Florence Co. death cert. no. 3954; 1930 U.S. Census (Florence Co., SC), which notes both parties. Emanuel's death certificate erroneously states that he was aged 65.

Monroe Stewart (black, age 21). *Murder.* The crime was committed on 3/19/1935 in Calhoun County. Executed for the murder of about 60-year-old Edward Hayne (black, the proprietor of a so-called "colored" poolroom), who was beaten on the head with an iron spike. Motive: robbery. The killer was put to death on July 26, 1935. Sources: *Calhoun (SC) Times*, 3/28/35 (1:1) & 5/30/35 (1:4); *Florence (SC) Morning News*, 7/27/35 (1:4); *The State* (Columbia, SC), 7/27/35 (12:5).

David M. Blanden (black, age 19). *Murder.* The crime was committed on 7/2/1934 in Spartanburg County. Handgun slaying of 25-year-old Benjamin F. Sims (white). Motive: mugging. This killer was executed on August 16, 1935. Sources: *Spartanburg Journal*, 7/3/34 (1:8) & 7/10/34 (1:8); *Spartanburg Herald*, 7/4/34 (1:5); *The State* (Columbia, SC), 8/17/35 (14:1). Appeal: 177 SC 1–32. See also: 1934 Spartanburg Co. death cert. no. 11582, and 1935 Richland Co. death cert. 12540. Blanden came from Anderson County.

Cornell Luster (black, age 29) **and Harry Hill** (black, age 24). *Murder.* Their crime was committed on 12/25/1934 in Greenville County. Cop killers. Both executed for the Christmas Day murder of 25-year-old Edwin D. Milam (white), a South Carolina state trooper. Motive: resisting arrest. The officer was responding to a call about two rowdies who had disrupted a church service. These were later identified as Luster and Hill. They overpowered Milam, beat him up, stabbed him, bludgeoned him with a rock and shot him three times with his own service weapon that they had wrested from him. The South Carolina electric chair ended their careers on December 20, 1935. Sources: *Kingsport (TN) Times*, 12/26/34 (3:4); *Greensboro (NC) Record*, 12/20/35 (1:7). See also: 1934 Greenville Co. death cert. no. 19610, and 1935 Richland Co. death cert. nos. 20289 and 20310.

1936

Robert Ashley, alias "William Brown" (black, age 17). *Murder.* The crime was committed on 3/12/1936 in Richland County. Prison guard killer. Executed for the ax murder of 42-year-old Joe Byrd (white), whose remains were found in his burning automobile. Motive: escape from custody. The killer had been classified as a so-called "low risk inmate" at the South Carolina State Penitentiary. He was therefore accorded the privilege of working the fields near the prison under Byrd's supervision. Ashley substantiated his "low risk" status in the manner described above. He was put to death on June 26, 1936. Source: *Florence (SC) Morning News*, 4/28/36 (2:4). See also: 1936 Richland Co. death cert. nos. 4785 and 9728.

Wash DeSaussure (black, age 24) **and James Mixon** (black, age 20). *Murder.* Their crime was committed on 2/28/1936 in Lee County. Both executed for the murder of 62-year-old Redic Johnson Kelley (white, a filling station owner), who was beaten on the head with a heavy wrench. Motive: robbery. The killers died in the electric chair on July 24, 1936. Source: *Florence (SC) Morning News*, 7/25/36 (1:8). See also: 1936 Richland Co. death cert. no. 11474, as well as Mr. Kelley's gravestone in Presbyterian Cemetery, Bishopville, South Carolina.

Sam Anderson (white, age 24) **and Sam Powell** (white, age 25). *Murder.* Their crime was committed on 1/11/1936 in Anderson County. Handgun slaying of 25-year-old Walter Anderson Daniel (white, a taxicab driver) who was shot nine times. Motive: carjacking. The killers were put to death on December 11, 1936. Source: *Augusta (GA) Chronicle*, 1/13/36 (2:5). See also: 1936 Anderson Co. death cert. no. 109, and Richland Co. death cert. nos. 20403 and 20404.

1937

George McDuffie (black, age 22). *Murder.* The crime was committed on 12/15/1936 in Lee County. Ax murder of 73-year-old Margie Ann Brown (white, a solitary widow), who was butchered in her bedroom. Motive: robbery. The killer was executed on April 9, 1937. Source: *Florence (SC) Morning News*, 12/17/36 (1:1) & 12/18/36 (1:5). See also: 1936 Lee Co. death cert. no. 19925, and 1937 Richland Co. death cert. no. 5896; 1920 & 1930 U.S. Census (Lee Co., SC), which note the killer's correct age.

Furman McDonald (white, age 54). *Murder.* The crime was committed on 9/29/1935 in Fairfield County. Child killer. Shotgun slaying of 13-year-old Hugh B. Thompson Jr. (white). Motive: overly righteous parent. McDonald's daughter had told him that the Thompson boy had pulled a knife on her. Whether this was true became irrelevant. The outraged father armed himself with a shotgun and stomped over to the Thompson residence. He walked right in like he owned the place. The boy's father was knocked out cold by a blow to the head when he confronted the intruder. Then espying the lad who he thought had caused the trouble, McDonald fatally blasted him with buckshot. This hothead was put to death on August 20, 1937. Source: *Greensboro (NC) Record*, 9/30/35 (1:3) & 8/20/37 (3:1). See also: 1935 Fairfield Co. death cert. no. 15020, and 1937 Richland Co. death cert. no. 12831.

1938

Ernest Gaines (black, age 28). *Murder.* The crime was committed on 1/30/1938 in Saluda County. Shotgun slayings of 28-year-old Brunson Edwin Coleman (white) and 45-year-old Carrie Myers Sullivan (black). Motive: probable larceny. The killer would only say that he had acted "to assert my rights," but the white man's money was found to be missing. The female victim was employed as a cook in Coleman's house. She was shot when she ran to alert the homeowner to the presence of an intruder. Coleman was shot when he came running in response to this. The killer was executed on April 13, 1938. Sources: *Augusta (GA) Chronicle*, 1/31/38 (1:6); *Florence (SC) Morning News*, 4/14/38 (1:3); *The State* (Columbia, SC), 1/31/38 (1:7). See also: 1938 Saluda Co. death cert nos. 2722 & 2723, plus Richland Co. death cert. no 6087.

Benjamin J. Rivers (black, age 45). *Murder.* The crime was committed on 7/14/1936 at Charleston. Cop killer. Handgun slaying of 44-year-old Purce A. Wansley (white), who was shot three times. Motive: resisting arrest. Rivers was executed on April 29, 1938. Source: *Florence (SC) Morning News*, 7/17/36 (1:3) & 7/21/36 (6:8). See also: 1936 Charleston Co. death cert. no. 10318, and 1938 Richland Co. death cert. no. 6123.

Luther G. Goodman (black, age 24). *Murder.* His crimes were committed on 6/9/1938 and on 6/10/1938 in Florence County. Shotgun slayings of 25-year-old Eloise Graham (black) and 30-year-old Eugene Lewellyn Singletary (white). Motive: sharecropper quarrel. This tragedy took place on a large plantation. The woman was slain because she had complained that Goodman was neglecting his crop. Her body was found in the fields on the following day, whereupon the superintendent of the farm (Singletary) set out to find the killer. Goodman saw him coming and concealed himself in a hayloft. The fact that the killer was lying in wait trumped whatever attempts were made to mitigate what he had done. Goodman was executed on July 29, 1938. Source: *Florence (SC) Morning News*, 6/11/38 (1:4) & 6/24/38 (1:8). See also: 1938 Florence Co. death cert. nos. 9027 and 9028, plus Richland Co. death cert. no. 13041; 1920 U.S. Census (Florence Co., SC), which notes the killer by more than just his initials.

George Gates (black, age 21). *Rape.* The crime was committed on 10/1/1938 in Darlington County. Indecent assault on the person of a 16-year-old white female (name withheld), who was found beaten unconscious with several of her teeth knocked out. The culprit was a short-order cook in a Darlington diner. The victim was a waitress there. The question of consent was rendered groundless by the victim's physical condition when she was found. The rapist was executed on December 9, 1938. Source: *Greensboro (NC) Daily News*, 10/2/38 (9:3) & 10/3/38 (3:8). See also: 1938 Richland Co. death cert. no. 19835.

1939

William B. Woods (white, age 24), **Jesse V. Bair** (white, age 28), **Clayton Crans** (white, age 29), **Herbert Moorman** (white, age 42), **Roy Suttles** (white, age 29) **and George Wingard** (white, age 23). *Murder.* Their crime was committed on 12/12/1937 in Richland County. Prison guard killers. All six executed for the fatal stabbing of 61-year-old John Olin Sanders (white), a guard captain at the South Carolina State Penitentiary. Motive: prison breakout gone awry. The electric chair did for these killers on March 24, 1939. Sources: *Dynamic Detective* (magazine), 3/38; *Master Detective* (magazine), 12/38. See also: 1937 Richland Co. death cert. no. 19755, and 1939 Richland Co. death cert. nos. 4011, 4012, 4013, 4014, 4015 and 4031.

Edward L. Humphrey (white, age 51). *Murder.* The crime was committed on 3/13/1938 in Dillon County. Uxoricide. Executed for the murder of 29-year-old Kathleen Harris Humphrey (white), who was beaten to death with a wrought iron poker. Motive: spousal abuse. The killer was executed on April 11, 1939. Sources: *The State* (Columbia, SC), 3/15/38 (1:7); *Florence (SC) Morning News*, 3/16/38 (3:7). See also: 1938 Florence Co. death cert. no. 3650, and 1939 Richland Co. death cert. no. 5611.

Joseph Broughton (black, age 39). *Murder.* The crime was committed on 7/31/1938 in Berkeley County. Shotgun slaying of 44-year-old James E. DuTart (white), a storekeeper. Motive: armed robbery. The killer was executed on June 23, 1939. Source: *Aiken (SC) Standard & Review*, 8/3/38 (7:6). See also: 1938 Berkeley Co. death cert. no. 10203, and 1939 Richland Co. death cert. no. 8872.

Otis McGill (white, age 35). *Murder.* The crime was committed on 2/18/1938 in Greenville County. Executed for the murder of 58-year-old Arthur P. Southerlin (white), who had both a wooden chair and a mailbox smashed over his head. Motive: tavern brawl. McGill paid with his life for this on July 28, 1939. Source: *Greensboro (NC) Record*, 2/19/38 (1:6) & 7/28/39 (3:1). See also: 1938 Greenville Co. death cert. no. 3801, and 1939 Richland Co. death cert. no. 10414.

Grover Cleveland Odom (white, age 50). *Murder.* The crime was committed on 4/5/1939 in York County. Shotgun slaying of 19-year-old Delbert Lee Cochran (white, his son-in-law) and partial cremation of his corpse. Motive: because the killer had felt affronted. According to published accounts, Odom had been in the habit of raping his own daughter. Finding her pregnant by incest, he duped young Cochran into marrying the girl. Then one day shortly afterward, Odom's new son-in-law came to visit bearing a loaded rifle. Nothing was actually said of this, but Odom suspected it to be a gesture of portent meant to convey the message that Cochran had become aware of what had occurred. So fearing that the situation might escalate, Odom lured the young fellow to his doom. He blasted him in the belly at point blank range while inside a fodder house and burned the place down in an attempt to cover up the crime. Odom died in the electric chair on October 24, 1939. Source: *Crime Detective* (magazine), 4/40. See also: 1930 U.S. Census (Rutherford Co., NC), which notes Odom, and (York Co., SC), which notes Cochran; 1939 Richland Co. death cert. no. 14737.

1940

Frank Dash, Jr. (black, age 22). *Murder.* The crime was committed on 8/20/1939 in Calhoun County. Fatal stabbing of 62-year-old Pizetta Haigler (black), she having been murdered in her cabin by an armed intruder. "Her throat was cut and her larynx torn out," according to one report. Motive: robbery and sexual assault. The killer was executed on January 19, 1940. Sources: *The State* (Columbia, SC), 8/22/39 (11:2) & 1/20/40 (14:4); *Greensboro (NC) Record*, 1/19/40 (1:3). See also: 1930 U.S. Census (Calhoun Co., SC), which notes Dash. See also: 1939 Calhoun Co. death cert. no. 10934, and 1940 Richland Co. death cert. no. 1317 which misstates the killer's age.

Press Bibbs (black, age 18). *Murder.* The crime was committed on 10/15/1938 in McCormick County. Shotgun slaying of 45-year-old James Lewis Leslie (white, a storekeeper), who was assassinated by three thugs who followed him home. Motive: robbery. The one who got caught (Bibbs) was executed on March 29, 1940. Sources: *Augusta (GA) Chronicle*, 10/19/38 (2:1); *Greensboro (NC) Record*, 3/39/40 (21:4). See also: 1938 Abbeville Co. death cert. no.

15048; 1930 U.S. Census (McCormick Co., SC), which note Mr. Leslie.

Will Lowry (black, age 18). *Rape.* The crime was committed on 2/12/1940 in York County. Indecent assault on the person of a 22-year-old white female (name withheld), who was attacked while walking home and mistreated to such an extent that she had to be admitted to a hospital in critical condition. The rapist was executed on June 14, 1940. Sources: *Greensboro (NC) Record*, 2/15/40 (2:3); *The State* (Columbia, SC), 2/13/40 (1:7) & 6/15/40 (7:8). See also: 1940 Richland Co. death cert. no. 10054.

Frank Ladson (black, age 26). *Murder.* The crime was committed on 3/30/1940 in Horry County. Ax murder of 65-year-old Joseph Pinkman Roberts (white), a farmer. Motive: robbery. The killer was executed on July 12, 1940. Source: *Greensboro (NC) Record*, 4/3/40 (8:5) & 7/12/40 (16:6). See also: 1940 Horry Co. death cert. no. 9665, and Richland Co. death cert. no. 11760.

George Abney (black, age 38). *Murder.* The crime was committed on 3/19/1940 in Saluda County. Uxoricide, etc. Shotgun slayings of 30-year-old Ella Abney and 41-year-old Mary Lois Long Rearden (white), his wife and landlady, respectively. Motive: supposedly because they had given the killer some medicine that did not taste right to him and he thought that it was poison. George Abney was executed on September 6, 1940. Sources: *Greensboro (NC) Record*, 3/22/40 (4:3); *Marietta (GA) Journal*, 9/6/40 (1:2). See also: 1940 Saluda Co. death cert. nos. 5170 and 5172, plus Richland Co. death cert. no. 14886.

1941

Joseph Woodward, alias "Woody Woodward," alias "Josiah Woodward," (black, age 21). *Attempted Rape.* The crime was committed on 10/9/1940 in Aiken County. Felonious assault on the person of a "young" white female (name withheld) with intent to commit rape. The victim "testified that the Negro stopped her as she was en route to work, choked her, and when she screamed dragged her about 85 yards from the road into a field of broom sage and threatened to kill her." In addition, "her clothes were badly torn" and bruises were evident on many parts of her person. The culprit was executed on January 31, 1941. Source: *Aiken (SC) Standard & Review*, 12/6/40 (1:1), 12/11/40 (1:3) & 2/5/41 (1:1).

Hugh Evans (white, age 22), **Willis Evans** (white, age 18) **and Hampton Lee** (white, age 25). *Rape.* Their crime was committed on 9/21/1940 in Richland County. Indecent assault on the person of 33-year-old Mary Ross Seibels Walker (white), the daughter of "a socially prominent insurance company executive." She and her male companion were attacked by the aforesaid trio with malicious intent. The man—Frank B. Gary Jr. (white, age 39) of Columbia, South Carolina—was knocked out cold by a blow on the head. The female party was then forcibly abducted and taken to a more remote spot where these "three Richland county farm boys" took turns raping her. They also slapped her around and stole every single item of intrinsic value that she had on her person: bracelet, rings and money. The three white rapists were led one by one to the electric chair on February 7, 1941. Source: *Greensboro (NC) Record*, 9/23/40 (3:6). See also:

1941 Richland Co. death cert. nos. 3040, 3042 & 3043; 1940 U.S. Census (Columbia, SC), which notes the victims of this outrage.

James Claudius Hann (white, age 27). *Murder.* The crime was committed on 6/6/1939 in Pickens County. Executed for the murder of 22-year-old Ruby Lee Bowling (white), she having been slashed to death with a razor and nearly decapitated. Motive: lovers' quarrel. The killer was electrocuted on February 7, 1941. Sources: *Greensboro (NC) Record*, 6/6/39 (1:8); *Florence (SC) Morning News*, 2/23/40 (1:8) & 2/8/41 (1:7); *Greenville (SC) News*, 2/8/41 (pg. 3), obituary. Also: 1939 Pickens Co. death cert. no. 11826, and 1941 Richland Co. death cert. no. 3041.

Will Hood, alias "Willie Dixon" (black, age 28). *Murder.* The crime was committed on 9/20/1940 in Fairfield County. Shotgun slaying of 62-year-old William Walter Lathan (white), a cotton grower. Motive: wage dispute. Mr. Lathan had just paid off his field hands and was walking homeward when he was shot. The killer was executed on April 11, 1941. Source: *The State* (Columbia, SC), 9/21/40 (1:5), 9/23/40 (1:5) & 4/12/41 (12:1). See also: 1940 Fairfield Co. death cert. no. 14177, and 1941 Richland Co. death cert. no. 6783.

Heywood Daniels, alias "String Beans" (black, age 28). *Attempted Rape.* The crime was committed on 2/14/1941 in Orangeburg County. Felonious assault on the person of a 73-year-old white female (name withheld) with intent to commit rape. The culprit had entered the victim's bedroom late that night and threatened her with death if she refused to comply with his demands. She was saved from further harm by the timely arrival of her son. The latter wounded the fleeing criminal with a shotgun blast, thus ensuring his capture. Daniels was executed on July 11, 1941. Source: *Times & Democrat* (Orangeburg, SC), 2/18/41 (1:2) & 7/12/41 (1:2).

Benjamin Heyward (black, age 32). *Murder.* The crime had been committed on 1/6/1925 in Beaufort County. Cop killer. Shotgun slaying of 22-year-old Benjamin Paul Carden (white). Motive: resisting arrest. Heyward was executed for this on August 15, 1941. Source: *Beaufort (SC) Gazette*, 1/8/25 (1:6) & 8/21/41 (1:5). See also: 1925 Beaufort Co. death cert. no. 5250, and 1941 Richland Co. death cert. no. 13286; 1920 U.S. Census (Charleston, SC), which notes Ben Heyward, the husband of Bertha Heyward.

Roy Long, alias "Roy Brooks," alias "Nudy Long" (black, age 27). *Rape.* The crime was committed on 3/30/1941 in Pickens County. Indecent assault on the person of a 74-year-old white female (name withheld), she having been attacked and beaten by a home intruder who made it a point to strike when nobody else was there. This rapist was executed on November 21, 1941. Source: *Pickens (SC) Sentinel*, 4/3/41 (1:6), 10/2/41 (1:6) & 11/27/41 (1:6).

1942

George Thomas (black, age 23). *Rape.* The crime was committed on 12/14/1940 in Georgetown County. Indecent assault on the person of a "young married" white female (name withheld), she having been grabbed as she was walking home and dragged into tall weeds. The rapist was executed on February 20, 1942. Sources: *Georgetown (SC) Times*, 12/20/40 (1:6); *The State* (Columbia, SC), 12/16/40 (1:1) & 2/21/42 (2:1).

Monroe Bounds (black, age 23). *Murder.* The crime was committed on 12/14/1935 in Florence County. Handgun slaying of 63-year-old Spy W. Farmer (white, a grocer), who was shot three times in the back. Motive: because the murdered man had balked at an attempt to sell him stolen goods. The killer was executed on March 13, 1942. Source: *Florence (SC) Morning News*, 12/15/35 (1:5) & 1/10/42 (1:5). See also: 1935 Florence Co. death cert. no. 18541, and 1942 Richland Co. death cert. no. 3804.

Cyrus Pinckney (black, age 28). *Attempted Rape.* The crime was committed on 7/9/1940 in Berkeley County. Felonious assault on the person of 15-year-old Jessie Lee Cumbee (white female) with intent to commit rape. The trial record does not contain additional details but they must have been highly egregious given the fact that they resulted in two executions. Pinckney was executed on July 10, 1942. Source: original case file (Berkeley General Sessions) Oct. Term, 1940; South Carolina State Archives; *The State* (Columbia, SC), 7/11/42 (12:2).

Richard Gaymon (black, age 21). *Attempted Rape.* The crime was committed on or about 6/1/1942 in Clarendon County. Felonious assault on the person of a white female (name withheld and age not recorded) with intent to commit rape. She was attacked in her own home. It was only the timely arrival of a housemaid that prevented the culprit from fully accomplishing his purpose. He was executed on August 7, 1942. Source: *The State* (Columbia, SC), 8/8/42 (5:1). An attempt to locate the original trial papers in this case proved unsuccessful even though Clarendon County courthouse personnel were friendly and willing to help.

Alchrist Grant (black, age 29). *Attempted Rape.* The crime was committed on 7/9/1940 in Berkeley County. Accomplice in a felonious assault on the person of 15-year-old Jessie Lee Cumbee (white female) with intent to commit rape. He was executed on September 11, 1942. Source: *The State* (Columbia, SC), 9/12/42 (4:8). See: PINCKNEY, Cyrus (executed 7/10/42).

John K. Robinson (white, age 17). *Murder.* The crime was committed on 1/4/1942 in Spartanburg County. Handgun slaying of 56-year-old Kenneth Jerome Wofford (white), a taxi driver. Motive: armed robbery. The killer was executed on December 11, 1942. Source: *The State* (Columbia, SC), 12/12/42 (12:7). See also: 1942 Spartanburg Co. death cert. no. 1337, and Richland Co. death cert. no. 15714.

Zonnie Frazier, Jr. (black, age 19). *Murder.* The crime was committed on 7/2/1942 in Darlington County. Cop killer. Executed for the handgun slaying of 58-year-old Claude R. DuBose (white), who was shot multiple times with his own service weapon. Motive: tavern brawl. The killer was executed on December 11, 1942. Source: *The State* (Columbia, SC), 12/12/42 (12:7). See also: 1942 Darlington Co. death cert. no. 8824, and Richland Co. death cert. no. 15703.

1943

Clarence Bagwell (white, age 32), **George R. Logue** (white, age 53) **and Sue Stidham Logue** (white female, age 41). Murder. Their crimes were respectively committed on 9/17/1941 and 11/16/1941 in Edgefield County. Contract killers and cop killers. Bagwell was executed for being the triggerman in the handgun slaying of 42-year-old Davis W. Timmerman (white, a store keeper), who was shot five times in his place of business at the behest of George R. Logue and Sue Stidham Logue. Motive: vendetta. Venue changed from Edgefield County to Lexington County. The trouble began when a mule belonging to Davis Timmerman fatally kicked a prize pig belonging to John Wallace Logue (white, age 41), the husband of Sue Stidham Logue. The pig's owner demanded monetary compensation for his loss. Timmerman agreed to pay what he felt was a reasonable amount: $40. John Wallace Logue accepted this, but later decided that the amount was inadequate. So he stomped into Timmerman's country store on 9/30/1940 and demanded additional payment. Timmerman balked at this. An argument flared. Logue lost his temper. He then assaulted Timmerman with an ax handle, whereupon the storekeeper grabbed a pistol from under his counter and shot John Wallace Logue in self-defense. The bullet was fatal. Enraged by this, Logue's widow and brother (Sue and George Logue) began a blood feud with the death of Davis Timmerman as its sole objective. They enlisted a third family member (who had hitherto been a respected member of the Spartanburg Police Department) to aid their nefarious plan. This accomplice (Joe Frank Logue) in turn knew Clarence Bagwell, a pub owner who was very much in need of money. The Logues paid $1,500 to finance the contract killing of Davis Timmerman. The crooked cop reportedly pocketed 2/3 of this money and offered Bagwell $500 to carry out the hit. Bagwell agreed. So on 9/17/1941 (nearly a year after the feud began) he went to Timmerman's store and pumped five bullets into the man, killing him on the spot. The Logues had gotten their revenge, but they paid a terrible price for it in terms of more than just dollars and cents. An intense police investigation implicated them, and on 11/16/1941 warrants were issued for their arrest. It fell to Edgefield County Sheriff Ward Day Allen (white, age 55) and his deputy William Lloyd Clark (white, age 50) to bring in the Logues. They approached the Logue farmhouse on that date and were at first received cordially by Sue Stidham Logue. The officers had unknowingly walked into a pre-arranged trap. George R. Logue and one of his tenants named William Fred Dorn (white, age 44) had positioned themselves in such a way (respectively armed with a pistol and a shotgun) as to catch the lawmen in a crossfire. Horrific was the fusillade as the weapons of all four men spat death inside the Logue farmhouse. Sue Stidham Logue made herself conspicuous by smashing a chair over the deputy's head. The latter got off several shots which killed Dorn the tenant. Sheriff Allen died at the scene. Deputy Clark succumbed to wounds two days later. All four culprits (including the Spartanburg policeman) were sentenced to die in the electric chair. Executive clemency saved the condemned cop, but he lost both his career and his freedom. The other three convicts were executed on January 15, 1943. The final tally was eight people dead because a mule had kicked a pig. Sources: *Augusta*

(GA) Chronicle, 11/11/41 (1:1) & 11/17/41 (1:7); *Official Detective*, 4/42; *Crime Detective*, 10/42; *Master Detective*, 6/69. See also: 1940 Edgefield Co. death cert. 14160; 1941 Greenwood Co. death cert. no. 17722 and Edgefield Co. death cert. nos. 14239 and 17495; 1943 Richland Co. death cert. nos. 887, 888 and 889; 1940 U.S. Census (Edgefield Co., SC), which notes Deputy Clark. Appeal: 201 SC 387–403.

Jesse Jones (black, age 18). *Murder.* The crime was committed on 2/24/1942 in Spartanburg County. Executed for the ax murders of 67-year-old James Leard Hughes and 64-year-old Mary Wooten Hughes (whites), a married couple. Motive: robbery. Confirmed to have also murdered another farm couple named Landrum Columbus Petrie and Ida Petrie (whites, siblings, ages 86 and 72), by the same means and for the same purpose, in Spartanburg County on 2/14/1942. All of the victims were tortured first to make them reveal the whereabouts of their money. The killer was executed on April 2, 1943. Sources: *Greensboro (NC) Daily News*, 2/25/42 (2:7:2); *Augusta (GA) Chronicle*, 2/27/42 (2:4) & 2/28/42 (2:1). Appeal: 201 SC 403–417. See also: 1942 Spartanburg Co. death cert. nos. 2662, 2663, 7182 and 7183, plus 1943 Richland Co. death cert. no. 4915. Also see the gravestone of Mr. and Mrs. Hughes in Cannon's Camp Ground United Methodist Church Cemetery, Spartanburg, South Carolina.

Johnny Sims (black, age 17) **and Sylvester McKinney** (black, age 21). *Murder.* Their crime was committed on 2/23/1942 in Spartanburg County. Ax murder of 59-year-old Walter Cox (white), a grocer. Motive: armed robbery. They were executed for this on July 16, 1943. Source: *The State* (Columbia, SC), 7/17/43 (10:4). See also: 1942 Spartanburg Co. death cert. no. 15985, and 1943 Richland Co. death cert. nos. 8759 & 8760.

Samuel Osborne (black, age 17). *Murder.* The crime was committed on 8/17/1941 in Barnwell County. Shotgun slaying of 58-year-old William P. Walker (white), a farm manager. Motive: because Walker had remonstrated with him for shirking his responsibilities, or so he said. This killer was executed on November 19, 1943. Source: *Augusta (GA) Chronicle*, 8/18/41 (2:5). Appeal: 202 SC 474–486. See also: 1943 Richland Co. death cert. no. 13456.

1944

Sammy Joe Timmons, alias "Frank Timmons" (black, age 19). *Attempted Rape.* The crime was committed on 9/8/1943 in Horry County. Felonious assault on the person of 31-year-old Pearl Prince (white, a married woman) with intent to commit rape. No other details are found in the court record. Timmons was executed for this on May 12, 1944. Sources: Horry County Court of General Sessions Case No. 7054 (original file), which is still in the courthouse there; *Columbia (SC) Record*, 5/12/44 (3:3); *The State* (Columbia, SC), 5/13/44 (10:2).

George Junius Stinney (black, age 14). *Murder.* The crime was committed on 3/24/1944 in Clarendon County. Child killer. Executed for the murders of 11-year-old Betty June Binnicker and 7-year-old Mary Ruth Thames (whites), whose skulls were smashed with what was believed to be an iron railroad spike and their bodies tumbled into a ditch. Motive: attempted sexual assault, or so it was alleged. The real motive, however, could well have been an overdeveloped sense of territorialism. Stinney was reported to have made a verbal confession to the local sheriff and to have also led lawmen to the spot where he hid the murder weapon. The victims had gone to a weed patch near some railroad tracks in search of wildflowers. Stinney used to graze a cow on that ground (or so it has been said) and was fiercely protective of it, regarding it as his exclusive turf, again as reports have alleged. The girls had reportedly asked him about wildflowers that were growing there. It is conjectured that he became enraged at their presence, his adolescent mind regarding them as trespassers. Both victims were reportedly found with their bicycles thrown atop them. Autopsies reportedly found no evidence of sexual assault. This, of course, made the establishment of a motive problematic. Sexual assault was the first thing everyone thought at the time, as they no doubt would today. The forensic evidence, however, suggests a different motive. Efforts to overturn the evidence in this case have so far fallen short of their goal of securing a posthumous pardon for Stinney. The case remains controversial and a favorite target for activists seeking to discredit capital punishment in general. A convicted double murderer, the boy was executed on June 16, 1944. He was *not* the youngest person to be legally put to death in the USA during the 20th century. A 13-year-old had been legally hanged in Georgia on 1/12/1917. Sources: *New Orleans Times-Picayune*, 3/26/44 (9:6); *The State* (Columbia, SC), 3/26/44 (1:5) & 6/17/44 (1:2). See also: 1944 Clarendon Co. death cert. nos. 3377, and 3378 plus Richland Co. death cert. no. 7339.

Bruce Hamilton (black, age 22). *Attempted Rape.* The crime was committed on 2/2/1944 in Spartanburg County. Felonious assault on the person of Josephine Walker (white, age not recorded) with intent to commit rape. She was the wife of a soldier stationed at Camp Croft. Further details of this case were censored—probably to forestall racial tension on a wartime military base. The attacker was executed on June 16, 1944. Sources: original court file (Spartanburg General Sessions, April 1944), South Carolina State Archives; *Columbia (SC) Record*, 6/16/44 (8:4); *Spartanburg Herald*, 2/3/44 (2:4).

Hurley Jones (black, age 22). *Rape.* The crime was committed on 5/1/1944 in Greenville County. Indecent assault on the person of a 17-year-old white female (name withheld). She was waiting at a trolley stand when Jones walked up to her and hit her in the face with enough force to knock her out. She later awoke to find herself in a locked garage where the attacker had had his way with her while she was unconscious. Jones was put to death for this on November 3, 1944. Sources: *Greenville (SC) Piedmont*, 5/2/44 (1:3) & 5/3/44 (1:3); *The State* (Columbia, SC), 11/4/44 (2:8).

1945

Charles Gilstrap (white, age 27). *Rape.* The crime was committed on 2/4/1944 in Greenville County. Indecent assault on the person of an 11-year-old white female (name withheld), she having been stalked on her way home from school. The rapist was put to death on February 9, 1945. Source: *Greensboro (NC) Record*, 2/9/45 (7:4). Appeal: 205 SC 412–423. See also: 1945 Richland Co. death cert. no. 2112.

George Carter (black, age 29). *Attempted Rape.* The crime was committed on 9/26/1945 in Greenville County. Felonious assault on the person of a 62-year-old white female (name withheld) with intent to commit rape. The rapist was then a "trusty" on the Greenville County chain gang. He had been sentenced to 40 years at hard labor for a previous sexual assault. The white lady in the present case was attacked in the kitchen of her home. Carter was executed for this on December 14, 1945. Sources: *Greenville (SC) Piedmont*, 11/1/45 (5:3); *The State* (Columbia, SC), 12/15/45 (7:5); *Florence (SC) Morning News*, 12/14/45 (1:4). See also: 1945 Richland Co. death cert. no. 14320.

1946

Wash Pringle (black, age 31). *Rape.* The crime was committed on 10/23/1945 in Sumter County. Indecent assault on the person of 39-year-old Annie S. Heriot (white), the details being unfit for publication. She died in 1976. The rapist was executed on January 25, 1946. Sources: original trial record (Sumter General Sessions, Nov. Term, 1945) located in the old Sumter County courthouse (which is closed to the public) and had to be retrieved by special request; *Columbia (SC) Record*, 1/25/46 (12:2); *The State* (Columbia, SC), 1/26/46 (2:7).

Junius A. Judge (black, age 24). *Murder.* The crime was committed on 4/16/1945 at Charleston. Handgun slaying of 25-year-old Alric Aaron Gore (white), a bus driver. Motive: a dispute over bus fare. The killer was executed on July 12, 1946. Source: *Florence (SC) Morning News*, 6/8/46 (1:5). See also: 1945 Charleston Co. death cert. no. 3614, and 1946 Richland Co. death cert. no. 13675.

Louis C. Gatlin (black, age 19). *Rape.* The crime was committed on 3/31/1945 at Charleston. Indecent assault on the person of a white female (name withheld and age not specified), she having been jumped as she walked home from a bus stop. The violence of the attack was such that the victim "had to be hospitalized for some time afterwards." The rapist was executed on July 19, 1946. Sources: *Charleston News & Courier*, 7/20/46 (12:1); *The State* (Columbia, SC), 7/20/46 (10:3). Appeal: 208 SC 414–421.

Charles T. Smith (black, age 66). *Murder.* The crime was committed on 5/25/1946 in Berkeley County. Cop killer. Fatal stabbing of 57-year-old William Calhoun Guerry (white), a magistrate's constable at Jamestown. Motive: resisting arrest. The killer was executed on November 29, 1946. Source: *The State* (Columbia, SC), 5/27/46 (2:6) & 11/30/46 (2:1). See also: 1946 Berkeley Co. death cert. no. 15990.

Lewis Scott (black, age 27). *Murder.* The crime was committed on 9/14/1945 in Williamsburg County. Cop killer. Handgun slaying of 45-year-old Walter Evans (white, the night policeman for Greeleyville), who was shot with his own service weapon after it had been wrested from him in a brawl. The killer was executed on December 20, 1946. Sources: *The State* (Columbia, SC), 9/16/45 (2:3); *Florence (SC) Morning News*, 12/21/46 (1:5). See also: 1945 Williamsburg Co. death cert. no. 15798, and 1946 Richland Co. death cert. no. 15407.

1947

Cleve Covington (black, age 24). *Murder.* The crime was committed on 8/13/1945 in Marion County. Executed for the murder of 48-year-old Watt N. Martin (white, a tobacco agent from Winston-Salem), whose "paper wrapped" body was found in a barn. He had been beaten to death with a wooden tobacco roller. Motive: presumed robbery. The killer was executed on January 3, 1947. Sources: *Greensboro (NC) Daily News*, 9/2/45 (12:4); *Greensboro (NC) Record*, 10/4/45 (14:4); *The State* (Columbia, SC), 1/4/47 (10:7). See also: 1945 Marion Co. death cert. no. 15329.

Rose Marie Stinnette (black female, age 48). *Murder.* The crime was committed on 4/26/1946 in Florence County. Mariticide. Executed for orchestrating and fully participating in the murder of 29-year-old Charles Stinnette (black), her husband. The man was lured to a railroad siding by four conspirators: his wife and three male accomplices who were said to be her lovers. Once there, Charles Stinnette was bludgeoned with a heavy pipe and his body rolled down an embankment to make it look like he had been hit by a train. Furthermore, all four conspirators climbed down the aforesaid embankment and took turns smashing the victim's head with the heavy pipe to make sure that no spark of life remained in him. The body was also stripped of valuables. Motive: too many roosters in the henhouse. Rose Marie Stinnette went to the electric chair on January 17, 1947. It is not certain what became of her three lackeys. Source: *Florence (SC) Morning News*, 4/28/46 (1:8), 4/30/46 (1:8) & 1/18/47 (1:3). See also: 1946 Florence Co. death cert. no. 5716, and 1947 Richland Co. death cert. no. 732.

Robert Jordan (black, age 21). *Murder.* The crime was committed on 12/19/1946 in Florence County. Executed for the murder of 53-year-old Irene Finklen Matthews (white), who was slashed to death with a butcher knife when she surprised a prowler in her home. The killer chased her from room to room inflicting numerous stab wounds before finally cutting her throat in the kitchen. That same killer was put to death on February 14, 1947. Source: *Florence (SC) Morning News*, 12/21/46 (1:4) & 2/15/47 (1:4). See also: 1940 U.S. Census (Florence Co., SC), which notes Mrs. Matthews.

Talmadge Haggins (black, age 22). *Murder.* The crime was committed on 9/19/1946 in Lancaster County. Handgun slaying of 28-year-old Oliver Benjamin Powers (white), a taxi driver. Motive: robbery and carjacking. The killer was executed on April 18, 1947. Source: *The State* (Columbia, SC), 9/21/46 (1:6) & 4/19/47 (2:6). See also: 1930 U.S. Census (York Co., SC), which notes Powers as a minor.

Freddie Jones (black, age 18). *Murder.* The crime was committed on 11/13/1945 in Chester County. Executed for the mutilation murder of 23-year-old Gladys Smith Woods (black), she having been stabbed "and the skin cut away from her face to make her unrecognizable." Motive: possibly deranged. Jones was executed on April 25, 1947. Source: *The State* (Columbia, SC), 11/16/45 (3:5) & 4/26/47 (12:6). See also: 1945 Chester Co. death cert. no. 11541, and 1947 Richland Co. death cert. no. 5092.

John Dickerson (black, age 35). *Murder.* The crime was committed on 9/13/1946 at Charleston. Fatal stabbing of 24-year-old Louise Stevens (black). Motive: flare-up in a lovers' lane. The couple had been "drinking and fussing" (in the killer's own words) at a sandpit near town. Their tryst somehow got out of hand and both ultimately wound up dead for it—the woman at the scene and Dickerson in the electric chair on May 2, 1947. He came from Manning, South Carolina. Source: *The State* (Columbia, SC), 5/3/47 (12:8). See also: 1946 Charleston Co. death cert. no. 10420.

William A. Davis (black, age 24). *Rape.* The crime was committed on 4/15/1947 in Sumter County. Indecent assault on the person of a white female (name withheld and age not specified), she having been attacked in her home during a nightlong spree in which the culprit burglarized at least two other private residences. Davis was executed on June 20, 1947. Sources: *Florence (SC) Morning News*, 4/17/47 (1:5); *The State* (Columbia, SC), 6/21/47 (10:2); *Augusta (GA) Chronicle*, 5/15/47 (2:1) & 6/21/47 (3:5). See also: 1947 Richland Co. death cert. no. 7875.

J.C. Sims (black, age 36). *Murder.* The crime was committed on 4/15/1947 in Anderson County. Cop killer. Handgun slaying of 41-year-old Willis Edwin Sanders (white). Motive: thief caught in the act. Sims (who was probably a moonshiner) was attempting to heist several 100-pound bags of sugar from an ice cream manufacturer when he was spotted by policemen on patrol. A gun battle then erupted with fatal consequences for both the thief and one of the lawmen. Sims was never identified by his full name. He reportedly came from Waynesville, North Carolina. He was executed on July 11, 1947. Source: *Augusta (GA) Chronicle*, 4/16/47 (2:1). See also: 1947 Anderson Co. death cert. no. 6905, and Richland Co. death cert. no. 9147.

Bert Grant, Jr. (black, age 18). *Attempted Rape.* The crime was committed on 5/24/1947 in Darlington County. Felonious assault on the person of a 35-year-old white female (name withheld) with intent to commit rape. The circumstances were of such an aggravated nature that news thereof was suppressed until after the culprit had been safely whisked away to a safe location. He was legally executed on July 25, 1947. Sources: *Greensboro (NC) Record*, 5/27/47 (B:8:5); *Augusta (GA) Chronicle*, 6/21/47 (3:7). See also: 1947 Richland Co. death cert. no. 9187.

Willie Pooler (black, age 19). *Rape.* The crime was committed on 5/25/1947 in Darlington County. Indecent assault on the person of a 67-year-old white female (name withheld) who was physically overpowered and "dragged into a thicket despite her struggles and screams." The rapist was executed on August 1, 1947. Source: *Augusta (GA) Chronicle*, 5/26/47 (2:4), 6/21/47 (3:7) & 8/1/47 (13:1). See also: 1947 Richland Co. death cert. no. 10417.

Leonard Arthur Pringle (black, age 23) **and Ernest Willis** (black, age 26). *Murder.* Their crime was committed on 4/15/1947 in Chester County. Fatal stabbing of 51-year-old Willie Reed (black), a taxi driver. Motive: robbery and carjacking. Both of the killers were executed on August 15, 1947. Source: *Augusta (GA) Chronicle*, 8/15/47 (20:1) & 8/16/47 (1:3). See also: 1947 Chester Co. death cert. no. 5805, and Richland Co. death cert. nos. 10429 & 10430.

Roosevelt Miller, alias "Robert Teasley" (black, age 20). *Rape.* The crime was committed on 11/20/1946 in Greenville County. Serial rapist. Executed for an indecent assault on the person of a white female (name withheld and age not specified) who was jumped near her home and left in a ditch. This was among a series of such attacks in the area around Fountain Inn that month. Miller had been sent to the chain gang in September 1944 for attempted rape but escaped. He apparently had no sense of restraint. He was executed on December 12, 1947. Sources: *Greenville (SC) Piedmont*, 11/21/46 (1:6); *The State* (Columbia, SC), 12/13/47 (6:5).

1948

Ernest Howard (black, age 25). *Attempted Rape.* The crime was committed on 10/10/1947 in Chesterfield County. Felonious assault on the person of 18-year-old Jennie Crowley (white) with intent to commit rape. The culprit was a "trusty" on the Chesterfield County chain gang, having drawn a sentence of life imprisonment three years earlier for killing another man in a brawl. He had "slipped away from" the road crew on the above date and gone to the Crowley residence. Howard knocked on the door and asked for a match. Then he forced his way inside and beat the young lady unconscious. He was executed on January 2, 1948. Sources: original court file, Case No. 4541 (Chesterfield General Sessions, Fall Term, 1947), South Carolina State Archives; *Chesterfield (SC) Advertiser*, 10/16/47 (1:6); *The State* (Columbia, SC), 1/3/48 (12:6). See also: 1948 Richland Co. death cert. no. 805.

Willie Gidron (black, age 18). *Murder.* The crime was committed on 4/30/1947 in Calhoun County. Cop killer, etc. Executed for the handgun slaying of 47-year-old George David Tilley (white), a local sheriff. Motive: escape from custody. Also confirmed to have murdered a storekeeper named William L. Riley (black, age 61) the previous day by stabbing him with an ice pick. Sheriff Tilley had arrested Gidron for that homicide and was in the act of bringing him to jail when the handcuffed prisoner somehow pulled a small-caliber handgun from his boot and opened fire. Gidron was put to death on January 9, 1948. Source: *Florence (SC) Morning News*, 5/8/47 (1:3). See also: 1947 Orangeburg Co. death cert. no. 6410, Calhoun Co. death cert. no. 4022, and 1948 Richland Co. death cert. no. 826.

Lawrence Davis (black, age 22). *Murder.* The crime was committed on 1/2/1947 in Marlboro County. Executed for the killing of 66-year-old Luther Ransome (white, a night watchman), who was battered about the head with the butt of a shotgun. Motive: burglary. Davis was executed for this on September 17, 1948. Source: *Florence (SC) Morning News*, 9/18/48 (1:5) & 3/24/50 (1:3). See also: 1947 Marlboro Co. death cert. no. 595, and 1948 Richland Co. death cert. no. 12136.

Matthew Jamison (black, age 17). *Rape.* The crime was committed on 7/5/1948 in Lexington County. Indecent assault on the person of a 21-year-old white female (name withheld), she and three companions having been carjacked by an armed assailant (Jamison) and forced to drive to a remote site where the others were tied up and robbed and the young lady raped. This daring young predator was executed on December 3, 1948. Source: *Florence (SC) Morning*

News, 9/17/48 (1:3). See also: 1948 Richland Co. death cert. no. 16788.

Leroy Grant Troy (black, age 22). *Rape.* The crime was committed on 6/16/1948 in Horry County. Indecent assault on the person of 23-year-old Myrtis Kissinger (white) under circumstances that are better left unsaid. This rapist was put to death on December 31, 1948. Sources: original court file (Horry Co. General Sessions, Oct. 1948, Case. no. 9402), Horry County Courthouse; *Columbia (SC) Record*, 12/31/48 (1:7); *The State* (Columbia, SC), 1/1/49 (11:4).

1949

Willie Lincoln (black, age 23). *Murder.* The crime was committed on 11/15/1947 in Orangeburg County. Shotgun slayings of 32-year-old Willie Lee Adams and 40-year-old Alberta Adams Johnson (blacks). Motive: because they had dared to give refuge to the killer's estranged wife. Willie Lincoln was executed for this on February 4, 1949. Source: *Charleston News & Courier*, 11/20/47 (B:11:3). Appeal: 213 SC 553–557. See also: 1947 Orangeburg Co. death cert. nos. 14445 and 14446, plus 1949 Richland Co. death cert. no. 2048.

Willie Junior Tolbert (black, age 22). *Rape.* The crime was committed on 8/8/1949 in Greenwood County. Indecent assault on the person of a 16-year-old white female (name withheld) who was forcibly abducted when the culprit carjacked the sedan in which she was a passenger, involuntarily driven around the countryside and raped twice during an hours long ordeal of terror. The attacker was executed on October 28, 1949. Source: *Augusta (GA) Chronicle*, 8/13/49 (10:4) & 9/14/49 (1:6). See also: 1949 Richland Co. death cert. no. 13229.

1950

Charles Walter Butler (black, age 37). *Murder.* The crime was committed on 1/2/1947 in Marlboro County. Accomplice in the killing of 66-year-old Luther Ransome (white, a night watchman), who was battered about the head with the butt of a shotgun. Motive: burglary. This offender was executed for his part in that crime on June 2, 1950. Source: *Florence (SC) Morning News*, 3/24/50 (1:3). Also: 1950 Richland Co. death cert. no. 8144. See: DAVIS, Lawrence (executed 9/17/48).

Ernest T. Preylow (black, age 32). *Murder.* The crime was committed on 4/2/1950 in Saluda County. Shotgun slaying of 34-year-old Fred Simpkins, alias "Horse Simpkins" (black), who was blasted with buckshot for the sake of a dollar. The killer was executed on June 30, 1950. Sources: original case file (*State vs. Preylow*), Saluda County Courthouse; *Columbia (SC) Record*, 6/30/50 (3:1). See also: 1950 Richland Co. death cert. nos. 6648 and 8195, the murdered man having died in the "colored" hospital there.

Larry Elmore (black, age 42). *Murder.* The crime was committed on 11/26/1949 in Laurens County. Shotgun slaying of 65-year-old Virgil Martin Betsill (white, a storekeeper), who was blasted twice behind his counter. Motive: armed robbery. The killer was executed on August 4, 1950. Source: *Augusta (GA) Chronicle*,

11/29/49 (1:1). See also: 1950 Richland Co. death cert. no. 10968; 1940 U.S. Census (Laurens Co., SC), which notes the murdered man.

1951

Carroll Gantt (black, age 18). *Murder.* The crime was committed on 6/30/1951 in Orangeburg County. Cop killer, etc. Shotgun slayings of 39-year-old James W. Etheridge (white, the police chief of Branchville), and 18-year-old Randolph D. Varn (black), a bystander. Motive: temper tantrum. Gantt was an unstable character who became enraged when his song did not play on a jukebox in the order that he was expecting. He then got his hands on a loaded shotgun and started shooting up the place, a so-called "negro café." The lawman was killed when he ran to the scene in response to the sound of gunfire. Gantt wound up in the electric chair on November 16, 1951. Sources: *Charleston News & Courier*, 7/1/51 (1:1) & 7/2/51 (1:3); *Columbia (SC) Record*, 11/16/51 (6:5). See also: 1951 Orangeburg Co. death cert. nos. 10537 and 10538, plus 1951 Richland Co. death cert. no. 17091.

1952

Smith Harvey (black, age 39). *Murder.* The crime was committed on 2/17/1951 in Beaufort County. Handgun slayings of 29-year-old Aubrey Godley, 25-year-old Lonnie Godley and 21-year-old Wilson McAlhaney (whites), who were described as "three members of a barbershop quartet." Motive: because he didn't like their singing. The killer was executed on January 25, 1952. Source: *Greensboro (NC) Record*, 2/20/51 (3:1) & 1/25/52 (13:4). See also: 1952 Richland Co. death cert. no. 899.

Frank J. Cox (white, age 39). *Murder.* The crime was committed on 10/10/1950 in Spartanburg County. Uxoricide and filicide. Executed for the shotgun slayings of 27-year-old Neola S. Cox (née Neola Range) and 22-month old Sandra Cox (whites, his wife and baby daughter), who were both blasted from behind. Motive: deadbeat dad and deadbeat husband. Cox had been brought to task for non-support. Ordered to contribute ten dollars weekly, he beat up his wife instead. That earned him 60 days on the chain gang. Enraged yet further by this, Cox then went on to commit the greater crime that cost him his life. He was put to death on February 15, 1952. Source: *Florence (SC) Morning News*, 10/12/50 (1:6). See also: 1950 Spartanburg Co. death cert. nos. 13753 and 13754, plus 1952 Richland Co. death cert. no. 2137.

William Perry Blassingame (white, age 31). *Murder.* The crime was committed on 5/19/1951 in Spartanburg County. Baby killer. Traumatic and fatal rape of 2-year-old Donna Kay Dobbins (white), the apparently illegitimate offspring of a fallen woman who said that she had been compelled to live with the killer or starve. Further details of this case are unprintable. The pervert turned murderer was put to death on April 18, 1952. Source: *Florence (SC) Morning News*, 7/24/51 (10:8), 7/26/51 (2:4) & 3/4/52 (10:5). See: 1951 Spartanburg Co. death cert. no. 6634, and 1952 Richland Co. death cert. no. 5523.

James H. Priester (black, age 24) **and John P. Priester** (black, age 26). *Murder.* Their crime was committed on 11/7/1951 in Beaufort County. Both executed for the torture killing of 50-year-old Harry E. Wilson (white), the postmaster at Lobeco. Motive: robbery. The culprits (siblings) did atrocious things to force the murdered man into surrendering his money. They shot him with a rifle first. Then they stabbed him multiple times with an ice pick in a slow, excruciating manner that was worthy of Torquemada. The South Carolina electric chair ended the lives of this pair on April 18, 1952. Source: *Augusta (GA) Chronicle*, 11/10/51 (2:7). See also: 1951 Beaufort Co. death cert. no. 18313, plus 1952 Richland Co. death cert. nos. 9644 and 9645; 1930 U.S. Census (Allendale Co., SC), which notes the correct names and ages of the Priesters.

Roland Wyatt (black, age 27). *Rape.* The crime was committed on 5/3/1951 in Spartanburg County. Indecent assault on the person of a 41-year-old white female (name withheld) who was attacked in her own home. The rapist had slipped into the lady's house while she was outdoors working in her yard. He threw a sheet over her head when she re-entered the place and accomplished his purpose right there on the floor. He was put to death on June 13, 1952. Source: *Florence (SC) Morning News*, 5/6/51 (1:1). See also: 1952 Richland Co. death cert. no. 11090.

1953

South Carolina did not execute any criminals this year.

1954

Lander Ray Gantt (white, age 27) **and Shelton H. Gainey** (white, age 19). *Murder.* Their crime was committed on 6/27/1949 in Horry County. Both executed for the murder of 27-year-old Robert D. Oliver (white, a taxi driver), who was severely beaten, robbed and locked in the trunk of his cab. The culprits took off to Pennsylvania in the stolen taxi. They were caught two days later. Mr. Oliver had remained locked in the trunk throughout that journey. He succumbed to internal injuries that were aggravated by being physically bumped around in the confined space for a distance of several hundred miles. His abductors (and killers) were executed on March 5, 1954. Source: *Greensboro (NC) Record*, 7/4/49 (B:1:8). See also: 1954 Richland Co. death cert. nos. 3337 and 3338.

Otis Glenn (black, age 21). *Murder.* The crime was committed on 4/28/1953 in Orangeburg County. Rifle slaying of 40-year-old Walter Herald Lee (white), his employer. Motive: carjacking and gross perfidy. Mr. Lee owned a small meatpacking company. It was agreed that he should give Glenn a ride to work that day. Lee met Glenn in front of the latter's house. Glenn shot Lee through the head, pulled his body out of the car and then drove away in it. He paid with his life for this, in the electric chair on March 12, 1954. Source: *Charleston News & Courier*, 9/14/53 (B:7:8). See also: 1953 Orangeburg Co. death cert. no. 5288, and 1954 Richland Co. death cert. no. 3339.

Raymond Corney, known to some as "Carney" (black, age 29). *Murder.* The crime was committed on 12/6/1953 in Florence County. Executed for the murders of 22-year-old Henry Bennett Allen and 15-year-old Betty Claire Cain (whites), a courting couple. Both were shot in the head with a handgun as they sat parked in a lovers' lane. The body of the male victim was then dragged to an abandoned well and dumped into it head first. The girl was decapitated by means of a sharp instrument. The killer threw her head into the well. Then he dragged the rest of her (presumably by the ankles) to an area that was more deeply wooded and there disposed of the remains in a shallow grave. Motive: robbery. The additional fact that the headless girl was found with her panties around her ankles suggested sexual assault, but it can be argued that the undergarment was already in that position when she was shot. The killer was put to death on May 7, 1954. Source: *Florence (SC) Morning News*, 12/11/53 (B:9:1), 12/12/53 (8:1), 12/13/53 (B:5:1) & 12/20/53 (1:4). See also: 1954 Richland Co. death cert. no. 8825.

Willie Hayden (black, age 35). *Murder.* The crime was committed on 3/11/1954 in Lancaster County. Executed for the ax murder of 66-year-old Murdock Johnson (white), a prison camp trusty. Motive: robbery. This was a chain gang killing. The victim was serving a short term for assault. He had received a Social Security stipend during that time. He had $22 in his pockets ten days prior to his scheduled date of release. Hayden and a fellow prisoner named William Lewis McDow (black, age 32) knew this. They lured Johnson to a site where prisoners (themselves included) were assigned to cutting wood and murdered him there. His $22 was split between them. Both were recidivist killers. Hayden was already serving a 12-year term for homicide. McDow was a lifer; he hanged himself on 6/12/1954. Hayden was electrocuted pursuant to law on August 27, 1954. Sources: *Panama City (FL) News*, 3/16/54 (2:7); *Augusta (GA) Chronicle*, 8/27/54 (8:1) & 8/28/54 (14:6). See also: 1954 Richland Co. death cert. no. 8846.

1955

Arthur Waitus, alias "Fat Eye" (black, age 33). *Murder.* The crime was committed on 4/30/1951 in Georgetown County. Strangulation of 35-year-old Maylees Cribb Coker (white), she having been jumped while walking home from the movies, forcibly dragged through a cemetery and into the parish house of a church, where her body was found several hours later. Motive: sexual assault. The killer was executed on April 15, 1955. Source: 224 SC 12 (Appeal). See also: 1951 Georgetown Co. death cert. no. 5841, and 1955 Richland Co. death cert. no. 5219.

Marvin H. Chasteen (white, age 38). *Murder.* The crime was committed on 11/5/1953 in McCormick County. Rifle slaying of 49-year-old Roy D. Wiggins (white), who was lured from his home under false pretenses. Motive: adultery with the dead man's wife, or so it was alleged. The killer was executed on October 7, 1955. Source: *Augusta (GA) Chronicle*, 12/17/53 (8:5), 12/18/53 (D:8:3) & 6/18/54 (1:1). See also: 1955 Richland Co. death cert. no. 13670.

Clay Daniels (black, age 23) **and Willie Daniels** (black, age 24). *Rape.* Their crime was committed on 8/12/1955 in Lee County. Indecent assault on the person of an 18-year-old white female (name withheld) and concomitant battery on the person of her 22-year-old male companion. The violated pair were seated in a parked car enjoying each other's company at the time. The culprits (who were siblings) attacked them. The male victim was dispatched by being "knocked unconscious with a steel bar." Then the assailants took turns raping the girl. They were legally put to death for this on December 2, 1955. Source: *Augusta (GA) Chronicle*, 12/3/55 (1:2). See also: 1955 Richland Co. death cert. nos. 17050 and 17051.

1956

Samuel Wright (black, age 21). *Murder.* The crime was committed on 2/26/1955 in Orangeburg County. Ax murder of 75-year-old Mary Lee Bannister Stroman (white) and concomitant maiming of that woman's invalid husband; they were attacked while in the sanctity of their own house. Motive: attempted robbery. The killer was the grandson of their maid. He was executed for this atrocity on January 13, 1956. Sources: *Aiken (SC) Standard & Review*, 3/2/55 (1:3); *Daily Independent* (Kannapolis, NC), 1/13/56 (1:3). See also: 1955 Orangeburg Co. death cert. no. 3616.

Henry Lee Boone (black, age 31). *Murder.* The crime was committed on 8/21/1954 in Cherokee County. Fatal stabbing of 32-year-old Agnes Irene Willard Webb (white, a mother of seven children) who was attacked with a sharpened piece of iron as she walked along a road. Motive: obnoxious drunk. The killer was executed on January 20, 1956. Sources: *Augusta (GA) Chronicle*, 8/23/54 (1:1); *Columbia (SC) Record*, 1/20/56 (1:6). Appeal: 228 SC 438–448.

Raymond Fuller (black, age 23). *Murder.* The crime was committed on 8/13/1952 in Spartanburg County. Rifle slaying of 26-year-old Lynn Baxter Moorman (white). Motive: robbery. The victim had parked his car in an area frequented by young couples. He was accompanied by a white female. The killer knew that the site had a reputation and deliberately went there armed for the purpose of marauding. Fuller smashed the driver's-side window of Moorman's car with the butt of his rifle. Then he fired a shot through Moorman's head at point-blank range. Both occupants of the car were also stripped of their personal valuables, but the female victim was not otherwise mistreated. Raymond Fuller paid with his life for this on July 27, 1956. Source: *Columbia (SC) Record*, 7/27/56 (1:6). Appeal: 229 SC 439–447. See also: 1952 Spartanburg Co. death cert. no. 12715.

Harold Byrd (black, age 23). *Murder.* The crime was committed on 1/22/1955 in Spartanburg County. Executed for the murder of 40-year-old Curtis Moss (black), a cab driver. Motive: robbery. The victim was carjacked. Then his hands were bound to render him helpless. Not satisfied, the killer stabbed the cabbie multiple times with an ice pick and heaved his body over a bridge railing. Moss fell 30 feet down into a wintry stream. He somehow managed to crawl out of the numbing water and drag himself to a nearby house, where he collapsed with the ice pick protruding from his throat. Black-on-black killer Harold Byrd died in the electric chair on August 31, 1956. Source: *Columbia (SC) Record*, 8/31/56 (1:1). Appeal: 229 SC 593–603. See also: 1955 Spartanburg Co. death cert. no. 2475.

1957

Willie Marion Daniels (black, age 30). *Rape.* The crime was committed on

2/26/1956 in Allendale County. Indecent assault on the person of a "middle aged" white female (name withheld), she having been attacked in her own house by an armed intruder (Daniels), who not only forced himself on her but also stole all of her money at gunpoint. Initial reports censored the fact that the victim had been sexually assaulted, a common practice designed to tamp down lynch mindedness. This rapist was legally executed on June 7, 1957. Source: *Augusta (GA) Chronicle*, 2/27/56 (3:1), 2/28/56 (3:2), 2/29/56 (D:6:1) & 6/8/57 (3:5).

James Eugene Smith (black, age 31). *Murder.* The crime was committed on 11/22/1952 in Abbeville County. Executed for the murder of 39-year-old Frank Lloyd Pardue (white, a grocer), who was "beaten to death with a stick." Motive: disgruntled employee. The killer was put to death on July 5, 1957. Source: *Columbia (SC) Record*, 7/5/57 (1:6). See also: 1952 Abbeville Co. death cert. no. 18261.

1958 and 1959

South Carolina did not execute any criminals during these two years.

1960

Robert Johnson (black, age 28). *Attempted Rape.* The crime was committed on 7/6/1959 in Orangeburg County. Felonious assault on the person of a 51-year-old white female (name withheld) with intent to commit rape. The victim (a maiden woman) was beaten bloody inside her own home. The culprit had gone there under the pretense of buying eggs. The fact that he was wearing socks over his hands was taken as evidence of evil intent. Robert Johnson was executed on May 13, 1960. Sources: *Spartanburg (SC) Herald*, 7/8/59 (1:1); *Greensboro (NC) Record*, 5/13/60 (2:4).

1961

Quincy Bullock (black, age 46). *Murder.* The crime was committed on 8/3/1958 in Dillon County. Handgun slaying of 28-year-old Carolyn Barfield Walshock (white), she having been shot four times as she ran from the scene of a lovers' lane ambush. Motive: attempted sexual assault. The killer was executed on April 28, 1961. Sources: *Spartanburg Herald*, 8/9/58 (1:4); *Sumter (SC) Daily Item*, 4/28/61 (1:2). Appeal: 235 SC 356–380.

Charlie Robinson (black, age 25). *Rape.* The crime was committed on 12/5/1959 in Calhoun County. Indecent assault on the person of a 58-year-old white female (name withheld) during the course of a nocturnal burglary. The victim was raped twice in her own bed and robbed of her money as well. Venue changed from Calhoun County to Orangeburg County. The attacker was executed on May 26, 1961. Source: *High Point (NC) Enterprise*, 5/26/61 (1:3). Appeal: 238 SC 140–166.

William Otis Britt (white, age 25) **and Douglas Westbury** (white, age 27). *Murder.* Their crime was committed on 9/7/1958 in Orangeburg County. Cop killers. Handgun slaying of 31-year-old Harry Boyd Ray (white), who was shot multiple times with weapons that included his own. Motive: bandits on the run. Both were executed on June 19, 1961. Sources: *Florence (SC) Morning News*, 9/13/58 (1:2); *Aiken (SC) Standard & Review*, 6/20/61 (1:5).

Walter James Outen (black, age 29). *Rape.* The crime was committed on 11/11/1959 in Richland County. Indecent assault on the person of a 30+-year-old white female (name withheld) described as "a widow and the mother of two children." She was grabbed as she stepped off a bus, dragged into a thicket and there raped at knifepoint. The attacker was legally put to death on July 14, 1961. Sources: *Columbia (SC) Record*, 11/12/59 (1:5) & 7/14/61 (1:5); *The State* (Columbia, SC), 11/12/59 (1:4) & 11/13/59 (1:6). Appeal: 237 SC 514–532.

1962

Ray Landy Young (black, age 27). *Murder.* The crime was committed on 4/4/1959 in Greenville County. Fatal stabbing of 63-year-old John S. Kehayas (white, a liquor store owner), the victim having been attacked with an ice pick. Motive: attempted robbery. The killer was executed on April 20, 1962. Sources: *Augusta (GA) Chronicle*, 4/20/62 (7:1); *Charleston News & Courier*, 4/21/62 (1:1). Also see the gravestone of John Kehayas in Rosemont Cemetery, Newberry, South Carolina.

Douglas Clee Thorne (white, age 24). *Rape.* The crime was committed on 3/13/1959 in Greenville County. Indecent assault on the person of a 16-year-old white female (name withheld) who was abducted from a parking lot on her birthday and raped three times in a sodomitical way. The attacker paid for this in the electric chair on April 20, 1962. Sources: *Florence (SC) Morning News*, 9/11/59 (B:5:6); *Augusta (GA) Chronicle*, 4/20/62 (7:1); *Charleston News & Courier*, 4/21/62 (1:1). Appeal: 239 SC 164–170.

Index

www.ingramcontent.com/pod-product-compliance
Ingram Content Group UK Ltd.
Pitfield, Milton Keynes, MK11 3LW, UK
UKHW041835100926
8556IPUK00018B/971

9 780786 495399